Nick Engler's
WEEKEND PROJECTS
PLUS

Nick Engler's
WEEKEND PROJECTS
PLUS

40 Great Woodworking Projects

PLUS *a Jig and a Technique to Help You Build Each One*

Nick Engler

Rodale Press, Inc.
Emmaus, Pennsylvania

OUR PURPOSE

"We inspire and enable people to improve their lives and the world around them."

The author and editors who compiled this book have tried to make all of the contents as accurate and as correct as possible. Plans, illustrations, photographs, and text have all been carefully checked and cross-checked. However, due to the variability of local conditions, construction materials, personal skill, and so on, neither the author nor Rodale Press assumes any responsibility for any injuries suffered or for damages or other losses incurred that result from the material presented herein. All instructions and plans should be carefully studied and clearly understood before beginning construction.

Printed in the United States of America on acid-free ∞ , recycled ♻ paper

Bookworks Staff
Designer: Linda Watts
Illustrator and Project Designer: Mary Jane Favorite
Art assistance: David Van Etten
Interior and Cover Photographer: Karen Callahan
Master Craftsman: Jim McCann

Rodale Press Home and Garden Books Staff
Vice President and Editorial Director: Margaret J. Lydic
Managing Editor, Woodworking Books: Kevin Ireland
Editor: Bob Moran
Director of Design and Production: Michael Ward
Associate Art Director: Carol Angstadt
Design assistance: Dale Mack
Studio Manager: Leslie M. Keefe
Cover Designer: Dale Mack
Copy Director: Dolores Plikaitis
Copy Editor: Nancy N. Bailey
Production Editor: Barbara McIntosh Webb
Book Manufacturing Director: Helen Clogston
Manufacturing Coordinator: Patrick T. Smith
Indexer: Diane Benison
Office Manager: Karen Earl-Braymer
Editorial assistance: Lori Schaffer

Special thanks to:

Wertz Hardware Store
West Milton, Ohio

Wertz Variety Store
West Milton, Ohio

Cincinnati Woodworking Club

Columbus Woodworking Club

Western Ohio Woodworkers' Club

We're happy to hear from you.

For questions or comments concerning the editorial content of this book, please write to:

Rodale Press, Inc.
Book Readers' Service
33 East Minor Street
Emmaus, PA 18098

For a complete list of Rodale woodworking books, access to our woodworking discussion forum, and a variety of other resources, visit our World Wide Web site at:

http://www.woodforum.com

Library of Congress Cataloging-in-Publication Data
Engler, Nick.
  Weekend projects plus : 40 great woodworking projects : plus a jig and a technique to help you build each one / by Nick Engler.
    p.   cm.
  Includes bibliographical references and index.
  ISBN 0–87596–785–X (alk. paper)
  1. Woodwork—Amateurs' manuals. 2. House furnishings—Amateurs' manuals. I. Title.
TT185.E545 1997
684'.08—dc21   97–34609

Distributed in the book trade by St. Martin's Press

2 4 6 8 10 9 7 5 3 1   hardcover

Contents

PART FOUR: FOR READING AND WRITING

PART FIVE: FOR SITTING AND PASSING TIME

PART SIX: FOR DRESSING AND SLEEPING

PART SEVEN: FOR YARD AND GARDEN

PART EIGHT: FOR CELEBRATION AND DECORATION

PART NINE: FOR CHILD'S PLAY

Contributors

Charles Bales got his first taste of woodworking at the knee of his father, who taught woodworking and drafting. He took woodworking classes in junior high school just for a few days — long enough to find out that his skills were already way beyond the class. He went on to start his own woodworking business in Dayton, Ohio, where he builds, repairs, and restores furniture.

Mike Boggs is a metallurgical engineer for the Stanley Works in Columbus, Ohio. He maintains and improves the quality of the metals in the Stanley tool line. However, he caught the woodworking bug in 1976. Starting with just a few hand tools, a jigsaw, and a Skil saw, he taught himself to work wood and by the 1980s was making what he calls "real furniture." Today he builds mostly Shaker and Early American pieces.

Larry Callahan learned woodworking from his father and soon found that he could build things better than what he could buy. To this day, he builds much of his own furniture and cabinets for his home in West Milton, Ohio. He does this not to save money but because it's the only way to get exactly what he wants. Not surprisingly, he's chosen an exacting line of work making electronic circuits for the U.S. Air Force.

Marion Curry is a retired technical editor for the Environmental Protection Agency and the National Institute of Occupational Safety and Health. She began woodworking in Cincinnati, Ohio, about 25 years ago when her granddaughters asked for a dollhouse. With no previous training, she managed to put two houses together. "Then they wanted me to fill the homes with doll furniture," says Marion. She decided to get some formal shop training, learned to build full-sized furniture, "and I haven't made a piece of dollhouse furniture since." Marion makes all types of furniture for her family.

Andy Fischer has been a golf instructor for the past 31 years and has toured professionally with the LPGA. When she wasn't on the fairways, she was woodworking. "I've always loved wood," says Andy. She began making wooden models from scraps of pine when she was seven years old,

then made a display stand to hold them. Today she teaches golfing and spends much of her spare time turning wood and making wooden boxes and small pieces of furniture. She has made a few pieces on commission, but she gives most of her stuff away. "I do woodworking because it's fun — and it's challenging," she says.

Paul Garbon is a firefighter for the Cincinnati Fire Department. He's been working with his hands most of his life and spent some

time working as both a rough and a finish carpenter. But he didn't get interested in fine woodworking until he inherited his grandfather's tools. "Both my grandfather and my great uncle made furniture," says Paul. He read everything he could on woodworking, then began to follow in his grandfather's footsteps, making his own furniture.

Peter Holt spent 30 years teaching himself woodworking while he developed and marketed products all over the world for National Cash Register. Then he retired to start his own wood-

working business in Lebanon, Ohio, English Accents. He makes small furniture, toys, and musical instruments.

Jim McCann is a master craftsman, tool engineer, and inventor. His father taught him the basics of woodworking, and he finished his shop education at Eastern Kentucky University. He spent time as a craftsman and designer for *Hands*

On! magazine, then went to work as an engineer for Shopsmith, Inc., designing and testing new tools. Today, he's back at work as a woodworker, and his craftsmanship has been featured in dozens of books and magazines.

Dr. Gopala Murthy came to this country from India, earned a Ph.D. in dairy technology, and worked at the Food and Drug Administration until he retired several years ago. For most of that time, he's worked with wood, making furniture. He started out big — his first project was a desk and chair. Since then he's built mostly classical furniture, including a Duncan Phyfe dining table with eight hand-carved chairs.

Paul Rising is a mechanical engineer specializing in automatic assembly and test equipment. He learned woodworking from "a great teacher" — his own father. He also admits to being a voracious reader of woodworking books. When he isn't busy at his day job, Paul builds custom cabinets and furniture part-time at his own business, Rising Custom Woodworks in Dayton, Ohio.

David T. Smith is the proprietor and master craftsman of The Workshops of David T. Smith, an organization of prolific woodworkers and potters who make museum-quality reproductions of early American artifacts just outside of Morrow, Ohio. There are over a dozen craftsmen at The Workshops, but each piece is built by just one woodworker, in a manner similar to the large furniture shops of Philadelphia and Newport in the 1700s. *American Country Furniture,* a collection of David's designs, has just been released in paperback from Rodale Press.

Ralph Sprang is an electronics engineer with a master's degree from Johns Hopkins University. He's a self-taught woodworker who has been turning wood and making period furniture reproductions for 20 years. He's also a gregarious woodworker, regularly attending meetings of several different woodworking clubs, including Western Ohio Woodworkers Club, the Ohio Valley Woodturners' Guild, the Cincinnati Woodworking Club, and the Cincinnati Wood Carvers Guild.

Eldon Studebaker is a retired potato farmer, schoolteacher, and nurseryman. He owned and operated Studebaker Nursery with his brother in New Carlisle, Ohio, for 40 years. He's always been good with his hands — he even taught shop for a few years — but really didn't start to get serious about woodworking until he retired. He likes to work "wood with history," particularly wood harvested from trees that he planted as a young nurseryman 40 to 50 years ago.

Pat Ventrone owns and operates Pat's Custom Cabinetry in Hillsboro, Ohio. He got his  start as a craftsman almost half a century ago in a fifth-grade shop class, and that was his last formal shop training. "I learned most of my trade by working with other cabinetmakers," he says. Pat sharpened his skills as a model maker for the U.S. Army and for RCA. Today he restores antique furniture and is hard at work developing his own special style of functional furniture.

David Wakefield is a native of Australia and the son of Oliver Wakefield, a famous  English comedian. His family traveled extensively, but David eventually came to roost in Athens, Ohio. He operates Howling Wolf Woodworks, manufacturing wood toys, and teaches at Hocking Valley Technical College. David has published two collections of his toy designs, *Animated Toys* and *Making Dinosaur Toys in Wood.*

Fred Weissborn has "always been interested in woodworking, as far back as I can remember." And he has always managed to make time to work with tools in between raising a family and pursuing a career as a design engineer for General Electric. After he retired, he began to pursue his avocation seriously. He is president of the Cincinnati Woodworking Club in Cincinnati, Ohio — and has been for 10 years!

Joe Zwiesler first started woodworking at age six, turning bowls at the East Dayton Boys Club, where his father was the director. He got formal training in woodworking at Western Kentucky University. For many years, he worked for Shopsmith, Inc., demonstrating their power tools, training their salespeople, and managing a Shopsmith Woodworking Store. Today, he works at The Hardwood Store in New Carlisle, Ohio, and continues to build furniture in his spare time.

Working Smart

*O**nce upon a time,** I had the honor of spending a pleasant afternoon with one of the grand old men of how-to journalism, Harry Wicks. Those of you who can still remember life before biscuit joiners and Super Glue may also recall that Harry was the workshop editor of the granddaddy of all how-to magazines, *Mechanics Illustrated.* You may also remember that Harry was a fine woodworker as well as a lucid writer. He was just thinking about winding up a career which, according to him, had spanned two thirds of the Iron Age when I met him in 1984.

Among the things that Harry and I discussed that afternoon were "weekend projects." Harry claimed to have invented the term and made it a running feature in Mechanics Illustrated. He was proud of the concept, but he lamented the fact that weekend projects had become synonymous with carnival crafts, 2 × 4 furniture, and other knocked-together designs.

"That was never my intention," Harry explained. "Weekend projects were supposed to show readers examples of *efficient craftsmanship.*" Woodworkers shouldn't have to compromise good design to build a project in a weekend. They just have to *work smart.*

And he's right. Take a tour of some of the great furniture collections in this country, such as the Winterthur Museum in Winterthur, Delaware. Many of the pieces on display were built in a few days. The craftsmen who made them were businessmen as well as artisans; most couldn't afford to spend weeks or months on a single project. So they evolved appealing designs and timesaving methods of work.

For those of us who don't have to make a living from our woodworking, you'd think that the time it takes to build a project would become less of an issue, but exactly the opposite is true. Efficient craftsmanship becomes doubly important when you work wood for pleasure because then time is *more* precious than money. The time I spend in my shop is often the most satisfying time of my day precisely because I can get a lot done and I'm proud of the results.

Working efficiently doesn't mean hurrying. The best craftsmen I know don't work briskly; they work carefully and steadily. They get a lot done for two reasons. The first is that they've learned a few tricks and know how to incorporate them in their projects. And the second is that they work "ahead of the project." When a student pilot learns to fly an airplane, his or her instructor drills in the importance of "staying ahead of the aircraft," anticipating what comes next. That same technique is essential in woodworking. You may build a project a step at a time, but you get better results and finish sooner if you arrange those steps in an efficient order.

This is a book of what I know Harry would consider weekend projects. Some are my designs; others I've collected from woodworkers whose work — and methods of working — I admire. There are obvious examples of fine woodworking; others are utilitarian, clever, or whimsical. All can be built in a few days, provided you're reasonably efficient.

To that end, I've included something extra with each of these projects. I've identified the important techniques that you need to know to get a job done quickly, and I've provided the information you need to apply these methods to any project. Additionally, I've included at least one timesaving fixture with each project. These jigs are, in most cases, just three or four scraps of wood. I thought long and hard to make them as simple as possible so you could build *both* the project and the jigs needed in a weekend.

Finally, the procedure for each project is divided into mornings, afternoons, and evenings — the way most of us work in real life. Usually, there are no more than two or three steps to be accomplished in each four-hour block of time. Once again, you don't have to hurry; just have fun and work smart.

With all good wishes,

PART ONE

For Cooking
and Eating

Breakfast Table

To make the bent aprons on this table, I cut multiple kerfs in the boards, almost sawing through the wood. This made the boards flexible enough to bend. To get the curve I wanted, I pressed them in a bending jig (a kind of mold), gluing two kerfed boards back to back. When the glue dried, the kerf-bent aprons held the curve.

MATERIALS LIST

Finished Dimensions in Inches

Parts

A.	Top	1½″ × 16″ × 29″
B.	Legs (4)	1½″ × 1½″ × 34½″
C.	Back aprons/rails (4)	¾″ × 4″ × 10¾″
D.	Center apron/rail (2)	¾″ × 4″ × 11½″
E.	Curved aprons* (4)	½″ × 4″ × 20″

* *Cut these parts to their final length after bending them.*

Hardware

#12 x 2″ Roundhead wood screws (5)
#20 Biscuits (16)

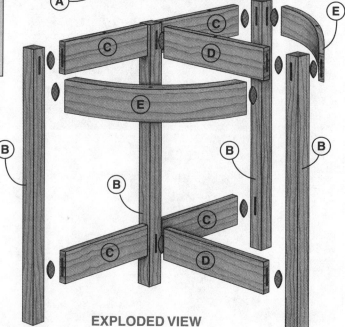

EXPLODED VIEW

The biscuit joinery that holds this table together simplifies it considerably. If you made traditional mortises and tenons, they would require a great deal of time. Furthermore, you would have to make a special jig to cut the tenons on the ends of the curved parts. But you can cut all the biscuit slots without any special fixtures or techniques.

Friday Evening

1 Prepare the materials, and cut the parts to size.
To make the table as designed, you need approximately 12 board feet of 8/4 (2-inch-thick) stock, and 6 board feet of 4/4 (1-inch-thick) stock. The table shown has a maple "butcher-block" top, and the legs, aprons, and rails are poplar. However, you can use any cabinet-grade wood.

Plane the 8/4 stock to 1½ inches thick, and rip it into pieces 1½ inches wide. Cut four pieces to the length needed to make the legs. Glue the remaining pieces edge to edge to make the wide board needed for the butcher block top. As you glue up the pieces, turn them so the annual rings run *vertically,* from top to bottom.

Plane the 4/4 stock to ¾ inch thick, and cut the rails, back apron, and center apron. Plane the remaining ¾-inch-thick wood to ½ inch thick, and cut the parts to make the curved aprons.

2 Glue up stock for the bending jig. Also, glue up scraps of plywood or particleboard to make a block 4½ inches thick, 6 inches wide, and 21 inches long. Tomorrow morning, you'll fashion a bending jig from this block.

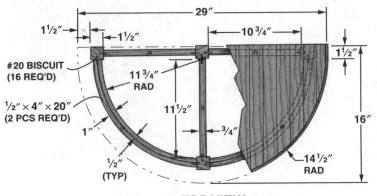

TOP VIEW

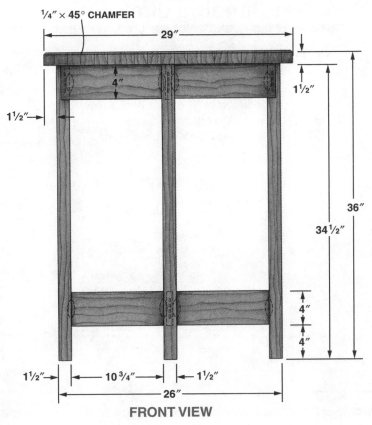

FRONT VIEW

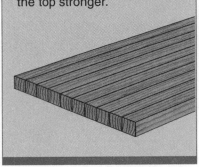

TRY THIS

MAKING BUTCHER BLOCKS

Glue up butcher-block tops so the annual rings in the wood strips run vertically, as shown. Because wood expands less across the annual rings than it does tangent to them, this arrangement makes the top more stable. In some hardwood species, it also makes the top stronger.

Saturday Morning

3 **Make the bending jig.**
You want to glue up the curved aprons as soon as possible, so make the bending jig first thing in the morning. Lay out the curve, as shown in the *Bending Jig Layout,* then cut it with a band saw or frame saw.

4 **Bend one curved apron.** Cut ⅜-inch-deep saw kerfs in one face of each curved apron board. Space the kerfs every ¾ inch as shown in the *Kerfing Detail.* Glue two of the boards back to back and press them in the bending jig, bending them through a 90-degree arc.

5 **Cut the biscuit joints.**
As shown in the *Joinery Detail,* the legs, aprons, and rails are assembled with biscuit joints — wooden plates in semicircular slots. This is quicker to make than mortises and tenons and it's just as strong.

Carefully mark the locations of the slots on the legs, as shown in the *Top View* and *Front View.*

Using a biscuit cutter, cut slots for number 20 biscuits. Cut matching slots in the ends of the straight rails and aprons.

See Also:
"Biscuit Joinery" on page 248.

Center the biscuit slots in the adjoining surfaces of the legs and rails. Because these parts are different thicknesses, you must readjust the fence of the biscuit jointer when switching from legs to rails.

Quick FIXTURE: Two-Part Bending Jig

When gluing kerf-bent boards back to back, you must bend them in a two-part form — one part to mold the inside of the curve, and the other to mold the outside, with space in between for the bent wood. To make this form, glue up a block of plywood or particleboard large enough to make both parts. Lay out both the outside and inside curve of the wood on the face of the block. Using a band saw, cut both curves. Discard the waste between the curves.

← 4½" →

SIDE VIEW

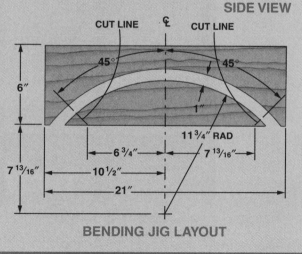

CUT LINE   ℄   CUT LINE

45°   45°

6"

1"

11¾" RAD

6¾"   7¹³/₁₆"

7¹³/₁₆"   10½"

21"

BENDING JIG LAYOUT

Saturday Afternoon

6 Cut and chamfer the top. Scrape the glue from the top stock and sand it smooth. Lay out the shape of the top, as shown in the *Top View,* and cut it with a band saw or saber saw. Sand the sawed edges.

To "soften" the top and make the table more comfortable to use, chamfer the top edge, as shown in the *Front View.* Rout the chamfer with a chamfering bit.

7 Bend a second curved apron. Remove the first curved apron from the bending jig. To make sure it holds the bend until you're ready to cut it, wrap a band clamp around it lengthwise and tighten the band. Then glue up the second set of kerfed boards, and clamp them in the bending jig.

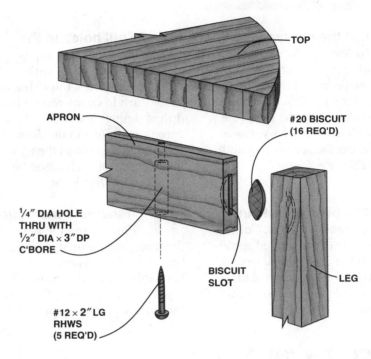

TOP

APRON

#20 BISCUIT (16 REQ'D)

¼" DIA HOLE THRU WITH ½" DIA × 3" DP C'BORE

BISCUIT SLOT

LEG

#12 × 2" LG RHWS (5 REQ'D)

JOINERY DETAIL

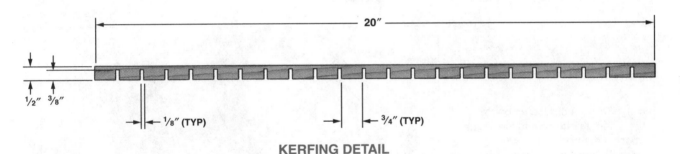

20"

½" ⅜"

⅛" (TYP)

¾" (TYP)

KERFING DETAIL

TRY THIS

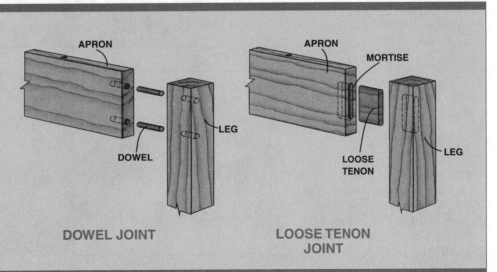

ALTERNATE JOINERY

If you don't have a biscuit joiner, you can also join the parts with dowels or "loose tenon" joints.

APRON

APRON

MORTISE

LEG

DOWEL

LEG

LOOSE TENON

LEG

DOWEL JOINT

LOOSE TENON JOINT

Sunday Afternoon

8 Cut the curved aprons to length. Remove the second curved apron from the bending jig, and remove the band clamp from the first one. Using the *inside* part of the form (the part with a convex curve) as a holder, cut the aprons to length on a table saw.

9 Cut biscuit slots in the curved aprons. Cut slots in the ends of the curved aprons for number 20 biscuits. Dry assemble the legs, rails, and aprons *without glue* to test the fit of the biscuit joints.

10 Drill holes in the aprons. The top is attached to the aprons with roundhead wood screws. These screws rest in counterbored holes drilled through the *width* of the aprons, as shown in the *Joinery Detail.* Drill a hole in the approximate center of each apron, as shown in the *Top View.*

11 Assemble the table. Finish sand the parts of the table, then glue up the three back legs, back aprons, and back rails. Hold the parts together with clamps, then glue the front leg, center apron, center rail, and curved aprons to the assembly. Let the glue dry at least an hour before removing the clamps. Fasten the top to the completed frame with round-head wood screws.

At Your Leisure

12 Finish the table. Remove the top from the frame and do any necessary touch-up sanding. Apply a finish. As shown the table top is stained and finished with tung oil, while the frame is painted.

EXTRA INFO

CUTTING A CURVED APRON TO LENGTH

1 To cut a curved apron to length, attach it to the *inside* part of the bending jig with double-faced carpet tape. Tilt the blade of your table saw to 45 degrees. Clamp the jig to your miter gauge, aligning the first cut line with the blade. Cut one end, as shown.

2 Then loosen the clamp, turn the jig around, and align the second cut line with the blade. Tighten the clamp, and cut the opposite end of the curved apron to length.

Pro SKILL: Kerf Bending

One of the easiest ways to bend a board is to make saw kerfs in one face, almost cutting through the wood. The board is very thin at each kerf, and this makes it flexible enough to bend.

To determine the correct depth for a kerf, cut test boards. Most hardwoods must be thinned down to at least 3/16 inch before they become flexible enough, but this varies with the species. The spacing between the kerfs depends on the radius of the curve and the width of the kerfs. The smaller the radius and the narrower the kerfs, the closer the kerfs should be. Don't make the kerfs too far apart, however. The closer the kerfs, the smoother the bend will appear.

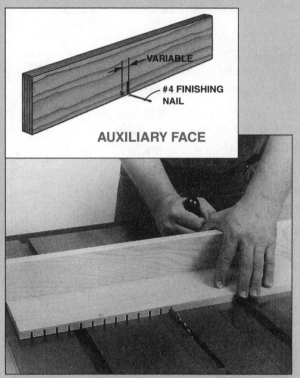

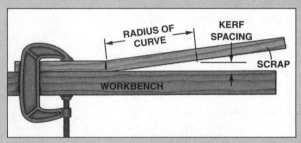

1 To find the maximum kerf spacing for a bend, cut a scrap as thick as the wood you want to bend and about a foot longer than the radius of the bend. Cut a kerf in the board about 6 inches from one end. Measure and mark the length of the radius out from the kerf. Clamp the end of the board to your workbench. Lift up on the other end until the kerf closes. The distance between the board and the bench top at the radius mark is the *maximum* kerf spacing.

2 To space the kerfs evenly, attach an auxiliary face to the miter gauge of your table saw. Cut a single kerf in the board, then drive a finishing nail in the auxiliary face, near the bottom edge. The distance from the nail to the blade should be equal to the kerf spacing. Place the kerf you just cut over the nail and cut another. Repeat until you have cut all the kerfs.

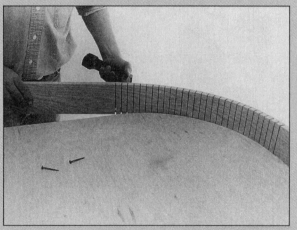

3 Laminate two kerfed boards back to back, clamping them in a bending jig while the glue dries. When you remove the clamps, the laminated parts will hold their curve.

4 You can also bend a kerfed board around a curved brace with the solid surface facing out. To hold the bend, attach the wood to the brace.

Nut Tray

The decorative corner joints on this nut tray are simple miters with multiple splines. Using a splined miter jig to hold the tray on the table saw, I cut the spline grooves at opposing angles to create a "shoelace" effect.

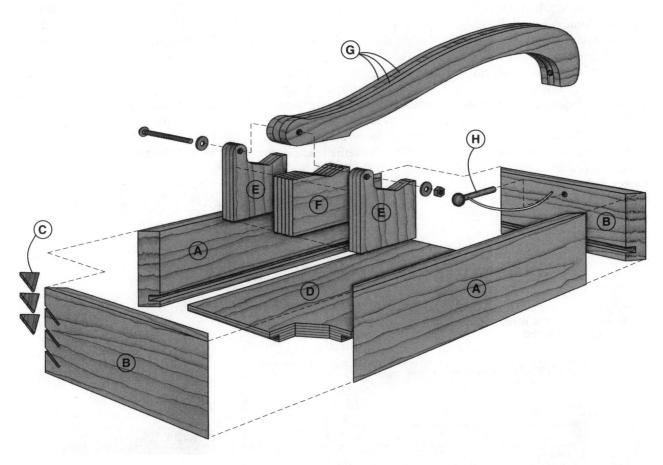

EXPLODED VIEW

MATERIALS LIST

Finished Dimensions in Inches

Parts

A.	Sides (2)	$\frac{1}{2}" \times 4" \times 12"$
B.	Ends (2)	$\frac{1}{2}" \times 4" \times 7"$
C.	Splines (24)	$\frac{1}{8}" \times 1" \times 1\frac{1}{4}"$
D.	Bottom*	$\frac{1}{2}" \times 6\frac{1}{2} \times 11\frac{1}{2}"$
E.	Pivot end parts† (6)	$\frac{3}{16}" \times 3" \times 4\frac{1}{2}"$
F.	Anvil parts† (5)	$\frac{3}{16}" \times 3" \times 3"$
G.	Lever sides† (3)	$\frac{5}{16}" \times 4" \times 13\frac{5}{8}"$
H.	Pin	$\frac{1}{4}"$ dia. $\times 1\frac{1}{4}"$

* Make this part from plywood.

† See text for grain direction.

Hardware

$\frac{1}{4}" \times 2\frac{1}{2}"$ Roundhead machine screw

$\frac{1}{4}"$ Flat washers (2)

$\frac{1}{4}"$ Stop nut

Nylon string (6")

The perennial problem with traditional nut trays is that the nut cracker seems to disappear with alarming regularity. This particular tray solves that problem with a built-in cracker. Set the nut on the anvil and apply pressure with the lever to crack the shell. When you're not cracking nuts, slip the pin in place to secure the lever in the "down" position, and use it as a handle to carry the tray.

Friday Evening

1 Prepare the materials, and cut the parts to size.
To make the nut tray, you need approximately 4 board feet of 4/4 (1-inch-thick) stock and a scrap of $\frac{1}{2}$-inch plywood. On the box shown, the ends and sides are made from ash; the anvil, pivots, and lever are made from white oak (less prone to splitting); and the splines are made from walnut and cherry. I suggest you choose species for the splines that contrast dramatically with the sides and ends. However, you can choose any combination of cabinet-grade woods that tickles your fancy.

Cut up the stock and set aside the lumber you will use to make the anvil, pivots, and lever. Plane the remaining 4/4 stock to ½ inch thick, and cut the sides and ends to size, mitering the ends at 45 degrees.

Resaw the stock you have set aside to make the remaining parts, and plane it to 5/16 inch thick. Cut the lever parts ½ inch longer and wider than specified in the Materials List. Plane the remaining stock to 3/16 inch thick.

Cut the anvil parts and pivot parts about ½ inch wider and longer than specified. As you cut these parts, pay careful attention to the grain direction. The wood grain in the lever middle should run perpendicular to the grain in the sides. This will reinforce the lever and prevent it from splitting. For the same reason, the grain direction in the pivot parts and anvil parts should alternate with each layer, just like plywood.

2 Glue up the stock for the pivots, anvil, and lever. Glue the oversize anvil, pivot, and lever parts face to face so the grain direction in the adjoining parts alternates. Remember, you must make two pivots from the six parts you have cut — one to attach to each side of the anvil.

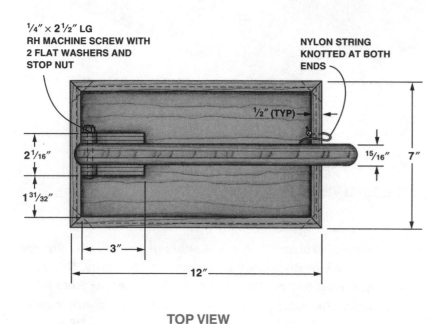

TOP VIEW

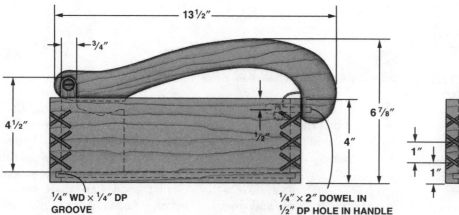

SIDE VIEW

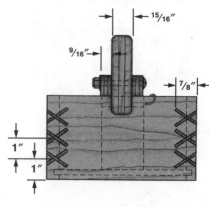

END VIEW

Saturday Morning

3 Cut rabbets and grooves in the bottom, sides, and ends. The plywood bottom rests in grooves in the sides and ends. Cut a ¼-inch-wide, ¼-inch-deep rabbet in the ends and edges of the bottom, creating a tongue all around the perimeter. Then make a matching groove in the inside surfaces of the sides and ends to fit the tongue.

4 Assemble the tray. Drill a ¼-inch-diameter hole through one end where shown in the *Side View.* (This hole holds the pin that locks down the lever.) Finish sand the sides, ends, and bottom. Assemble the parts with glue to make a box-shaped assembly.

5 Cut the shapes of the pivots, anvil, and lever. While the glue in the box assembly is drying, trim the pivot, anvil, and lever stock to the width and length specified in the Materials List. Mark the hole location, and lay out the profile of the lever, as shown in the *Lever Pattern* and the profiles of the anvil and pivots, as shown in the *Anvil and Pivot Layout.* Drill the holes in the lever and pivots, then cut the profiles with a scroll saw or band saw. Sand the sawed edges.

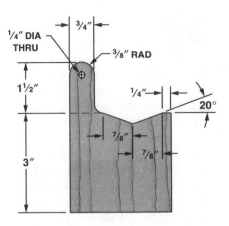

ANVIL AND PIVOT LAYOUT

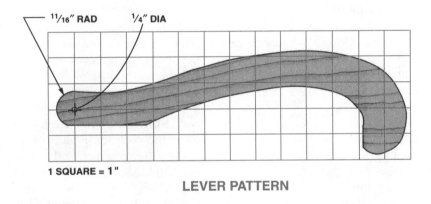

1 SQUARE = 1"

LEVER PATTERN

Quick FIXTURE: Splined Miter Jig

To cut spline grooves or slots in an assembled corner, you must hold the assembly at the proper angle to the saw blade or bit in a carriage. The splined miter jig is designed to do just that — it cradles the corner of a box or frame-shaped assembly as you cut.

Make the jig from scraps of ¾-inch plywood, mitering the ends of the braces and supports. Assemble the parts with glue and wood screws. The angle between the supports must be precisely 90 degrees to properly cradle a corner of a box or frame. Sand the edges of the jig flush and straight so you can guide it along a fence.

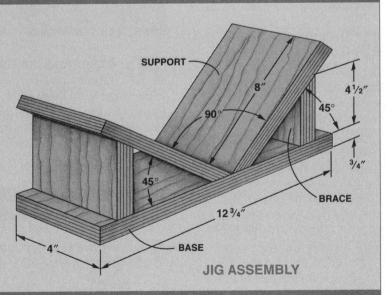

JIG ASSEMBLY

Saturday Afternoon

6 Assemble the pivots and anvil. Glue the pivots to each face of the anvil, using the roundhead machine screw to align the pivot holes. This should make a block with two "horns" on either side.

7 Install half the splines in the tray. Cut three angled spline slots in each corner of the tray, spacing them 1 inch apart. Each slot should be approximately 7/8 inch deep, as measured along the surface — not quite deep enough to cut through the inside surfaces of the tray assembly.

Plane stock thin enough to fit the spline slots. Most saw blades cut a 1/8-inch-wide kerf, but not all. You may have to cut the splines a little thicker or thinner than 1/8 inch depending on the blade used. Cut the splines into rectangles slightly larger than needed to fill the slots, then glue them in the tray.

See Also:
"Making Decorative Splined Miters" on page 13.

Saturday Evening

8 Drill the pin hole in the lever. Sand the surfaces of the anvil/pivot assembly flush and clean. Temporarily clamp the anvil/pivot assembly in the tray assembly, and install the lever between the pivots with the roundhead machine screw. The inside edge of the "hook" at the handle end of the lever should fit over the outside face of the tray end opposite the pivots. If it doesn't, sand or file the hook until it fits properly.

Place the lever in the down position, with the end hooked over the edge of the tray. Drill a

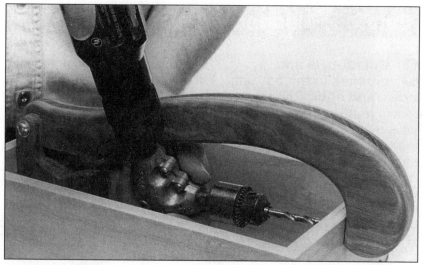

To drill the pin hole in the tray and the lever, mount a 1/4-inch bit and a right-angle drilling attachment in your drill. Bore the hole through the tray and partway into the lever.

1/4-inch-diameter hole through the tray from the inside and partway into the lever. Remove the lever.

9 Install the remaining splines in the tray. Cut away the protruding parts of the splines that you installed earlier and sand them flush. Cut a second set of spline slots in the corners of the tray, angled in the opposite direction from the first. Glue splines in the slots.

Sunday Afternoon

10 Assemble the tray. Trim the second set of splines and sand them flush. Finish sand the tray, anvil/pivot assembly, and lever. Glue the anvil/pivot assembly in the tray.

Sunday Evening

11 Install the lever and pin. After the glue dries, attach the lever to the pivots with a roundhead machine screw, two

washers, and a stop nut. (The stop nut prevents the machine screw from coming loose as you use the lever.)

Drill a 1/8-inch-diameter hole through the tray about 1 inch to the left or right of the 1/4-inch-diameter hole, and another through the pin near one end. When inserted in the 1/4-inch-diameter hole, the pin locks the lever in place so you can use it like a handle. Later on, you'll use the 1/8-inch-diameter holes to tie the pin to the tray so it won't get lost.

At Your Leisure

12 Finish the nut tray. Remove the lever and pin from the tray. Do any necessary touch-up sanding, then apply a nontoxic finish such as shellac or "salad bowl dressing." After the finish has dried and you have rubbed it to the desired luster, replace the lever. Thread a piece of nylon string through the 1/8-inch-diameter holes in the pin and the tray end. Knot the ends to prevent the string from pulling out of the holes.

Pro SKILL: Making Decorative Splined Miters

There are two types of splined miter joint. In some, the spline grooves are cut in the adjoining edges before the joints are assembled. Once the joints are glued together, the splines are hidden from sight. In others, slots or grooves are cut after the joint is assembled, and the installed splines are in full view. In these joints, the splines are decorative as well as functional.

To make the decorative "shoelace" splined miters in the nut tray, you must install two sets of splines in each mitered corner.

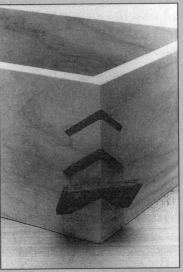

1 To install the first set, saw three angled slots across each corner, perpendicular to the miter joint. Tilt the saw blade at 45 degrees, adjust the depth of cut, and position the rip fence for the first cut. Place the spline jig on the worktable, against the fence. Rest the tray in the jig, holding it against the fence, too. Cut the first slot, guiding the jig along the fence. Rotate the tray so another corner faces down, and cut a second slot. Continue until you have cut all four corners. Then move the fence over 1 inch and repeat, cutting all four corners again. Move the fence another inch, and repeat a third time.

2 Glue splines in the slots you have made. Let the glue dry, then cut them nearly flush with the wood surface, using a hand saw or a band saw. Finally, sand them flush.

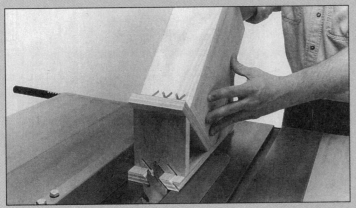

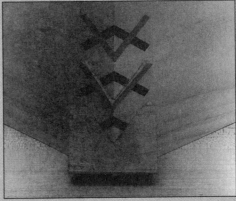

3 Cut a second set of spline slots in the same manner as the first. But this time, turn the tray around in the splined miter jig so the open top faces in the opposite direction. The slots will be angled in the opposite direction as the first set.

4 Glue the second set of splines in place, let the glue dry, then cut and sand them flush. The two sets of splines will appear to cross each other at the corners like shoelaces.

Spoon Rack

■ **QUICK FIXTURE**
Distressing Tool
■ **PRO SKILL**
Antique Finishes

This is a copy of a historical piece from the early nineteenth century. To make it look like the original, I treated the wood with acid to artificially age it, "distressed" the wood surface to simulate wear and tear, and applied a glaze over the finish to add the ground-in dirt that accumulates after a century or two.

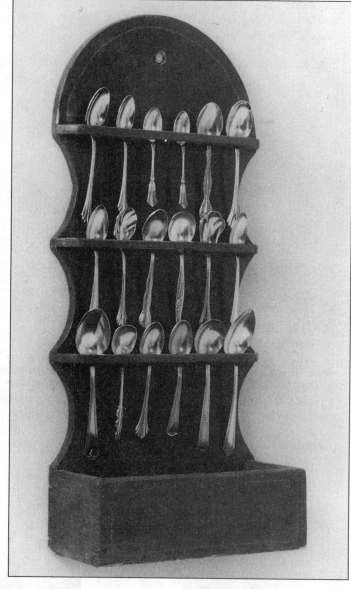

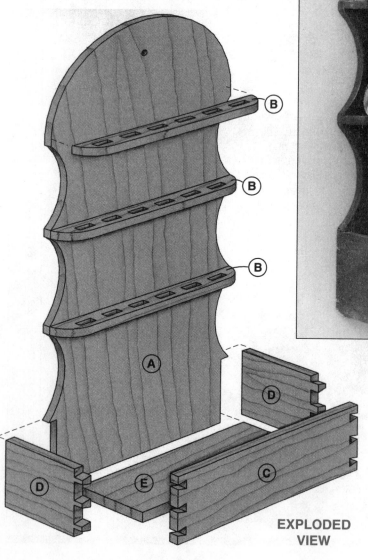

EXPLODED VIEW

MATERIALS LIST

Finished Dimensions in Inches

Parts

A.	Back	½″ × 12″ × 26¾″
B.	Racks (3)	½″ × 1¼″ × 12″
C.	Bin front	½″ × 4″ × 12″
D.	Bin sides (2)	½″ × 4″ × 5″
E.	Bin bottom	½″ × 4″ × 11″

Hardware

6d Square-cut nails (18–24)

At first glance, this design goes against everything you've been taught about joining wood. The wood grain in many of the parts opposes adjoining parts. The grain in the racks is perpendicular to the back; the bin sides are opposed to the back; the bottom fights with both the sides and the back. You wonder that this project held together for two centuries.

Well, it did. And the reason is that, with the exception of the dovetail joints on the bin, none of the parts are glued together. They are assembled with nails. Old-time craftsmen knew that small nails bent a little as the wood expanded and contracted, allowing the parts to move independently.

Friday Evening

1 Prepare the materials, and cut the parts to size. To reproduce the spoon rack, you need approximately 5 board feet of 4/4 (1-inch-thick) stock. The original box is made from white pine; I built the copy shown from poplar. You can use any attractive cabinet-grade wood. After planing the stock to ½ inch thick, saw the parts to size.

2 Lay out the profiles of the back and racks. Lay out the profile of the back, as shown in the *Front View.* While you're at it, mark the profile of *one* rack, as shown in the *Rack Layout.* There's no need to lay out the others, as you'll see when you cut the shapes.

Resources Antique nails may be purchased from:

Tremont Nail Company
P.O. Box 111
Wareham, MA 02571

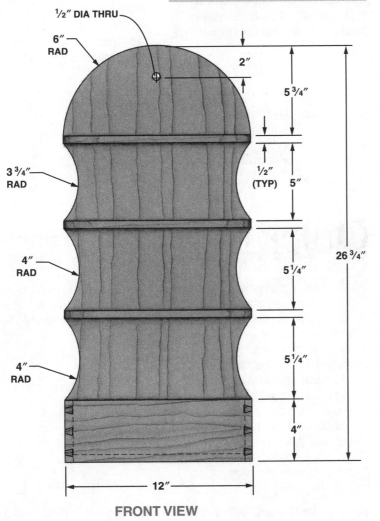

FRONT VIEW

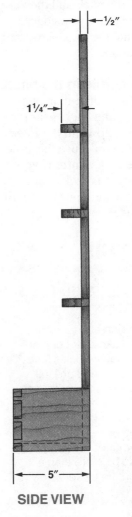

SIDE VIEW

Saturday Morning

3 Cut the mortises in the racks. Stack the rack parts face to face with the ends and edges flush. The rack that's marked should be on top. Hold the stack together with double-faced carpet tape.

To make the mortises that hold the spoons, drill overlapping ⅜-inch-diameter holes inside each rectangle that you've marked. Drill down through the entire stack, boring all three racks at once. This will remove most of the waste. Clean up the sides and square the corners with a chisel and a rasp.

4 Cut the profiles of the back and racks. Using a band saw or a saber saw, cut the profiles of the back and the racks. Sand the sawed edges, then separate the rack parts, and discard the tape.

5 Drill a hole in the back. Drill a ½-inch-diameter hole through the back, near the top edge, as shown in the *Front View.* Later, you'll use this hole to hang the rack. **Note:** If you wish to hang this rack over a standard "Shaker" peg, you will have to make the hole larger.

Saturday Afternoon

6 Cut the dovetail joints. Lay out the tails on the bin front, and cut them on a table saw. Use the completed tails as templates to mark the pins on the sides, then cut them.

See Also:
"Cutting Dovetails" on page 38.

Sunday Afternoon

7 Assemble the spoon rack. Finish sand all wooden surfaces. Glue the bin front to the bin sides, then nail the bottom in place. Attach the racks to the back, nailing through the back and into each rack. Finally, attach the assembled bin to the back with nails.

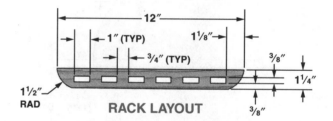

RACK LAYOUT

12″
1″ (TYP)
1⅛″
¾″ (TYP)
⅜″
1¼″
1½″ RAD
⅜″

At Your Leisure

8 Finish the rack. Do any necessary touch-up sanding and apply a finish. To artificially age the spoon rack with an "antique" finish, follow the instructions on the next page.

Quick FIXTURE: Distressing Tool

Antiquing a project usually begins with "distressing" the wood surface — creating the little nicks and dings that a piece accumulates over time. One of the easiest ways to do this is to strike the surface with keys. Wire a dozen or more keys to the end of a stick or dowel to serve as a handle. If you don't have enough old keys lying around, ask the folks at your local hardware store to save the keys that they misgrind.

Pro SKILL: Antique Finishes

To apply an antique finish — a finish that looks scores of years old — you must duplicate the aging process. This means creating a believable surface history. The surface must show what would have happened to the project if it really had weathered a century or two.

To do this, think about what happens to furniture as it's passed down through generations. The wood surfaces darken, wear, and collect chips and dings. The finishes become discolored, worn, and scratched.

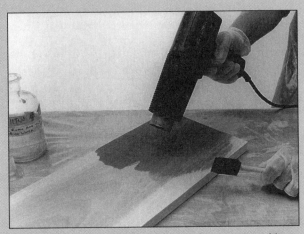

1 As wood ages, the exposed surfaces react with light and air, darkening or changing the color. The thin layer of darkened wood at the surface is called the patina. To create an instant patina, paint the raw wood with a dilute solution of nitric acid, then gently warm the surface with a heat gun. As the wood heats up, the color will develop. **Warning:** Purchase laboratory-grade acid from a chemical supply house, and dilute it 7 to 1 with distilled water. Add the acid to the water (not the other way around) to avoid unwanted reactions. When handling the acid, wear rubber gloves and a full face shield.

2 Distress the wood surface. Let it dry completely, then lightly beat the surface with the distressing tool. Don't overdo this! You mustn't make too many marks or mark the wood too deeply. The surface should look well used, but it shouldn't look like it's been through a war.

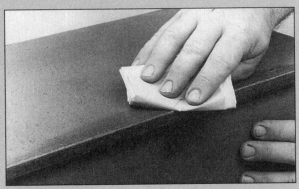

3 Wood furniture wears most at the edges and corners, especially in the vicinity of pulls and latches. The corners of table tops, the front edges of shelves, and chair seats also see lots of wear. Lightly sand away the patina in these areas, exposing raw wood. Don't worry if you cut through the patina; the last step will take care of that.

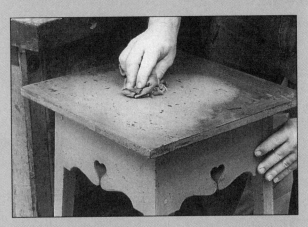

4 Finally, cover the surface with a dark glaze, then wipe most of it away. The glaze will remain in the cracks and crevices in the surface — the very same places that dirt and grime would accumulate. There are several commercial glazes available, or you can make your own. Mix 2 ounces of Burnt Umber and 2 ounces of Burnt Sienna artist's oil paints. Thin them with 8 ounces of turpentine, 3 ounces of boiled linseed oil, and ¼ ounce of japan drier. This will complete the antique finish, making your project seem much older than it really is.

Trivets

Although they look to be glued up from many small pieces of wood, these trivets are each made from a single board. I cut a series of intersecting grooves on both sides of the boards, using a notch jig to hold the stock at an angle to the cutter. Where the grooves meet, they create openings. The openings form a lacelike pattern.

Note: There's no need for a Materials List for this project; each trivet may be as large or as small as you wish to make it. The trivets shown are ¾ inch thick and 6 inches square.

Saturday Morning

1 Prepare the materials.
Decide how many trivets you'd like to make, then plane the material to the desired thickness, and cut it up into uniform squares. You can use any cabinet-grade wood, provided it's reasonably free of defects such as knots or splits.

2 Make the notch jig. To create the patterns shown, you must cut grooves in the trivet stock at a 45-degree angle from the edges. The easiest way to do this is to build a *Notch Jig* that holds the stock at the proper angle. Use this jig to guide the wood as you cut it. Make the notch jig shown on the opposite page from a scrap of plywood. The trivet stock must fit the notch in the jig loosely. There should be just a little gap so you can easily remove the stock from the jig. The gap won't interfere with the accuracy of the operation.

18

3

Cut the grooves. Set up to cut ½-inch-wide grooves on your table saw (using a dado cutter) or your router table (using a straight bit). Adjust the depth of cut to half the thickness of the stock plus ¹⁄₃₂ inch.

Place a trivet blank in the notch jig, rest the jig against the fence, and position the fence so the cutter will make a groove down the center of the stock, cutting diagonally from corner to corner. Starting in the center of the stock and working out toward the corners, cut a series of intersecting grooves. Before making each groove, you must turn the stock, flip it face for face, move the fence, or some combination of the above. The sequence in which you turn, flip, and move determines the pattern in the completed trivet. The drawings on pages 20 and 21 show the sequences for making crisscross and checkerboard patterns.

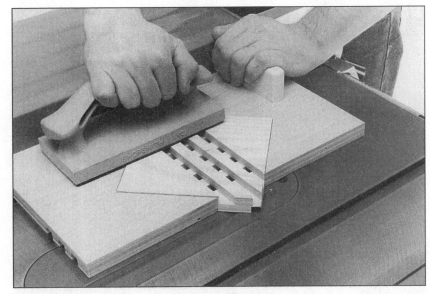

When cutting the grooves in the trivets, place the stock in a notch jig and guide the jig along a fence. Use a miter gauge to help feed the stock and the jig over the cutter.

Note: On the crisscross pattern, all the grooves on one side of the trivet stock are parallel to one another. In the checkerboard pattern, the grooves on any given side cross each other at right angles.

Quick FIXTURE: Notch Jig

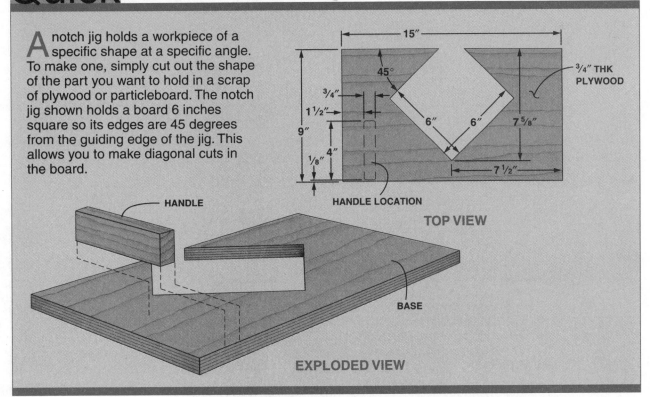

A notch jig holds a workpiece of a specific shape at a specific angle. To make one, simply cut out the shape of the part you want to hold in a scrap of plywood or particleboard. The notch jig shown holds a board 6 inches square so its edges are 45 degrees from the guiding edge of the jig. This allows you to make diagonal cuts in the board.

15"

45°

¾"

1½"

9"

4"

⅛"

6"   6"

7⅝"

¾" THK PLYWOOD

7½"

HANDLE LOCATION

TOP VIEW

HANDLE

BASE

EXPLODED VIEW

HOW TO: Making the Trivets

CRISSCROSS PATTERN

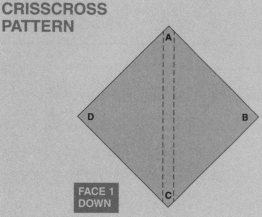

FACE 1 DOWN

1 Cut a diagonal groove down the center of the first face.

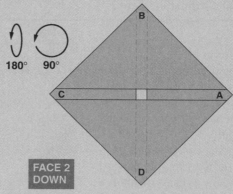

FACE 2 DOWN

2 Flip the board face for face, turn it 90 degrees, and cut a diagonal groove down the center of the second face.

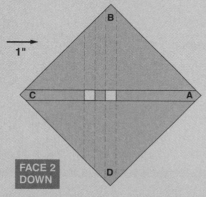

FACE 2 DOWN

3 Move the fence 1 inch further from the cutter. (If it's 3½ inches away, move it to 4½ inches.) Cut a groove in the second face parallel to the center groove.

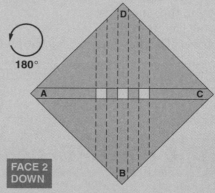

FACE 2 DOWN

4 Turn the board 180 degrees, and cut another groove parallel to the center groove.

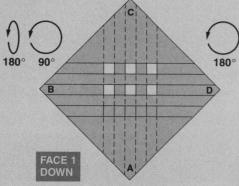

FACE 1 DOWN

5 Flip the board face for face, turn it 90 degrees, and repeat steps 3 and 4, cutting parallel grooves in the first face.

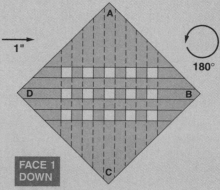

FACE 1 DOWN

6 Move the fence over 1 inch again, and repeat steps 3, 4, and 5. Continue until the crisscross pattern extends to the corners.

CHECKERBOARD PATTERN

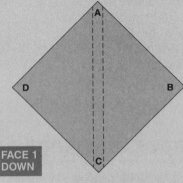

FACE 1 DOWN

1 Cut a diagonal groove down the center of the first face.

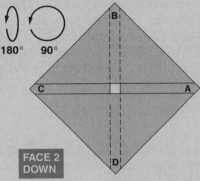

180° 90°

FACE 2 DOWN

2 Flip the board face for face, turn it 90 degrees, and cut a diagonal groove down the center of the second face.

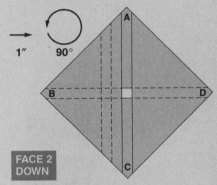

1" 90°

FACE 2 DOWN

3 Move the fence 1 inch further from the cutter. Turn the board 90 degrees, and cut a groove perpendicular to the center groove in the second face.

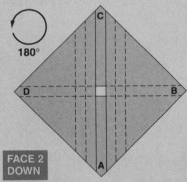

180°

FACE 2 DOWN

4 Turn the board 180 degrees, and make another groove in the second face perpendicular to the center groove.

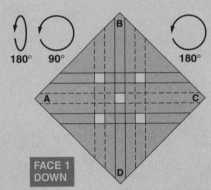

180° 90° 180°

FACE 1 DOWN

5 Flip the board face for face, turn it 90 degrees, and repeat steps 3 and 4, cutting grooves perpendicular to the center groove in the first face.

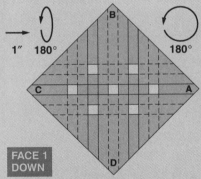

1" 180° 180°

FACE 1 DOWN

6 Move the fence 1 inch further from the cutter. Flip the board face for face, and cut a groove parallel to the center groove in the second face. Turn it 180 degrees, and cut another.

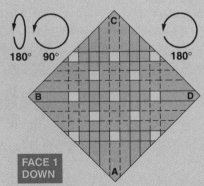

180° 90° 180°

FACE 1 DOWN

7 Flip the board face for face, and turn it 90 degrees. Cut a groove parallel to the center groove in the first face, turn it 180 degrees, and cut another.

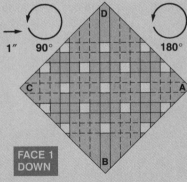

1" 90° 180°

FACE 1 DOWN

8 Repeat steps 3 through 7 until the checkerboard pattern extends to the corners.

At Your Leisure

4 Apply a finish. Lightly sand the completed trivets, then apply a finish. Because the trivets will be subjected to extreme heat from time to time, don't apply a building finish (a finish that builds up on the sur- face of the wood such as shellac or varnish). These will bubble and melt when you set hot pans on them. Instead apply one or two coats of a *penetrating* finish such as tung oil or Danish oil.

Pro SKILL: Handling Odd Shapes and Angles

Use a notch jig to hold two-dimensional shapes or work at odd angles. This simple fixture is invaluable not only for cutting, but also for sanding, drilling, routing, and other woodworking operations.

1 In most cases a notch jig serves as a moving car- riage to guide a workpiece past a cutter. You might push a notch jig along a table saw fence to cut the corners off a square board, creating an octagon (left).

Or guide it along a router table fence to create an angled slot in a workpiece (above).

2 However, you can also use a notch jig as a stationary cradle to help posi- tion parts during an operation. This jig is clamped to a drill press table to locate the holes in octagonal parts. By turning and flipping each part in the jig, you can drill eight identical holes, all precisely the same distance away from the nearest corner.

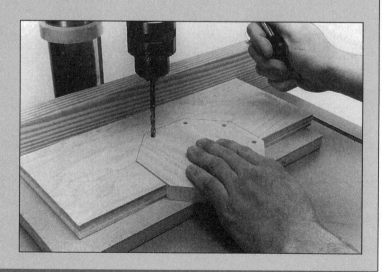

Silverware Caddy

■ **QUICK FIXTURE**
Mortising Jig

■ **PRO SKILL**
Routing Mortises

A mortising jig simplifies mortising operations, letting you rout precise mortises no matter what the shape of the cut or the workpiece. The mortises in the caddy handle are a good example. Without a jig, it's tricky to rout mortises in round stock. With one, it's just a simple matter of tracing the outline of the mortise with your router.

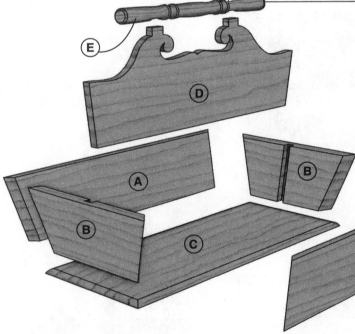

EXPLODED VIEW

MATERIALS LIST

Finished Dimensions in Inches

Parts

A.	Sides (2)	⅜″ × 3½″ × 13½″
B.	Ends (2)	⅜″ × 3½″ × 7″
C.	Bottom	⅜″ × 6″ × 12½″
D.	Divider	⅜″ × 5⅛″ × 13⅛″
E.	Handle	⅝″ dia. × 7¾″

Hardware

½″ Wire brads (24)
1″ Wire brads (8)

The caddy shown is a replica of an antique that's been in the family of Eldon Studebaker since they helped settle the Ohio wilderness in the early nineteenth century. Eldon has made about a dozen of these handsome carryalls from a scarlet oak that he planted on the Studebaker homestead 40 years ago.

Eldon makes his carryalls with compound mitered rabbet joints at the corners, as you can see in the photo. I simplified his design somewhat and used ordinary compound miter joints.

Friday Evening

1 Prepare the materials, and cut the parts to size.
To make this caddy, you need approximately 3 board feet of 4/4 (1-inch-thick) stock. If you resaw the stock into two boards, then you only need 1½ board feet. Choose an attractive cabinet grade wood. The caddy shown is made from scarlet oak (a variety of red oak), but you can use almost any species.

Rip a small turning square to make the handle, then plane the remaining stock to ⅜ inch thick. Cut the bottom and divider to the sizes shown in the Materials List. Rip the stock for the sides and ends to width, beveling both edges at 15 degrees. Cut the sides and ends about an inch longer than specified.

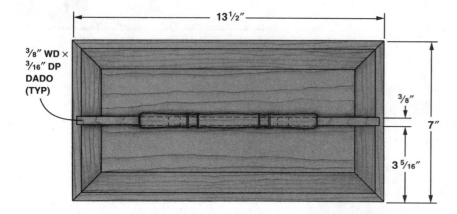

3/8″ WD × 3/16″ DP DADO (TYP)

13½″

⅜″

7″

3 5/16″

TOP VIEW

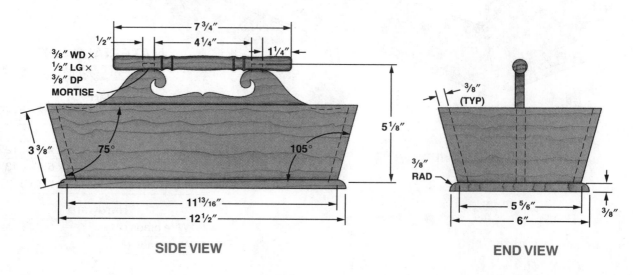

3/8″ WD × 1/2″ LG × 3/8″ DP MORTISE

7 ¾″

½″

4 ¼″

1¼″

3 ⅜″

75°

105°

5 ⅛″

11¹³/₁₆″

12½″

SIDE VIEW

⅜″ (TYP)

⅜″ RAD

5 ⅚″

6″

⅜″

END VIEW

Saturday Morning

2 Cut the compound miters in the sides and ends. The sides and ends are sloped at 75 degrees (15 degrees off vertical). Because of this, they are joined by *compound miters* — a combination of a miter and a bevel.

To make a compound miter, tilt your saw blade and angle the miter gauge. The settings are determined by the slope of the work. For a slope of 15 degrees, set the blade tilt to 43½ degrees and the miter gauge to 78¼ degrees. Miter and bevel the ends of the tray parts.

See Also: "Compound Miters" on page 221.

3 Cut the dadoes in the ends. Using a router or a dado cutter, cut the ³⁄₈-inch-wide, ³⁄₁₆-inch-deep dadoes in the inside faces of the ends, where shown in the *Top View.* These hold the divider.

4 Cut the profile of the divider. Lay out the profile of the divider on the stock, as shown in the *Divider Pattern.* Cut the shape with a scroll saw or band saw, then sand the sawed edges.

Saturday Afternoon

5 Assemble the sides, ends, and divider. Finish sand the sides, ends, and divider, then assemble the parts with glue. Clamp them together with a band clamp. Wipe away any glue that squeezes out of the joints with a wet rag.

6 Shape ends and edges of the bottom. The ends and edges of the bottom are rounded, as shown in the *End View* and *Side View.* Shape the ends first, then the edges, using a router and a ³⁄₈-inch roundover bit.

TRY THIS

STRONG END GRAIN GLUE JOINTS

When joining the parts of a mitered box or frame, you must glue end grain surfaces together. These joints tend to be weak because the end grain soaks up the glue. To make a stronger joint, coat the surfaces *twice.* Apply a thin coat of glue to the adjoining end grain surfaces, and let them dry unassembled for 15 to 20 minutes. Then apply a second coat and clamp the parts together. The first coat prevents the second from being absorbed.

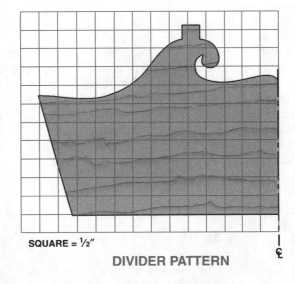

SQUARE = ½"

DIVIDER PATTERN

TRY THIS

CONTINUOUS WOOD GRAIN

Trays and boxes look best if you make the wood grain continuous around the perimeter. Cut the sides and ends from the same board, then join them as if you had bent the board at the corners.

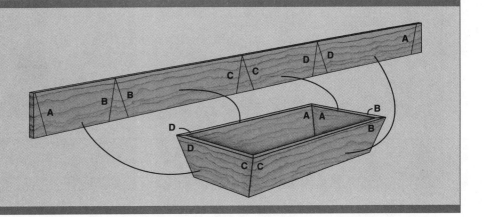

7 **Turn the handle.** Turn the cylindrical shape of the handle, as shown in the *Handle Layout.* Sand the handle smooth on the lathe.

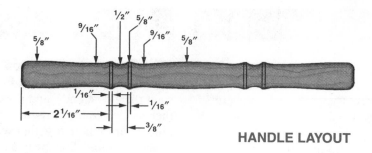

HANDLE LAYOUT

Quick FIXTURE: Mortising Jig

When routing mortises — even when routing just one mortise — you can simplify the operation and increase the accuracy by making a mortising jig. The simple jig shown below automatically positions the mortise and controls its length and width.

The slot in the jig guides the router. You can follow the edges of the slot with a *pattern-routing bit* or a *guide bushing.* The slot must be sized differently for each tool.

■ The guide bearing on a pattern-routing bit (also called an *overbearing*) is the same diameter as the bit. When using this tool, make the slot exactly the same size as the mortise you want to cut. You must also make the template as thick as the bit is long. The cutting flutes on most pattern-routing bits are 1 inch long, so the template must be at least that thick. If it isn't, the bearing won't touch the edges of the slot when making shallow cuts.

■ A guide bushing is a hollow tube that surrounds an ordinary straight bit. Its diameter is slightly larger than the bit, so you must make the slot larger than the mortise you want to cut. How much larger? Subtract the diameter of the bit from the diameter of the guide bushing. Make the slot longer and wider than the mortise by that amount. For example, if you're using a ½-inch bit and a ⅝-inch bushing, make the slot ⅛ inch longer and wider than the mortise you wish to rout.

You can cut the slot in the template with a saber saw or a scroll saw, but there's a simpler and more accurate way to make it. Rip the board that will become the template into three pieces. The middle piece must be exactly as wide as the slot you need. Cut this middle piece into three pieces and discard the middle. Glue the remaining four pieces back together so the distance between the two middle pieces is equal to the length of the slot needed.

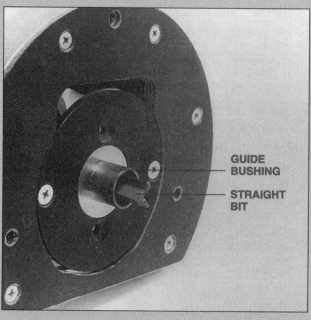

Saturday Evening

8 Cut the mortises in the handle. Make the *Mortising Jig* shown below. Mount the turned handle in the jig, and rout the mortises, as shown in the *Side View.* Use a ½-inch guide bushing to guide the router and a ⅜-inch straight bit to do the cutting. Square the corners of the mortises with a chisel.

See Also:
"Routing Mortises"
on page 28.

Sunday Afternoon

9 Assemble the remaining parts of the caddy. Remove the clamps from the caddy assembly. If necessary, do a little touch-up sanding at the corners to make the joints clean and flush.

Mark the center of the slot on the template (both the length and the width). Mark a mortise on the first part you want to rout, and mark the center of the mortise. Position the template over the mortise layout, and clamp it to the stock.

Attach one or more cleats to the template, aligning the cleats with the ends and edges of the stock. If you're mortising round stock, cut V-grooves in the cleats before you attach them. Use the cleats to position the template on the work and secure it in place.

Note: The mortising jig shown is designed and sized specifically for routing the mortises in the caddy handle, using a ⅜-*inch straight bit* and a ½-*inch guide bushing.* Modify this design as needed for the mortise you want to rout and the equipment you will use.

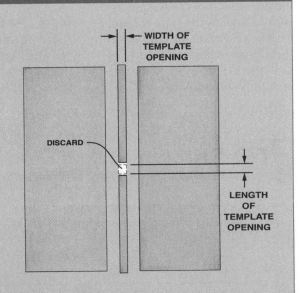

WIDTH OF
TEMPLATE
OPENING

DISCARD

LENGTH
OF
TEMPLATE
OPENING

TEMPLATE DETAIL

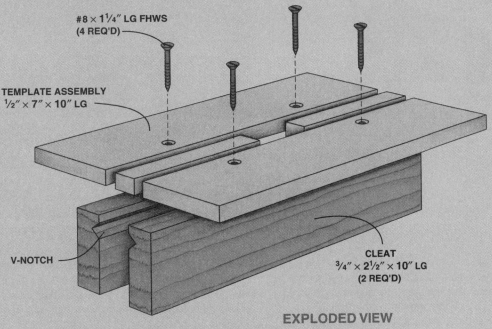

#8 × 1¼" LG FHWS
(4 REQ'D)

TEMPLATE ASSEMBLY
½" × 7" × 10" LG

V-NOTCH

CLEAT
¾" × 2½" × 10" LG
(2 REQ'D)

EXPLODED VIEW
(SIZED FOR ROUTING SLOTS IN CADDY HANDLE)

Reinforce the miter joints by *crossnailing* them with ½-inch wire brads, as shown in the **Corner Joinery Detail.** Drive brads at right angles to one another, locking the parts together.

Finish sand the bottom, and attach it to the caddy assembly with 1-inch wire brads. *Don't glue it in place!* The wood grain on the bottom runs perpendicular to the ends. If you glue the parts together, the ends will restrict the movement of the bottom as it shrinks and swells. The bottom may split, buckle, or pull loose. Wire brads will bend slightly as the wood moves, and the assembly will remain sound.

Glue the handle to the divider, inserting the tenons in the mortises. To prevent it from pulling loose, pin it in place by driving a ½-inch wire brad through each mortise and tenon.

Set the heads of the brads slightly below the wood surface.

At Your Leisure

10 **Finish the silverware caddy.** Do any necessary touch-up sanding, then apply a finish to all wooden surfaces. If you plan to use this

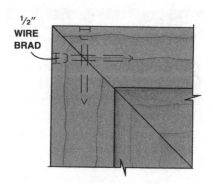

CORNER JOINERY DETAIL

caddy to hold foodstuffs (it makes a great serving tray for crackers and rolls), apply a nontoxic finish such as shellac or "salad bowl dressing."

Pro SKILL: Routing Mortises

When routing mortises, the rules are the same as for any routing operation. Make deep cuts in several passes, removing no more than ¼-inch stock at a time from softwoods and ⅟₁₆ to ⅛ inch from hardwoods. Follow the edge of the template so you're cutting against the rotation of the bit. (The bit rotates clockwise as you look at the top of the router.)

1 Use the cleats to secure the mortising jig to the work, either clamping them or squeezing them in a vise (shown). Check that the slot in the template is properly centered over the mortise layout, then rout the mortise, following the sides of the slot.

2 If necessary, square the corners of the mortise with a mortising chisel. Use a scrap board to guide the chisel, holding the back flat against the sides of the board.

PART TWO

For Storing
and Keeping

Cigar Humidor

■ *QUICK FIXTURE*
Table Saw Dovetail Jig

■ *PRO SKILL*
Cutting Dovetails

Contrary to popular belief, dovetail joints don't require tedious handwork or expensive routing equipment. The tails and pins that join the parts of this humidor were cut on a table saw with an ordinary rip blade and a super-simple two-piece jig.

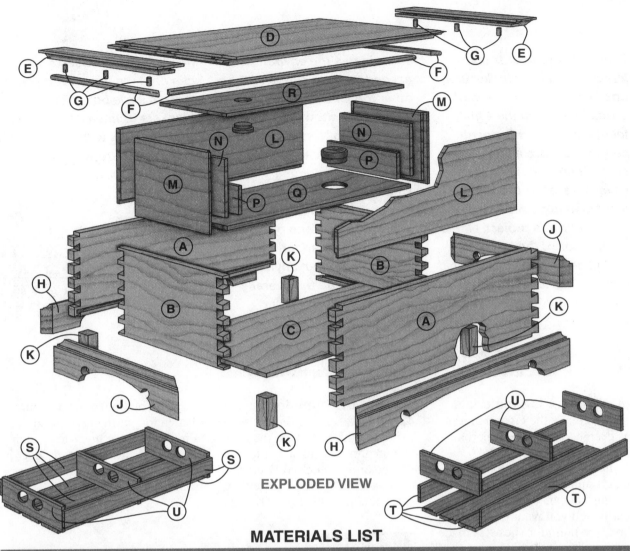

EXPLODED VIEW

MATERIALS LIST

Finished Dimensions in Inches

Box Parts

A.	Front/back (2)	½″ × 7⅜″ × 16″
B.	Sides (2)	½″ × 7⅜″ × 8″
C.	Bottom	¼″ × 7⅜″ × 15½″
D.	Lid	⅝″ × 8⅞″ × 16¼″
E.	Breadboards (2)	⅝″ × 1¼″ × 8⅞″
F.	Beading (total)	¼″ × ⅜″ × 36″
G.	Dowels (6)	3/16″ dia. × ½″
H.	Front/back feet (2)	½″ × 2½″ × 17″
J.	Side feet (2)	½″ × 2½″ × 9″
K.	Glue blocks (4)	½″ × ½″ × 2″

Liner and Tray Parts*

L.	Front/back liners (2)	¼″ × 6⅝″ × 15¼″
M.	Side liners (2)	¼″ × 6⅝″ × 7″
N.	Tall ledges (2)	¼″ × 4½″ × 6½″
P.	Short ledges (2)	¼″ × 2¼″ × 6½″
Q.	Bottom liner	¼″ × 6½″ × 13¾″
R.	Lid liner	¼″ × 7″ × 15″
S.	Top tray battens (5)	¼″ × 1½″ × 14⅜″

T.	Bottom tray battens (5)	¼″ × 1½″ × 13⅞″
U.	Tray ends/dividers (6)	¼″ × 2″ × 5¾″

* Make the liners and trays from Spanish cedar.

Hardware

#4 × ½″ Flathead wood screws (4)
¾″ Wire brads (60)
7/16″ × 1¼″ Stop hinges and mounting screws
Hygrometer
Humidifier

Resources Purchase the stop hinges (#HBB), hygrometer (#HHYG), and humidifier (#HNH3) from:

Beal Tool Company
541 Swans Road NE
Newark, OH 43055

They also sell Spanish cedar in small amounts if you don't have a source for it locally.

This cigar humidor is fashioned after a classic "keeping box." Craftsmen made small boxes like this in the eighteenth and early nineteenth century to store all manner of small items, including jewelry, silverware, scientific equipment, and important documents. For this project, I lined the interior of the box with unfinished wood and installed a humidifier to raise the relative humidity inside the box.

This creates the environment needed to store cigars and other tobacco products.

Note: As shown, the humidor is a "long weekend" project — you can make the box itself in an ordinary weekend, but it takes an extra day to install the liners and trays.

If you're not fond of cigars, you can easily adapt this plan to hold just about anything. Simply change the overall dimensions to suit your

needs. In most cases, you can omit the liner, but if you make a large box to store blankets or linens, you may wish to line it with aromatic red cedar. Here are some suggested sizes:

	H	D	L
Jewelry Box	10″ ×	8″ ×	16″
Document Box	10″ ×	10″ ×	16″
Hope Chest	20″ ×	20″ ×	32″
Blanket Chest	26″ ×	24″ ×	45″

Before You Begin

1 Prepare the materials. To make the cigar humidor as designed, you need approximately 7 board feet of 4/4 (1-inch-thick) hardwood stock and 8 square feet of ¼-inch-thick Spanish cedar. You can use any hardwood you want to make the box (the humidor shown is made from mahogany), but cigar lovers insist on storing cigars in boxes made from or lined with unfinished Spanish cedar.

Resaw and plane the Spanish cedar to ¼ inch thick. Cut the liner parts about 1 inch wider and longer than specified in the Materials List, and wipe them down with water. Seal the parts in a plastic bag along with the hygrometer. Check the parts every day, and add water until the humidity inside the bag is 70 percent. Keep the humidity at this level for at least three days before you cut and install the lining.

See Also:
"Lining Humidors" on page 40.

Friday Evening

2 Cut the humidor parts to size. Plane the 4/4 stock to ⅝ inch thick, and cut the lid and breadboards to size. Plane the remaining stock to ½ inch thick, and cut the front, back, sides, and glue blocks. Also cut

the feet, but make them about 1 inch longer than specified. Finally, plane a piece to ¼ inch thick, and cut the bottom. Set aside some ¼-inch-thick scraps to make the beading.

TRY THIS

VARIATIONS

If you don't want to make the dovetail joints shown, you can join the sides of the humidor with finger joints or splined miter joints. Instructions for making finger joints are on page 64, and the procedure for making the splined miter is on page 13.

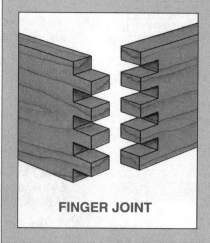

FINGER JOINT

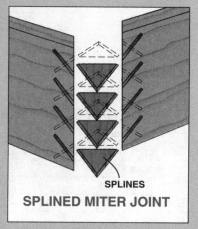

SPLINES

SPLINED MITER JOINT

Saturday Morning

3 Rout the grooves in the front, back, and sides.

The bottom rests in ¼-inch-wide, ¼-inch-deep grooves around the inside of the box. The ends of these grooves are stopped ⅛ inch before the ends of front, back, and sides as shown in the *Dovetail and Groove Layout*. Otherwise, you'd see them at the corners when you assemble the box. Rout these grooves with a router and a straight bit.

4 Cut the dovetail joints.

Lay out the tails on the front and back as shown in the *Dovetail and Groove Layout,* then cut them on a table saw. Use the tails as templates to mark the pins on the sides, then cut the pins to interlock with the tails. The complete procedure is explained on pages 38 and 39.

Saturday Afternoon

5 Assemble the box.

Finish sand the front, back, sides, and bottom. Assemble the front, back, and sides with glue. As you do so, slide the bottom into the grooves in the other parts. However, don't glue it in place. Let the bottom "float" in the grooves so it can expand and contract.

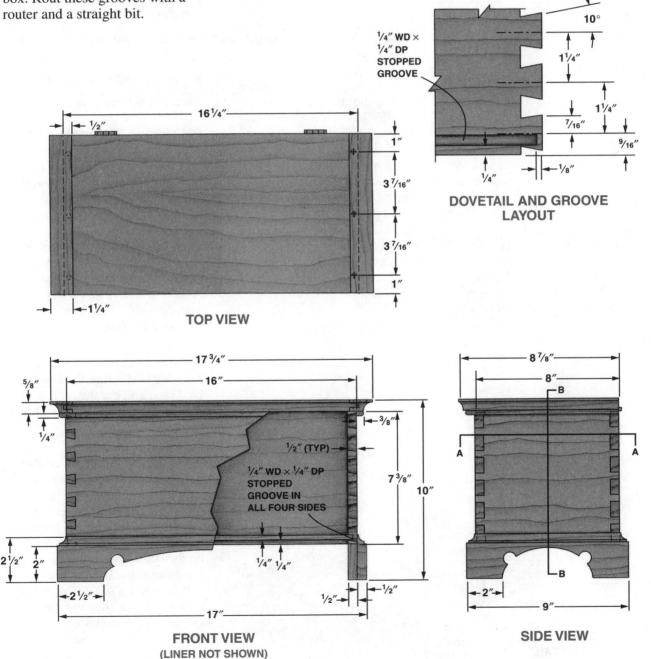

¼" WD × ¼" DP STOPPED GROOVE

10°

1¼"

1¼"

⁷/₁₆"

⁹/₁₆"

¼"

⅛"

DOVETAIL AND GROOVE LAYOUT

16¼"

½"

1"

3⁷/₁₆"

3⁷/₁₆"

1"

1¼"

TOP VIEW

17¾"

16"

⅝"

¼"

3/8"

½" (TYP)

¼" WD × ¼" DP STOPPED GROOVE IN ALL FOUR SIDES

7⅜"

10"

2½"

2"

¼" ¼"

2½"

½"

½"

17"

FRONT VIEW
(LINER NOT SHOWN)

8⅞"

8"

B

A   A

B

2"

9"

SIDE VIEW

As you clamp up the box, make sure the members are square to one another. Clamp *Corner Squares,* shown on page 135, to the assembly to hold the parts square until the glue dries.

6 **Join the breadboards to the lid.** The wood grain in the breadboards runs perpendicular to the grain in the lid. This keeps the lid flat. However, you must join the breadboards in such a way that the lid can still expand and contract.

To do this, cut ¼-inch-thick, ½-inch-long tongues in the ends of the lid and matching grooves in the inside edges of the breadboards, as shown in the *Lid Detail.* Temporarily assemble the lid and breadboards. From the bottom surface of the assembly, drill ³/₁₆-inch-diameter, ½-inch-deep holes where shown on the *Top View.* These holes must go through the tongues and grooves.

Disassemble the lid and breadboards. With a small round file, elongate four of the six holes in the tongues — the middle holes and those nearest the back edge. Turn the holes into slots ³/₈ inch long. However, be careful not to widen the holes. They must remain ³/₁₆ inch wide, as shown in the *Dowel Joint Detail.*

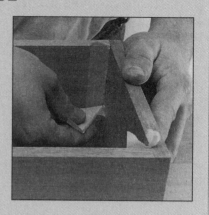
Assemble the lid and breadboards, gluing just the first 2 inches of each tongue-and-groove joint nearest the front edge. Glue the dowels in the holes, but be careful not to get any glue on the tongue as you do so.

This arrangement keeps the breadboards in place, but still allows the lid to move toward the back edge. And when the box lid is closed, the dowels are not visible.

Saturday Evening

7 **Shape the edges of the lid and feet.** When the glue has dried sufficiently on the box and lid assemblies, sand the joints flush and clean. Using a table-mounted router, cut a cove in the front edge of the lid assembly, then the breadboard ends as shown in the *Lid Detail.* (Leave the back edge square.) Also rout a cove and a step in the top edges of the feet, as shown in the *Foot Profile.*

8 **Miter the ends of the feet.** Measure the assembled box, and cut the feet to fit around the outside surface. Miter the adjoining ends.

9 **Cut the profiles of the feet.** Place the feet face to face, the front and back feet in one stack and the side feet in another. Tape the stacks together.

Lay out the profiles of the feet on the stacks, as shown in the *Foot Patterns.* Drill ¾-inch-diameter holes where specified in the patterns, then cut the elliptical profiles with a band saw or coping saw. Sand the sawed edges.

LID DETAIL

⅛″   ⅛″
³/₈″ RAD   ⅛″
⅛″

FOOT PROFILE

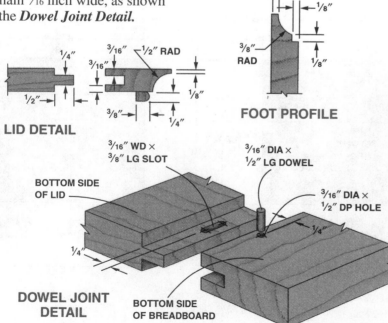

³/₁₆″ WD × ³/₈″ LG SLOT

³/₁₆″ DIA × ½″ LG DOWEL

BOTTOM SIDE OF LID

³/₁₆″ DIA × ½″ DP HOLE

¼″

DOWEL JOINT DETAIL

BOTTOM SIDE OF BREADBOARD

10 Assemble the base. Finish sand the feet and glue them together to form a frame. Reinforce the miter joints in this base frame with glue blocks.

Sunday Afternoon

11 Attach the lid. Mortise the lid and the back for hinges. If you wish, use the *Router Plane* shown on page 84 to help cut the hinge mortises to a uniform depth. Install the hinges and check the action. Make sure the lid rests flat against the top of the box when it's closed — you want to get a good seal to keep the humidity in the box.

Note: As long as you're making a fairly small box, you don't need lid supports (metal braces that hold the lid open). The stop hinges specified in the Materials List will support the lid for you. But if you make the box much larger than the one shown, you should install supports.

12 Make and install the beading. Round over the edge of a ¼-inch-thick scrap, then rip a ⅜-inch-wide strip from the edge to make the beading. Turn the assembled box and lid upside down on the workbench. Cut the beading to fit around the front and side of the box, mitering the adjoining ends. Glue the beading to the lid and bread-boards. (It won't interfere with the movement of the lid.)

Although you can round over the edge of the beading with a router and a small roundover bit, it's faster to do it by hand. Set a block plane to make a very shallow cut, then plane away the sharp corners on the edge, rounding it over. Finish up with 100-grit sandpaper and a sanding block.

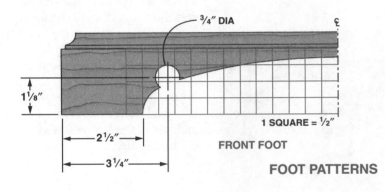

FOOT PATTERNS

FRONT FOOT — ¾" DIA — 1 SQUARE = ½" — 1⅛" — 2½" — 3¼"

SIDE FOOT — ¾" DIA — 1 SQUARE = ½" — 1⅛" — 2" — 2⅜"

Quick FIXTURE: Table Saw Dovetail Jig

When cutting the tails and pins in the front, back, and sides, you must line up the layout lines on the boards precisely with the saw blade. This jig makes it a snap. Just attach the jig to your miter gauge and run it over the blade to cut a kerf in the base. Use this kerf as an indicator to align the stock before each cut.

The jig is made from two pieces of plywood glued together in an L-shaped assembly. The horizontal base must be slightly wider than the thickness of the boards you are joining. (Otherwise, you won't be able to see the kerf.) The vertical face must be tall enough to support the boards on end.

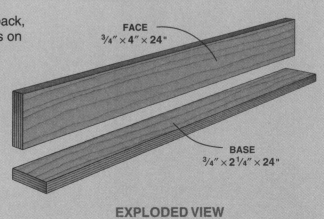

FACE
¾" × 4" × 24"

BASE
¾" × 2¼" × 24"

EXPLODED VIEW

Sunday Evening

13 **Cut the liner parts to size.** Measure the inside of the box — it probably won't be exactly as shown in the drawings. Make the necessary adjustments to the sizes of the liner and tray parts in the Materials List, then remove them from their plastic bag, and cut them to size. **Note:** Spanish cedar dries out quickly, so after you cut each part, replace it in the bag to prevent it from losing its moisture content and shrinking.

14 **Cut the rabbets in the front and back liners.** Cut ¼-inch-wide,

⅛-inch-deep rabbets in the ends of the front and back liners, as shown in *Section B*.

15 **Assemble the side liners and ledges.** Glue the side liners, tall ledges, and short ledges together, making two stair-step assemblies, as shown in *Section A*. The steps or ledges on these assemblies support the trays inside the humidor. Note that the ends of the side liners must protrude ⅛ inch past the ends of the ledges.

When you knock off for the evening, put all the liner parts back in the plastic bag and seal it.

Monday Morning

16 **Install the liner, hygrometer, and humidifier.** Using a hole saw, cut a hole through the bottom liner near one corner to hold the humidifier. Attach the bottom liner to the humidor bottom with two #4 brass screws. Position the screws in the center of the liner part so it can expand toward the edges. Slip the front and back liners into the box, then the side assemblies. Put the lid liner in place, and stick a few pieces of double-faced carpet tape to the top surface. Shut the lid, and press down for a moment.

When you open the lid, the lid liner should be stuck to it. Fasten the lid liner to the lid with two #4 screws. Remove the screws and liner, and discard the tape.

Cut a hole through the lid liner for the hygrometer. It doesn't matter where you put this instrument, but it shouldn't hit the liners or tray when the lid is closed. Replace the lid liner, and install the hygrometer and the humidifier.

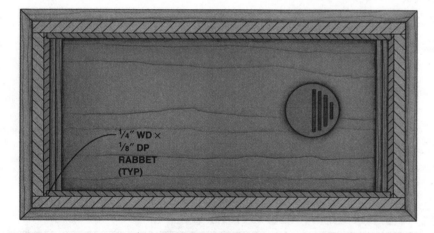

¼″ WD × ⅛″ DP RABBET (TYP)

SECTION A

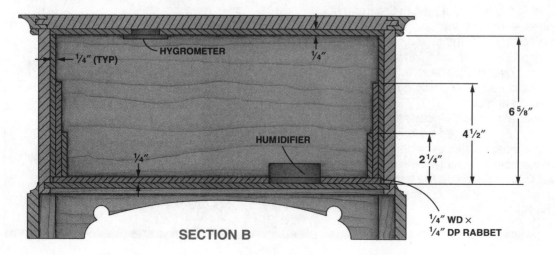

HYGROMETER

¼″ (TYP)

¼″

HUMIDIFIER

¼″

6⅝″

4½″

2¼″

¼″ WD × ¼″ DP RABBET

SECTION B

17 **Make the trays.** Drill 1-inch-diameter holes in the tray ends and dividers, as shown in the ***Tray Detail/Side View.*** Then nail together the ends, dividers, and battens with wire brads. Rest the trays on the ledges inside the lined humidor.

Note: As shown, the dividers are positioned right in the middle of the battens. These can be moved to one side or eliminated, depending on the length of the cigars you want to store.

When you've completed the liner and the trays, remove them from the humidor and seal them in their plastic bag. Keep the humidity inside the bag at 70 percent while you finish the humidor.

Make an assembly jig from scraps of wood, as shown, to hold the dividers and ends as you nail on the battens.

At Your Leisure

18 **Finish the hardwood surfaces.** Remove the lid from the humidor. Finish sand the surfaces, then glue the base frame to the box. (It's much easier to sand the box without the base attached.) Apply a finish to the hardwood surfaces inside and out, but do not coat the cedar liners or trays.

Rub out the finish to the desired gloss. Replace the liners in the box. Also replace the lid, hygrometer, and humidifier.

Keep the humidifier filled with water until the humidity inside the box stabilizes at 70 percent. If you need to raise the humidity quickly, wipe one or both of the trays with water and place them inside the humidor.

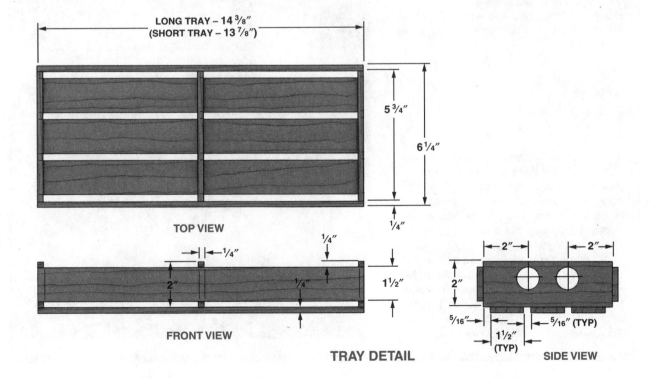

LONG TRAY – 14 3/8"
(SHORT TRAY – 13 7/8")

5 3/4"

6 1/4"

1/4"

TOP VIEW

1/4"

1/4"

2"

1/4"

1 1/2"

FRONT VIEW

TRAY DETAIL

2"   2"

2"

5/16"   5/16" (TYP)

1 1/2"
(TYP)

SIDE VIEW

Pro SKILL: Cutting Dovetails

The front, back, and sides of the humidor are joined with "through" dovetails. The pins and tails go completely through each other so you can see them on both surfaces of the corner. There are many, many ways to make dovetails, but one of the easiest is to cut them on a table saw.

Before you begin, there are several things you should know about dovetails. First of all, they seem to look better if the pins are narrower than the tails. It's traditional to end a dovetail joint at the edge in a half pin rather than a half tail — this, too, seems to look better. Finally, the pins and tails should be just a little longer (about $1/32$ inch) than the boards are thick. They will protrude past each other when you assemble the joint, but you can easily sand them flush.

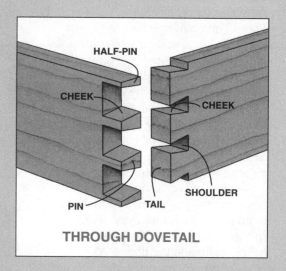

THROUGH DOVETAIL

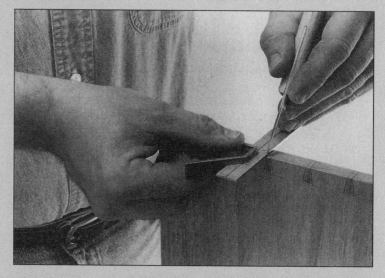

1 Begin by laying out the tails on the front and back parts. Layout is the most critical part of this operation, so take your time and get it right.

Mark the shoulders of the tails on both faces of each board with a mortising gauge. Then mark the cheeks on one face, using a sliding T-bevel to trace the angles precisely. With a square, transfer the cheek layout lines to the opposite faces, and mark the cheeks on that surface as well. Shade the areas between the tails so you know what to cut away.

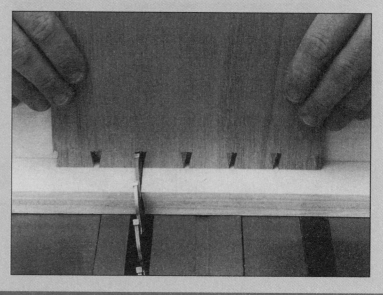

2 Mount a rip blade on your table saw. Attach the table saw dovetail jig to your miter gauge, tilt the saw blade to 10 degrees, and pass the jig over the saw blade to cut a kerf in the base. Adjust the depth of cut so the blade will cut up to the shoulder of each tail, but no higher. Place a board on end in the jig and cut all the cheeks that lean in one direction. Then turn the board face for face and cut the cheeks that lean in the opposite direction. Before each cut, line up the layout lines with the appropriate side of the saw kerf.

3 After cutting the cheeks of the tails, go back and make multiple passes over the saw blade to clean out as much waste from between the tails as you possibly can. You won't be able to get it all. Because the blade is tilted, it will leave little triangular steps in the shoulders. Trim these steps away with a chisel. Place the back of the chisel against a square block to hold it straight up and down, then cut downward, cutting the shoulders flat and true.

4 It's a fair bet that the layout of the dovetail joint will change slightly as you cut the tails. So use the completed tails as a template to mark the pins. Use *Corner Squares* (shown on page 135) to hold the boards in the proper position while scoring the shapes of the tails in the sides with a chisel. Score the pin shoulders with a mortising gauge, then mark the cheeks with a square. Once again, mark both faces of each board, and shade the waste areas.

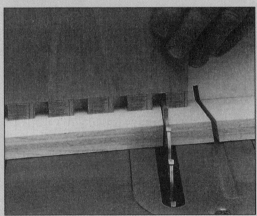

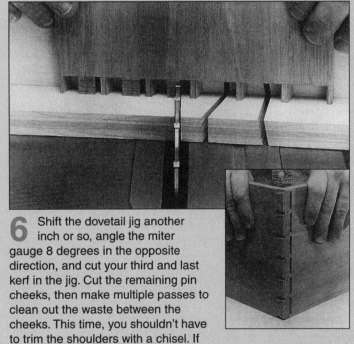

5 Detach the dovetail jig from the miter gauge, move it sideways an inch or so, and attach it again. Angle the miter gauge left or right 8 degrees. Return the saw blade to its normal position (square to the table), and cut another kerf in the jig. Readjust the depth of cut to saw up to the shoulder mark. Place a piece of wood in the jig, and cut all the cheeks that face in the direction that you've angled the miter gauge.

6 Shift the dovetail jig another inch or so, angle the miter gauge 8 degrees in the opposite direction, and cut your third and last kerf in the jig. Cut the remaining pin cheeks, then make multiple passes to clean out the waste between the cheeks. This time, you shouldn't have to trim the shoulders with a chisel. If you're cutting with a rip blade, the teeth will cut parallel to the shoulder line, with no steps. When you have finished cutting the pins, assemble the dovetail joint.

Bonus SKILL: Lining Humidors

You'd think lining a humidor would be a simple matter. After all, you're just building a box inside a box. But the inside box must be made of a specific material and maintained at a much higher moisture content than the outside box. This presents some thorny problems.

FINDING SPANISH CEDAR

The first problem is finding the proper material. Cigar lovers insist that their cigars be stored in Spanish cedar. The reason? I wish I could tell you. I consulted several tobacconists, and no one told me the same story. One said that Spanish cedar regulated moisture better than other species (true), another said it didn't matter, mahogany was an acceptable substitute (true, but not for purists). One said the cedar was neutral and imparted no flavor to the tobacco (not true), and another said the cedar gave a tobacco a mild, spicy flavor (true again).

I'm convinced that the real reason is that when Latin American countries began to export cigars in the nineteenth century, they looked around for something to pack them in. Native cedar was plentiful, cheap, and easy to work, so they made cigar boxes from it. As the reputation of their cigars grew, the cedar packing boxes became part of the mystique.

Where do you get Spanish cedar? With the popularity of cigars growing, dozens of lumber retailers now carry it. But be warned — not all Spanish cedar is suitable for humidor linings. Many craftsman have had unfortunate experiences with cedar that begins to ooze or "weep" sap after they complete the humidor, sometimes ruining the cigars inside.

Why so? It seems there are two types of Spanish cedar. (And neither one is a true cedar, by the way. They are members of the mahogany family.) The type you don't want — the weepy type — is South American cedar, *Cedrela fissilis,* which grows in Brazil and other South American countries. Honduras cedar, *Cedrela odorata,* which grows in Central America is much less likely to weep. How do you tell the difference between the two? Inspect the wood with a magnifier. South American cedar is orange-brown in color and has small dark brown flecks in the grain. Honduras cedar is lighter and pinker (much like the color of fresh-cut cherry) and has no flecks.

FITTING THE LINER

Once you have the proper lining material, the next dilemma you face is how tight the liner should fit inside the box. As you bring the inside of the humidor up to 70 percent relative humidity, the liner will swell. If it's too tight, it will buckle. It may even pop the joints of the humidor.

There is a misconception that Spanish cedar is a stable wood and you don't need to worry about expansion and contraction. This is hogwash. Plain-sawn Spanish cedar will move across the grain as much as 6.3 percent and quartersawn 4.2 percent. Compared to other woods, that's good stability, but not great. Furthermore, this species moves more along the grain than many others. I've seen an 18-inch-long piece expand just under 0.05 inch parallel to the grain after I wiped it with water and let it sit in a sealed container overnight. With any other wood, I would have expected about 0.005 inch of movement, one-tenth as much! Regardless of its relative stability, you are torturing this wood when you raise the humidity inside the humidor to 70 percent. Any wood, no matter how stable, is going to move in this extreme environment.

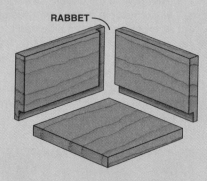

LINER PARTS JOINED WITH RABBETS

So how do you allow for movement when you cut the parts of the liner? The answer is — you don't need to. Instead of trying to guesstimate how much the wood is going to move after it's sawed, cut it after it moves.

Plane the liner parts to the proper thickness, and cut them slightly longer and wider than needed. Wipe them down with water, and seal them in a plastic bag with the hygrometer you bought for your humidor. Check the bag every day and continue to wipe the wood with water until you raise the humidity inside the bag to 70 percent. Hold it there for a few days to give the cedar a chance to reach equilibrium with the humidity, then remove it from the bag, cut the liner parts to size, and install them immediately. As long as you cut to fit, the parts will be the correct size.

There are advantages to this technique. When you install the cedar, it will be at 14 to 15 percent moisture content. (The moisture content of wood rises or falls about 1 per cent for every 5 percent change in relative humidity.) The moisture in the wood will quickly establish the humidity inside the humidor at 70 percent, or close to it. You won't have to wait weeks and weeks while the tiny humidifier strains to create the steamy climate inside the box that cigars need. And the high moisture content helps prevent the wood from weeping.

FINISHING THE HUMIDOR

Next problem: You are installing wood at 15 percent moisture content inside a case made from expensive hardwoods at 8 percent moisture content, and that can hurt. The moisture that creeps through the lining and into the humidor is going to cause it to

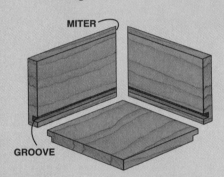

LINER PARTS JOINED WITH MITERS AND GROOVES

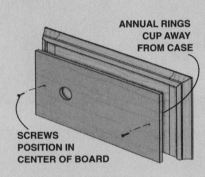

LINER PART SCREWED TO CASE

expand, stressing the joints of the case. Furthermore, the inside surfaces will swell more than the outside. Parts will warp, joints will pop, and teeth will gnash unless you seal the inside of the humidor before you install the lining. The finish will not stop the migration of moisture, but it will slow it down and give it a chance to dissipate.

What should you use? Your choice is complicated because Spanish cedar contains volatile oils. These oils, which give the wood its aroma and flavor the cigars also react with many finishes. In some cases they dissolve them! One craftsman told me that he finished the inside of his humidor case with polyurethane. A few weeks after lining it, the cedar oils reduced the finish to a gummy mess. What finish won't react with the cedar? Your safest choice is shellac. It's affected by very few chemicals other than alcohol. Three or more coats will form an acceptable moisture barrier.

JOINING THE LINING

Should you attach the lining to the inside of the humidor? Not if you don't have to. Because the lining and the humidor case have two different moisture contents, you should let the lining "float" inside the case as much as possible. Where you do attach it, use screws, not glue. Drive the screws near the center of the boards so they can expand and contract toward the edges. Don't screw them down at the edges or the corners; the wood may buckle or split.

Where the parts of the lining meet, use joinery that prevents the wood from cupping or bowing inward. Remember, the humidifier is on the inside of the lining, so there will always be more moisture on the inside surfaces of the lining than on the outside. This, in turn, will cause the parts to cup unless they interlock somehow. Simple rabbets are a good choice; so are miters, finger joints, and dovetails. The adjoining boards brace each other and keep their neighbors straight and true.

What if you can't join a liner part to its neighbors? When this is the case, screw the liner to the humidor so the annual rings curve away from the case. Wood tends to cup opposite its annual rings. This tendency, combined with the fact that there's more moisture on the inside surface, will make the liner pull away from the case near the middle of the board. But the screws in the middle will prevent this, and the edges and corners of the liner will simply press harder against the case. As long as the humidor case doesn't warp, the liner will remain flat.

LOOKING TO THE FUTURE

There's one more thing to consider when lining a humidor. The cigar craze isn't going to last forever. Like any fad, the public will lose interest and move on, stashing their unsmoked cigars with their hula hoops and disco albums. When that happens, you want to be able to remove the liner from your humidor so you still have a small, handsome chest instead of flea market fodder. To this end, use as few screws as possible. Install the hygrometer and the humidifier in the lining; don't cut into the case itself.

CD Candle Box

■ **QUICK FIXTURE**
Tall Fence

■ **PRO SKILL**
Making Raised Panels

When cutting the beveled edges of the sliding lids on this box, I turned the stock on edge. To help support the stock in this position, I attached an auxiliary "tall fence" to my table saw fence. I also used this tall fence to cut the angles in the end wedges.

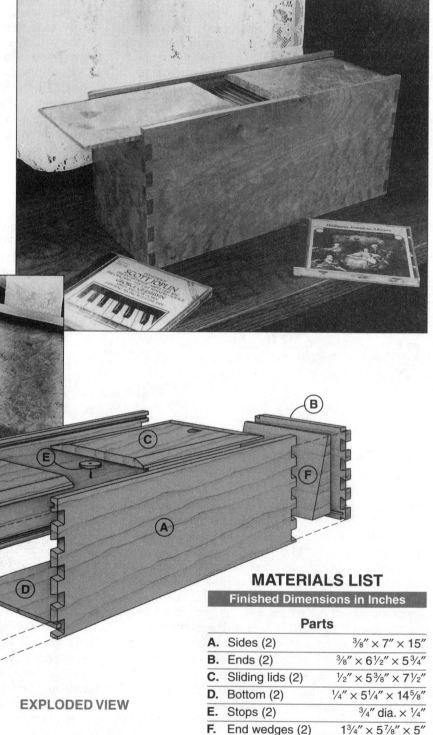

EXPLODED VIEW

MATERIALS LIST

Finished Dimensions in Inches

Parts

A.	Sides (2)	$\frac{3}{8}'' \times 7'' \times 15''$
B.	Ends (2)	$\frac{3}{8}'' \times 6\frac{1}{2}'' \times 5\frac{3}{4}''$
C.	Sliding lids (2)	$\frac{1}{2}'' \times 5\frac{3}{8}'' \times 7\frac{1}{2}''$
D.	Bottom (2)	$\frac{1}{4}'' \times 5\frac{1}{4}'' \times 14\frac{5}{8}''$
E.	Stops (2)	$\frac{3}{4}''$ dia. $\times \frac{1}{4}''$
F.	End wedges (2)	$1\frac{3}{4}'' \times 5\frac{7}{8}'' \times 5''$

Hardware

#4 $\times \frac{1}{2}''$ Flathead wood screws (2)

This is an old-time "candle box" with a new twist — the lid is split so you can open it from either end. The design will store jewelry, recipe cards, computer discs, almost any small item. As you can see, I've adapted this particular box for compact discs. As drawn, the box will hold about 25 CDs. The optional wedges at either end of the box support the discs at a slight angle, letting you flip through them like a card file.

Friday Evening

1 Prepare the materials, and cut the parts to size.

To make the candle box as designed, you need approximately 4 board feet of 4/4 (1-inch-thick) stock and a scrap of 8/4 (2-inch-thick) stock. On the box shown, the ends and sides are made from "quilted" soft maple. (The rare figure in this wood is thought to be caused by a fungus.) The sliding lids are made from a maple burl. However, you can use any attractive wood.

Plane the scrap of 8/4 stock to 1¾ inches thick, and rip it to 5⅞ inches wide. Don't cut the wedges to size yet.

Plane the 4/4 stock to ½ inch thick, select wood for the lids, and cut them to size. Plane the remaining stock down to ⅜ inch thick, and cut the sides and ends to size. Finally, plane what's left to ¼ inch thick, and cut the bottom. Set aside some ¼-inch-thick scraps to make the stops.

Resources Figured maple may be purchased from:

Maple Specialties, Inc.
43306 S.E. North Bend Way
Suites 1 and 2
North Bend, WA 98045

TRY THIS

BOOKMATCHING

When making the lids, resaw the stock and open it like a book, as shown. The grain pattern on each lid will be a mirror image of the other. Together, they will create a pleasing design.

See Also:
"Resawing" on page 107.

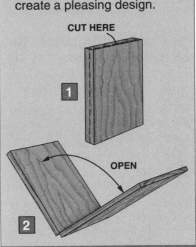

CUT HERE

OPEN

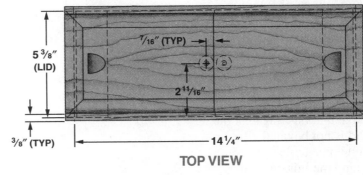

TOP VIEW

7/16″ (TYP)

5 3/8″ (LID)

2 11/16″

3/8″ (TYP)

14 1/4″

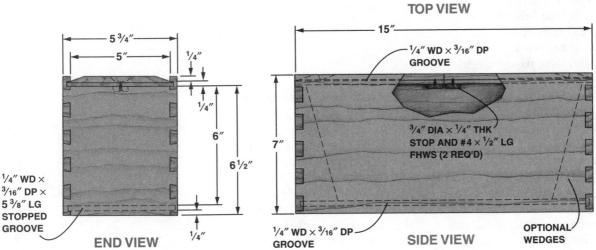

END VIEW

5 3/4″

5″

1/4″

1/4″

6″

6 1/2″

1/4″

¼″ WD × ³/₁₆″ DP × 5 ³/₈″ LG STOPPED GROOVE

SIDE VIEW

15″

7″

¼″ WD × ³/₁₆″ DP GROOVE

¾″ DIA × ¼″ THK STOP AND #4 × ½″ LG FHWS (2 REQ'D)

¼″ WD × ³/₁₆″ DP GROOVE

OPTIONAL WEDGES

2 **Cut the grooves in the sides and ends.** Rout ¼-inch wide, ³⁄₁₆-inch-deep grooves in the sides and ends to hold the bottom and the lids, as shown in the *Side View* and *End View.* Note that the grooves in the ends are stopped so you don't see them when the box is assembled.

Saturday Morning

3 **Cut the dovetails in the sides and ends.** Lay out the dovetail pins on the sides, as shown in the *Dovetail Layout.* Cut the pins, then use them as a template to mark the tails on the ends. Cut the tails and fit them to the pins.

See Also:
"Cutting Dovetails" on page 38.

Saturday Afternoon

4 **Bevel the edges of the lids.** Three out of four edges on each sliding lid are beveled at 20 degrees, as shown in *Section A* of the *Lid Layout.* (The edge that butts against the other lid is not beveled.) To cut this angle on a table saw, you must stand the lids on their edges and ends. To do this safely, first make an auxiliary *Tall Fence* (see page 46) and attach it to your table saw fence.

Because the lids are relatively small, the sawing operation will be safer if you attach them to a larger "carriage" board. Select a plywood scrap at least 8 inches wide and 16 inches long to serve as the carriage. Stick the lids to this board with carpet tape and cut the bevels, guiding the carriage along the tall fence.

5 **Cut the end wedges.** If you elect to make the end wedges, leave the tall fence attached to the table saw fence. Attach the wedge stock to the carriage board, and rip the stock at a 15-degree angle, guiding the carriage along the tall fence. Cut the angled stock into two 5-inch-long, 6-inch-wide segments.

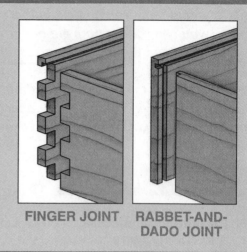

TRY THIS

A SIMPLER STYLE
If you don't want to make the dovetail joint shown, you can join the sides and ends of the box with finger joints or rabbet-and-dado joints.

FINGER JOINT **RABBET-AND-DADO JOINT**

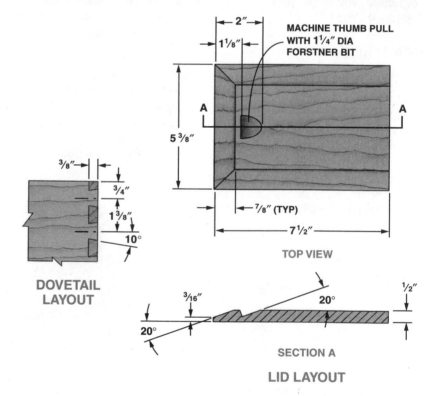

DOVETAIL LAYOUT

2"
1¹⁄₈"
MACHINE THUMB PULL WITH 1¼" DIA FORSTNER BIT

A   A

5³⁄₈"

⁷⁄₈" (TYP)

7¹⁄₂"

TOP VIEW

³⁄₈"
³⁄₄"
1³⁄₈"
10°

³⁄₁₆"
20°
20°
½"

SECTION A

LID LAYOUT

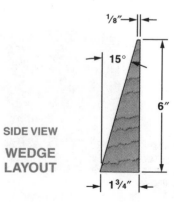

¹⁄₈"
15°
6"

SIDE VIEW

WEDGE LAYOUT

1³⁄₄"

To bevel the lids, secure a tall fence to your table saw. Attach the lids to the face of a carriage board with double-faced carpet tape. The ends or edges you wish to cut must be flush with the lower edge of the carriage board. Tilt the saw blade to 20 degrees, and cut the bevels, guiding the carriage board along the tall fence. Cut the bevels in the ends of the lids first, then the bevels in the edges. Remember, do not cut bevels in the adjoining ends of the lids.

Rip the wedge stock in four passes. First, attach it to a carriage board with double-faced carpet tape. Tilt the saw blade to 15 degrees and adjust the depth of cut to 1½ inches. **(1)** Make the first pass, guiding the carriage along the tall fence. **(2)** Then raise the depth of cut to 3 inches and make the second pass. **(3)** For the third pass, remove the stock from the carriage, flip it edge for edge, and reattach it to the carriage. Readjust the fence, change the depth of cut to 1½ inches, and feed the stock over the saw blade. **(4)** Finally, raise the depth of cut to 3 inches, and make the final pass. By cutting the wedge stock in stages like this, you reduce the chances of kickback.

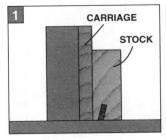
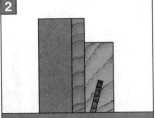
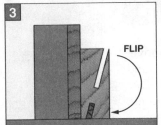
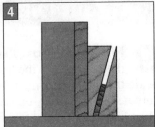

6 Cut the fingerholds in the lids. The fingerholds in the lids are half-round recesses cut in the same manner as the pocket hole in a screw pocket. In fact, you can use the *Screw Pocket Jig* shown on page 89 to hold the board while you cut the recesses with a 1¼-inch-diameter drill bit.

7 Assemble the box. Finish sand the sides, ends, and bottom. Glue the sides to the ends. As you join them, slide the bottom into its grooves. Do not glue the bottom in place; let it "float" in the grooves so it can expand and contract.

To cut a fingerhold, clamp the lid in the screw pocket jig. Position the jig and the lid under the drill bit and clamp the jig to the drill press table. Feed the drill into the wood very slowly so the cutting edges don't catch on the wood.

Sunday Afternoon

8 Install the lids. Sand the corner joints flush and smooth, then fit the lids to the grooves near the top edges of the sides.

Using a hole saw or a plug cutter, make two ¾-inch-diameter discs from a scrap of the ¼-inch-thick stock. Drill and countersink a pilot hole for a #4 screw in the center of each disc. Also drill a pilot hole partway through the bottom face of each lid, ½ inch in from the square edge (the edge without the bevel).

Slide the lids into the box, and attach the stops to the bottom faces with flathead woods screws. Use a short-shank or offset screwdriver to drive the screws.

At Your Leisure

9 Finish the box. Remove the stops from the lids, and slide the lids out of the box. Do any necessary touch-up sanding, then apply a finish. After the finish has dried and you have rubbed it to the desired luster, replace the lids in the box.

As shown, the box is finished with a mixture of tung oil and spar varnish (1 cup oil to 1 table-spoon varnish), rubbed to a high gloss. I like this combination for highly figured woods because it shows off the grain so nicely.

Quick FIXTURE: Tall Fence

When cutting the bevels on the lids in the *CD Candle Box*, you must balance the boards on their ends and edges. Unfortunately, table saw fences are too short to safely support the boards as you do this. You must extend the guiding surface vertically with a *tall fence*.

The fence face must be perfectly straight and flat to guide the work accurately. To ensure that it is, clamp the face to a flat surface (such as the saw table) as you glue the stiffener to it. Attach the fixture to the table saw fence with bolts or screws, then check that it's square to the worktable.

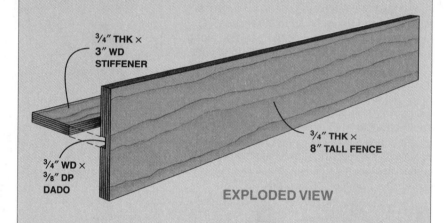

¾" THK × 3" WD STIFFENER

¾" WD × ⅜" DP DADO

¾" THK × 8" TALL FENCE

EXPLODED VIEW

Use a square to check that the tall fence is square to the saw table. If not, shim the tall fence by sticking pieces of tape above or below the mounting screws until it rests at the proper angle.

Pro SKILL: Making Raised Panels

The lids on the *CD Candle Box* are small *raised panels* — boards with bevels or tapers cut around the circumference. This "thins out" the panels at the edges and ends. The edges of the lids, for example, fit a ¼-inch-wide groove, even though the lid is ½ inch thick. Raised panels are commonly used for drawer bottoms, door panels, and frame-and-panel assemblies.

1 When cutting a raised panel, the bevel angle is critical. If it's too steep, as shown on the left, the panel could split the groove that it rests in. If it's too shallow, as shown in the middle, the panel will be loose in the groove — it will rattle every time you move the assembly. The bevel must be angled so it barely touches the side of the groove, as shown on the right. To find the proper bevel angle, draw up a full size (or even twice size) section view of the assembly, and measure the angled surface with a protractor.

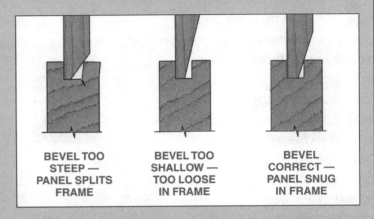

BEVEL TOO STEEP — PANEL SPLITS FRAME

BEVEL TOO SHALLOW — TOO LOOSE IN FRAME

BEVEL CORRECT — PANEL SNUG IN FRAME

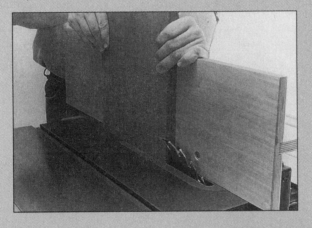

2 Attach a tall fence to your table saw fence to help support the stock as you cut the ends and edges. Cut the ends first, sawing across the grain.

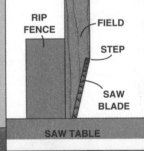

RIP FENCE
FIELD
STEP
SAW BLADE
SAW TABLE

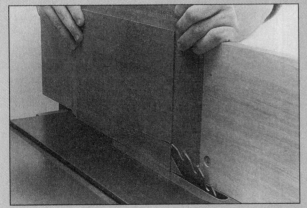

3 Then cut the edges, ripping with the grain. The reason that you cut the ends before the edges is that the wood is more likely to tear as the saw exits a crosscut. By saving the rip cuts till last, you will cut away any torn grain.

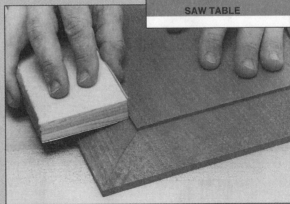

4 Raised panels often have a step between the field (the flat part of the panel) and the bevels. To make this step, adjust the depth of cut so just the outside corners of the sawteeth break through the surface as you cut. After cutting, sand or file the step square to the field.

Chimney Cupboard

■ *QUICK FIXTURE*
Parallel Rules

■ *PRO SKILL*
Cutting Coves

To cut a large cove molding, pass the molding stock across your table saw at an angle to the blade. Instead of cutting the wood in two, the blade will create a deep hollow. To help set up the table saw for a coving cut, use a set of parallel rules — two straightedges joined so they are always parallel.

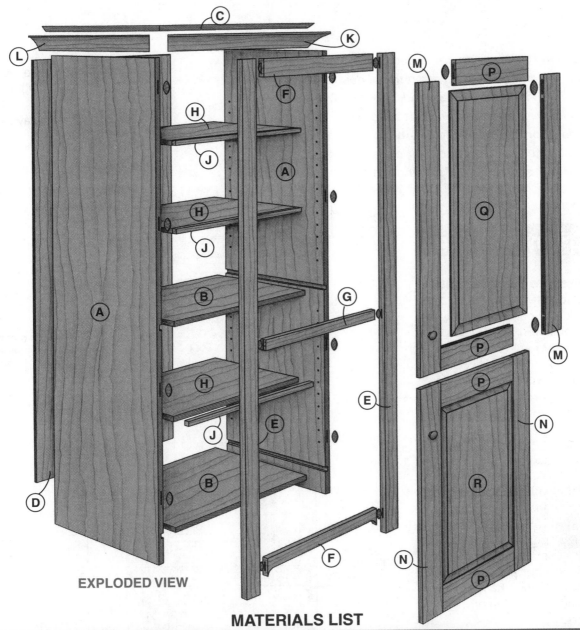

EXPLODED VIEW

MATERIALS LIST

Finished Dimensions in Inches

Parts

A.	Sides* (2)	$3/4'' \times 17\frac{1}{4}'' \times 74\frac{1}{4}''$
B.	Fixed shelves* (2)	$3/4'' \times 17'' \times 22\frac{1}{4}''$
C.	Top*	$3/4'' \times 19\frac{11}{16}'' \times 26\frac{3}{8}''$
D.	Back*	$1/4'' \times 22\frac{1}{4}'' \times 70\frac{7}{8}''$
E.	Face frame stiles (2)	$3/4'' \times 2'' \times 74\frac{1}{4}''$
F.	Face frame top/bottom rails (2)	$3/4'' \times 2\frac{1}{2}'' \times 19''$
G.	Face frame middle rail	$3/4'' \times 1\frac{1}{2}'' \times 19''$
H.	Adjustable shelves* (2–4)	$3/4'' \times 16\frac{5}{8}'' \times 21\frac{3}{8}''$
J.	Shelf trim (2–4)	$1/4'' \times 3/4'' \times 21\frac{3}{8}''$
K.	Front cove molding	$3/4'' \times 3\frac{1}{2}'' \times 28''$
L.	Side cove moldings (2)	$3/4'' \times 3\frac{1}{2}'' \times 20\frac{1}{2}''$
M.	Top door stiles (2)	$3/4'' \times 3'' \times 36\frac{5}{8}''$
N.	Bottom door stiles (2)	$3/4'' \times 3'' \times 28\frac{7}{8}''$
P.	Door rails (4)	$3/4'' \times 3'' \times 12\frac{7}{8}''$
Q.	Top door panel	$1/2'' \times 13\frac{3}{8}'' \times 31\frac{3}{8}''$
R.	Bottom door panel	$1/2'' \times 13\frac{3}{8}'' \times 23\frac{3}{8}''$

Make these parts from plywood.

Hardware

#8 × 1½" Flathead wood screws (5)

#18 × ¾" Wire brads (14–16)

#20 Biscuits (16)

#00 Biscuits (6)

4d Finishing nails (12–16)

1" Wooden knobs (2)

Magnetic catches (2)

Flush-mount rat-tail hinges (4)

Shelf support pins (12)

Craftsman Pat Ventrone combined old and new materials and techniques in this traditional design so you could finish it in a long weekend. The door frames, for example, are assembled with biscuits, eliminating the need for mortises and tenons. And those old-fashioned rat-tail hinges not only add a bit of decoration; they eliminate the necessity of making hinge mortises.

Resources Purchase the rat-tail hinges (#H41-C04) from:

Ball and Ball
463 W. Lincoln Highway
Exton, PA 19341

Friday Evening

1 Prepare the materials, and cut the parts to size.

To make the chimney cupboard, you need approximately 18 board feet of 4/4 (1-inch-thick) stock, two 4×8-foot sheets of ¾-inch plywood, and a single 4×8-foot sheet of ¼-inch plywood. The cupboard shown is made

See Also:
"Cutting Plywood"
on page 204.

from red oak and red oak plywood, but you can use a variety of other woods and veneered plywoods. Bear in mind that oak- and birch-veneered plywoods are readily available and (relatively) inexpensive. You may pay through the nose for plywoods covered in other veneers.

Plane the 4/4 stock to ¾ inch thick. Cut the sides, top, back, shelves, shelf trim, and face frame parts, as specified in the Materials List. Bevel the front and side edges of the top at 45 degrees as you cut it. Rip the cove molding stock to width but don't cut it to length yet. Don't do anything about the door parts until after the case is assembled.

2 Attach the shelf trim.

Glue the shelf trim to the front edges of the adjustable shelves. This will hide the plies when the shelves are installed in the case.

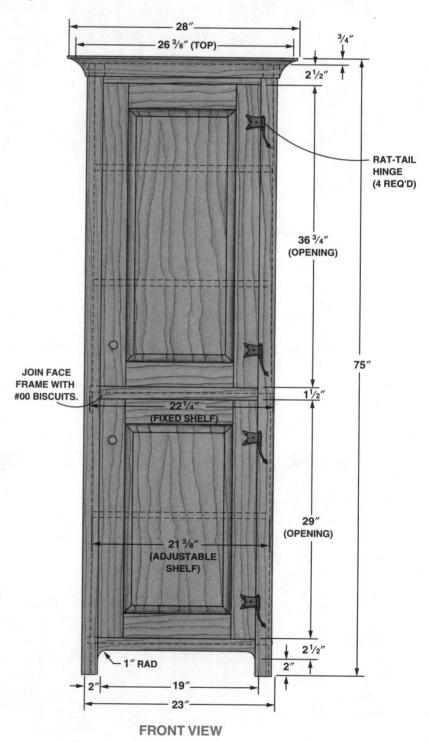

FRONT VIEW

Saturday Morning

3 **Cut the dadoes and rabbets in the case parts.** Using a router, cut the dadoes and rabbets needed in the sides and top:

See Also:
"Routing Dadoes and Rabbets" on page 59.

■ ³⁄₄-inch-wide, ³⁄₈-inch-deep dadoes in the sides, as shown in the *Side Layout*

■ ¹⁄₄-inch-wide, ³⁄₈-inch-deep rabbets in the back edges of the sides

■ ¹⁄₄-inch-wide, ³⁄₈-inch-deep rabbets in the back edge of the top, as shown in the *Side View*

4 **Drill holes for shelf supports.** The adjustable shelves rest on shelf support pins. The pins themselves fit into ¹⁄₄-inch-diameter holes in the sides. Drill the holes, as shown in the *Side Layout*.

See Also:
"Drilling Guide" on page 127.

5 **Cut the profile of the bottom rail.** Lay out the profile of the bottom rail, as shown in the *Front View.* Cut the shape with a scroll saw or band saw, then sand the sawed edges.

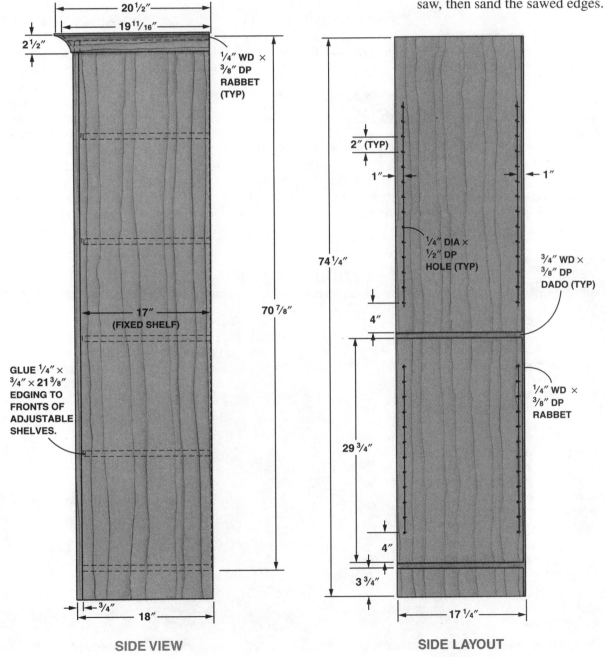

20¹⁄₂″
19¹¹⁄₁₆″
2¹⁄₂″

¹⁄₄″ WD × ³⁄₈″ DP RABBET (TYP)

17″ (FIXED SHELF)

70⁷⁄₈″

GLUE ¹⁄₄″ × ³⁄₄″ × 21³⁄₈″ EDGING TO FRONTS OF ADJUSTABLE SHELVES.

³⁄₄″
18″

SIDE VIEW

2″ (TYP)
1″
1″

¹⁄₄″ DIA × ¹⁄₂″ DP HOLE (TYP)

³⁄₄″ WD × ³⁄₈″ DP DADO (TYP)

74¹⁄₄″

4″

¹⁄₄″ WD × ³⁄₈″ DP RABBET

29³⁄₄″

4″

3³⁄₄″

17¹⁄₄″

SIDE LAYOUT

Saturday Afternoon

6 **Assemble the face frame.** Cut biscuit joints in the ends of the face frame rails and the edges of the face frame stiles. Assemble the face frame with glue and #00 biscuits. The middle rail is narrower than the biscuit is long, so a small portion of the biscuit will protrude on both sides of the joint. When the glue dries, remove the protruding portion of the biscuits with a flush-cut saw or a file.

7 **Cut the coves in the molding stock.** While you're waiting for the glue to dry on the face frame, cut the coves in the molding stock. Pass the wood across the table saw at a 37-degree angle to the blade to cut a cove ½ inch deep and 3⅛ inches wide.

See Also:
"Cutting Coves"
on page 55.

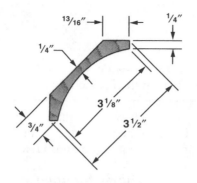

MOLDING PROFILE

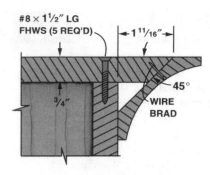

TOP ASSEMBLY DETAIL

Double-bevel the edges of the stock at 45 degrees, as shown in the *Molding Profile.*

Saturday Evening

8 **Assemble the case.** Finish sand the surfaces of the face frame, sides, fixed shelves, top, and back. Dry assemble (*without* glue) the sides and the fixed shelves. Fit the face frame to the front edges of the case, and cut slots for #20 biscuits to join the face frame to the case. Glue together the sides, fixed shelves, and face frame.

Attach the top to the case with glue and flathead wood screws. The top must be flush with the back edge of the case and should overhang the side and front edges by 1¹¹⁄₁₆ inches, as shown in the *Top Assembly Detail.*

Quick FIXTURE: Parallel Rules

A set of parallel rules is a flexible parallelogram. Two straightedges are joined by two stretchers so all the joints pivot. As you pull the rules farther apart or push them closer together, they remain absolutely parallel. These rules were once common drafting tools, but they are becoming hard to find. No matter — you can make your own from four narrow strips of hardwood. Joint the strips straight and true, then join them at the ends with flathead wood screws. The screws serve as pivots.
Note: The distance between the screw holes on the two straightedges must be exactly the same. Likewise for the holes in the stretchers. To make sure they're equal, stack each pair of parts and drill both of them at once.

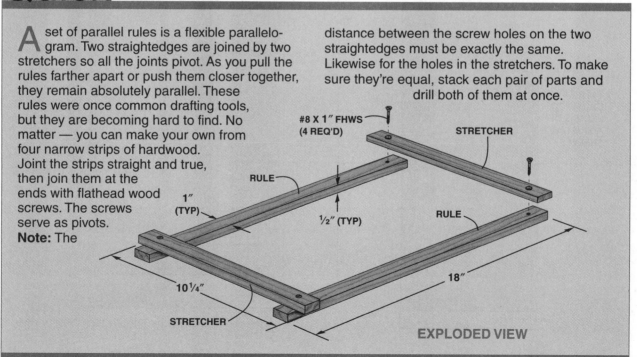

EXPLODED VIEW

Sunday Afternoon

9 **Install the cove molding.** Cut the cove molding to the proper length, mitering the adjoining ends. Nail and glue the molding to the top, sides, and face frame, as shown in the *Top Assembly Detail.*

10 **Cut the door parts.** Measure the openings for the doors just in case you got them a little different from what is shown in the drawings. Adjust the dimensions of the door rails, stiles, and panels as needed, then cut the rails and stiles to size. Plane the remainder of the ¾-inch-thick stock to ½ inch thick. Glue the boards edge to edge to make the wide door panels.

When mitering the cove molding, hold it at a 45-degree slope so one of the long bevels (in the back of the molding) rests flat against the miter gauge face. If you have trouble holding the work at this angle, adhere the molding to a beveled scrap board with double-faced carpet tape. *Saw guard removed for clarity.*

Sunday Evening

11 **Cut the door frame joinery.** The door frames are assembled with biscuit joints, while the panels "float" in grooves, as shown in the *Top Door Layout* and *Bottom Door Layout.* Cut:

■ Semicircular slots for #20 biscuits in the ends of the rails and the edges of the stiles
■ ¼-inch-wide, ¼-inch-deep grooves in the edges of the rails
■ ¼-inch-wide, ⅜-inch-deep *stopped* grooves in the edges of the stiles. These grooves should stop before they cut through the biscuit slots.

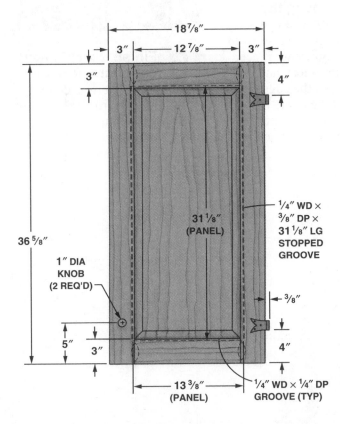

TOP DOOR LAYOUT

- 18⁷⁄₈″
- 3″ — 12⁷⁄₈″ — 3″
- 3″
- 4″
- 36⁵⁄₈″
- 31⅛″ (PANEL)
- ¼″ WD × ⅜″ DP × 31⅛″ LG STOPPED GROOVE
- 1″ DIA KNOB (2 REQ'D)
- 5″ 3″
- ⅜″
- 4″
- 13⅜″ (PANEL)
- ¼″ WD × ¼″ DP GROOVE (TYP)

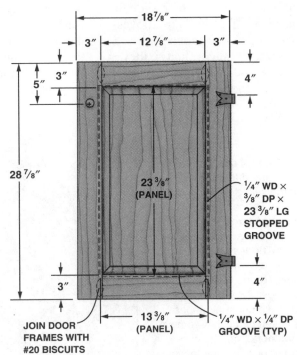

BOTTOM DOOR LAYOUT

- 18⁷⁄₈″
- 3″ — 12⁷⁄₈″ — 3″
- 5″ 3″
- 4″
- 28⁷⁄₈″
- 23⅜″ (PANEL)
- ¼″ WD × ⅜″ DP × 23⅜″ LG STOPPED GROOVE
- 3″
- 4″
- JOIN DOOR FRAMES WITH #20 BISCUITS
- 13⅜″ (PANEL)
- ¼″ WD × ¼″ DP GROOVE (TYP)

TRY THIS

MAKING AND FITTING DOORS

As shown in the drawings, the doors are ⅛ inch shorter and narrower than the openings. This provides 1/16 inch "clearance" around the perimeter of the door frames so the doors can be opened and closed easily. Rather than make the doors to clear the openings, many craftsmen prefer to make them the *same size* as the openings, then shave down the edges of the frame to fit. This offers two advantages. It prevents you from making the doors too small and getting a sloppy fit, and it allows you to fit the doors to openings that may not be precisely square.

12 **Cut the raised panels.** Cut the beveled edges of the panels, as shown in the **Panel Profile.** Position the fence so the saw blade leaves a small step around the perimeter of the "fields" (the raised parts of the panels). Bevel the ends of the panels first, then the edges.

See Also:
"Making
Raised Panels"
on page 47.

PANEL PROFILE

1¼"   3/16"   ½"

13 **Assemble the doors.** Finish sand the door parts, then assemble the frames with glue and biscuits. As you put the frames together, slide the panels in place in their grooves. *Do not* glue the panels in the grooves; let them float so they can expand and contract with changes in the weather.

Monday Morning

14 **Fit and hang the doors on the cupboard.** Remove the clamps from the assembled doors and, if need be, sand the joints clean and flush. Shave down the edges of the frames until the doors fit their openings with no more than 1/16-inch clearance all around the perimeter.

Mount the leaves of the rat-tail hinges on the door frames. About ⅜ inch of each leaf (the rounded portion or *barrel*) must protrude beyond the edge of the frame.

Temporarily insert the doors in their openings, and secure them with small wooden wedges. Insert the posts in the leaves, and mark their position on the face frame. Remove the doors and mount the posts. Then hang the doors by slipping the barrels over the posts. Also install knobs and magnetic catches.

15 **Install the adjustable shelves.** Insert shelving support pins in the holes in the interior of the case. Rest the shelves on the pins, making sure they fit properly.

At Your Leisure

16 **Finish the chimney cupboard.** Remove the adjustable shelves, doors, knobs, and all hardware. Do any necessary touch-up sanding, then apply a finish to all wooden surfaces, inside and out.

The *post* of a rat-tail hinge is mounted to the face frame with a screw and a *collar.* The tabs on the collar go through the frame and are clinched over. The *leaf* is mounted to the door frame, and the *barrel* of the leaf slips over the post. One advantage of these unusual hinges is that you can easily remove the doors from the cupboard by lifting the leaves off the posts.

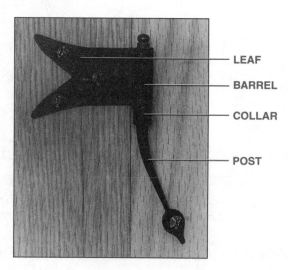

LEAF
BARREL
COLLAR
POST

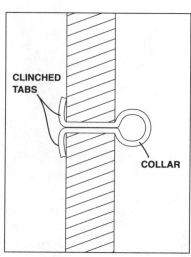

CLINCHED
TABS
COLLAR

Pro SKILL: Cutting Coves

To cut a large cove in a board with a table saw, pass the stock over the saw blade at an angle to the blade body. Use a *combination* blade and guide the stock along a fence. (Make a fence by jointing a straight edge on a long scrap of hardwood.) The height of the blade determines the depth of the cove, the angle determines its width, and the position of the fence controls the position of the cove on the stock.

1 Find the coving angle — the angle at which the work will cross the blade — with parallel rules. Adjust the blade to the desired depth of cut, and set the rules to the width of the cove. Place the rules on the table saw, straddling the blade. Turn them at various angles while rotating the blade by hand. Find the position where the teeth of the saw brush both the front and back straightedges. Using a grease pencil or some other nonpermanent marker, trace the inside edge of each straightedge, making two lines on the saw table.

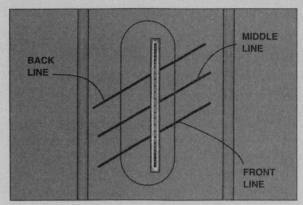

BACK LINE

MIDDLE LINE

FRONT LINE

2 Measure the distance between the front and back lines, then draw a third halfway between them. This marks the center of the cove cut. Use all three lines as references to determine the angle and position of the fence board that guides the work. For example, if you want to cut a cove down the middle of a 3½-inch-wide board, the fence must be 1¾ inches away from the middle reference line and parallel to it. Fasten the fence to the table with double-faced carpet tape on the "front" side of the middle line so the rotation of the blade pulls the work against it.

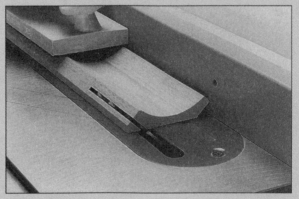

3 Adjust the blade so it projects no more than ¹⁄₁₆ inch above the saw table. Turn on the saw, and place the stock against the fence. Slowly feed the stock, cutting against the rotation of the blade. After completing the first pass, raise the saw blade another ¹⁄₁₆ inch, and make a second pass. Repeat until you have cut the cove to the desired depth. On the last pass, make a very shallow cut, and feed the stock very slowly — this will make the cove as smooth as possible.

4 If you are making a molding, bevel or shape additional surfaces after cutting the cove. Then smooth the cove with a scraper or sandpaper.

Vegetable Bin

When routing the dadoes that hold the shelves in this bin, I guided the router along a shopmade T-square. The crossbar or "head" of the square aligned the straightedge so the resulting dadoes were precisely 90 degrees to the edge.

EXPLODED VIEW

MATERIALS LIST

Finished Dimensions in Inches

Parts

A.	Sides* (2)	$\frac{3}{4}$" × $9\frac{3}{4}$" × $35\frac{1}{4}$"
B.	Top shelf*	$\frac{3}{4}$" × $10\frac{1}{4}$" × $13\frac{1}{4}$"
C.	Lower shelves* (3)	$\frac{3}{4}$" × $9\frac{1}{2}$" × $13\frac{1}{4}$"
D.	Top	$\frac{3}{4}$" × $11\frac{1}{4}$" × $15\frac{3}{4}$"
E.	Back*	$\frac{1}{4}$" × $13\frac{1}{4}$" × $31\frac{1}{4}$"
F.	Top shelf trim (2)	$\frac{3}{4}$" × $\frac{3}{4}$" × $4\frac{3}{4}$"
G.	Top bin front	$\frac{3}{4}$" × $2\frac{1}{2}$" × 14"
H.	Middle bin front	$\frac{3}{4}$" × 4" × 14"
J.	Bottom bin front	$\frac{3}{4}$" × 10" × 14"

Make these parts from plywood.

Hardware

4d Finishing nails (8–10)

6d Finishing nails (40–48)

This storage unit offers a single shelf and three bins of various sizes. It's built to countertop height so the top can be used as a work surface. Although it's designed for foodstuffs, it will hold many other items. My wife and I use one to separate and store recyclables. A friend built a wider version for his potting shed.

Quick FIXTURE: T-Square Gu

This handy jig can be used to guide routers, sa circular saws, and other cutting tools in a st straightedge serves as a fence or guide, whil square the straightedge to the work. Cut bo of wood or plywood, then screw them to another. Don't glue them. The head of up with use, and you may need to r time to time.

HEAD

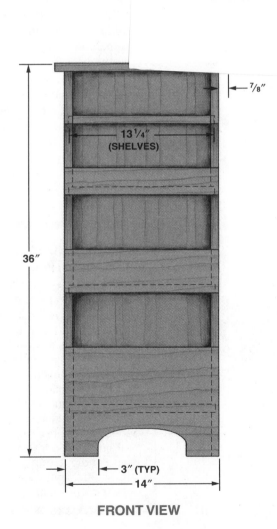

13 1/4"
(SHELVES)

7/8"

36"

3" (TYP)

14"

FRONT VIEW

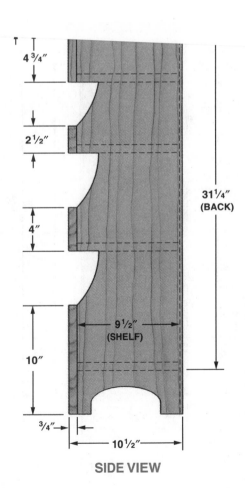

4 3/4"

2 1/2"

4"

31 1/4"
(BACK)

9 1/2"
(SHELF)

10"

3/4"

10 1/2"

SIDE VIEW

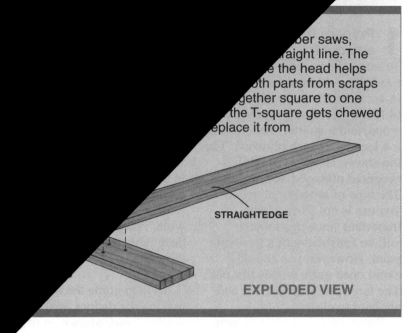

...ber saws,
...raight line. The
...e the head helps
...th parts from scraps
...gether square to one
...the T-square gets chewed
...eplace it from

STRAIGHTEDGE

EXPLODED VIEW

3 **Cut the profiles of the sides and bottom bin front.** To save time, "pad saw" the profiles of the sides, sawing both pieces at once. To do this, stack the sides face to face with the ends and edges flush. Hold the stack together with double-faced carpet tape. Lay out the profiles on the top piece, as shown in the *Side Layout* and *Foot Pattern*, then cut the sides with a saber saw or band saw. Sand the sawed edges, take the pieces apart, and discard the tape.

Also lay out and cut the profile of the bottom bin front. Use the same *Foot Pattern* that you used for the sides.

4 **Assemble the bin.** Finish sand the parts, then assemble the sides and shelves with glue and 6d finishing nails. Fasten the back in its rabbets with glue and 4d nails — this will also square the assembly. Finally, attach the bin fronts, shelf trim, and top with glue and 6d nails. Set the heads of the nails below the surface.

TRY THIS

PREPARING PLYWOOD FOR PAINTING

Where the plies show, coat them with auto-body filler. Sand the filler smooth and apply shellac. The filler prevents the plies from showing through the paint; the shellac keeps the chemicals in the filler from reacting with the paint. After you paint the project, the edges will be perfectly smooth.

Paint all wooden surfaces, inside and out. Apply at least three coats, lightly sanding between the coats.

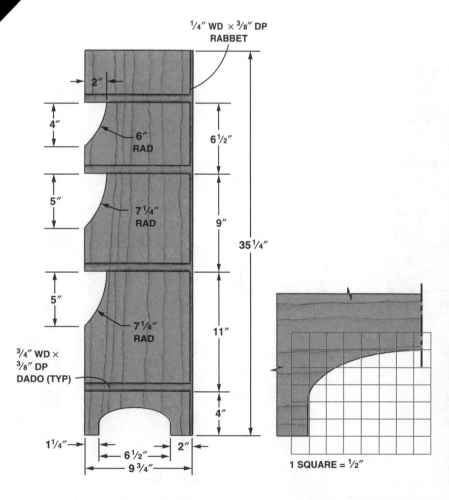

¼" WD × ⅜" DP RABBET

2"

4"

6" RAD

6½"

5"

7¼" RAD

9"

35¼"

5"

7¼" RAD

11"

¾" WD × ⅜" DP DADO (TYP)

4"

1¼" →

6½"

2"

9¾"

SIDE LAYOUT

1 SQUARE = ½"

FOOT PATTERN

At Your Leisure

5 Finish the vegetable bin. I recommend that you paint this project with a washable latex paint to make it easy to clean — especially if you plan to use it for vegetables and fruits. To prepare the assembled bin for painting, fill all the nail holes with wood putty. Inspect the plywood edges that show. If there are any voids (gaps between the plies), fill these with wood putty. Let the putty dry, then sand all surfaces flush and clean.

Pro SKILL: Routing Dadoes and Rabbets

A T-square guide saves setup time when routing joinery in large parts. All you have to do is position the jig, clamp it to the work, and guide the router along it. It won't work for extremely long joints, such as the rabbets in the back edge of the vegetable bin. But it's a real boon when cutting dadoes and end rabbets across wide boards.

1 Before you cut the joinery, make a gauge to help position the T-square accurately. Clamp the T-square guide to a large scrap. Stick a piece of thin hardboard to the scrap with one edge against the straightedge. Mount the bit that you plan to use in the router. Rout through the hardboard, guiding the router along the straightedge. Save the strip between the straightedge and the bit — this is your gauge.

2 Lay out the cut you want to make on the work. If you're making a dado, mark both sides or shoulders. Position the T-square on the work so the straightedge is offset from the *nearest* side by the width of the gauge. Clamp the T-square to the work.

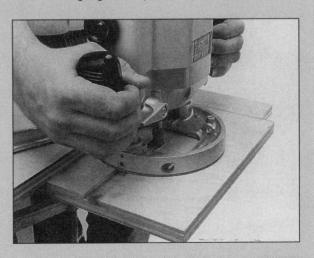

3 Rout the dado or rabbet, keeping the router firmly against the straightedge as you cut. Make deep cuts in several passes, routing just ¹⁄₁₆ to ⅛ inch deeper with each pass. **Tip:** Feed the router from left to right as you face the T-square guide. The rotation of the bit will help keep the router against the straightedge.

Southwest Box

The corners of this small box are joined with interlocking "fingers" — multiple tenons with spaces between them. To get the width of the fingers and the spacing just right, use a finger joint jig to position the boards as you cut them.

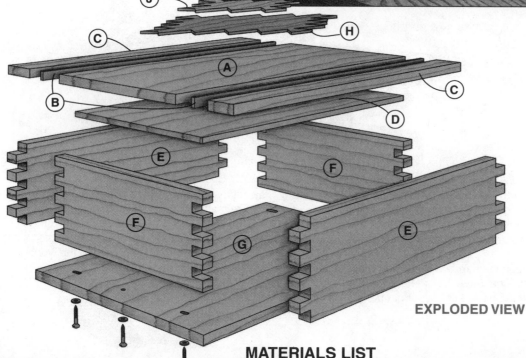

EXPLODED VIEW

MATERIALS LIST
Finished Dimensions in Inches

Parts

A. Top middle	½″ × 6¼″ × 13″
B. Top banding (2)	⅛″ × ½″ × 13″
C. Top edges (2)	½″ × 1¼″ × 13″
D. Lip	¼″ × 6⅞″ × 10⅞″
E. Sides (2)	½″ × 4½″ × 12″
F. Ends (2)	½″ × 4½″ × 8″
G. Bottom	½″ × 9″ × 13″
H. Large appliqué	⅛″ × 4½″ × 9″
J. Small appliqué	⅛″ × 2½″ × 5″

Hardware

#8 × 1″ Roundhead wood screws (6)

#8 Flat washers

60

In 1521, when the Spanish conquered New Spain — the area we know as Mexico, California, Arizona, and New Mexico — they taught native craftsmen to build European furniture. The Spanish designs were a unique blend of European and African art forms. When the African Moors ruled Spain during medieval times, the Spanish adopted the Moorish design tradition, the mujedar. Native American woodworkers found these geometric designs remarkably similar to their own, and the two decorative styles, Islamic and Indian, combined to create the unique Southwest style.

When craftswoman Andy Fischer made this box, she used a traditional Southwest pattern, the stepped "cloud form," to decorate the top. She chose finger joints to join the corners because their geometry echoed the stylized clouds.

Friday Evening

1 Prepare the materials, and cut the parts to size.
To make this box, you need approximately 5 board feet of 4/4 (1-inch-thick) stock, preferably two or three different species of contrasting colors. The box shown is made from white oak and walnut, a light and a dark wood. But you might also combine light, dark, and medium-colored woods, such as maple, walnut, and cherry.

Resaw the stock you will use to make the appliqués, and plane or sand it to ⅛ inch

> See Also:
> **"Resawing"** on page 107.

thick. Plane the remaining 4/4 stock to ½ inch thick, and cut the parts for the sides, ends, top, and bottom. Make the sides and ends 1/16 inch longer than specified to allow extra stock for the finger joints. Plane a ½-inch-thick piece to ¼ inch thick, and cut the lip.

2 Glue up the top parts.
The top is assembled from five pieces glued edge to edge, as shown in the *Top View* — middle, bandings, and edges. To create the best visual effect, the bandings should be a contrasting color from the middle and

> See Also:
> **"Gluing Stock Edge to Edge"** on page 74.

edges. Glue the parts together edge to edge with the wood grain parallel.

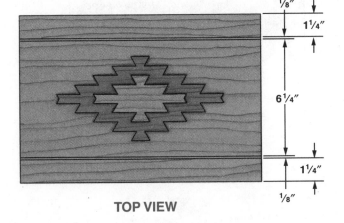

TOP VIEW

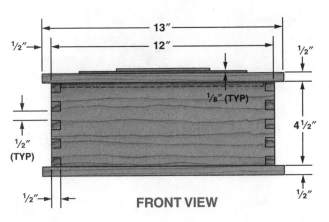

FRONT VIEW

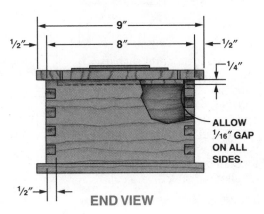

ALLOW 1/16" GAP ON ALL SIDES.

END VIEW

Saturday Morning

3 **Cut the finger joints.** To create the finger joints that join the sides and ends, you must cut a series of notches in the ends of the boards. Cut these notches and the fingers between them exactly the same width so the parts will interlock. To do this quickly and precisely, make a *Finger Joint Jig* and use it to guide the wood as you cut the notches.

See Also:
"Making Finger Joints" on page 64.

Saturday Afternoon

4 **Cut the appliqués.** Enlarge the *Appliqué Patterns,* and lay out the shapes on the ⅛-inch-thick stock. For the best visual effect, the large appliqué should contrast with both the lid and the small appliqué. The small appliqué and the lid may be the same color or different colors; it doesn't matter. (On Andy's box, they are the same color.) But the large appliqué should be different enough to stand out clearly from both parts.

Cut the appliqués with a coping saw, scroll saw, or band saw. Sand the sawed edges smooth.

TRY THIS

PRESANDING SMALL PARTS

Small, delicate parts such as the appliqués are difficult to sand after they are cut. When you can, sand the surfaces up to the final grit even before you lay out the shapes. Then you'll only have a small amount of edge sanding to do after the shapes are cut.

5 **Drill the holes and slots in the bottom.** The bottom is held to the sides and ends with screws, as shown in the *Screw Slot Detail.* To allow the bottom to expand and contract, only the middle screws are set in holes. The *outside* screws (those nearest the sides) rest in small slots. The bottom slides past these screws when it expands and contracts.

Make both the pilot holes and the slots on a drill press. First, cut the counterbores with a ½-inch-diameter flat-bottom bit such as a brad-point bit or a Forstner bit. Then drill the pilot holes and slots with a ³⁄₁₆-inch-diameter bit. To make the slots

and the elongated counterbores around them, cut a series of overlapping holes, then clean up the straight edges of the slots and counterbores with a chisel.

TRY THIS

DRILLING SLOTS

When drilling a series of overlapping holes to make a slot, drill the first and last hole in the series, then go back and drill out the waste between them. This helps you cut slots to precise lengths.

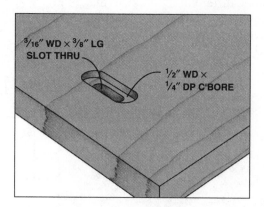

³⁄₁₆″ WD × ³⁄₈″ LG SLOT THRU

½″ WD × ¼″ DP C'BORE

SCREW SLOT DETAIL

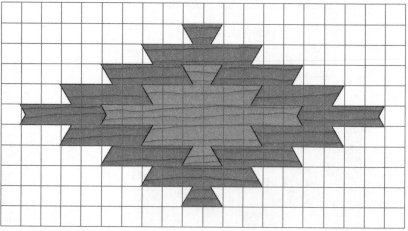

1 SQUARE = ½″

APPLIQUÉ PATTERNS

Saturday Evening

6 Assemble the box.
Do any necessary touch-up sanding, then glue the sides and the ends together. Make sure the parts are square to one another as you clamp them together and test-fit the lip in the box opening to make sure it fits without rubbing. Then glue the lid assembly, lip, and appliqués together.

When the glue dries, sand the finger joints clean and flush. Attach the bottom to the box with roundhead wood screws and flat washers. Tighten the screws so they're snug, but don't make them so tight that the bottom can't expand and contract.

At Your Leisure

7 Finish the box. Apply a finish to all wooden surfaces, inside and out. This is especially important when finishing the lid. If you don't apply the same number of coats to both surfaces of the lid, they will absorb and release moisture at different rates. One surface will expand or contract more quickly than the other, and this will cause the lid to cup. Finishing both surfaces evenly helps ensure that the lid will remain flat.

Quick FIXTURE: Finger Joint Jig

This fixture is an adjustable miter gauge extension with a stop to position the wood before each cut. One face is fixed; the other slides left and right so you can adjust the position of the stop relative to the cutter. When mounted on a miter gauge, it will work with either a table saw and a dado cutter or a table-mounted router and a straight bit.

Make the stop the same size as the fingers you want to cut. If you want to cut different sizes of fingers, make several sliding faces, each with a stop the appropriate size.

When setting up the fixture, use the adjustment screw to fine-tune the position of the stop. One turn of the screw will move the sliding face and its stop 1/32 inch.

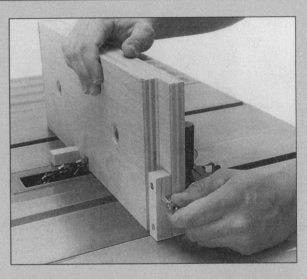

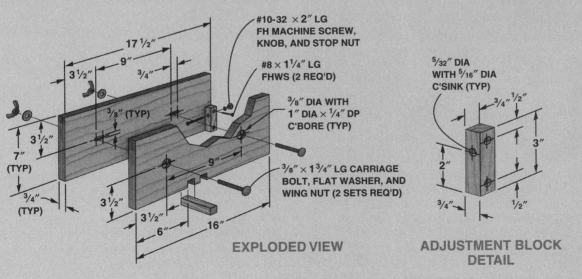

#10-32 × 2" LG
FH MACHINE SCREW,
KNOB, AND STOP NUT

#8 × 1 1/4" LG
FHWS (2 REQ'D)

3/8" DIA WITH
1" DIA × 1/4" DP
C'BORE (TYP)

3/8" × 1 3/4" LG CARRIAGE
BOLT, FLAT WASHER, AND
WING NUT (2 SETS REQ'D)

17 1/2"
9"
3/4"
3 1/2"
3/8" (TYP)
3 1/2"
7"
(TYP)
3/4"
(TYP)
9"
3 1/2"
3 1/2"
6"
16"

EXPLODED VIEW

5/32" DIA
WITH 5/16" DIA
C'SINK (TYP)

3/4"   1/2"
3"
2"
3/4"   1/2"

**ADJUSTMENT BLOCK
DETAIL**

Pro SKILL: Making Finger Joints

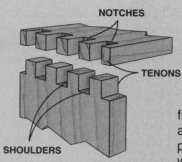

NOTCHES

TENONS

SHOULDERS

FINGER JOINT

Finger joints are interlocking tenons and notches at the ends of adjoining boards. Usually, the fingers are spaced evenly and they are all the same width. When making finger joints:

■ Rip the adjoining boards so their width is a multiple of the finger width. There should be no "half fingers" in the joint.

■ Cut the fingers 1/32 inch longer than the thickness of the adjoining board. After assembly, sand the protruding ends of the fingers flush.

■ Scribe the shoulders of the fingers, and back up the boards with a scrap as you cut them. This will prevent the cutter from tearing the wood grain.

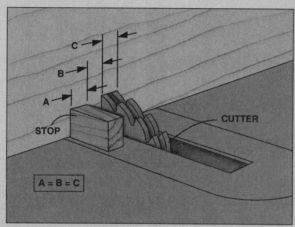

C

B

A

STOP

CUTTER

A = B = C

1 If you're using a table saw, set up the dado blade so it's exactly the same width as the stop on the jig. If you're using a router table, select a straight bit that's the same width. Adjust the distance between the stop and the cutter equal to the width of the cutter (and stop).

2 Place the first board end-down against the face of the jig, and slide it sideways until it butts against the stop. Clamp the board to the jig, and feed it forward, cutting the first notch.

3 Place the second board against the first, and align the edge with the side of the notch nearest the stop. Clamp the second board to the first, and cut a notch in the corner of the second board.

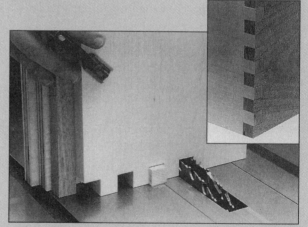

4 Loosen the clamp, and move both boards sideways until the notches you just cut fit over the stop. Tighten the clamp, and cut another set of notches. Repeat until you have cut all the notches in both boards. Assemble the joint. If it's too tight, move the stop *toward* the cutter slightly. If it's too loose, move it *away* from the cutter.

PART THREE

For Display
and Entertainment

Coffee Table

Both the top and the trestles of this table are made from narrower boards glued edge to edge. A clamp holder comes in handy when assembling these large, flat parts. This jig holds and spaces the clamps so you can give your full attention to positioning and aligning the stock.

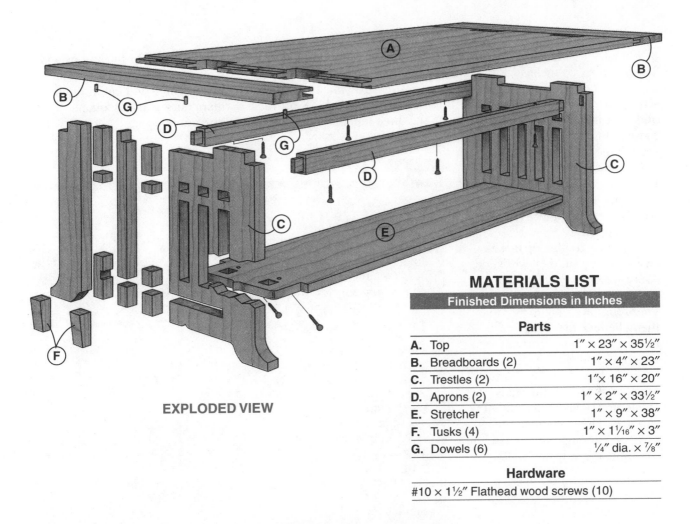

EXPLODED VIEW

MATERIALS LIST

Finished Dimensions in Inches	
Parts	
A. Top	$1'' \times 23'' \times 35\frac{1}{2}''$
B. Breadboards (2)	$1'' \times 4'' \times 23''$
C. Trestles (2)	$1'' \times 16'' \times 20''$
D. Aprons (2)	$1'' \times 2'' \times 33\frac{1}{2}''$
E. Stretcher	$1'' \times 9'' \times 38''$
F. Tusks (4)	$1'' \times 1\frac{1}{16}'' \times 3''$
G. Dowels (6)	$\frac{1}{4}''$ dia. $\times \frac{7}{8}''$
Hardware	
#10 $\times$ $1\frac{1}{2}''$ Flathead wood screws (10)	

This coffee table is a variation on a knockdown "trestle" table design. The tusks hold the trestles, stretcher, and aprons together, and the top fits over the tenon in the trestles. To take the wiggle out of the assembled table — and to keep the top from coming off every time you try to move it, I added a few screws in the aprons and the stretcher. Remove the tusks and the screws, and the table comes apart and stores flat.

Friday Evening

1 Prepare the materials, and cut the parts to size.
To make this coffee table, you need approximately 22 board feet of 5/4 (1¼-inch-thick) stock. The table shown is made from Kentucky coffeetree, a hardwood with a strong grain pattern, a creamy tan color, and a pungent aroma. However, you can use any attractive wood.

Plane the 5/4 stock to 1 inch thick, and study the lumber for a moment. Plan what boards you will use to make what parts, and how you will orient the grain. Glue up stock to make a wide

See Also:
"Gluing Stock Edge to Edge" on page 74.

board for the top. Cut all the parts to size except for the tusks and the trestles.

Saturday Morning

2 Glue up the trestles.
Like the top, the trestle ends of the table are wide boards made from narrower stock. However, these parts have a decorative pattern of rectangular openings, as shown in the *End View.* Rather than cut the openings after you glue up the stock, it's easier to create the pattern as you assemble the trestles.

For each trestle, cut two strips 1 inch thick, 3½ inches wide, and 20 inches long and nine strips 1 inch thick, 1 inch wide, and 18½ inches long. Arrange these with the narrow strips in the middle, the wide strips on either side, and the top ends flush. Lay out the pattern on the assembly, then cut every other narrow strip into pieces to create the openings.

If you try to glue up these strips as they sit, they will slide every which way when you tighten the clamps. You'll lose your religion trying to align them, believe me. To save frustration, drive brads partway into the edges and cut them off close to the surface. Press the parts together so the cut-off brads create tiny holes in the adjoining surfaces. The brads function as tiny "positioning pins" when you assemble the strips.

Warning: Remember, you have some more work to do on the trestles. You must cut the tenons in each top edge, profiles in the three remaining edges, and mortises for the aprons and stretcher. Position the brads where you won't cut through them during a subsequent operation.

TRY THIS

MATCHING GRAIN EDGE TO EDGE

To get the best possible grain match on the trestles, pick a board at least 9 inches wide and 41 inches long. Cut it into two 20-inch lengths and "fold" one edge as shown to make a wide board. Rip the strips from this wide board in order, numbering them as you cut them. When you glue them back together, they will look like a single board.

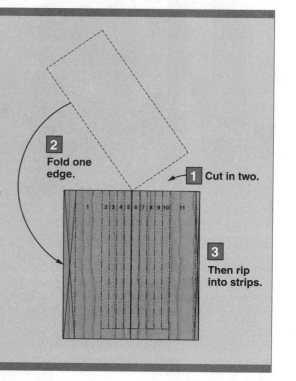

2 Fold one edge.

1 Cut in two.

3 Then rip into strips.

Quick FIXTURE: Clamp Holder

When gluing up the top and the trestles of the coffee table, you must arrange the clamps parallel to one another, space them evenly, and place the jaws so they face up. This is often an exercise in frustration if you're using pipe clamps. The round pipes always want to roll over. This simple clamp holder, however, keeps them in place. Additionally, the plastic laminate surface on the base makes it easy to clean up glue that squeezes out of the joints.

Make the base from a "sink cutout." (These are available at most building supply companies.) To make the holders, drill 1-inch-diameter holes through a strip of wood, spacing them evenly along the length. Then rip the strip in two.

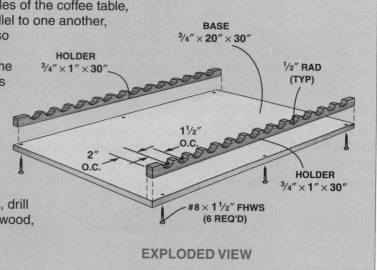

BASE
¾″ × 20″ × 30″

HOLDER
¾″ × 1″ × 30″

½″ RAD (TYP)

1½″ O.C.

2″ O.C.

HOLDER
¾″ × 1″ × 30″

#8 × 1½″ FHWS (6 REQ'D)

EXPLODED VIEW

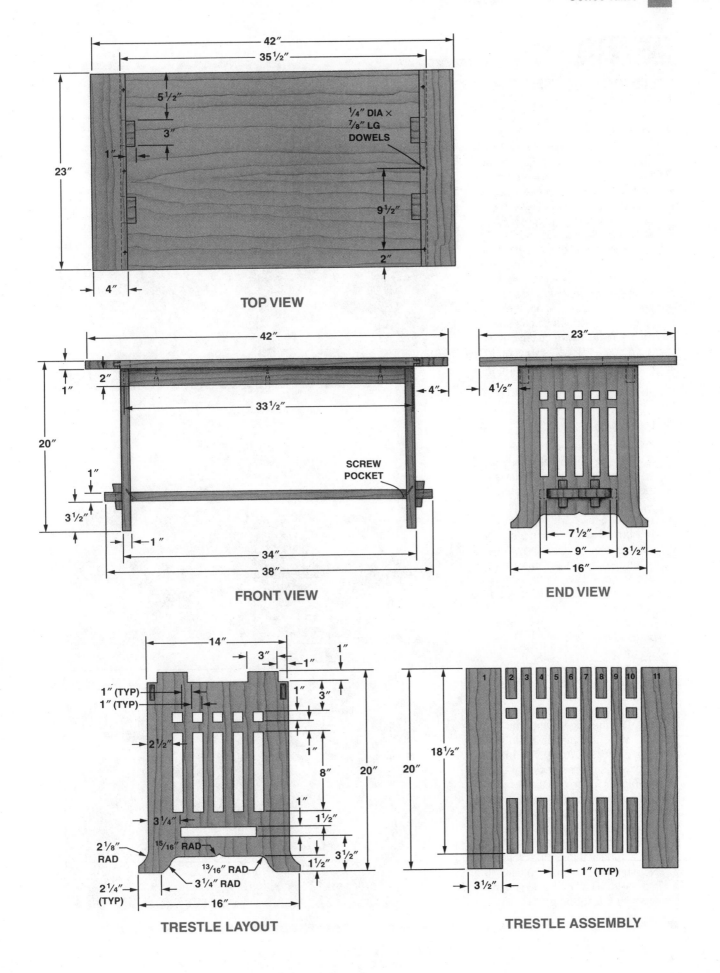

TOP VIEW

FRONT VIEW

END VIEW

TRESTLE LAYOUT

TRESTLE ASSEMBLY

EXTRA INFO

GLUING UP TRESTLES

1 Number the strips 1 through 11, beginning with a wide strip on one side. Lay out the pattern on the strips, drawing the horizontal lines completely across the assembly. Mark the waste on the even-numbered strips (#2, #4, #6, #8, and #10). On each strip (except for #11), drive wire brads partway into one edge. Drive two brads between each set of horizontal lines where there is no waste (where the wood is continuous across the trestle). With a wire cutter, cut off the brads as close as you can to the wood surface, leaving sharp nubs just above the surface.

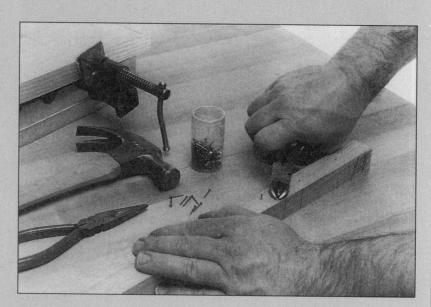

2 Arrange several bar clamps on the clamp holder shown on page 68. Lay strip #1 across the clamps, then position strip #2 beside it. Tighten the clamps, squeezing the parts together. The cut-off brads in one piece will bite into the adjoining edge of the other, creating small depressions. Loosen the clamps, position strip #3 next to #2, and tighten the clamps again. Continue until all the strips are pressed together.

3 Cut the even-numbered strips into pieces and discard the waste. Apply glue to the adjoining surfaces and arrange the pieces in the clamps. As you position each one, align the cut-off brads with their respective depressions — you can feel when each piece slides into place. Finally tighten the clamps. Nothing will slide out of place; the parts will all be held in alignment by the cut-off brads.

Saturday Afternoon

3 **Attach the breadboards to the top.** The wood grain in the breadboards runs perpendicular to the grain in the top, keeping the top flat. However, you must join the breadboards in such a way that the top can still expand and contract.

To do this, cut ⅜-inch-thick, ¾-inch-long tongues in the ends of the top and matching grooves in the inside edges of the breadboards, as shown in the *Top Detail.* Temporarily assemble the top and breadboards, and clamp them together. From the bottom surface of the assembly, drill ¼-inch-diameter, ⅞-inch-deep holes where shown in the *Top View.* These holes must go through the tongues and grooves.

Disassemble the top and breadboards. With a small round file, elongate four of the six holes in the tongues —those nearest the edges. Turn the holes into slots ½ inch long. However, be careful not to widen the holes. They must remain ¼ inch wide, as shown in the *Dowel Joint Detail.*

Using a band saw, cut the mortises for the trestles, as shown in the *Top View.* Cut

through the tongues as you do this; it won't weaken the tongue-and-groove joints overmuch if you remove small sections.

Assemble the top and breadboards, gluing just 2 or 3 inches of each tongue-and-groove joint around the middle dowel hole. Glue the dowels in their holes,

but be careful not to get any glue on the tongues as you secure the dowels nearest the edges.

This arrangement keeps the breadboards in place, but still allows the top to move toward the front and back edge. And when the table is assembled, the dowels are hidden from sight.

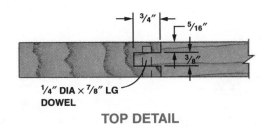

TOP DETAIL

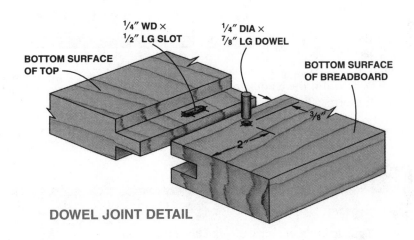

DOWEL JOINT DETAIL

Bonus FIXTURE: Mortising Template

To make the through mortises in the trestles for the stretcher, make a mortising template with an opening 1 inch wide and 7½ inches long. For the smaller stopped mortises for the aprons, make a template with an opening ½ inch wide and 1½ inches long. These templates are designed to work with pattern-routing bits. To work properly, they must be as thick as the cutting flute is long. For detailed instructions on how to rout mortises with templates, see page 28.

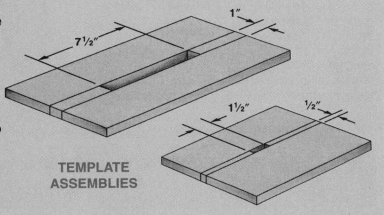

TEMPLATE ASSEMBLIES

4 Rout the mortises in the trestles. Remove the trestles from the clamps, and sand the faces smooth and clean. Make the mortising templates shown on page 71, and rout the mortises with a pattern-cutting bit. Note that the mortises for the stretcher go through the wood, but those for the aprons are only ¾ inch deep, as shown in the *Trestle Detail.*

See Also:
"Routing Mortises" on page 28.

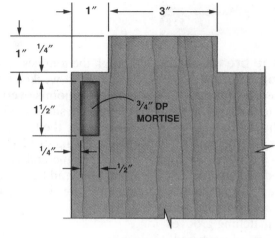

TRESTLE DETAIL

Saturday Evening

5 Cut the tenons in the aprons. Saw or rout tenons in the ends of the aprons, as shown in the *Apron Layout.* Fit the tenons to the small mortises in the trestles.

See Also:
"Tenoning Jig" on page 120.

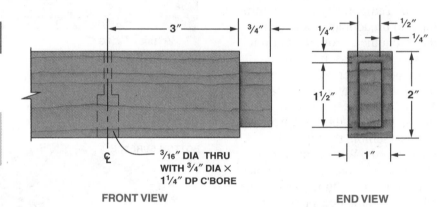

FRONT VIEW

³/₁₆" DIA THRU WITH ¾" DIA × 1¼" DP C'BORE

END VIEW

APRON LAYOUT

TRY THIS

NIBBLING

It's difficult to cut a perfectly straight line on a band saw, so you may not get the top edges of the trestles perfectly flat. No matter, to clean up these surfaces you can "nibble" them flat, if necessary. With double-faced carpet tape, attach a fence to your band saw table just behind the blade and perpendicular to it. The distance from the fence to the front of the teeth on the blade should be 1 inch. Rest a trestle on the table so the tenons are against the fence. Turn on the saw and feed the trestle left and right, letting the teeth nibble the stock. Don't try to remove more than ¹/₃₂ inch of stock at a time. To cut a smooth surface, feed the wood very slowly.

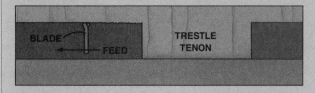

BLADE   FEED   TRESTLE TENON

6 Drill the pocket holes in the aprons. The top is attached to the aprons with screws. To hide the screws from sight, drill 3 counterbored holes through the bottom edge of each apron, as shown in the *Apron Layout* and the *Front View*.

7 Cut the profiles of the trestles and stretcher. Lay out the tenons and the profile of the trestles as shown in the *Trestle Layout* and the stretcher as shown in the *Stretcher Layout*. Cut the shapes with a band saw or coping saw, then sand the sawed edges.

Sunday Afternoon

8 Cut the tusks and tusk mortises. Finish sand the trestles and stretcher, and fit the stretcher to the mortises in the trestles. Mark where the outside surface of each trestle meets the stretcher. This should be approximately 1 inch from the shoulders on the stretcher.

Disassemble the parts and mark a second line on each end of the stretcher $\frac{1}{16}$ inch in from the first (or about $\frac{15}{16}$ inch from the shoulders).

This second line marks the inside surfaces of the tusk mortises. Lay out 1-inch-square holes for each mortise, as shown in the *Stretcher Layout*. Drill 1-inch-diameter holes through each mortise to remove most of the waste, then square the corners with a coping saw and a file.

Cut the tusks on a band saw, as shown in the *Tusk Layout.* Reassemble the trestles and stretcher, then insert the tusks in their mortises. They probably won't sit as shown in the *End View.* In fact, if you've cut them precisely as shown in the layout, they will ride high in the mortises. Carefully sand the angled sides until as much of each tusk shows below its mortise as shows above it when the tusk is snug.

Tip: Mark the tusks and the mortises so you can get the same tusk in the same mortise each time you assemble the table.

Sunday Evening

9 Assemble the table. Assemble the trestles, aprons, stretcher, and tusks. Carefully fit the tenons on the trestles to the mortises in the table top, then drive flathead wood screws through the pocket holes in the aprons and into the bottom face of the top.

If the table is still a little wobbly (and it's likely to be), drill and countersink screw holes through the stretchers and into the trestles, as shown in the *Trestle Joinery Detail.*

At Your Leisure

10 Finish the table. Disassemble the parts of the table, and finish sand any wooden surfaces that still need it. Apply a finish to the parts, then rub it out to the desired luster.

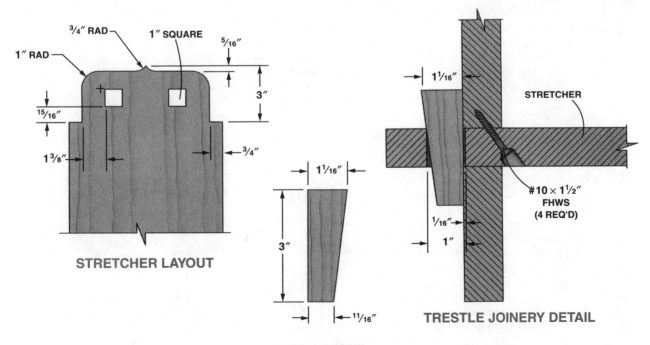

STRETCHER LAYOUT

TUSK LAYOUT

TRESTLE JOINERY DETAIL

STRETCHER

#10 × 1½" FHWS (4 REQ'D)

Pro SKILL: Gluing Stock Edge to Edge

When gluing up wide stock from narrow boards, there are several ways in which you might arrange the wood grain. Your choice depends on how the assembly will be used and how the wood is cut.

■ If you're using plain-sawn wood (in which the annual rings run side to side) and the wide stock will be braced in some way (as a table top is braced when it's attached to the aprons), arrange the boards so the annual rings cup up or out. The assembly will tend to cup up in the center, but this can be easily controlled by bracework.

■ If you're using plain-sawn stock and the wide stock will not be braced (like the leaves of a table), alternate the direction of the annual rings. The individual boards may cup in the opposite direction from the rings, but the overall assembly will remain flat.

■ If stability is critical, use quartersawn wood (in which the annual rings run face to face). This type of lumber expands and contracts half as much as plain sawn. Furthermore, it has little tendency to cup.

PLAIN-SAWN, ANNUAL RINGS CUP UP
Assembly tends to cup, rising in middle.

PLAIN-SAWN, ANNUAL RINGS ALTERNATE
Individual boards cup in alternating directions.

**QUARTERSAWN, ANNUAL RINGS IN
NO PARTICULAR ORDER**
Assembly remains flat.

1 Once the boards are arranged, use a pencil to make two diagonal marks across them, forming a large "V." The marks will show you which edges to joint and help you to align the parts during glue-up.

2 Joint the adjoining edges straight. Adjust the bar clamps so you can apply pressure to the assembly as soon as possible. Apply glue to one edge of each board (except for the last one), then press the board together in the clamps.

3 Arrange the bar clamps so they alternate between the top and bottom surfaces. This evens out the pressure and keeps the assembly from buckling. If the boards shift or slide as you apply pressure, straddle the joints with C-clamps and cauls near the ends. Wrap the cauls in plastic wrap or wax paper to keep them from sticking to the assembly. **Warning:** Don't let the iron parts of the clamps touch the wood where the glue squeezes out from the joints — they will leave black marks.

Adjustable Collector's Rack

■ **QUICK FIXTURE**
Miter Gauge Extension and Stop

■ **PRO SKILL**
Making Multiple Cuts

Many of the pieces and the joints in this small shelving unit are exactly the same — I had to make the same cuts over and over again. To make these repetitive cuts accurately, I used a miter gauge extension and a stop block.

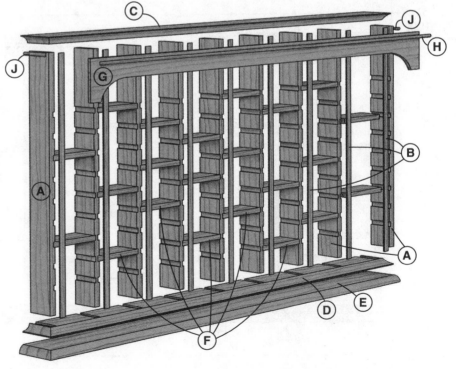

MATERIALS LIST

Finished Dimensions in Inches

Parts

A.	Supports (9)	½″ × 1⅞″ × 24¼″
B.	Support trim (9)	⅛″ × ½″ × 24¼″
C.	Top	¾″ × 3⅜″ × 38¾″
D.	Bottom	¾″ × 2¾″ × 38″
E.	Base	¾″ × 3⅛″ × 38¾″
F.	Shelves (20-40)	½″ × 1⅞″ × 4¼″
G.	Valance	¼″ × 4″ × 36½″
H.	Top front molding	⅜″ × ⅜″ × 37¼″
J.	Top side moldings (2)	⅜″ × ⅜″ × 2⅝″

Hardware

4d Finishing nails (36)

EXPLODED VIEW

Collections of small objects are constantly changing. Every birthday and holiday seems to bring a new addition, and you have to rearrange the collection to make room for it. This small shelving unit is designed to accommodate these changes — you can add or rearrange the shelves as needed.

Friday Evening

1 Prepare the materials, and cut the parts to size.
To make this rack, you need approximately 12 board feet of 4/4 (1-inch-thick) stock. The rack shown is made from mahogany, but you can use any cabinet-grade wood. Because the parts of this project are small and narrow, it's possible to make it from scraps left over from larger projects.

Plane the 4/4 stock to ¾ inch thick, then cut the top and base to the sizes specified in the Materials List; however, *cut the bottom to the same size as the*

top. Later on, you'll trim the bottom to size, but for now make both parts the same.

Plane the remaining stock to ½ inch thick, and cut the supports, support trim, and shelves. To help cut these parts quickly and accurately, use a miter gauge extension and a stop block to gauge the length of each part before you cut it.

Select a board at least 2 inches wide and 38 inches long, and plane it to ⅜ inch thick. Set this aside to make the moldings. Finally plane a board to ¼ inch thick, and cut the valance.

Saturday Morning

2 Cut the dadoes in the top, bottom, and supports. The supports fit in stopped dadoes in the top and bottom, and the shelves rest in dadoes in the supports. There are lots of dadoes to cut, but you need to make only two setups:

■ Cut the ½-inch-wide, ¼-inch-deep stopped dadoes in the top and bottom, as shown in the *Top Layout* and *Bottom Layout*. You must make 18 of these.

■ Cut the ½-inch-wide, ⅛-inch-deep dadoes in the supports, as shown in the *Support Layout*. There are 144 of these to make.

Cut both sets of dadoes with a table-mounted router and a straight bit. Use the miter gauge extension and stop to position the dadoes precisely the same on each board.

See Also:
"Making Multiple Cuts" on page 80.

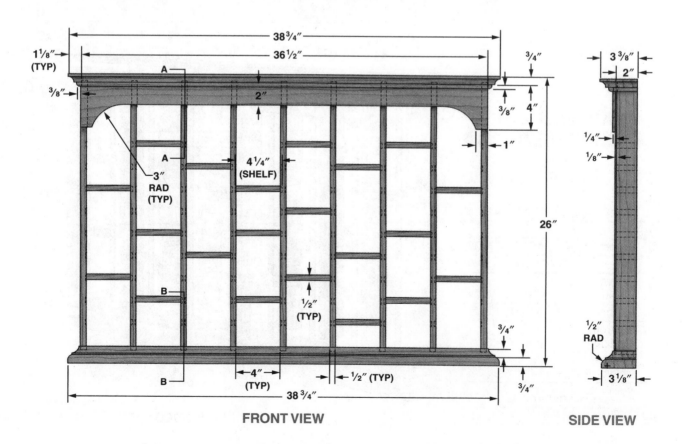

FRONT VIEW   **SIDE VIEW**

Saturday Afternoon

3 **Trim the bottom to size.** After cutting the dadoes, trim the bottom to the size shown in the Materials List. Cut ⅜ inch off each end, and rip ⅝ inch off the front edge.

4 **Rout the molding and edge profiles.** Using a router, shape the edges of the top, bottom, and base. Also cut the shape of the top moldings. You'll need to make three shapes:

■ Cut ½-inch-radius coves in the front edge and both ends of the top and bottom, as shown in the ***Top/Bottom Edge Profile.***

■ Round the front edge and both ends of the base, cutting a ½-inch-radius roundover, as shown in the ***Side View.***

EXTRA INFO

ROUTING STOPPED DADOES

1 To make the stopped dadoes, attach an extension to the miter gauge you use with your router table. Clamp a stop to the extension to position the work before you cut the dado. Secure another stop to the router table itself on the outfeed side of the router bit to halt the cut when the dado is 2 inches long.

2 Hold the top board firmly against the extension and the stop that's attached to it. Turn on the router, and feed the work forward slowly until it butts against the stop that's attached to the router table. Set the top aside, and repeat with the bottom board. Then move the stop on the extension to cut the next set of dadoes, and continue.

3 When you have cut all the stopped dadoes, square the blind ends with a chisel.

■ Round both edges of the molding stock, cutting a ⅜-inch-radius roundover, as shown in the *Molding Detail.*

When shaping the top, bottom, and base, cut the ends first, then shape the front edges. After shaping the molding stock, rip ⅜-inch-wide strips from each edge to make the moldings.

SAFETY FIRST

MAKING NARROW MOLDINGS

To make small, narrow moldings, always shape the edge of a wide board, then rip the molding free of the board. Never try to shape slender stock; it may break apart in your hands.

5 Cut the profile of the valance. Lay out the profile of the valance on the stock, as shown in the *Front View.* Cut the shape with a band saw or scroll saw, then sand the sawed edges.

6 Assemble the base and bottom. Glue the base and bottom face to face with the back edges flush. Let the glue dry overnight.

Sunday Afternoon

7 Assemble the rack. Finish sand all the wooden parts, then assemble the top, base/bottom, supports, and valance with glue and 4d finish nails. Set the heads of the nails.

Cut the moldings to size, mitering the adjoining ends. Attach the top front molding with glue and wire brads. Attach the side moldings with wire brads *only.* The wood grain in these moldings runs perpendicular to the top and sides. If you

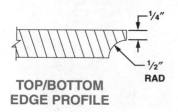

TOP/BOTTOM EDGE PROFILE

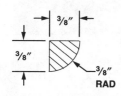

MOLDING DETAIL

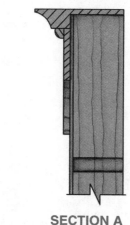

SECTION A

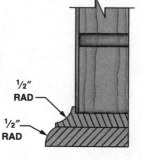

SECTION B

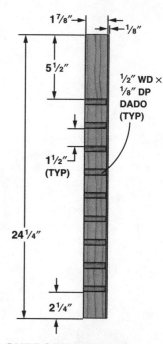

SUPPORT LAYOUT

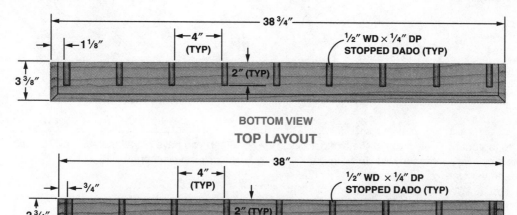

BOTTOM VIEW

TOP LAYOUT

BOTTOM LAYOUT

glue them in place, the side moldings will restrict the movement of the adjoining parts. If the moldings are held by brads only, the wire brads will bend slightly as the top and supports expand and contract.

At Your Leisure

8 **Finish the rack.** Do any necessary touch-up sanding, then apply a finish to the wooden surfaces of the assembled rack. You'll find a penetrating finish such as tung oil or Danish oil works best. If you use a finish that builds up on the surface of the wood (such as varnish), it may interfere with the fit of the shelves in the dadoes.

TRY THIS

HIDING NAIL HEADS

Many woodworkers avoid using nails and brads because they don't like the holes that these fasteners leave in the wood surface. However, you can hide a nail or brad head completely by lifting a sliver from the wood with a small gouge. Drive the nail into the depression and set the head, then glue the sliver back in place.

 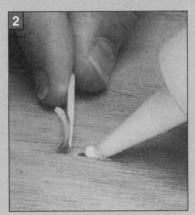

Quick FIXTURE: Miter Gauge Extension and Stop

This T-shaped assembly extends the length of your miter gauge face, giving you more control when cutting long parts. It also gives you a long surface to which you can attach stops. This, in turn, lets you duplicate parts and make multiple cuts.

You can use almost any small scrap of wood as a stop, but a block with a double-mitered edge that comes to a blunt point works best. Sawdust builds up on flat surfaces, comes between the stop and the work, and interferes with the accuracy of the cut. If the edge is pointed, the sawdust builds up behind the point. Small amounts won't affect accuracy.

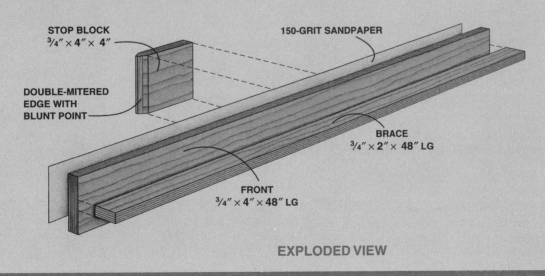

STOP BLOCK
3/4" × 4" × 4"

DOUBLE-MITERED EDGE WITH BLUNT POINT

150-GRIT SANDPAPER

BRACE
3/4" × 2" × 48" LG

FRONT
3/4" × 4" × 48" LG

EXPLODED VIEW

Pro SKILL: Making Multiple Cuts

When duplicating parts or joints, use a stop to position the work before each cut. This stop may be attached to an extended miter gauge face, a fence, or the worktable.

1 The easiest and the most versatile method is to attach the stop to a miter gauge extension. The distance from the edge of the stop to the blade or cutter determines the length of the cut or the position of the joint. An added benefit to this setup is that you can position the extension to support the work on both sides of the cut, as long as you don't mind cutting into your extension. This extra support reduces tear-out and produces a cleaner cut.

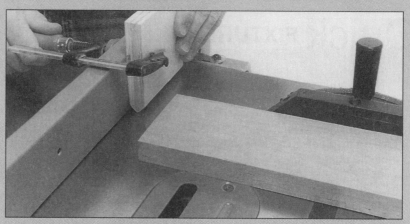

2 You can also use a fence as a stop when making kerfs or joinery cuts that don't go completely through the board. When cutting duplicate parts, you must attach a stop to the fence, as shown. Otherwise, the wood may be pinched between the fence and the blade as you cut through it, and the saw will fling the cut-off part back at you.

3 Occasionally, you may have to make multiple cuts where you don't have a miter gauge or fence where you can attach a stop. When this is the case, attach your stops directly to the worktable. Either clamp them in place or secure them with double-faced carpet tape.

Divider Screen

- ■ **QUICK FIXTURE**
  Router Plane
- ■ **PRO SKILL**
  Setting Hinges

*O*ne of the trickiest tasks in setting a hinge is cutting the hinge mortise. For the hinge to look good and operate properly, the bottom must be cut to the precise depth and shaved dead flat. A router plane makes this chore a no-brainer.

EXPLODED VIEW

Resources You can purchase double-action hinges (#29033) from:

The Woodworkers' Store
4365 Willow Drive
Medina, MN 55340

MATERIALS LIST
Finished Dimensions in Inches

Parts

A. Stiles (6)		³/₄″ × 2″ × 65¹/₈″
B. Top rails (3)		³/₄″ × 7⁷/₈″ × 21¹/₂″
C. Bottom rails (3)		³/₄″ × 6¹/₈″ × 21¹/₂″
D. Panels* (3)		¹/₄″ × 21³/₈″ × 59¹/₁₆″

Make these parts from plywood.

Hardware

Double-action hinges and mounting screws
(6 sets)

This simple screen blends with almost any decor, classic or contemporary. Just change the panels to suit your tastes, says the designer and builder, Mike Boggs. They can be covered with veneer, cloth, paint, even wallpaper to blend with or complement their surroundings.

Friday Evening

1 Prepare the materials, and cut the parts to size.
To make this screen, you need approximately 15 board feet of 4/4 (1-inch-thick) stock and two 4 × 8-foot sheets of ¼-inch plywood. The screen shown is made from cherry and birch veneer plywood covered in cloth, but you can use most cabinet-grade materials.

Plane the 4/4 stock to ¾ inch thick, and cut the rails and stiles to the sizes specified in the Materials List.

Saturday Morning

2 Cut the tenons in the rails and the grooves in the stiles. The screen frames are joined with tenons and grooves. Cut ¼-inch-wide, ¾-inch-deep grooves in the inside edges of the stiles, using a router or a dado cutter. Then cut matching ¼-inch-thick, ¾-inch-long tenons in the ends of the rails. Use a tenoning jig to hold the rails vertical as you make the cuts that form the tenons.

See Also:
"Cutting Tenons"
on page 121.

Note: If you plan to cover the panels with cloth or wallpaper, you may have to cut both the tenons and the grooves slightly wider than specified.

3 Cut the arcs in the rails.
Make a beam compass from a long, narrow scrap of wood. Use it to scribe 19-inch- and 15-inch-radius arcs on one top rail, and 48-inch- and 43-inch-radius arcs on one bottom rail.

Stack the top rails and bottom rails face to face in two separate stacks, with the marked rails on top. Hold the stacks together with double-faced carpet tape. Using a band saw or a saber saw, cut the arcs, sawing through all three parts in each stack. With the rails still stacked, sand the sawed edges. Then take the stacks apart, and discard the tape.

To scribe an arc with the beam compass, first clamp the pivot board to a workbench, and place the beam over the pivot. Place the rail beneath the pencil at the end of the beam, and adjust its position. When scribing the bottom arc on a rail, the pencil should cross the two bottom corners (where the tenons begin). When scribing the top arcs, the pencil should brush the top edge at the middle, and the two points where it crosses the ends of the rail should be equidistant from the top edge. When a rail is properly positioned, clamp it to the bench and scribe the arc.

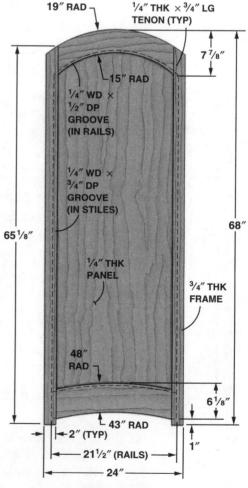

19" RAD
¼" THK × ¾" LG TENON (TYP)
7⅞"
15" RAD
¼" WD × ½" DP GROOVE (IN RAILS)
¼" WD × ¾" DP GROOVE (IN STILES)
65⅛"
68"
¼" THK PANEL
¾" THK FRAME
48" RAD
6⅛"
43" RAD
2" (TYP)
1"
21½" (RAILS)
24"

SINGLE SCREEN
FRONT VIEW

Saturday Afternoon

4 **Cut the grooves in the rails.** Using a piloted slot cutter with a bearing to follow the radius of the rails, rout the ¼-inch-wide, ½-inch-deep slots in the inside edges of the rails.

5 **Cut the profile of the panels.** Lay out the panel profile on one panel, as shown in the *Panel Layout.* Stack the panels face to face with the marked panel on top, and hold the stack together with double-faced carpet tape. Cut the profile with a saber saw or coping saw, sand the sawed edges, then take the stack apart.

6 **Cut the profiles in the top edges of the stiles.** Temporarily assemble the rails, stiles, and panels, and clamp them together. Using the beam compass, mark a 19-inch radius on the top ends of the stiles. These radii should appear continuous with the arched edges of the top rails. Disassemble the frame. Cut the arched stile ends with a band saw or saber saw, then sand the sawed edges.

Saturday Evening

7 **Cut the hinge mortises.** Line up the stiles edge to edge as they will be joined when the frames are assembled. Mark the locations of the hinges.

At the marks, cut mortises for the hinges. Use a router plane to shave the mortises to the proper depth, and level the bottoms.

Temporarily install the hinges in the mortises, and check the action. The stiles should swing easily both ways. When you're satisfied that the hinges work properly, remove them.

See Also:
"Setting Hinges" on page 85.

Sunday Afternoon

8 **Finish the panels and the inside edges of the rails and stiles.** However you plan to finish the panels, do it now. Apply veneer, clear finish, paint, cloth, or wallpaper. Also, finish sand the inside edges of the stiles and rails, and apply a finish to these surfaces.

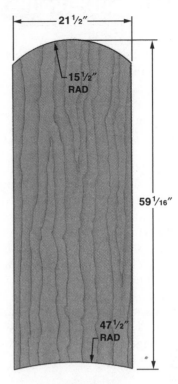

PANEL LAYOUT

Note: Depending on how you finish or cover the panels and the type of finish you apply to the frame members, it may take several days (working a few minutes each day) to get this project ready for assembly.

Bonus FIXTURE: Beam Compass

When scribing large arcs, make a beam compass from a long scrap of wood. Drill a hole in one end to hold a pencil, then drill pivot holes along the length. The distance from the pencil hole to a given pivot hole must be equal to radius of the arc you want to scribe. To swing the compass, install a dowel in a smaller board — this will serve as the pivot.

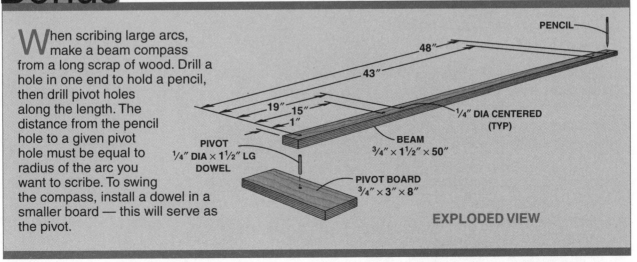

EXPLODED VIEW

At Your Leisure

9   Assemble the screens.
Glue the rails and stiles together. As you do so, insert the panels in their grooves. Do *not* glue the panels in place, however; let them float.

When the glue dries, sand the joints clean and flush. Then finish sand the faces and the outside edges of the frame members. Be careful *not* to sand the panels or the inside edges of the frame. You may want to mask off these surfaces to keep them clean.

Apply a finish to the faces and outside edges of the frame. When the finish has dried, install the hinges, joining the individual screens.

DOUBLE ACTION HINGES (6 SETS REQ'D)

72"

FRONT VIEW
ASSEMBLED SCREENS

Quick FIXTURE: Router Plane

A router plane is an old hand tool that allows you to clean out the bottoms of dadoes, grooves, and mortises. The L-shaped blade reaches into the recess, while the base slides along the surface.

You can still buy these planes for a reasonable price, but this shop-made design offers an advantage you won't find on the market. The base is made from clear plastic so you can see the cut as you make it.

Resources Purchase the plane iron (#23P10.02) from:

Garrett Wade
161 Avenue of the
Americas
New York, NY 10013

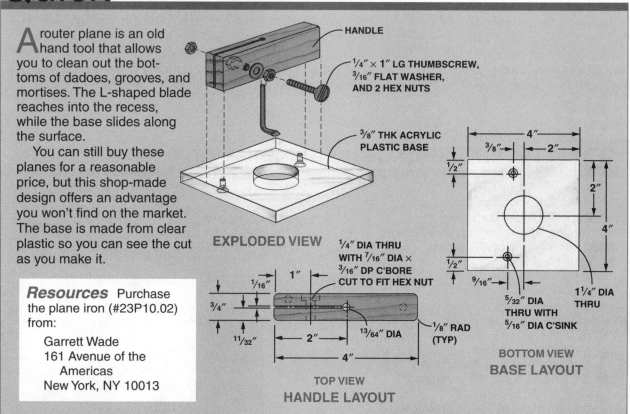

HANDLE

$1/4'' \times 1''$ LG THUMBSCREW, $3/16''$ FLAT WASHER, AND 2 HEX NUTS

$3/8''$ THK ACRYLIC PLASTIC BASE

EXPLODED VIEW

$1/4''$ DIA THRU WITH $7/16''$ DIA × $3/16''$ DP C'BORE CUT TO FIT HEX NUT

$1/16''$
$3/4''$
$11/32''$
$1''$
$2''$
$4''$
$13/64''$ DIA
$1/8''$ RAD (TYP)

TOP VIEW
HANDLE LAYOUT

$4''$
$3/8''$
$2''$
$1/2''$
$2''$
$4''$
$1/2''$
$9/16''$
$5/32''$ DIA THRU WITH $5/16''$ DIA C'SINK
$1 1/4''$ DIA THRU

BOTTOM VIEW
BASE LAYOUT

Pro SKILL: Setting Hinges

To install most hinges, you must cut *mortises* for the leaves. This procedure is similar to cutting a standard mortise, but there are two important differences. First, when setting a hinge with two identical leaves, you must make *matching* mortises in the adjoining parts. Second, cut the mortises very shallow so the wooden parts almost touch when the hinge is closed. How shallow? That depends on the hinge. For some, the depth of the mortise must be equal to the thickness of the hinge leaves; for others, it must be half the diameter of the barrel.

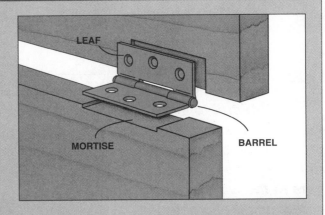

1 Measure and mark the locations of the hinges on one of the adjoining surfaces, then place both surfaces together. When joining two frames with hinges, clamp the stiles edge to edge. If you're installing a lid, clamp it to the case. If you're hanging a door, wedge it in place with slivers of wood or cardboard. Transfer the marks across the seam from one surface to the other.

2 Remove the clamps or wedges, and disassemble the parts. Position the hinge leaf on one part, and trace around it. Cut the edges of the hinge mortise, and remove most of the waste with a chisel. However, don't cut it to its full depth yet.

3 Set the router plane to the depth you want to cut, and shave the bottom of the mortise. It's easiest to do this with a pivoting motion. Press down on one side of the plane's base to hold it flat on the wood surface, then pivot the blade into the mortise. When the mortise is cleaned out, drill pilot holes for the hinge screws and install the hinges. **Note:** Although you also perform this chore with a router, it's often much easier to grab your router plane than it is to set up the router, rig the proper support, and cut a mortising template. And the router plane will cut into square corners!

Hall Table

■ **QUICK FIXTURE**
Screw Pocket Jig

■ **PRO SKILL**
Making Screw Pockets

Screw pockets are difficult to make on a standard drill press — the table is hard to tilt and the column gets in the way. This screw pocket jig gets around those limitations. It holds the work at an angle so there's no need to tilt the table, and you can position it so the column won't interfere.

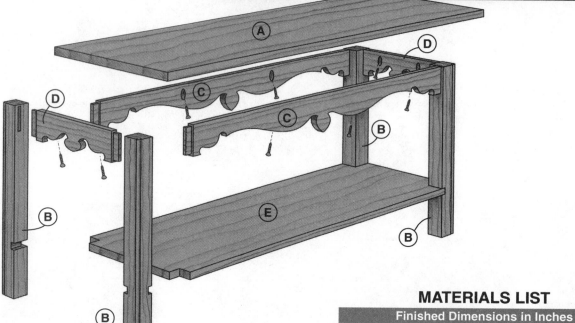

EXPLODED VIEW

MATERIALS LIST

Finished Dimensions in Inches	
Parts	
A. Top	1″ × 18″ × 50″
B. Legs (4)	2″ × 2″ × 28″
C. Front/back aprons (2)	¾″ × 5½″ × 41″
D. Side aprons (2)	¾″ × 4½″ × 13″
E. Shelf	1″ × 15″ × 43″
Hardware	
#8 × 1½″ Roundhead wood screws (12)	

This long, narrow table looks good in a hallway and lets you display collectibles without taking up too much space. It can also be used in a living room as a sofa table or in a dining room as a serving table.

The scrollwork on the table gives it a country look, but you can easily change the style by changing the shapes of the aprons. Straight aprons will blend with both classic and contemporary surroundings, while jagged "cloud steps" create a Southwest feel.

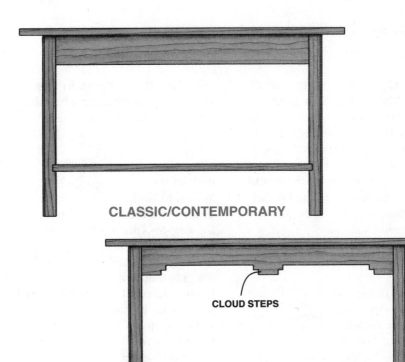

CLASSIC/CONTEMPORARY

CLOUD STEPS

SOUTHWEST

Friday Evening

1 Prepare the materials, and cut the parts to size.

To make this table as shown, you need approximately 6 board feet of 4/4 (1-inch-thick) stock to make the aprons, 16 board feet of 5/4 (1¼-inch-thick) stock to make the top and shelf, and 5 board feet of 10/4 (2½-inch-thick) stock to make the legs. If your lumberyard doesn't carry

10/4 stock, purchase 6 board feet of 12/4 stock. Or, you may be able to get by with stock that measures a "strong" 8/4 (that is, approaching 9/4). Often-times, you can plane stock like this to a full 2 inches thick if it's reasonably straight to begin with.

See Also:
"Gluing Stock Edge to Edge" on page 74.

The table shown is made from curly cherry, but you can use any cabinet-grade wood.

Plane the 4/4 stock to ¾ inch thick, and cut the aprons to the sizes specified in the Materials List. Plane the 5/4 stock to 1 inch thick, and glue up the wide boards needed for the top and the shelf. Plane the 10/4 stock to 2 inches thick, and cut the legs.

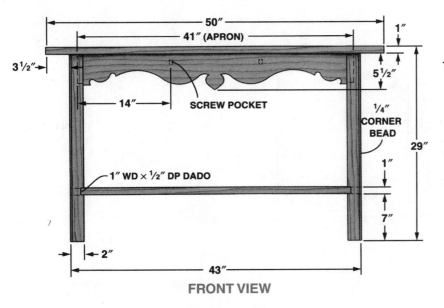

FRONT VIEW

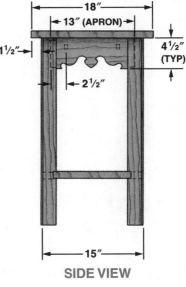

SIDE VIEW

Saturday Morning

2 Cut the mortises and dadoes in the legs.

Carefully examine the legs and chose the front and back, right and left. Also decide which surfaces will face out and which will face in. Clearly mark the inside corner on each leg, and lay out the mortises and dadoes on the *inside* surfaces.

Rout ¼-inch-wide, 4-inch-long, 1¹⁄₁₆-inch deep mortises in the legs, as shown in the *Leg-to-Apron Joinery Detail.* Also cut 1-inch-wide, ½-inch-deep dadoes, as shown in the *Front View.*

> See Also:
> **"Routing Mortises"**
> on page 28.

Saturday Morning

3 Cut the tenons in the aprons and notches in the shelf.

Cut ¼-inch-thick, 4-inch-wide, 1-inch-long tenons in the ends of the aprons to fit the mortises in the legs, as shown in the *Leg-to-Apron Joinery Detail.* Use a tenoning jig to hold the board vertically as you make the cuts that will form the tenons. Also cut 1½-inch-square notches in the corners of the shelf, as shown in the *Shelf Corner Layout.* These notches fit the dadoes in the legs.

> See Also:
> **"Cutting Tenons"**
> on page 121.

After cutting the joinery, dry assemble (that is, assemble *without* glue) the legs, aprons, and shelf to check the fit of the parts.

Saturday Afternoon

4 Cut the screw pockets in the aprons.

Make the *Screw Pocket Jig* shown on the opposite page to help hold the aprons at the proper angle while drilling the screw pockets. Mark the locations of the screw pockets on the inside surfaces of the aprons, as shown in the *Front View* and *Side View.* On a drill press, drill the pocket holes and shank holes.

> See Also:
> **"Making Screw Pockets"**
> on page 91.

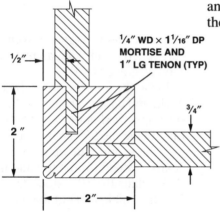

¼" WD × 1¹⁄₁₆" DP MORTISE AND 1" LG TENON (TYP)

½"

2"

2"

¾"

LEG-TO-APRON JOINERY DETAIL

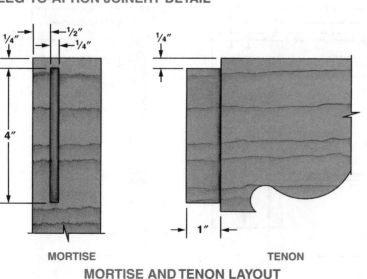

¼"   ½"
       ¼"

¼"

4"

1"

MORTISE   TENON

MORTISE AND TENON LAYOUT

←1½"→

1½"

SHELF CORNER LAYOUT

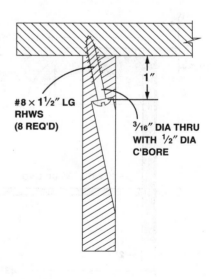

#8 × 1½" LG RHWS (8 REQ'D)

1"

³⁄₁₆" DIA THRU WITH ½" DIA C'BORE

SCREW POCKET DETAIL

5 Cut the beads in the outside corners of the legs.

The legs have decorative corner beads (or *rolls*, as they're sometimes called) on the outside corners, as shown in the *Side View.* Molders and shapers cut beads with dedicated beading knives and cutters, but if you don't have one of these tools, use a table-mounted router with a small *point-cut* roundover bit. Make each bead in three passes, cutting 90 degrees of the rounded shape with each pass.

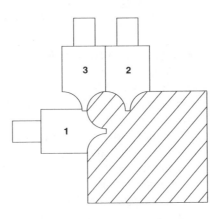

ROUTING CORNER BEADS

To make a corner bead or roll with a router, use a *point-cut* roundover bit — a bit without a pilot post or bearing. Make the beads in three passes. On the first pass, cut one outside surface of each leg. Then turn the legs end for end, and cut the other outside surfaces. Finally, reposition the fence or guide, and round over the outside corners.

Quick FIXTURE: Screw Pocket Jig

This jig is an L-shaped carriage tilted at 20 degrees. It cradles the work and holds it at a slight angle to the drill bit as you bore screw pockets or other angled holes.

To make the jig, first assemble the back and the support to make the carriage. Attach the wedges to the base, then secure the carriage assembly to the wedges.

To use the jig, position it so the bit will exit the stock in the middle of the edge, then clamp it to your drill press table.

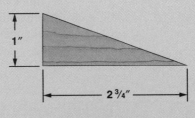

WEDGE LAYOUT

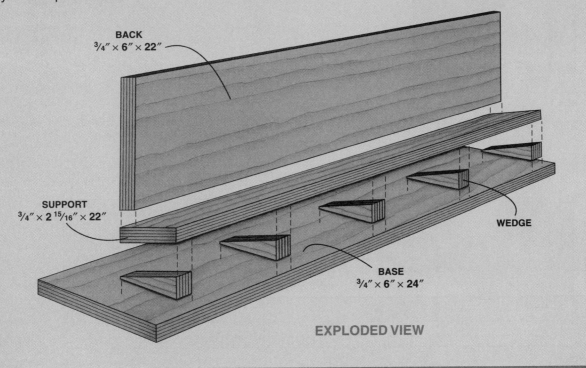

BACK
$3/4'' \times 6'' \times 22''$

SUPPORT
$3/4'' \times 2^{15}/16'' \times 22''$

WEDGE

BASE
$3/4'' \times 6'' \times 24''$

EXPLODED VIEW

Saturday Evening

6 **Cut the profiles of the aprons.** Enlarge the *Front/Back Apron Pattern,* and trace it on the front or back apron. (There's no need to trace it on both.) Also enlarge the *Side Apron Pattern,* and trace it on one of the side aprons. Stack the front/back aprons face to face in one stack and the side aprons in another, so the marked aprons are on top of each stack. Hold the stacks together with double-faced carpet tape.

Cut the profiles of the aprons in both stacks using a band saw or a scroll saw. Sand the sawed edges, then take the stacks apart and discard the tape.

Sunday Afternoon

7 **Assemble the table.** Finish sand all the wooden parts, then assemble the legs, aprons, and shelf with glue. To help anchor the shelf to the legs, drive roundhead wood screws up through the bottom of the shelf and into the leg at a 25- to 30-degree angle, as shown in the *Shelf-to-Leg Joinery Detail.* Counterbore each screw.

Attach the top to the table by driving roundhead wood screws up through the screw pockets and into the top, as shown in the *Screw Pocket Detail.* Do not glue the top in place. The shank holes in the screw pockets are larger than the screw shanks, and this lets the top "float," expanding and contracting with changes in the relative humidity.

At Your Leisure

8 **Finish the table.** Remove the top from the table. Do any necessary touch-up sanding, then apply a finish to all wooden surfaces. Be sure to apply the same number of coats to both the top and bottom surfaces of the table top and the shelf. Even though the bottom surfaces won't show, it's important that they absorb and release moisture at the same rate as the top surfaces. If they don't, these parts may cup or warp. When the finish dries, rub it out and replace the top.

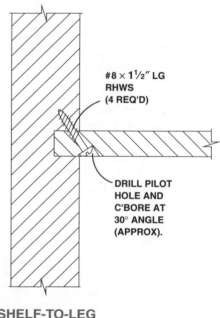

#8 × 1½" LG
RHWS
(4 REQ'D)

DRILL PILOT HOLE AND C'BORE AT 30° ANGLE (APPROX).

SHELF-TO-LEG JOINERY DETAIL

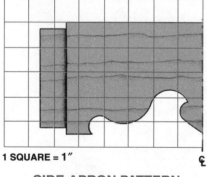

1 SQUARE = 1″

SIDE APRON PATTERN

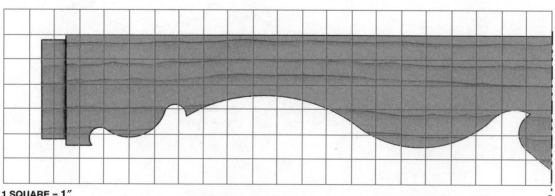

1 SQUARE = 1″

FRONT/BACK APRON PATTERN

Pro SKILL: Making Screw Pockets

Screw pockets are used in furniture construction to attach table tops to apron-and-leg assemblies. The screw passes through a *shank hole* in the apron and into the underside of the table top. The head rests in a counterbore or *pocket hole.* These holes are drilled at an angle (usually between 15 and 25 degrees) on the inside of the apron, where they won't be seen when the table is assembled. The shank hole exits the edge of the apron about halfway between the faces.

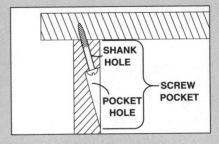

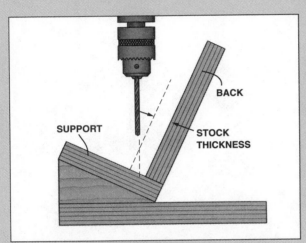

1 To make a screw pocket using the screw pocket jig, position it so that when you extend the quill, the drill bit contacts the support, not the back of the carriage. The distance from the back to where the tip of the bit touches the support should be approximately equal to one-half the thickness of the stock. Clamp the jig to the drill press table.

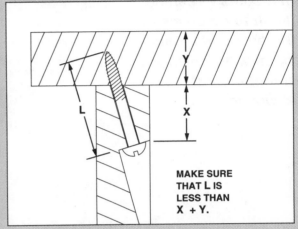

2 Adjust the drill press depth stop for the depth of the pocket hole. This must be deep enough that the screws will get a good bite in the table top but not so deep that the screws will go all the way through the table top.

3 Rest the work top edge down in the carriage. Slide it along so the bit will enter where you want the screw pocket, and clamp the work to the back of the carriage. Drill the pocket holes. A Forstner bit works best for this task.

4 Without changing the position of the jig, switch drill bits and bore the shank holes in the center of the pocket holes. A brad-point or twist bit works well for this task. Drill completely through the work so the bit exits the top edge. **Note:** Make the shank hole slightly larger than the diameter of the screw. This lets the table top move.

Clock Shelf

Making a "fair" curve — a curve without any noticeable bumps or flat spots — can be difficult to do on a saw. With the aid of a router compass, however, you can rout perfect arcs and circles.

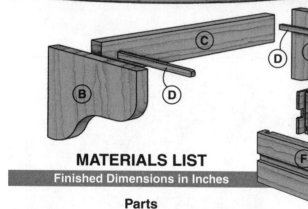

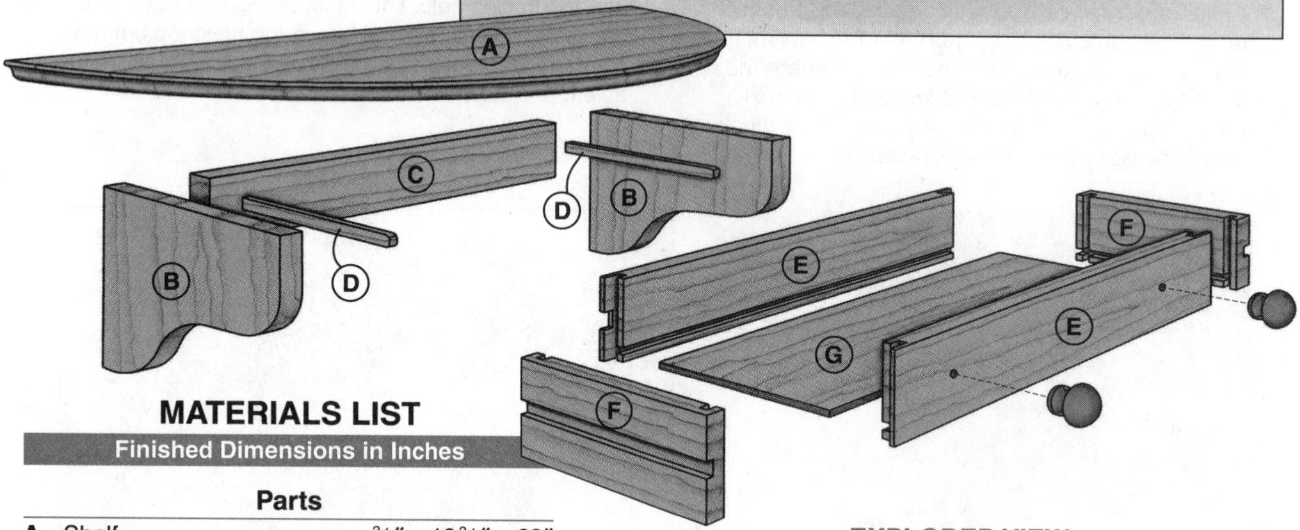

EXPLODED VIEW

MATERIALS LIST
Finished Dimensions in Inches

Parts

A.	Shelf	¾″ × 10¾″ × 22″
B.	Brackets (2)	¾″ × 7″ × 7″
C.	Cleat	¾″ × 2½″ × 13″
D.	Drawer guides (2)	¼″ × ½″ × 5¾″
E.	Drawer front/back (2)	½″ × 2½″ × 13″
F.	Drawer sides (2)	½″ × 2½″ × 6″
G.	Drawer bottom	¼″ × 5⅝″ × 12½″

Hardware

¾″ Wire brads (4–6)
¾″ Drawer knobs (2)

It's called a "clock shelf" because it was originally designed to hold small case clocks. The drawer under the shelf was intended to hold the winding key. Today, there are more uses for these small shelves than ever. They can be used to hold any small or medium-size item, whether decorative or practical.

Friday Evening

1 Prepare the materials, and cut the parts to size.
To make this shelf, you need approximately 5 board feet of 4/4 (1-inch-thick) stock. The clock shelf shown is made from mahogany, but you can use any cabinet-grade wood.

Plane the 4/4 stock to ¾ inch thick, and cut the brackets and cleat to the sizes specified in the Materials List. Also cut the shelf, but make it about 1 inch wider than specified.

Plane the remaining stock to ½ inch thick, and cut the drawer guides, front, back, and sides. You can make the drawer bottom from a scrap of ¼-inch plywood, or plane a small piece of the ½-inch-thick stock to ¼ inch thick and cut it from that.

Note that the drawer parts are sized so the drawer will fill the space between the brackets with no clearance for the drawer to slide freely. After assembling all of the parts, you will plane or sand the drawer for a perfect fit.

2 Cut the profiles of the brackets and shelf. Lay out one bracket, as shown in the *Bracket Pattern*. Stack the bracket stock face to face with the marked bracket on top, holding them together with double-faced carpet tape. Cut the bracket profile with a band saw or saber saw, sand the sawed edges, and take the stack apart.

To cut the shelf, first make a *Router Compass* and fasten your router to it. Mount a ½-inch straight bit in the router. Fasten the compass to the shelf stock by driving a #10 screw through the pivot hole and into the shelf. Swing the router around the pivot screw, routing the arc in several shallow passes. When the arc is cut, rip the shelf to the proper width, removing the strip of wood with the pivot hole in it.

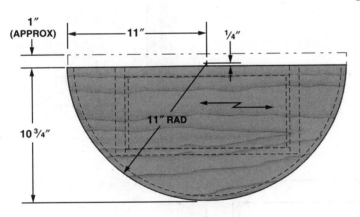

TOP VIEW

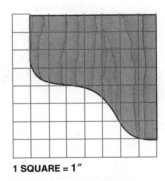

1 SQUARE = 1″

BRACKET PATTERN

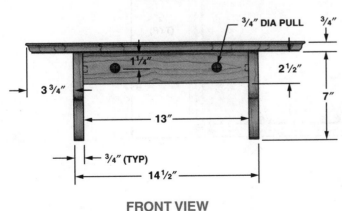

FRONT VIEW

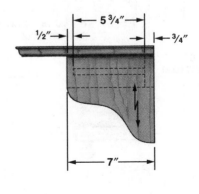

SIDE VIEW

Saturday Afternoon

3 **Cut the drawer joinery.**
The drawer front, back, and sides are joined with lock joints (also called tongue-and-dado joints). To make the lock joints, cut a ¼-inch-wide groove in the ends of the drawer front and back, as shown in the *Drawer Joinery Detail*. This will create two tongues in each end. Cut the *inside* tongues short so they are just ¼ inch long. Then cut a ⅛-inch-wide, ¼-inch-deep dado in the inside faces of the drawer sides. Each dado must be just ¼ inch from the end of the board.

See Also:
"Making Lock Joints" on page 106.

Also cut ¼-inch-wide, ¼-inch-deep grooves in the inside faces of the drawer front, back, and sides, ¼ inch from the bottom edges. These grooves will hold the drawer bottom.

Finally, cut ½-inch-wide, ¼-inch-deep grooves in the outside faces of the drawer sides, as shown in the *Drawer/Side View*. Notch the ends of the drawer back so the grooves are open at the back of the assembled drawer. These grooves fit over the drawer guides.

4 **Assemble the drawer.**
Finish sand the drawer

parts and assemble the front, back, and sides with glue. As you put these parts together, slip the bottom into its grooves but *don't* glue it in place. Let it float so it can expand and contract in the grooves.

Saturday Evening

5 **Shape the edge of the shelf.** Using a router and a piloted ogee bit, shape the curved edge of the shelf, as shown in the *Shelf Edge Profile*. Sand the shaped edge to remove the mill marks.

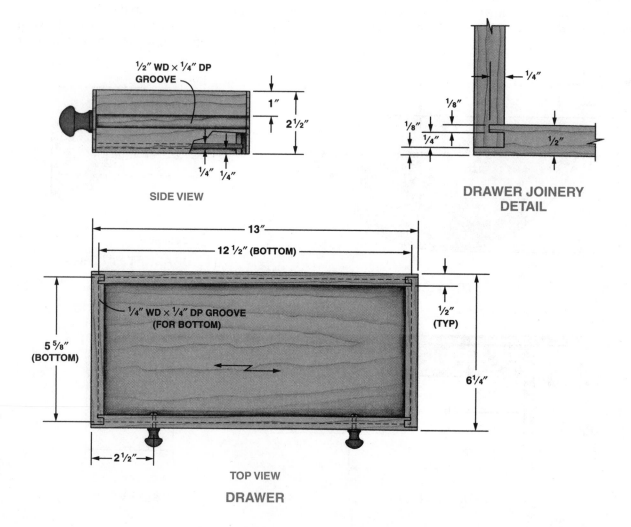

½″ WD × ¼″ DP GROOVE

1″

2½″

¼″   ¼″

SIDE VIEW

¼″

⅛″

⅛″

¼″

½″

DRAWER JOINERY DETAIL

13″

12½″ (BOTTOM)

¼″ WD × ¼″ DP GROOVE (FOR BOTTOM)

½″ (TYP)

5⅝″ (BOTTOM)

6¼″

2½″

TOP VIEW

DRAWER

6 **Assemble the shelf.**
Finish sand the parts of the shelf. Attach the drawer guides to the brackets with wire brads. *Don't* glue them in place. The wood grain in the guides is opposed to the brackets; if glued, the guides will restrict the movement of these parts, causing them to cup. The brads, however, will bend slightly as the brackets expand and contract.

Secure the brackets to the cleat with glue and screws, then attach the shelf to the bracket assembly in the same manner. Counterbore and countersink all screws, and fill the counterbores with wooden plugs to hide the screw heads.

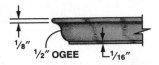

SHELF EDGE PROFILE

Sunday Afternoon

7 **Fit the drawer.** Insert the drawer between the brackets and test the sliding action. If the fit is too tight or the drawer binds as it slides in and out, determine what is causing the problem. Are the sides rubbing against the brackets or are the guides too tight in the grooves? If the sides are rubbing, sand or plane the outside surfaces to remove some stock. If the guides are tight, open up the grooves with a rasp or file.

When the drawer fits, install knobs in the drawer front.

At Your Leisure

8 **Finish the shelf.** Remove the drawer and the pulls. Do any necessary touch-up sanding to the wooden surfaces, then apply a finish to the assembled shelf and drawer. After rubbing out the finish, replace the pulls and install the drawer.

To hang the clock shelf, drill holes through the cleat and into the walls. Countersink or counterbore the holes in the cleat so the bolt heads will rest below the wood surface. If the shelf will hold only light objects (less than 20 pounds), you can attach it to the wall with molly anchors, toggle bolts, or similar "hollow wall" fasteners. If you plan to put anything heavier on the shelf, at least one hole should line up with a stud in the wall. Secure the cleat to the stud with a long screw.

Quick FIXTURE: Router Compass

This "compass" is just a scrap of ¼-inch plywood, slightly longer than the radius you want to cut and as wide as the base of your router. Remove the sole from the router base, and use it as a template to mark mounting holes on the router compass. Drill the mounting holes as well as a 1-inch-diameter access hole for the router bit.

Fasten the router compass to the base of the router in place of the sole. Mount a straight bit in your router, then drill a ³⁄₁₆-inch-diameter pivot hole in the compass. The distance from the *center* of the pivot hole to the *near edge* of the bit should be equal to the radius you want to cut.

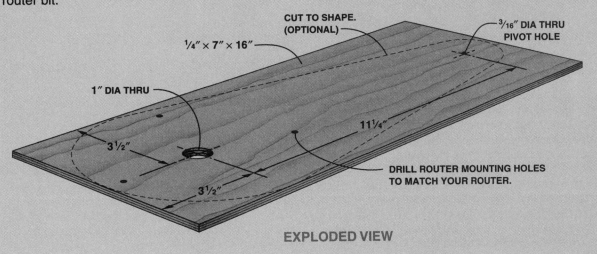

EXPLODED VIEW

Pro SKILL: Routing Circles and Arcs

To rout a circle, you must swing the router around a pivot on the end of a rigid compass. The same rules apply to this operation as apply to other routing tasks:

■ Cut against the rotation of the bit, swinging the router in one direction only. Remember, the bit turns clockwise as you look at it from above. Swing the router counterclockwise when cutting circular shapes, clockwise when making circular cutouts.

■ Cut through thick stock in several passes, routing just ⅛ to ¼ inch deeper with each pass.

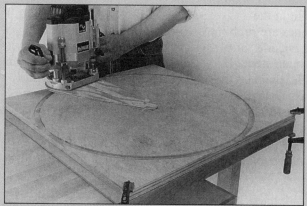

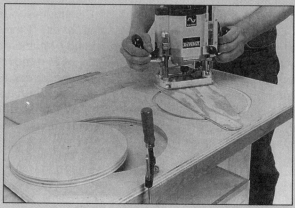

1 Mount the router to a router compass, and install a straight bit in the collet. Attach the work to a scrap of plywood with double-faced carpet tape, and secure the plywood to a workbench. (The plywood prevents you from cutting into the bench top.) Mark the pivot point on the work. Drive a screw through the router compass and into the work. When cutting a circular shape with a router, the distance from the pivot hole to the *inside* edge of the cutter should equal the radius you want to cut. When making a circular cutout, measure to the *outside* edge of the cutter. Adjust the depth of cut, turn the router on, and swing it around the pivot.

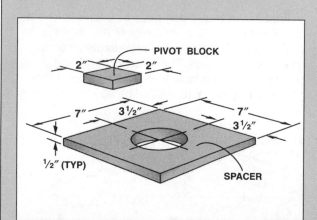

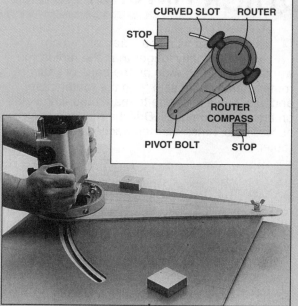

2 If you don't want to drive the pivot screw into the work, make a separate *pivot block* from a scrap of wood. Attach the pivot block to the work with double-faced carpet tape, then drive the pivot screw into the block. Also make a spacer block the same thickness as the pivot block and as wide as the router base. Drill an access hole in the spacer block for the router bit, and attach it to the bottom of the compass with carpet tape. When you've routed the circle, remove the pivot block from the work, and discard the tape.

3 You can also rout partial circles — arcs and curved slots — with a router compass. Just swing the router through part of the circle. Using double-faced carpet tape, attach stops to the work to limit the travel of the router — this will keep you from cutting the slot or arc too long.

PART FOUR

For Reading and Writing

Desk Organizer

The parts of this desk accessory are made of boards of different thicknesses. To make the best use of my lumber, I resawed it on a band saw, cutting through the width to make two or more thin boards from thick stock. Resawing also saved planing time because I didn't have to remove as much stock from the surface.

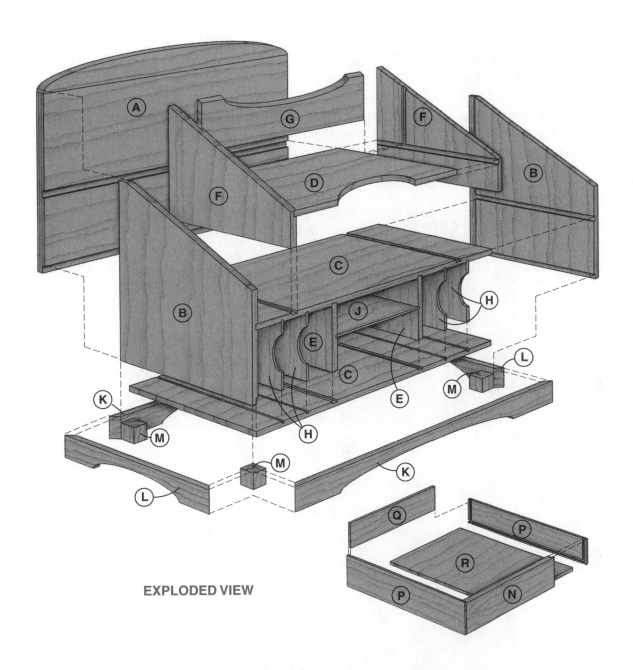

EXPLODED VIEW

MATERIALS LIST

Finished Dimensions in Inches

Parts

A. Back*	$3/8''$ × $12^3/4''$ × $17^1/4''$
B. Sides (2)	$3/8''$ × $9^1/8''$ × $11^3/4''$
C. Bottom/middle shelves (2)	$3/8''$ × $8^7/8''$ × $17^1/4''$
D. Top shelf	$3/8''$ × $8^3/4''$ × $11^3/4''$
E. Bottom dividers (2)	$3/8''$ × $8^3/4''$ × $4^3/4''$
F. Top dividers (2)	$3/8''$ × $8^3/4''$ × $6^5/8''$
G. Back divider	$3/8''$ × $3^7/8''$ × $11^3/4''$
H. Pigeonhole dividers (4)	$1/8''$ × $8^3/4''$ × $4^3/4''$
J. Drawer shelf	$1/8''$ × $8^3/4''$ × $6^1/4''$
K. Front/back feet (2)	$3/8''$ × $1^1/2''$ × $18^1/2''$

L. Side feet (2)	$3/8''$ × $1^1/2''$ × $9^7/8''$
M. Glue blocks (4)	$3/4''$ × $3/4''$ × $1^1/8''$
N. Drawer fronts (2)	$3/8''$ × $2^3/16''$ × $6''$
P. Drawer sides (4)	$1/8''$ × $2^3/16''$ × $8^5/8''$
Q. Drawer backs (2)	$1/8''$ × $1^{15}/16''$ × $5^7/8''$
R. Drawer bottoms (2)	$1/8''$ × $8^1/2''$ × $5^7/8''$

*Make this part from plywood edged (at the top) with solid wood.

Hardware

$1/4''$ Drawer pulls (2)

If you do any sort of paper-work, there are few things more useful than pigeon-holes — spaces and slots to organize letters, bills, stationery, stamps, notices that you may have won ten million dollars, junk mail, and all the other papers that clutter our lives. This is a set of pigeonholes that you can put anywhere you need them.

It's not a difficult project by any stretch of the imagination, but there are a lot of cuts to make. It will take you the better part of a day to make all the rabbets and dadoes. For this reason, it's a "long" week-end project.

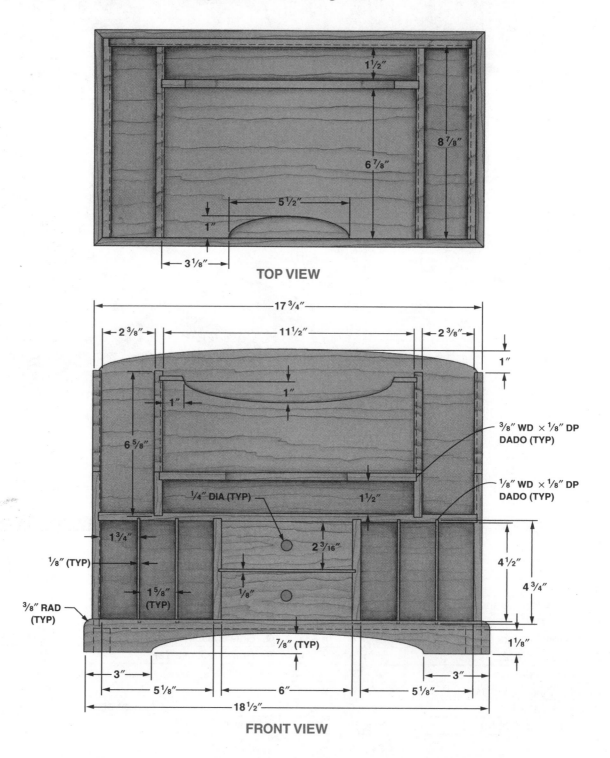

TOP VIEW

FRONT VIEW

1 Prepare the materials, and cut the parts to size.
To make the desk organizer, you need approximately 7 board feet of 4/4 (1-inch-thick) stock and a scrap of ⅜-inch plywood. This presumes that you plan to resaw the stock to make two or more thin boards from each thick one. If you don't, you'll need almost twice as much lumber. The desk organizer is made from quarter-sawn white oak and oak plywood, but you can use any attractive wood and matching plywood.

If you're new to resawing, I suggest you resaw the rough lumber to make boards ½ inch and ¼ inch thick. This will give you an extra ⅛ inch of thickness to remove on the planer, making the ⅜-inch and ⅛-inch-thick stock needed. If you've done this before and trust your equipment,

resaw the lumber to make boards ⁷⁄₁₆ inch and ³⁄₁₆ inch thick. Plane them to the thicknesses needed.

Cut the ⅜-inch and ⅛-inch-thick parts *except* for the drawer parts and feet. Wait until after

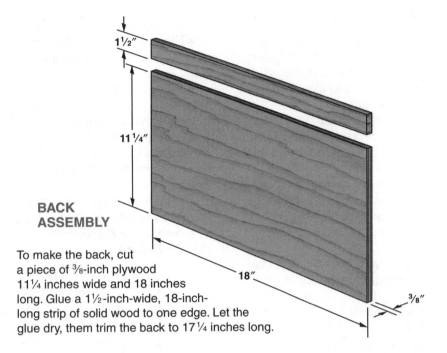

BACK ASSEMBLY

1½"

11¼"

18"

⅜"

To make the back, cut a piece of ⅜-inch plywood 11¼ inches wide and 18 inches long. Glue a 1½-inch-wide, 18-inch-long strip of solid wood to one edge. Let the glue dry, them trim the back to 17¼ inches long.

you've assembled the pigeon-holes to cut these. As you're cutting each part, pay careful attention to the grain direction. With the exception of the back, all the parts of the pigeonhole assembly must expand and contract front to back. To do this, the grain in the horizontal parts must run side to side, while that in the vertical parts runs up and down.

The back is the one part in the whole assembly that you can't orient to expand and contract with the other parts. For this reason, make the back from ply-wood and edge it with a strip of solid wood. When the organizer is assembled, the solid wood strip will become the top edge and hide the plies.

2 Lay out the joints and shapes on the pigeon-hole parts. Keeping track of which part gets what joint and what side to cut can be a night-mare. You can eliminate much of the confusion by laying out all the joints and profiles on the

9⅛"

⅜" (TYP)

28°

3⅞"

12¾"

8¾"

7⅛"

11¾"

3¼"

¾"

1½"

2"

5⅞"

¾" SQUARE

9⅞"

SIDE VIEW

parts *before* you cut them. Here's a checklist for the joinery:

■ $\frac{3}{8}$-inch-wide, $\frac{1}{8}$-inch-deep rabbet and groove in the inside face of the back, as shown in the *Back Layout*

■ $\frac{3}{8}$-inch-wide, $\frac{1}{8}$-inch-deep dadoes and rabbet on the inside face of the sides, as shown in the *Side Layout*

■ $\frac{3}{8}$-inch-wide, $\frac{1}{8}$-inch-deep dadoes and stop grooves in the inside faces of the top dividers, as shown in the *Top Divider Layout*

■ $\frac{3}{8}$-inch-wide, $\frac{1}{8}$-inch-deep dadoes in the top face of the middle shelf, as shown in the *Middle Shelf/Top Face Layout*

■ $\frac{3}{8}$-inch-wide, $\frac{1}{8}$-inch-deep dadoes and $\frac{1}{8}$-inch-wide, $\frac{1}{8}$-inch-deep dadoes in the bottom face of the middle shelf and the top face of the bottom shelf, as shown in the *Middle Shelf/Bottom Face* and *Bottom Shelf/Top Face Layout*

■ $\frac{1}{8}$-inch-wide, $\frac{1}{8}$-inch-deep dadoes in the bottom dividers, as shown in the *Bottom Divider Layout*

And another for the shapes:

■ Elliptical curve on the top edge of the back, as shown in the *Back Pattern*

■ Elliptical curve in the front edge of the top shelf, as shown in the *Top Shelf Pattern*

■ Elliptical curve in the top edge of the back divider, as shown in the *Back Divider Pattern*

■ Elliptical curves in the front edges of the pigeonhole dividers, as shown in the *Pigeonhole Divider Pattern*

■ Sloped top edges of the sides and top dividers (angled at 28 degrees), as shown in the *Side Layout* and *Top Divider Layout*

Check your joinery layout by stacking the parts in the same configuration in which you will join them. *Make sure you've marked the correct surfaces and that you know which are the front edges!*

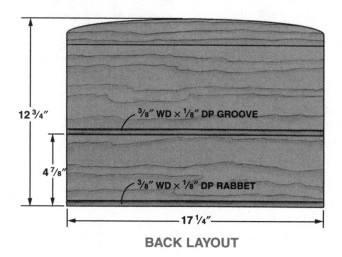

BACK LAYOUT

Quick FIXTURE: Resawing Fence

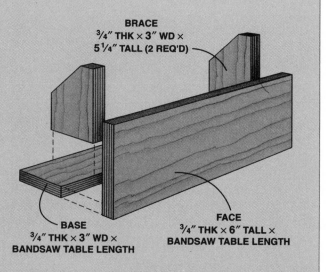

When you resaw wood, you must cut through its width, with the board standing on edge. Additionally, the face of the board must be parallel to the saw blade. To properly support a wide board in this position, make a tall *resawing fence* that you can attach to your band saw.

The fence face must be perfectly straight and flat to guide the work accurately. To ensure that it is, clamp the face to a flat surface (such as a saw table) as you glue the base and the braces to it. Secure the fence to the band saw table with clamps.

Note: If you have a fence accessory for your band saw, you don't need to make this fixture. Instead make the simpler *tall fence* shown on page 46 and attach it to your band saw fence to increase its height.

BRACE
$\frac{3}{4}$" THK × 3" WD ×
$5\frac{1}{4}$" TALL (2 REQ'D)

BASE
$\frac{3}{4}$" THK × 3" WD ×
BANDSAW TABLE LENGTH

FACE
$\frac{3}{4}$" THK × 6" TALL ×
BANDSAW TABLE LENGTH

EXPLODED VIEW

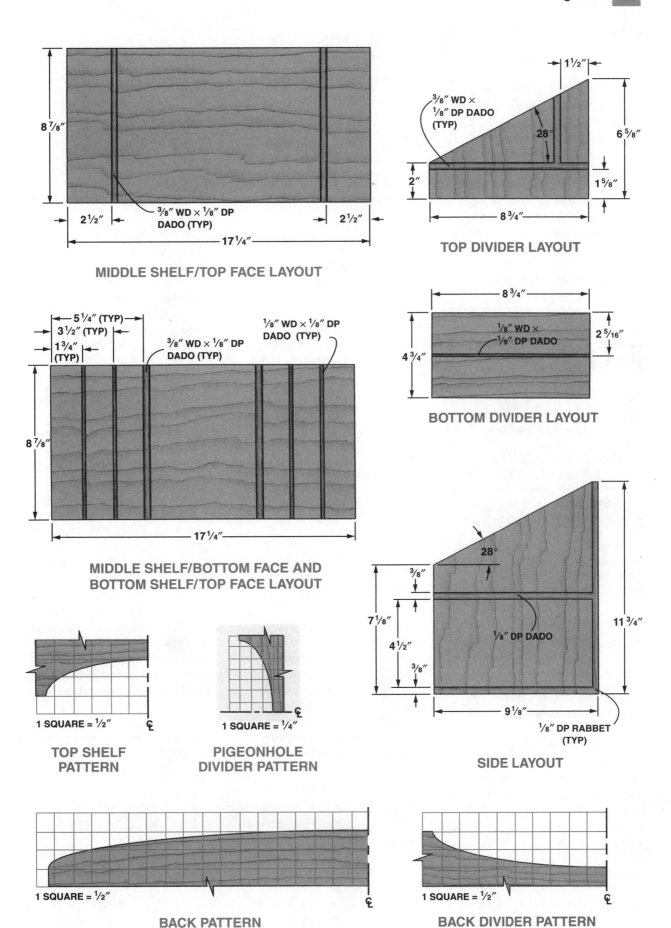

MIDDLE SHELF/TOP FACE LAYOUT

8 7/8″

2 1/2″   17 1/4″   2 1/2″

3/8″ WD × 1/8″ DP DADO (TYP)

TOP DIVIDER LAYOUT

1 1/2″
6 5/8″
28°
2″
8 3/4″
1 5/8″
3/8″ WD × 1/8″ DP DADO (TYP)

MIDDLE SHELF/BOTTOM FACE AND BOTTOM SHELF/TOP FACE LAYOUT

5 1/4″ (TYP)
3 1/2″ (TYP)
1 3/4″ (TYP)
3/8″ WD × 1/8″ DP DADO (TYP)
1/8″ WD × 1/8″ DP DADO (TYP)
8 7/8″
17 1/4″

BOTTOM DIVIDER LAYOUT

8 3/4″
4 3/4″
2 5/16″
1/8″ WD × 1/8″ DP DADO

TOP SHELF PATTERN

1 SQUARE = 1/2″

PIGEONHOLE DIVIDER PATTERN

1 SQUARE = 1/4″

SIDE LAYOUT

28°
3/8″
7 1/8″
4 1/2″
3/8″
1/8″ DP DADO
11 3/4″
9 1/8″
1/8″ DP RABBET (TYP)

BACK PATTERN

1 SQUARE = 1/2″

BACK DIVIDER PATTERN

1 SQUARE = 1/2″

Saturday Afternoon

3 **Cut the joinery.** Cut the joints in the back, sides, dividers, and shelves. Use a dado cutter or a router to make the ⅜-inch-wide joints, and a rip blade to make the ⅛-inch wide joints.

Note that the ⅜-inch-wide grooves in the top dividers are stopped. They end at the dado. Perhaps the easiest way to make these is with a router. First rout the dadoes across the grain of the parts. Then rout the grooves, starting or stopping at the dadoes.

TRY THIS

CUTTING JOINTS WITH RIP BLADES

A rip blade has saw teeth that are ground straight across the top and leave a flat-bottom kerf. Standard rip blades leave a kerf approximately ⅛ inch wide; narrow-kerf blades cut kerfs as small as 5/64 inch. In addition to ripping wood, you can use these blades to make very narrow dadoes and grooves. When cutting across the grain, feed the work slowly to avoid chipping.

Saturday Evening

4 **Cut the shapes.** Cut the angled top edges in the sides and top dividers. Also bevel the top edge of the back divider. Using a band saw, cut the elliptical profiles of the back, top shelf, back divider, and pigeonhole dividers. Sand the sawed surfaces.

5 **Assemble the pigeonholes.** Finish sand all the parts you've made so far. Temporarily, assemble the pigeonholes *without glue* to test the fit of the joints. When you're satisfied that the joints fit properly, assemble the parts with glue and clamp them together. You'll find that it helps to build this assembly from the bottom up, assembling the parts in this order:

■ Glue the drawer shelf between the bottom dividers.

■ Attach the bottom divider assembly to the bottom and middle shelves.

■ Glue the sides to the bottom and middle shelf.

■ Attach the back to the assembly.

■ Assemble the top dividers, top shelf, and back divider.

■ Glue the top divider assembly to the middle shelf and back.

The "open assembly time" (before you must apply the clamps) of most common woodworking glues is less than 15 minutes, so you must do this quickly. If you can't assemble the parts fast enough, use a glue with a longer open time such as liquid hide glue (30 minutes) or

TRY THIS

STAINING THE INSIDE

If you intend to stain this project, it's wise to apply a stain to the inside surfaces *before* you assemble them, even though it will cost you some time. Otherwise, you'll find it extremely difficult to reach into the deep recesses and spread the stain evenly. Use a water-soluble aniline dye to stain the wood. Oil-based stains prevent the glue from penetrating the wood and weaken the glue bonds.

slow-set epoxy (up to 1 hour). Do *not* glue the pigeonhole dividers in the assembly. If you do, it will be almost impossible to finish the inside surfaces of the pigeonholes. Just leave them loose for the time being.

Sunday Afternoon

6 **Make the feet.** Remove the clamps from the pigeonhole assembly. Sand the joints clean and flush where necessary, then carefully measure the outside dimensions. The accumulation of small errors may make these slightly different from those shown in the drawings.

Make the necessary adjustments in the length of the feet, then cut them to size, mitering the ends. Lay out the elliptical profiles of the feet, as shown in the ***Front and Back Feet Pattern*** and ***Side Feet Pattern.*** Cut the profiles on a band saw.

Assemble the feet with glue and glue blocks. However, do *not* attach them to the pigeonhole assembly yet.

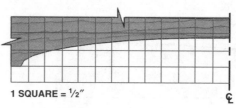

1 SQUARE = ½″

FRONT AND BACK FEET PATTERN

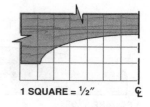

1 SQUARE = ½″

SIDE FEET PATTERN

Sunday Evening

7 Cut the drawer parts.
Measure the openings for the drawers in the pigeonhole assembly. Once again, it's likely that the dimensions will be slightly different from the drawings. Make the necessary adjustments to the measurements of the drawer parts, then cut them to size. Be sure to cut the drawer bottoms so the grain runs from side to side in the drawers.

The drawers have to be slightly smaller than their openings to work properly. However, it's usually a good idea to make the drawer parts to fit the opening exactly. The assembled drawer will be just a little too large, but you can easily fit the drawer to the opening by sanding or planing the surfaces until it slides smoothly.

8 Cut the drawer joinery.
Like the pigeonholes, it helps to lay out the joints on the parts, then cut them. They are:

■ Lock joints (also called tongue-and-dado joints) in the adjoining ends of the drawer front and drawer sides, as shown in the *Lock Joint Detail*

See Also:
"Making Lock Joints" on page 106.

■ ⅛-inch-wide, ⅛-inch deep dadoes near the ends of the drawer sides to hold the backs, as shown in the *Drawer/Side View*

■ ⅛-inch-wide, ⅛-inch-deep grooves near the bottom edges of the drawer fronts and sides to hold the bottoms

9 Assemble the drawers.
Finish sand the parts of the drawers. Assemble the front, sides, and back with glue. Apply a little glue to the grooves that hold the bottoms in the drawer fronts, then slide the bottoms in place. Do not glue any other surface but the front edge of the drawer bottoms. The bottoms must be left free to expand toward the back of the assembly.

Monday Morning

10 Fit the drawers to the pigeonholes.
Remove the clamps from the drawers and test fit them in their openings. Carefully sand stock from the top and side surfaces until the drawers slip in and out of the opening without sticking. Attach small drawer pulls to the fronts of the drawers.

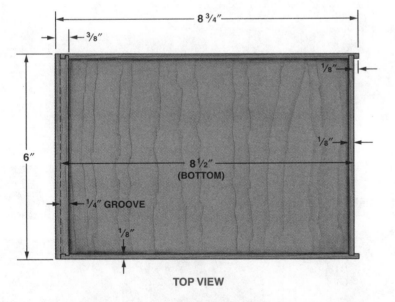

TOP VIEW

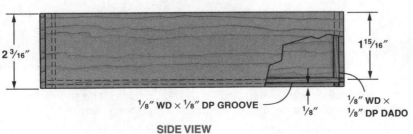

SIDE VIEW
DRAWER

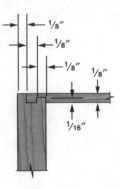

LOCK JOINT DETAIL

At Your Leisure

11 **Finish the organizer.** Remove the pulls from the drawers and do any necessary touch up sanding to the drawers, feet, and pigeonhole assembly. If you're applying a stain, touch up the areas you've sanded on the pigeonholes. Then apply a matching stain to the feet and drawers. When the stain dries, apply a finish to all wood surfaces.

Rub out the finish to the desired luster, then slide the pigeonhole dividers into their slots. Glue the pigeonhole assembly to the feet assembly with epoxy cement. (Don't use polyvinyl (white) or aliphatic (yellow) glue; the finish will prevent these adhesives from bonding properly. Finally, replace the drawer pulls and slide the drawers in place.

EXTRA INFO

MAKING LOCK JOINTS

1 To make lock joints, first cut ⅛-inch-wide, ⅛-inch-deep grooves in the ends of the drawer fronts. Use the tenoning jig shown on page 120 to hold the work vertically.

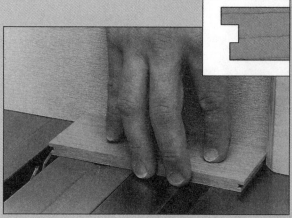

2 When you make the grooves, you'll create two ⅛-inch-long "tongues" on each end of the drawer fronts. Cut the inside tongues short, making them just ¹⁄₁₆ inch long.

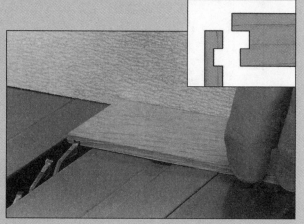

3 Cut ⅛-inch-wide, ¹⁄₁₆-inch-deep dadoes near the ends of the drawer sides. The short tongues on the drawer fronts fit into these dadoes.

Pro SKILL: Resawing

When you slice a board through its width, you are *resawing* the wood, making two thin boards out of a thick one. Unless the stock is very narrow (less than 3 inches), this is best done on a band saw. Use a *wide blade* (½ to 1 inch) for this operation; it's less likely to bow and twist.

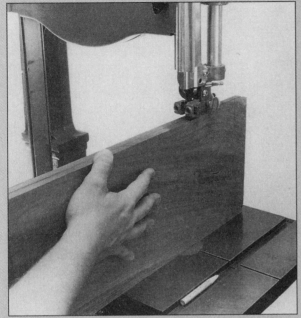

1 Before you can resaw accurately, you must first know the *blade lead*. Few band saw blades track parallel to their bodies. The teeth usually cut more aggressively on one side than the other. To cut a straight line, you must guide the wood past the blade in the same direction that the blade leads. To find this direction, scribe a line along the edge of a wide scrap, parallel to the face, and begin cutting along the line on the band saw.

2 Adjust the feed direction until the saw is cutting straight along the line, then stop cutting and turn off the machine. Don't let the scrap move! Using the scrap as a straightedge, mark a line on the table with a wax pencil. This is your lead line for that particular blade.

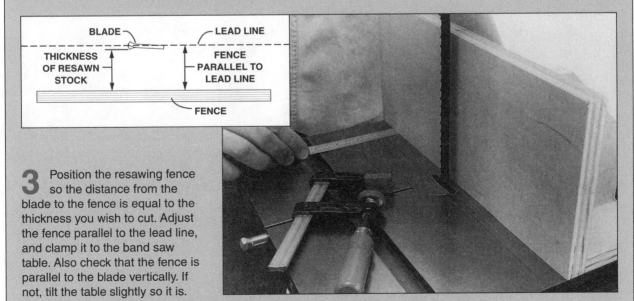

3 Position the resawing fence so the distance from the blade to the fence is equal to the thickness you wish to cut. Adjust the fence parallel to the lead line, and clamp it to the band saw table. Also check that the fence is parallel to the blade vertically. If not, tilt the table slightly so it is.

(continued)

Pro SKILL: Resawing — CONTINUED

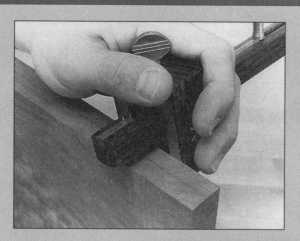

4 Joint at least one face and one edge of the board you wish to resaw. Scribe a line along the top edge to use as a reference.

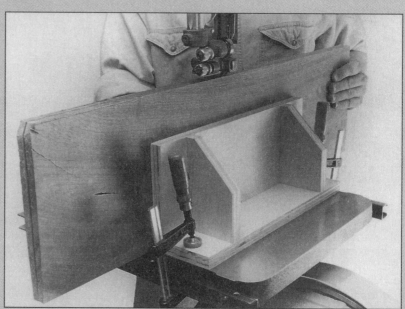

5 Place the jointed edge on the band saw table and the jointed face against the fence. Turn on the saw, and feed the wood into the blade. Keep the feed rate slow and even. Watch the reference line as you cut — this will tell you if the blade is cutting true. And be very careful to keep the stock pressed flat against the fence.

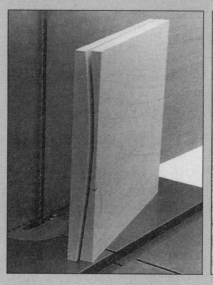

6 If the blade isn't tensioned properly, it may cup or "belly" in the cut *(left)*. Should this happen, increase the blade tension and decrease the feed rate. A rough, uneven cut (called "washboarding") is caused by the blade slapping back and forth in the cut *(right)*. If this is a problem, reduce the feed rate or use a wider blade.

Hanging Secretary

Hanging a cabinet or shelving unit on a wall can be an exercise in frustration, especially when you don't have adequate help. A pair of deadmen provide the assistance you need, holding the cabinet in place while you fasten it to the wall.

109

EXPLODED VIEW

MATERIALS LIST

Finished Dimensions in Inches

Parts

A. Shelving sides (2)	$\frac{3}{4}'' \times 7'' \times 43\frac{7}{8}''$	
B. Desk sides (2)	$\frac{3}{4}'' \times 10'' \times 10\frac{1}{2}''$	
C. Shelves (5)	$\frac{3}{4}'' \times 6\frac{3}{4}'' \times 21\frac{1}{4}''$	
D. Front	$\frac{3}{4}'' \times 5\frac{1}{2}'' \times 20\frac{1}{2}''$	
E. Bottom*	$\frac{3}{4}'' \times 16'' \times 21\frac{1}{4}''$	
F. Desk lid	$\frac{3}{4}'' \times 11\frac{13}{16}'' \times 20\frac{1}{2}''$	
G. Ledger	$\frac{3}{8}'' \times \frac{7}{16}'' \times 20\frac{1}{2}''$	
H. Top	$\frac{3}{8}'' \times 8\frac{3}{8}'' \times 24\frac{3}{4}''$	
J. Front molding	$1\frac{1}{8}'' \times 1\frac{1}{4}'' \times 24\frac{1}{4}''$	
K. Side moldings (2)	$1\frac{1}{8}'' \times 1\frac{1}{4}'' \times 8\frac{1}{8}''$	

L. Back*	$\frac{1}{4}'' \times 21\frac{1}{4}'' \times 43\frac{7}{8}''$
M. Valance rail	$\frac{3}{4}'' \times 1\frac{3}{4}'' \times 22''$
N. Nailing strip	$\frac{3}{4}'' \times 1\frac{3}{4}'' \times 20\frac{1}{2}''$

* Make these parts from plywood.

Hardware

4d Cut nails (24–30)

1″ Wire brads (18–24)

#8 × 1¼″ Flathead wood screws (4)

1½″ × 2″ Butt hinges and mounting screws (2)

This small secretary makes an excellent organizer for letters and bills or a display unit for collectibles. It can also be adapted as a phone desk and message center. The design was patterned after an early nineteenth-century secretary by David T. Smith of Morrow, Ohio. David and the craftsmen who work with him at his workshops are accomplished builders of American country-style furniture.

Friday Evening

1 Prepare the materials, and cut the parts to size.

To make this secretary, you need approximately 20 board feet of 4/4 (1-inch-thick) stock, a quarter sheet (2 × 4 feet) of ¼-inch plywood, and a small piece of ¾-inch plywood. The secretary shown is made from poplar and birch plywood, but you can use any cabinet-grade materials.

Plane the 4/4 stock to ¾ inch thick, and cut the sides, shelves, front, desk lid, rail, and nailing strip. When cutting the desk sides, miter the top ends at 20 degrees, as shown in the *Side*

Layout. Also bevel the top edge of the front and both edges of the lid at 20 degrees, as shown in the *Side View.* Cut the back and bottom from plywood.

Cut two strips of ¾-inch-thick stock 1½ inches wide and 48 inches long. Plane these to 9/16 inch thick, and set them aside. Later, you'll use these strips to make the moldings.

Select a ¾-inch-thick board large enough to make both the top and the ledger. Plane the board to ⅜ inch thick, and set it aside. *Don't* cut the top or the ledger to size just yet.

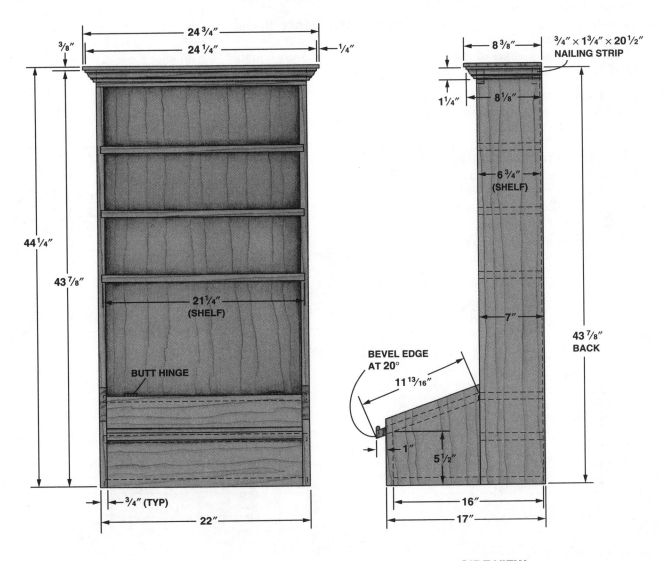

FRONT VIEW

SIDE VIEW

Saturday Morning

2 Cut the dadoes and rabbets in the sides.

For the most part, this project is assembled with simple dadoes and rabbets, and all of these are cut in the sides, as shown in the *Side Layout.* Using either a dado cutter or a router and straight bit, make:

- ¾-inch-wide, ⅜-inch-deep dadoes in the shelving sides to hold the shelves
- ¾-inch-wide, ⅜-inch-deep rabbets in the bottom ends of the shelving sides to hold the bottom
- ¾-inch-wide, ⅜-inch-deep *stopped* rabbets in the bottom ends of the desk sides to hold the bottom
- ¼-inch-wide, ⅜-inch-deep rabbets in the back edges of the shelving sides to hold the back

Note: As you cut the joinery, remember the sides are *mirror images* of each other.

3 Cut the notches in the sides.

Using a hand saw or a saber saw, cut ¾-inch-wide, 1¾-inch-long notches in the top front corners of the sides, as shown in the *Side Layout.* These notches hold the valance rail.

Saturday Afternoon

4 Assemble the sides.

Finish sand the shelving sides and the desk sides, then glue them edge to edge. The bottom edges must be flush.

5 Make the molding stock.

Cut a ¼-inch cove in the edge of one of the ⁹⁄₁₆-inch-thick strips, then rip the strip to 1¼ inch wide. Rout an ogee in the edge of the other strip, and rip the second strip to ¹³⁄₁₆ inch wide. Glue the two strips together face to face to make the top molding stock, as shown in the *Molding Profile.*

6 Make the ledger.

Round over the edge of the ⅜-inch-thick stock, as shown in the *Ledger Profile.* You can use a table-mounted router and a small roundover bit for this task, but you may find it faster and easier to knock the corners off the stock with a block plane, then round the surface with a file or scraper.

After rounding the edge, rip the ledger from the stock, beveling the edge at 20 degrees.

Saturday Evening

7 Assemble the case.

Remove the clamps from the side assemblies, and sand the glue joints clean and flush. Finish sand the sides, shelves, front, back, nailing strip, valance rail, and bottom. Assemble the sides and shelves with glue and cut nails. Then add the front, bottom, valance rail, and nailing strip, attaching each part with glue and nails. Attach the back to the case with wire brads and glue.

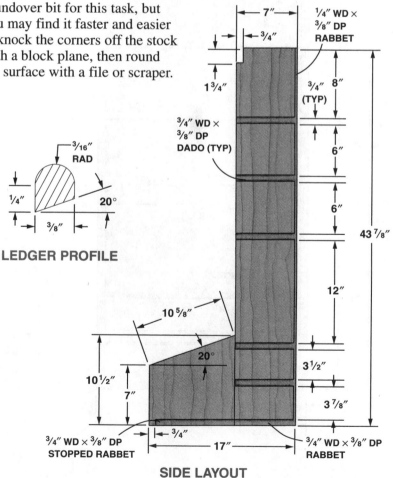

SIDE LAYOUT

LEDGER PROFILE

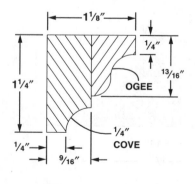

MOLDING PROFILE

Sunday Afternoon

8 Install the molding. Cut the moldings to length, mitering the adjoining ends. Glue the front molding to the valance rail. Glue the side moldings to the front molding, but *don't* glue them to the sides. The wood grain on the side moldings runs perpendicular to the grain in the sides. If you glue the two parts together, the moldings will restrict the natural expansion and contraction of the sides. Instead, attach the moldings with wood screws. Drill pilot holes slightly larger than the screw shanks through the sides. Drive the screws *from inside the case* through the sides and into the moldings. The oversize holes will allow the sides to move.

9 Install the top. Cut the top to size. (It should overhang the moldings by ¼ inch at the front and the sides.) Attach it to the sides and valance rail with glue and cut nails. Do *not* glue it to the side moldings.

10 Attach the desk lid. Mortise the edge of the desk lid and the adjoining shelf for hinges. Then attach the lid to the shelf. Secure the ledger to the desk lid with glue and wire brads.

See Also:
"Setting Hinges" on page 85.

At Your Leisure

11 Finish the secretary. Remove the desk lid from the case and set the hinges aside. Do any necessary touch-up sanding, then apply a finish to all wooden surfaces, inside and out. When the finish dries, replace the lid.

TRY THIS

USING CUT NAILS

Before wire-nail technology came along, nails were cut from plate and had a rectangular cross-section. They are still made and give your project an antique look. They also hold better than today's wire nails, if properly installed. Drill a pilot hole for each nail, slightly smaller than the nail shank. (This prevents the nail from splitting the wood.) Drive the nail home, and set the head.

12 Hang the secretary. To hang the secretary, drill two or three holes through the nailing strip and into the walls. At least one hole should line up with a stud in the wall frame to properly support the weight of the piece. Secure the nailing strip to the stud with a long wood screw or lag screw. In the remaining holes, use mollies or toggle bolts.

Quick FIXTURE: Deadman

How many woodworkers does it take to hang a cabinet? Sounds like the beginning of a bad joke, but for those of us who have been there, it's no laughing matter. Typically, this task requires two or three people— one to drive the fasteners, and the others to hold the cabinet in position. With a pair of these *deadmen*, however, you don't need quite so much help.

Deadmen are adjustable stands made from scraps of plywood and construction lumber. To use them, clamp the top and base assemblies together so the tops are the desired height above the floor. Double-check that the clamps are tight, then rest the cabinet on the deadmen. You'll still need a second person to help lift the cabinet onto the deadmen and to steady them while you drive the fasteners. But the cabinet will remain in one place and your help won't moan about how tired their arms are getting.

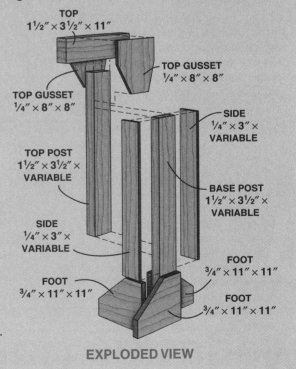

TOP 1½" × 3½" × 11"

TOP GUSSET ¼" × 8" × 8"

TOP GUSSET ¼" × 8" × 8"

SIDE ¼" × 3" × VARIABLE

TOP POST 1½" × 3½" × VARIABLE

BASE POST 1½" × 3½" × VARIABLE

SIDE ¼" × 3" × VARIABLE

FOOT ¾" × 11" × 11"

FOOT ¾" × 11" × 11"

FOOT ¾" × 11" × 11"

EXPLODED VIEW

Pro SKILL: Hanging Cabinets

When hanging a cabinet or shelving unit on a wall, you must adequately support the weight of the unit and whatever you intend to store in it. To do this, the cabinet must be properly designed and properly attached to the wall.

1 While most furniture bears its weight on its legs or feet, a hanging cabinet supports itself from its back. For this reason, most wall units have a sturdy *nailing strip* at the back top edge. (Heavy units may also have them at the bottom edge.) Hang these cabinets by driving nails, screws, or bolts through the nailing strips and into the wall.

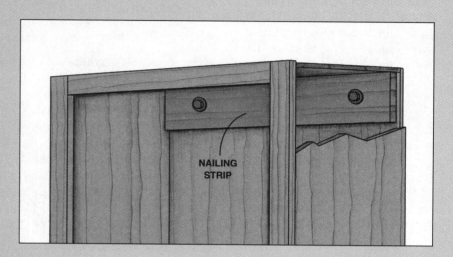

NAILING STRIP

2 You can also use *mounting strips* to hang cabinets. The adjoining edges of these strips are either beveled or shaped so they interlock. Attach the top strip to the cabinet and the bottom strip to the wall, then fit the top strip over the bottom one. The weight of the cabinet will hold it in place, or you can sink a nail or two through the top strip and into the wall to lock the parts together. **Note:** Cabinets with mounting strips often have no backs.

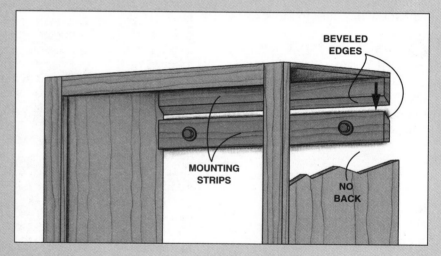

BEVELED EDGES

MOUNTING STRIPS

NO BACK

3 No matter what system you use, you must anchor the strip firmly to the wall. To attach a cabinet to a masonry wall, drill holes in the mortar with a masonry bit, and install lead anchors. Drive screws through the strip and into the anchors. To attach a cabinet to a frame wall, locate the studs. Then drive screws through the strip and the drywall (or plaster) and into the stud.

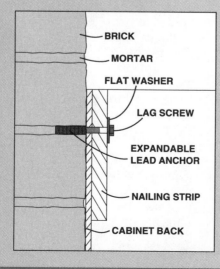

BRICK

MORTAR

FLAT WASHER

LAG SCREW

EXPANDABLE LEAD ANCHOR

NAILING STRIP

CABINET BACK

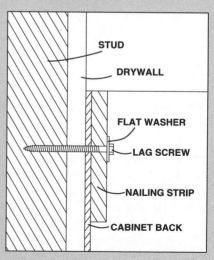

STUD

DRYWALL

FLAT WASHER

LAG SCREW

NAILING STRIP

CABINET BACK

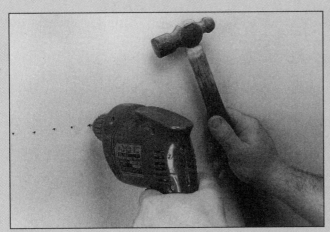

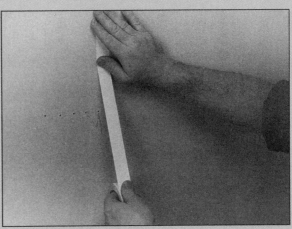

4 One of the most effective ways of finding studs in a wall is to tap for them with a hammer. Tapping will make a low-pitched hollow sound over areas between studs. As you tap near a stud, the sound pitch rises sharply. When you think you know the location of the stud, check by boring a small hole. The bit will bring back

a little sawdust with it if you're right. When you're sure of where the stud is, mark it. If you don't want to mark directly on the wall, apply a piece of *drafting tape* over the stud. This material looks like masking tape, but it peels up easily without ruining the surface beneath it.

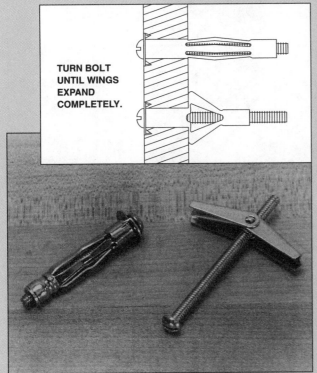

TURN BOLT
UNTIL WINGS
EXPAND
COMPLETELY.

5 Always fasten a cabinet to at least two points on a wall; otherwise the unit may tilt or swing. But what if the cabinet is narrow and you can only attach it to one stud? When this is the case, attach it to the stud *and* at another location on the drywall or plaster. Use *hollow wall anchors* such as mollies or toggle bolts. Drill holes in the wall, then insert the anchors, and tighten the bolts. The anchors expand on the inside of the wall, as shown.

6 To help support a cabinet while you drive fasteners through its nailing strip, adjust two or more *deadmen* to the desired height, then rest the cabinet on them. The deadmen should toe out from the wall slightly so the feet are an inch or two further from the wall than the tops. This will help hold the cabinet against the wall.

Side Table and Magazine Holder

■ **QUICK FIXTURE**
Tenoning Jig

■ **PRO SKILL**
Cutting Tenons

*T*he parts of this Arts-and-Crafts-style table are joined by mortises and tenons. To cut the tenons, master craftsman Larry Callahan made a simple tenoning jig. This held the boards vertically while he sawed their ends.

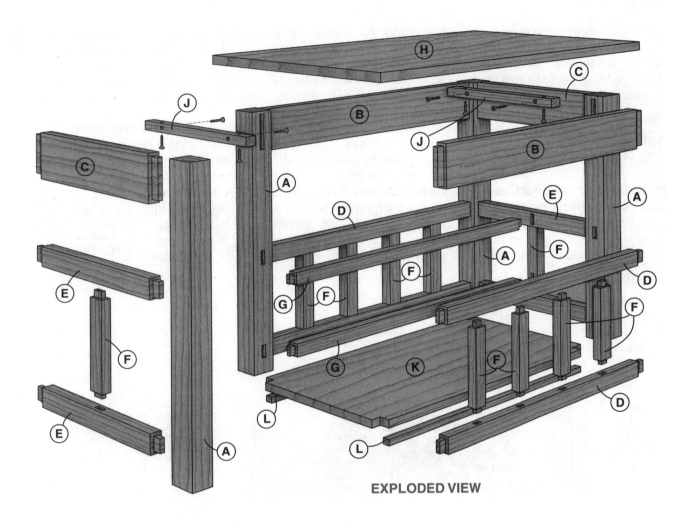

EXPLODED VIEW

MATERIALS LIST

Finished Dimensions in Inches		
Parts		
A. Legs (4)	$1\frac{1}{2}'' \times 1\frac{1}{2}'' \times 23\frac{1}{4}''$	
B. Front/back aprons (2)	$\frac{3}{4}'' \times 3\frac{3}{4}'' \times 18\frac{1}{2}''$	
C. Side aprons (2)	$\frac{3}{4}'' \times 3\frac{3}{4}'' \times 10\frac{1}{2}''$	
D. Front/back stretchers (4)	$\frac{3}{4}'' \times 1\frac{1}{2}'' \times 18\frac{1}{2}''$	
E. Side stretchers (4)	$\frac{3}{4}'' \times 1\frac{1}{2}'' \times 10\frac{1}{2}''$	
F. Slats (10)	$\frac{3}{4}'' \times 1'' \times 8''$	
G. Dividers (2)	$\frac{3}{4}'' \times 1\frac{1}{2}'' \times 19\frac{1}{4}''$	
H. Top	$\frac{3}{4}'' \times 14'' \times 22''$	
J. Top cleats (2)	$\frac{3}{4}'' \times \frac{3}{4}'' \times 9''$	
K. Bottom	$\frac{3}{4}'' \times 10'' \times 18\frac{3}{16}''$	
L. Bottom cleats (2)	$\frac{1}{2}'' \times \frac{1}{2}'' \times 17\frac{1}{2}''$	
Hardware		
#8 × 1¼″ Flathead wood screws (8)		

If you have more magazines and newspapers than places to put them, you'll appreciate this clever side table. The base sports a divided holder that will hold a surprising amount of reading material. You can also use it to store knitting or display potted plants. With a few more slats, it also makes a good toy bin.

Friday Evening

1 Prepare the materials, and cut the parts to size.
To make the side table, you need about 12 board feet of 4/4 (1-inch-thick) stock, and 4 board feet of 8/4 (2-inch-thick) stock. The table shown is made from white oak, but you can use any cabinet-grade wood.

Plane the 4/4 stock to ¾ inch thick and the 8/4 stock to 1½ inches thick. Cut all the parts to the sizes specified in the Materials List, except for the top and bottom. For these parts, glue up narrow boards to make wide stock. Later, when the glue is dry, you can trim them to the proper size. **Note:** To cut the ½-inch-

See Also:
"Making Multiple Cuts" on page 80.

square cleats from ¾-inch-thick material, rip the stock twice. There's no sense in planing a large board down to ½ inch thick for these two little parts.

Saturday Morning

2 **Lay out the mortises and tenons on the legs, stretchers, and slats.** With the exception of the cleats that hold the top and bottom, all the parts of the table are assembled with mortise-and-tenon joints. Inspect the parts, and choose which surfaces will be turned out, which will be turned in, which surfaces will face up, and which will face down. Carefully mark all surfaces.

Lay out the mortises and tenons on the parts, paying careful attention to the orientation of each part. When you've completed the layout, arrange the parts in the approximate configuration in which they will be assembled, and check your work. There are a lot of mortises and tenons to make; you don't want to remake a part because you cut the mortises in the wrong surface.

3 **Rout the mortises in the legs, stretchers, and slats.** When making mortise-and-tenon joints, most craftsmen prefer to begin with the mortises. It's easier to fit the tenons to

See Also:
"Routing Mortises" on page 28.

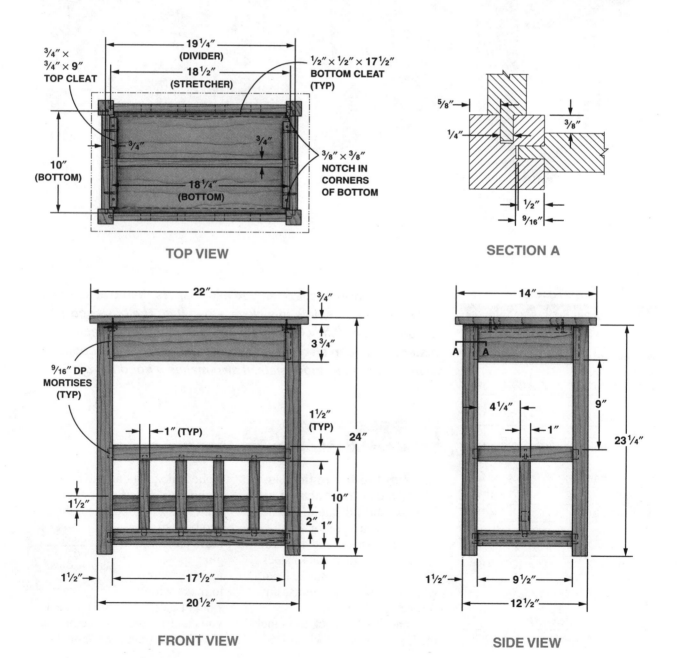

TOP VIEW

SECTION A

FRONT VIEW

SIDE VIEW

the mortises than it is to size the mortises to the tenons. Cut:

- ¼-inch-wide, 3¼-inch-long, ⁹⁄₁₆-inch-deep mortises in the inside surfaces of the legs to hold the aprons, as shown in the *Leg Layout*
- ¼-inch-wide, 1-inch-long, ⁹⁄₁₆-inch-deep mortises in inside surfaces of the legs to hold the stretchers, as shown in the *Leg Layout*
- ¼-inch-wide, 1-inch-long, ⁹⁄₁₆-inch-deep mortises in the inside face of the top side stretchers and the middle slats, as shown in the *Stretcher and Slat Layout.* These will hold the dividers. Note that the mortise in the stretcher face is turned so the

long dimension is *perpendicular* to the length of the part. All the other mortises are parallel.

- ¼-inch-wide, ½-inch-long, ⁹⁄₁₆-inch deep mortises in the bottom edges of the top stretchers and the top edges of the bottom stretchers to hold the slats, as shown in the *Front/ Back Stretcher Layout* and the *Side Stretcher Layout*

Saturday Afternoon

4 Cut the tenons in the aprons, stretchers, and slats.
All the tenons are ¼ inch thick, ½ inch long, and have ¼-inch shoulders, as shown in the *Tenon Detail.* This makes it possible to cut them all with just two setups — one to cut the shoulders and the other to cut the cheeks. First, make the *Tenoning Jig,* shown on page 120, to hold the parts vertically on your table saw. Cut the shoulders first; use the miter gauge to guide them over the saw blade. Then use the tenoning jig when cutting the cheeks.

See Also:
"Cutting Tenons" on page 121.

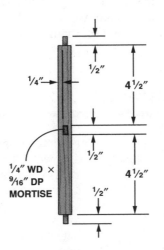

SIDE STRETCHER LAYOUT

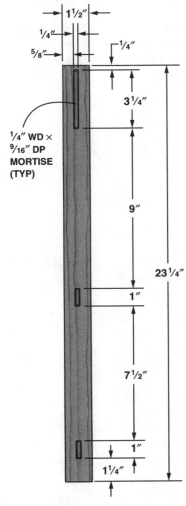

LEG LAYOUT

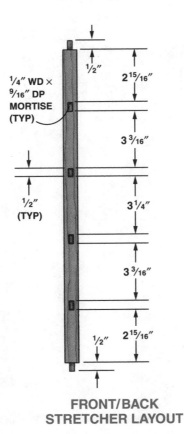

FRONT/BACK STRETCHER LAYOUT

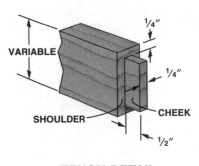

TENON DETAIL

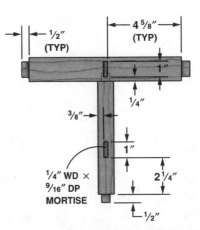

STRETCHER AND SLAT LAYOUT

Saturday Evening

5 Notch the middle slats.
As you've probably noticed, the mortises in the top short stretchers intersect. Because of this, you cannot insert the slats and dividers in these mortises without notching one set of tenons. Using a band saw or coping saw, cut a ¼-inch-wide, ¼-inch-deep notch in the top tenon of each middle slat, as shown in the *Middle Slat Tenon Notch Detail.*

6 Assemble the legs, stretchers, slats, dividers, and bottom cleats.
Finish sand the legs, stretchers, slats, dividers, and bottom cleats. Glue the slats and long stretchers together to make two ladderlike assemblies, and set them aside.

Then put together the legs, short stretchers, and middle slats to form the two sides of the table. Glue the long stretcher assemblies and dividers between the sides to make the table frame, square the frame, and clamp it together. Glue the bottom cleats to the inside surface of the bottom long stretchers, as shown in the *Bottom Cleat Detail.*

Quick FIXTURE: Tenoning Jig

A tenoning jig holds boards vertically as you cut their ends. It's especially useful for cutting boards that are too narrow to be supported safely and accurately by a fence or a tall fence extension.

When assembling the jig, don't attach the backstop permanently, just screw it in place. This lets you replace the backstop when it gets chewed up or when you need to hold the boards at a different angle. Assemble the remaining parts with glue and screws. Take special care that the face is square to the base, otherwise you won't be able to make square cuts.

To use the jig, rest the work against the backstop and clamp it in place — this will keep it from shifting. Guide the jig along a fence or straightedge as you cut.

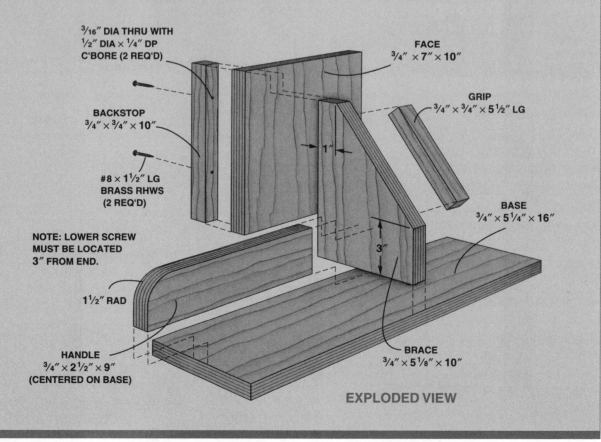

³/₁₆″ DIA THRU WITH ½″ DIA × ¼″ DP C'BORE (2 REQ'D)

BACKSTOP
¾″ × ¾″ × 10″

#8 × 1½″ LG BRASS RHWS (2 REQ'D)

NOTE: LOWER SCREW MUST BE LOCATED 3″ FROM END.

1½″ RAD

HANDLE
¾″ × 2½″ × 9″
(CENTERED ON BASE)

FACE
¾″ × 7″ × 10″

GRIP
¾″ × ¾″ × 5½″ LG

1″

BASE
¾″ × 5¼″ × 16″

3″

BRACE
¾″ × 5⅛″ × 10″

EXPLODED VIEW

Sunday Afternoon

7 **Cut and fit the bottom.**
Trim the bottom to the proper size, then cut ⅜-inch-square notches in the corners, as shown in the *Top View.* Place the bottom in the frame so it rests on the cleats.

8 **Attach the top.** Drill two sets of ³⁄₁₆-inch-diameter screw holes and countersinks in each of the top cleats. Each set should be perpendicular to the other, as shown in the *Front View.* Note that the holes are slightly larger than the shafts of the screws. This is to accommodate the expansion and contraction of the top.

Fasten the cleats to the inside surfaces of the side aprons with flathead wood screws, flush with the top edges. Trim the top to size, and secure it to the cleats.

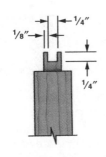

**MIDDLE SLAT TENON
NOTCH DETAIL**

At Your Leisure

9 **Finish the table.** Remove the top and bottom from the table. Do any necessary touch-up sanding, then apply a finish to the wooden surfaces. After the finish dries, replace the top and bottom.

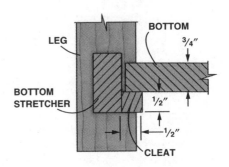

BOTTOM CLEAT DETAIL

Pro SKILL: Cutting Tenons

There are several techniques for cutting tenons. One of the most common methods is to cut the cheeks and shoulders in two steps on a table saw with a saw blade. Another is to cut each cheek and shoulder in one step with a dado cutter or a table-mounted router.

Which method you use depends on the results that you want and your own preferences. I use both. When I have just a few tenons to make, I'll use a dado cutter or a router. But the dado leaves a rougher surface than I'd like, and a router often requires multiple passes to remove all the stock. When I have a lot of tenons to make, I use my table saw and an ordinary combination blade. Even though this requires two setups to make the tenons, the cuts are clean, and you can remove a lot of stock with just two passes.

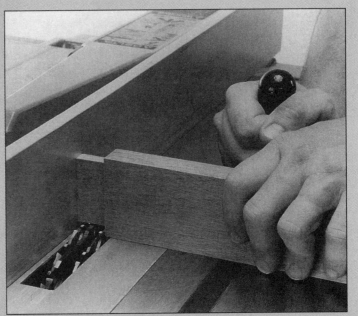

1 To cut a tenon with a dado cutter, guide the work with a miter gauge. Use a fence as a stop to set the length of the tenon. If the tenon is longer than the cutter is wide, make several passes, removing a little more stock with each pass. Cut a cheek and a shoulder in one face, then rotate the work 90 degrees and do the same in an edge. Continue cutting "around" the board until you have cut all the cheeks and shoulders.

(continued)

Pro SKILL: Cutting Tenons — CONTINUED

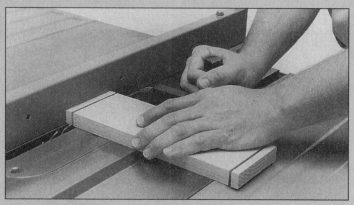

2 The procedure is almost exactly the same when cutting a tenon on a table-mounted router. Mount a wide straight bit in the router; use a miter gauge to guide the work and a fence as a stop. Feed the work so the rotation of the bit pulls the work toward the fence.

3 When cutting tenons on a table saw, first cut the shoulders. Guide the work over the blade with a miter gauge, using the fence as a stop. Cut around the boards, creating shoulders in both the faces and edges, as needed.

4 To cut the cheeks, use a tenoning jig to hold the work vertically. Guide the jig along the fence as you cut.

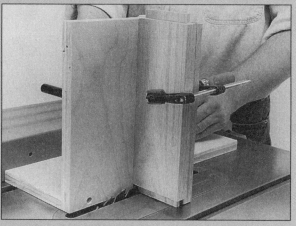

5 When cutting tenons in boards over 1½ inches wide (such as the aprons in the Side Table and Magazine Holder), attach a wide scrap to the back-stop of the tenoning jig. This provides additional support when cutting the cheeks in the edges of the work.

Expandable Shelves

■ **QUICK FIXTURE**
Drilling Guide

■ **PRO SKILL**
Spacing Holes Evenly

The adjustable shelves in this shelving system rest on pin-style supports. These support pins are inserted in stopped holes in the sides of each unit. To drill the many holes needed — and to space them all exactly the same — I made a drilling guide to position each row of holes.

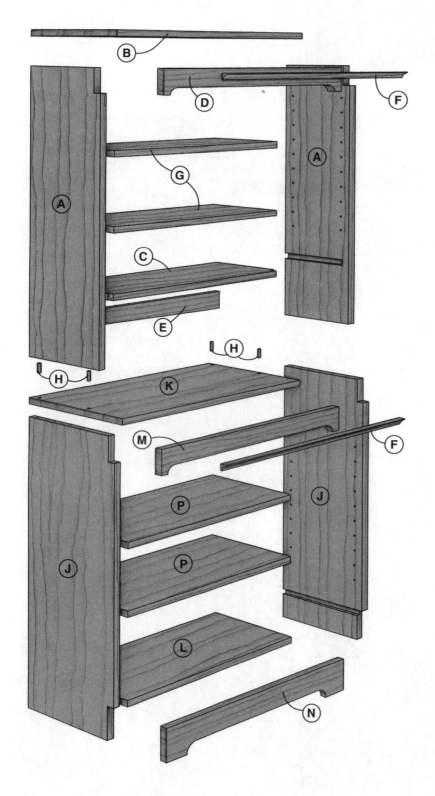

EXPLODED VIEW

MATERIALS LIST

Finished Dimensions in Inches

Top Unit Parts

A.	Top sides* (2)	¾″ × 9″ × 35¼″
B.	Top*	¾″ × 10″ × 24″
C.	Top fixed shelf*	¾″ × 9″ × 23¼″
D.	Valance	¾″ × 3″ × 24″
E.	Stretcher	¾″ × 2″ × 22½″
F.	Molding	¾″ × ¾″ × 24″
G.	Top adjustable shelves* (2)	¾″ × 9″ × 22⅜″
H.	Dowels (4)	¼″ dia. × 1¼″

Bottom Unit Parts

F.	Molding	¾″ × ¾″ × 24″
J.	Bottom sides* (2)	¾″ × 11″ × 35¼″
K.	Counter*	¾″ × 12″ × 24″
L.	Bottom fixed shelf*	¾″ × 11″ × 23¼″
M.	Waist	¾″ × 3″ × 24″
N.	Plinth	¾″ × 4″ × 24″
P.	Bottom adjustable shelves* (2)	¾″ × 11″ × 22⅜″

These parts can be made from solid wood or plywood. The remaining parts must be made from solid wood.

Top Unit Hardware

#8 × 1½″ Flathead wood screws (18–24)

¼″ Shelving support pins (8)

Bottom Unit Hardware

#8 × 1½″ Flathead wood screws (18–24)

¼″ Shelving support pins (8)

With this versatile design, you can make a handsome shelving system as tall or as long as you need. The top and bottom units fit together in many different configurations. Additionally, you can adjust the height and the width of the units to fit your space.

It's possible to make about four of these units in a weekend. Beyond that, it's best to spread the project over a longer period of time.

Friday Evening

1 Prepare the materials, and cut the parts to size.
To make each top unit, you need approximately 13 board feet of 4/4 (1-inch-thick) stock. Each bottom unit requires 17 board feet of 4/4 stock. Or, you can make the sides, shelves, top, and counter from ¾-inch plywood. If you do this, you can get one top and one bottom unit from 4 board feet of 4/4 stock and a 4 × 8-foot sheet of plywood. The shelving

units shown are made from hard maple and birch plywood.

If you make the shelves entirely from solid stock, plane the 4/4 stock to ¾ inch thick, and cut all the parts to size except for the moldings. For these slender parts, select a board at least 3 inches wide and 25 inches long, and set it aside. If you work with plywood, the procedure is similar — plane the solid stock, cut the valance, stretcher, waist, and

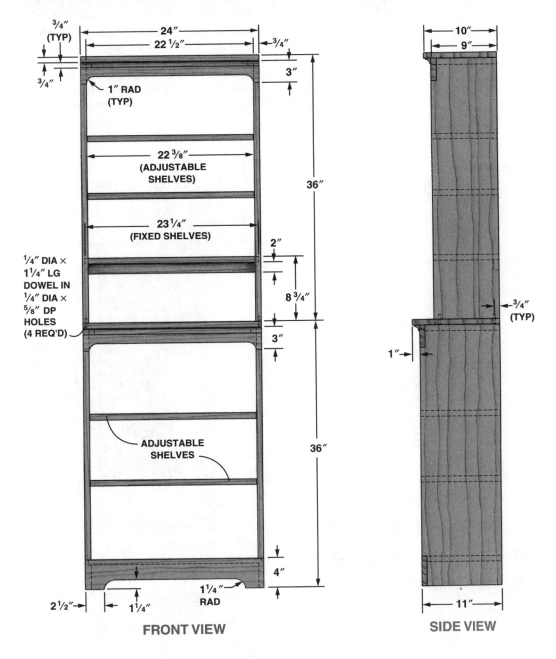

FRONT VIEW

SIDE VIEW

plinth to size, and set aside a board to make the moldings. Cut the plywood parts to size, but make the top and counter ¼ inch *shorter* than shown in the Materials List. From scraps of solid stock, rip ⅛-inch-thick, ¾-inch-wide strips. Glue these strips to the *outside* ends and edges of the plywood; that is, the surfaces that will show when the shelving units are assembled and the adjustable shelves are installed.

Note: If you want to wrap the molding around the sides of the top units, you'll have to make the tops longer than specified.

To hide the plies on the of the plywood parts, glue strips of solid wood to those edges that will be visible on the assembled units. You need only cover the front edges of the shelves and the sides, but you must cover the front edges and both ends of the tops and counters. Hold the strips in place with masking tape until the glue dries, then scrape the strips flush with the faces of the plywood parts. Be careful not to scrape through the veneer on the plywood.

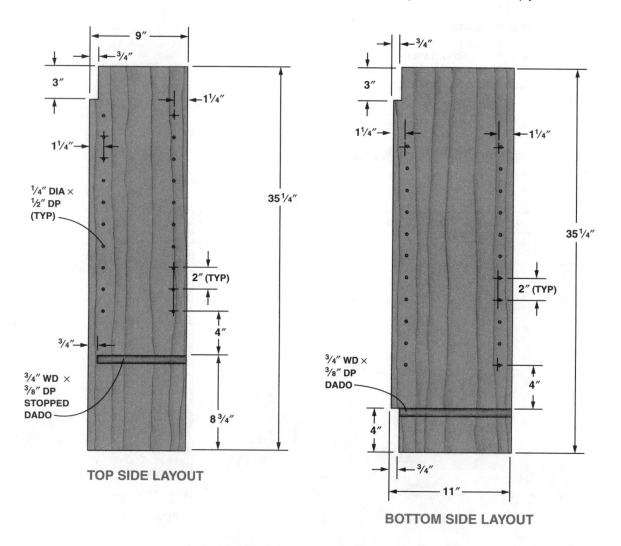

TOP SIDE LAYOUT

BOTTOM SIDE LAYOUT

Saturday Morning

2 Rip the plywood parts to the proper width.
When the solid-wood strips are attached to their edges, the plywood parts will be ⅛ inch wider than specified. Rip the parts to the correct width. (You could simply cut the plywood parts ⅛ inch narrower to begin with and not

See Also:
"Cutting Plywood" on page 204.

have to rip a second time. But it's more accurate to do it this way. By ripping the final width after the strips are attached, you compensate for any variations in the thickness of the strips.)

3 Cut the dadoes and notches in the sides and top fixed shelf. Lay out the dadoes and notches on the sides, as shown in the *Top Side*

Layout and *Bottom Side Layout.* If you've made the fixed shelves from plywood, you must adjust the width of the dadoes from what is shown in the drawings. Plywood is typically 1/32 inch smaller than its nominal dimension — ¾-inch plywood is usually 23/32 inch thick.

Also lay out notches on the front corners of the top fixed shelf to fit the stopped dadoes in

Quick FIXTURE: Drilling Guide

This jig positions shelving support holes and guides the drill bit as you bore them. It eliminates a lot of layout work and makes it easy to locate the holes accurately. The hole spacing on the jig is duplicated precisely every time you drill a set.

To make the jig, glue two long scraps of ¾-inch plywood together face to face. After the glue

dries, trim the assembly to size, mark the holes where you want them, and drill the holes. Then attach a lip to one edge. Note that the lip overhangs both the top and bottom faces of the guide. This lets you flip the jig over and align it with either the left or right edge of a board.

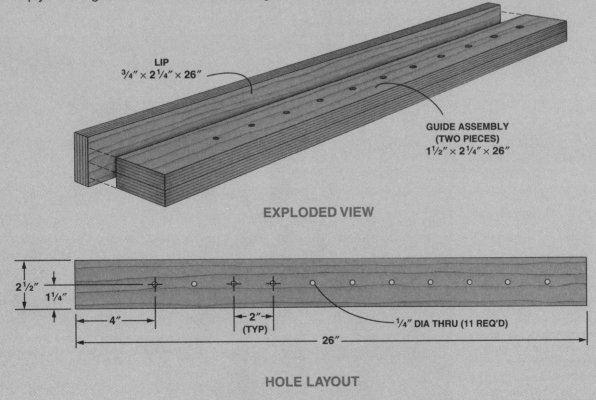

LIP
¾" × 2¼" × 26"

GUIDE ASSEMBLY
(TWO PIECES)
1½" × 2¼" × 26"

EXPLODED VIEW

2½"

1¼"

4"

2"
(TYP)

¼" DIA THRU (11 REQ'D)

26"

HOLE LAYOUT

the sides. These notches should be ³⁄₈ inch wide and ³⁄₄ inch long.

Rout the dadoes with a straight bit. Note the dadoes in top sides are *stopped* — they stop ³⁄₄ inch away from the front edges. After routing the dadoes, square the stopped ends with a chisel.

See Also:
"Routing Dadoes and Rabbets" on page 59.

Cut the notches with a band saw or a saber saw. You can save a little time by stacking the top sides face to face in one pile and the bottom sides in another. Tape the stacks together with the ends and edges flush, then cut the notches in each stack.

Saturday Afternoon

4 **Drill the holes in the sides.** Make a *Drilling Guide,* as shown on page 127, to help align and space the shelving support holes. Using a hand drill,

bore ¹⁄₄-inch-diameter, ¹⁄₂-inch deep holes in the sides. Take care to align each set of holes so they are exactly the same distance from the ends of the sides. Otherwise, the adjustable shelves will rock on their supports. The holes in the bottom sides must begin 8 inches from the bottom end, while those in the top sides begin 12³⁄₄ inches from the bottom ends.

5 **Drill dowel holes in the top sides.** If you plan to stack these units as shown in the photo, drill ¹⁄₄-inch-diameter, ⁵⁄₈-inch-deep holes in the bottom ends of the top sides, as shown in the *Front View.* Don't drill the matching holes in the counters just yet; wait until after you've assembled the units.

6 **Cut the profiles of the valances and plinth.** Lay out the profiles of the top valance, waist, and plinth, as shown in the *Front View.* Cut the profiles with a band saw or a

saber saw, then sand the sawed edges. Once again, you can save some time by stacking the valances with the ends and edges flush, then cut both parts at once.

Saturday Evening

7 **Assemble the shelving units.** Finish sand the sides, fixed shelves, top, counter, cleat, valances, and plinth. Assemble the parts with glue and screws. Counterbore and countersink each screw so the heads will rest about ¹⁄₈ inch below the wood surface, then cover the heads with wooden plugs. When the glue dries, sand the plugs flush with the surrounding surface.

Sunday Afternoon

8 **Drill the dowel holes in the counter.** Carefully measure the position of the

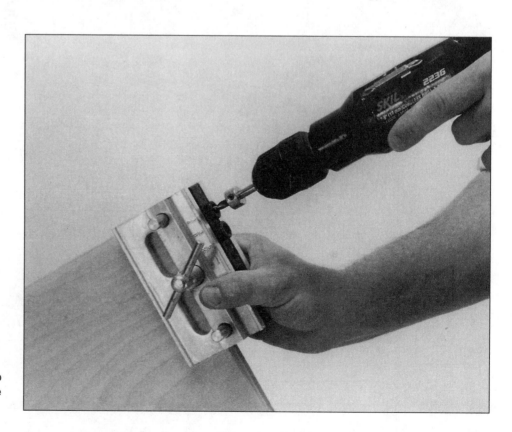

When boring the dowel holes in the bottom ends of the top sides, use a commercial *doweling jig* to locate the holes and guide the drill bit.

dowel holes in the top unit. Lay out and drill matching sets of holes in the counters. **Note:** Why should you wait until after you have assembled the top units to drill the holes in the counter? Because unless your construction methods are extremely precise, it's likely that the dowel holes on the assembled units will be off slightly from what is shown in the drawings. And even if the holes are displaced by as little as $1/32$ inch, it will be difficult to join the top and bottom units.

TRY THIS

USING DOWEL CENTERS

Use *dowel centers* to locate and mark the holes in the counters. Insert the centers in the holes in the top unit, position the top unit over the bottom unit it will be joined to, then press down firmly. The dowel centers will make small indentations in the counter, showing you where to drill the dowel holes.

EXTRA INFO

COVERING SCREW HEADS

1 To cover the heads of screws, cut plugs in a scrap of wood with a *plug cutter*. The scrap should be the same species and have the same grain pattern as the wood into which you have driven the screws. The plugs must be the same diameter as the screw counterbores.

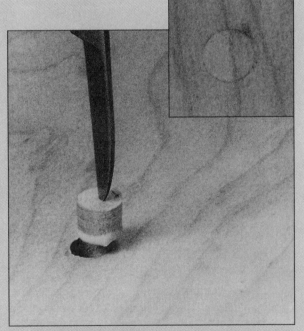

2 Dip the plugs in glue, align the grain direction with the wood, and press or tap them into the counterbores. Let the glue dry, then sand the plugs flush with the wood surface.

9 Make and install the moldings. Cut a ½-inch-radius cove in the edges of the molding stock you have set aside, then rip ¾-inch-wide strips from the shaped edges to make the moldings, as shown in the *Molding Detail.*

Finish sand the moldings. Cut them to length, and join them to the valances, top, and counter with glue.

Note: You may wish to wrap the molding around the right or left sides of the top end units, as shown in the *Optional Side Molding Detail.* If this is the case, you must cut the top 1 inch longer than specified.

Pro SKILL: Spacing Holes Evenly

When drilling holes for shelving support pins and similar hardware, you must space the holes evenly (usually every 1 to 2 inches, on center). You could do this by measuring and marking each hole, but this would be extremely time-consuming and prone to errors. There are better ways.

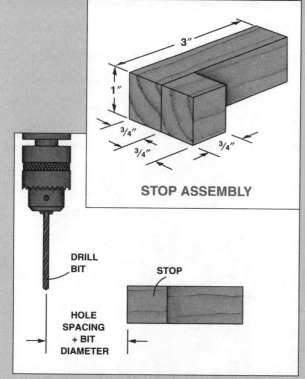

STOP ASSEMBLY

DRILL BIT

STOP

HOLE SPACING + BIT DIAMETER

1 When drilling a single row of holes, use a stop and a pin to position the work before drilling each hole. Clamp the stop to the drill press fence about ¹⁄₁₆ inch above the work. Adjust its horizontal position so the distance from the stop to the bit equals the desired spacing. (It's easier to measure the distance from the edge of the stop to the *far* edge of the bit. This should be the desired spacing *plus* the diameter of the bit.)

2 Drill a hole in the stock and insert a pin in it. Slide the work under the stop until the pin butts against it. Drill a second hole, move the pin to the new hole, and repeat.

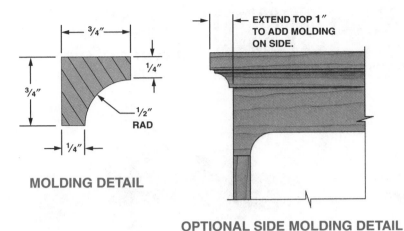

MOLDING DETAIL

EXTEND TOP 1″
TO ADD MOLDING
ON SIDE.

OPTIONAL SIDE MOLDING DETAIL

At Your Leisure

10 Finish the shelving units. Do any necessary touch-up sanding, then apply a finish to the wooden surfaces of the shelving units and adjustable shelves. When the finish dries, rub it out to the desired gloss. Insert shelving support pins in the holes where you want to hang the shelves, then rest the adjustable shelves on the pins.

3 When you must make several rows of *matching* holes, it's best to make a template or *drilling guide.* This is a thick board with a row of evenly spaced holes to position and guide the drill bit. If you wish, add a cleat or a lip to help position the guide. When using the guide, always align the bottom (or the top) with the same point on each board so the rows of holes all line up at the same height. For example, when making the Expandable Shelves, you should align the bottom end of the drilling guide with the dadoes for the fixed shelves.

4 If the drilling guide will be used over and over again, install steel drill guides in the template. These metal bushings line the holes, preventing the drill bit from reaming out the wooden template and enlarging the holes.

Calendar Frame

When assembling this frame, you want to be certain that the members are square to one another. Otherwise, the calendar won't fit properly. A set of corner squares will hold the frame members in position while the glue dries.

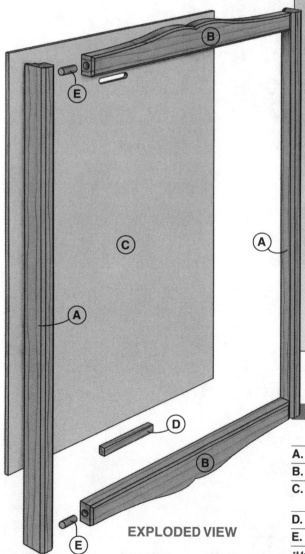

EXPLODED VIEW

MATERIALS LIST
Finished Dimensions in Inches

Parts

A.	Stiles (2)	¾″ × 1⅛″ × (Calendar length + 1½″)
B.	Rails (2)	¾″ × 2¼″ × (Calendar width - ½″)
C.	Back*	⅛″ × (Calendar width + ¾″) × (Calendar length + 1″)
D.	Stop	⅜″ × ½″ × 6″
E.	Dowels (4)	⅜″ dia. × 1″

*Make this part from hardboard.

This clever frame lets you quickly remove the calendar, turn it to the next month, and replace it in the frame in just a few seconds. Paul Rising, the craftsman who designed it, says he has a hard time keeping up with the demand. "People often buy the same type of calendar from year to year because they enjoy the artwork," says Paul. "This gives them a nice frame to protect and display it."

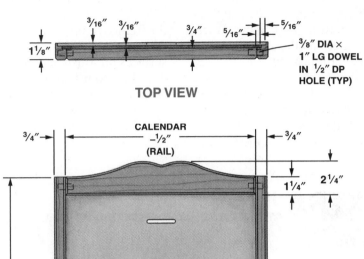

TOP VIEW

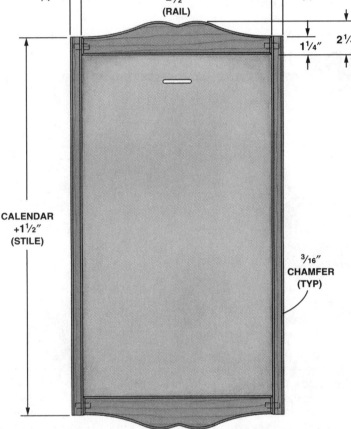

FRONT VIEW

Saturday Morning

1 Prepare the materials, and cut the parts to size.
To make a single frame, you need approximately 2 board feet of 4/4 (1-inch-thick) lumber and a small piece of ⅛-inch hardboard. You can use any cabinet-grade wood you'd like. The frame shown is made from poplar.

Measure your calendar "open," as it would normally hang on a wall. Use these dimensions to figure the sizes of the parts, as shown in the Materials List. Plane the 4/4 stock to ¾ inch thick, and cut the rails, stiles, stop, and back to size.

2 Cut the rabbets in the stiles. The back surfaces of the stiles are cut with "double rabbets," as shown in the *Top View.* One rabbet holds the back, while the other creates an opening that lets you slip the calendar in and out of the frame. Cut the rabbets with a dado cutter or a table-mounted router and a straight bit.

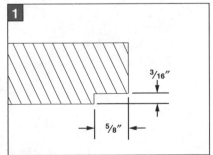

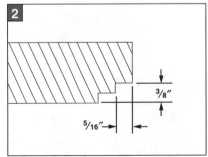

To create the double rabbets in the stiles, first cut a rabbet ⅝ inch wide and ³⁄₁₆ inch deep in the back surface. Cut the second rabbet in the bottom of the first, ⁵⁄₁₆ inch wide and ³⁄₁₆ inch deep (⅜ inch deep from the surface of the stock.)

3 **Trace the patterns on the rails.** Enlarge the *Rail Pattern,* and adjust the length to fit the rails in your frame. Trace the pattern on the stock, but don't cut it just yet.

4 **Drill the dowel holes in the rails and stiles.** The rails and stiles are joined by dowels, as shown in the *Front View.* To position these holes accurately, arrange the rails and stiles front faces down to form the frame. Temporarily, clamp the parts together so the front surfaces are flush, and mark the dowel locations across the seams between the rails and stiles. Drill ⅜-inch-diameter, 9/16-inch-deep dowel holes at your marks.

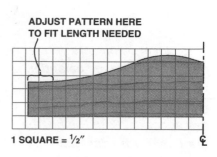

ADJUST PATTERN HERE
TO FIT LENGTH NEEDED

1 SQUARE = ½"

RAIL PATTERN

EXTRA INFO

DRILLING MATCHING DOWEL HOLES

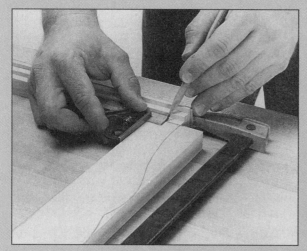

1 To assemble the frame, you must drill matching dowel holes in the adjoining rails and stiles. To do this, clamp the parts together temporarily and mark the locations of the dowels, drawing lines across the seams where the rails butt against the stiles.

2 Use a small square to transfer the marks to the edges of the stiles and the ends of the rails. Mark the locations of the dowel holes ⅜ inch from the front face of each part.

3 Drill the holes in the ends of the rails with a portable drill. Cut the hole parallel to the edge of the part, aligning the bit with your eye. It won't matter if you're off a degree or two. Drill the holes in the edges of the stiles on the drill press.

5 Cut the profiles of the rails. Cut the rail profiles with a band saw or saber saw. Since both parts are exactly the same, you can save some time by stacking the parts face to face, taping them together, and cutting both at once. After cutting the profiles, sand the sawed edges.

6 Chamfer the edges of the rails and stiles. Using a table-mounted router and a chamfering bit, cut $^3/_{16}$-inch chamfers in the edges of the stiles and the ends *and* edges of the rails, as shown in the *Front View.*

7 Assemble the frame. Finish sand the rails and stiles. Then assemble the frame with dowels and glue. To make sure the parts of the frame are 90

Quick FIXTURE: Corner Squares

This triangular jig has one perfectly square corner. Cleats on the sides allow you to clamp the jig to two boards that are joined at right angles. This, in turn, holds them square to one another. You'll need two jigs to clamp a square frame.

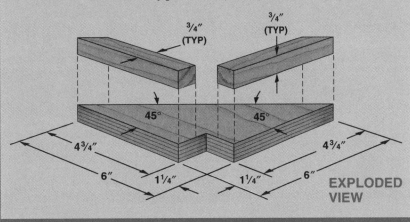

EXPLODED VIEW

degrees to one another, make a set of *Corner Squares.* Use these jigs to hold the parts in alignment until the glue dries.

Saturday Evening

8 Cut the slot in the back. The back is slotted, as shown in the *Back View,* so you can hang the frame on a nail, screw, or small peg. Cut the $^1/_4$-inch-wide, 2-inch-long slot with a router and a straight bit.

9 Attach the back to the frame. Remove the clamps and corner squares from the frame assembly. Glue the back to the stiles in the *rearmost* rabbets, flush with the back edge. Also glue the stop to the back face of the bottom rail, just below the back.

At Your Leisure

10 Finish the frame. Do any necessary touch-up sanding, then apply paint or a finish to the wooden surfaces that will show when the frame is hanging on a wall.

CALENDAR
+$^3/_4$"
(BACK)

$^1/_4$" 2"

2"
O.C.

CALENDAR
+1"
(BACK)

$^3/_4$"

$^1/_2$"

6"

BACK VIEW

Pro SKILL: Gluing Up Flat and True

When assembling frames, boxes, drawers, cases, and similar constructions, the corners must be square and the assembly must rest flat on the floor or against a wall. To achieve this, you must take some extra care when gluing up. After clamping the parts together, check the individual corners and the overall assembly.

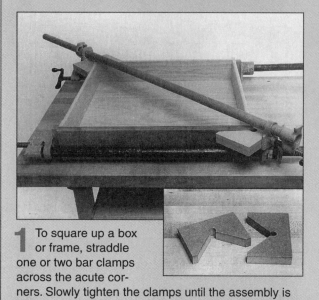

1 To square up a box or frame, straddle one or two bar clamps across the acute corners. Slowly tighten the clamps until the assembly is square. As you do so, protect the corners with corner cauls — small blocks of wood with a V-shaped notch in one side.

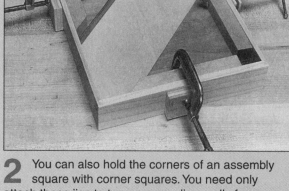
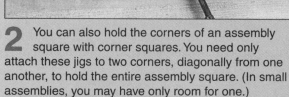

2 You can also hold the corners of an assembly square with corner squares. You need only attach these jigs to two corners, diagonally from one another, to hold the entire assembly square. (In small assemblies, you may have only room for one.)

3 Use two lengths of string to tell if an assembly has a twist or "wind" in it. Stretch the strings diagonally from corner to corner so they cross one another, and tape them in place to keep them taut. If the assembly is flat, both strings wil be straight and they will barely touch one another. If there's a gap between the strings or one string seems to lift another, the assembly is twisted.

4 To help keep an assembly flat while the glue dries, clamp it or weigh it down to a flat surface such as the top of your workbench. If your workbench is not especially flat, use the table of your table saw. Lower the blade below the surface, and spread a sheet of plastic over the tool to protect it from glue.

PART FIVE

For Sitting and Passing Time

Mantle Clock

■ *QUICK FIXTURE*
Tapering Jig

■ *PRO SKILL*
Cutting Tapers

The sides of this clock are slightly angled, and the face frame members are tapered to match. To cut these tapers, I mounted the frame members in a tapering jig. This jig is a carriage that holds the stock at an angle to the saw blade as you rip it.

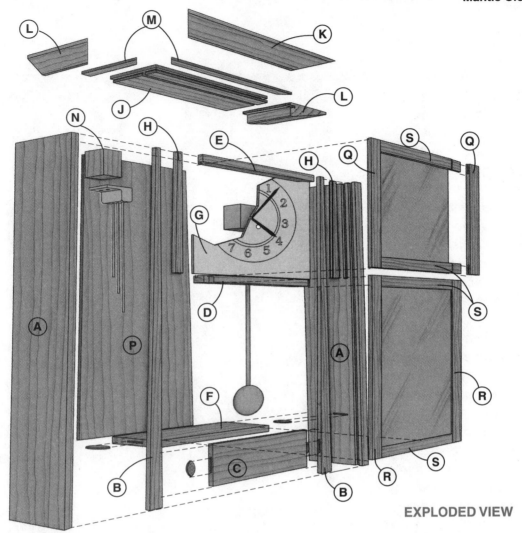

EXPLODED VIEW

MATERIALS LIST

Finished Dimensions in Inches		

Parts

A.	Sides (2)	¾″ × 6½″ × 39¼″
B.	Stiles (2)	½″ × 1½″ × 39¼″
C.	Bottom rail	½″ × 4¾″ × 12½″
D.	Middle rail	¾″ × 1½″ × 13⅝″
E.	Top rail	¾″ × 1″ × 13″
F.	Shelf	¾″ × 5¼″ × 14²³⁄₃₂″
G.	Clock board*	¼″ × 13″ × 13¾″
H.	Clock board holders (2)	½″ × ⅞″ × 13¼″
J.	Top*	¾″ × 6½″ × 14½″
K.	Top front molding	1½″ × 2″ × 18½″
L.	Top side moldings (2)	1½″ × 2″ × 8½″
M.	Spline* (total)	¼″ × 1″ × 30″
N.	Chime mount	2″ × 2″ × 2¾″
P.	Back*	¼″ × 15½″ × 34⅛″
Q.	Top door stiles (2)	½″ × 1½″ × 12½″
R.	Bottom door stiles (2)	½″ × 1½″ × 19″
S.	Door rails (4)	½″ × 1½″ × 12½″

Make these parts from plywood.

Hardware

#8 × 1¼″ Flathead wood screws (2)
#4 × ¾″ Flathead wood screws (6)
#2 × 1¼″ Roundhead wood screws (4)
1″ × 1½″ Butt hinges and mounting screws
#20 Biscuits (4)
½″ Door pulls (2)
Magnetic catches (2)
Clock movement (with chimes and 22½″ pendulum)
Shaker clock dial
Clock hands

Resources Order the movement (#3301x), dial (#7416S), and hands (#4970X) from:

Woodcraft Supply Corporation
210 Wood County Industrial Park
P.O. Box 1686
Parkersburg, WV 26102-1686

Be sure to ask to have the winding-key holes punched in the dial.

The clock shown is based on an Arts and Crafts (or Mission) design, built by Gustav Stickley in 1909. If you're not fond of the Arts and Crafts style, you can easily adapt this project by making straight sides. This will give you a more contemporary look. Or, get rid of the beveled top moldings and substitute a simple rectangular top to produce a Shaker-style clock.

All three styles are related. Many contemporary designers are influenced by the Arts and Crafts movement, while the Arts and Crafts style incorporates elements of Shaker design. Stickley, the patron saint of American Arts and Crafts furniture, learned his trade in a Shaker furniture factory.

CONTEMPORARY STYLE

SHAKER STYLE

WEEK 1

Friday Evening

1 Prepare the materials, and cut the parts to size. To make the mantle clock as designed, you need approximately 10 board feet of 4/4 (1-inch-thick) stock, 2 board feet of 8/4 (2-inch-thick) stock, a quarter sheet (2 × 4 feet) of ¼-inch plywood, and a scrap of ¾-inch plywood. On the clock shown, the sides are made from curly white oak and the back has been covered with curly white oak veneer to match. The face frame, top moldings, and door frames are made from quarter-sawn white oak. Oak was the favorite wood of Arts and Crafts furnituremakers, but they also worked in mahogany, walnut, and cherry.

Plane the 8/4 stock to 1½ inches thick, and rip it to 2 inches wide for the moldings, but don't cut them to size yet.

Plane the 4/4 stock to ¾ inch thick, and cut the sides to length, beveling the ends at 1¼ degrees. Cut the top rail, middle rail, and shelf about 1 inch longer than specified — you'll trim them to length later on. Plane the remaining stock to ½ inch thick and cut the bottom rail, stiles, and clock board holders. Rip 1½-inch-wide stock for the door frame members, but don't cut them to length just yet. Cut the top from ¾-inch plywood, making it about ½ inch longer than specified.

Saturday Morning

2 Cut the grooves and rabbets in the sides, top, middle rail, and clock board holders. The parts of the clock case are joined with grooves and rabbets. Cut these with a dado cutter or a table mounted router:

■ ½-inch-wide, ¼-inch deep grooves in the sides to hold the face frame and the clock board holders, as shown in the *Side Layout*

■ ¼-inch-wide, ⅜-inch deep rabbets in the sides and top to hold the back, as shown in *Section A*

■ ¼-inch-wide, ¼-inch deep grooves in the top, middle rail, and clock board holders to hold the clock board, as shown in *Section A,* the *Middle Rail Layout,* and *Section B.*

Note that the ½-inch-wide grooves in the sides that hold the clock board holders are stopped on one end.

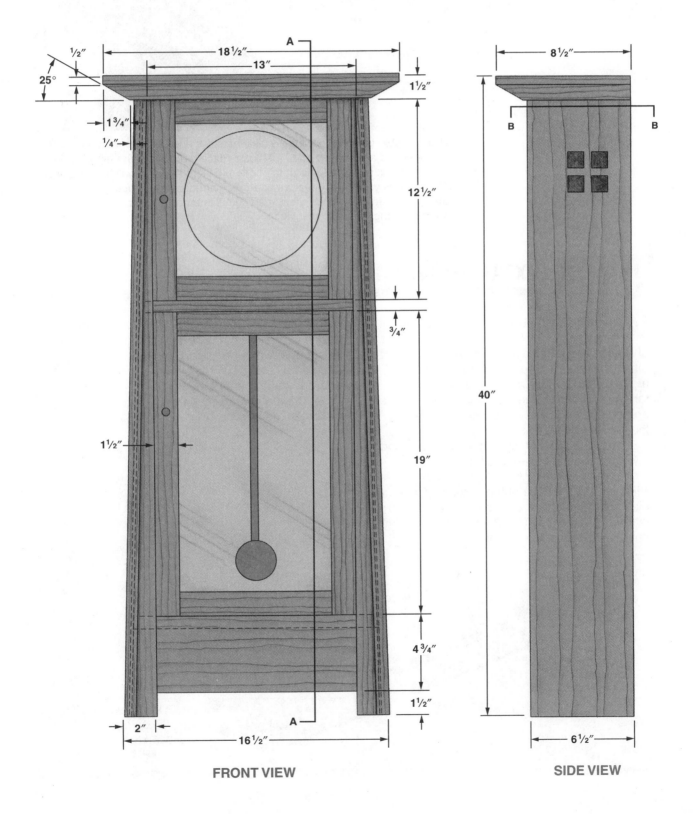

FRONT VIEW   **SIDE VIEW**

3 Taper the stiles and the clock board holders.

Make a tapering jig to cut 1¼ degree tapers in the stiles and clock board holders. To save time and ensure that the tapers are precisely the same, stack the parts in the jig and cut all four at once.

Using double-faced carpet tape, stack the stiles and clock board holder stock so the edges and the top ends are flush. Place the stack in the tapering jig with the clock board holders at the bottom (where the taper will be narrowest). The grooves you cut in the clock board holder edges must face in, toward the jig. Tighten the clamp screw, then cut all four parts at once, guiding the taper jig along the table saw fence.

Quick FIXTURE: Tapering Jig

When cutting the tapers in the face frame stiles and clock board holders, you must rip one edge at a slight angle (1¼ degrees) to the other, making the stile wider at the bottom than at the top. To do this, mount the boards in a tapering jig, a carriage that holds the boards at an angle to the blade as you guide the jig along the table saw fence.

To make a tapering jig, cut a piece of ¼-inch plywood about 6 inches wide and 3 inches longer than the piece you want to taper — this will serve as the base of the carriage. Cut a piece of ¾-inch plywood the same width and length. On the face of the ¾-inch plywood, lay out the tapered shape you want to cut. The tapered surface must be flush with and parallel to one long edge of the board, as shown. Cut out this shape with a band saw or hand saw, creating a long, angled notch. Fasten the notched board to the base so the ends and edges are flush. Drive a wood screw through the top end of the notch, as shown.

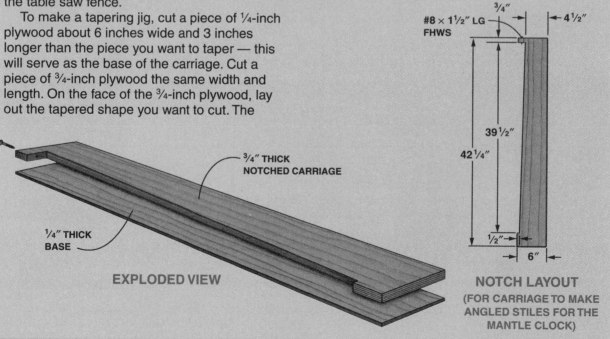

¾″ THICK NOTCHED CARRIAGE

¼″ THICK BASE

EXPLODED VIEW

#8 × 1½″ LG FHWS

¾″

4½″

39½″

42¼″

½″

6″

NOTCH LAYOUT
(FOR CARRIAGE TO MAKE ANGLED STILES FOR THE MANTLE CLOCK)

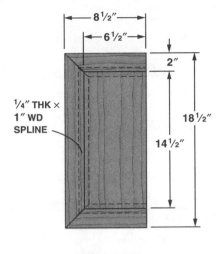

8¹⁄₂″

6¹⁄₂″

2″

¹⁄₄″ THK ×
1″ WD
SPLINE

18¹⁄₂″

14¹⁄₂″

TOP VIEW

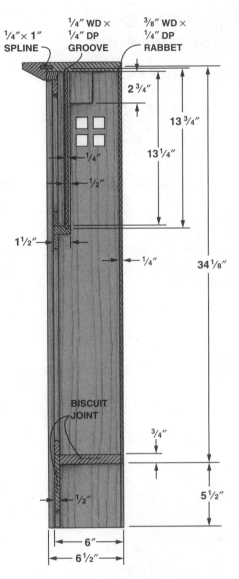

¹⁄₄″× 1″
SPLINE

¹⁄₄″ WD ×
¹⁄₄″ DP
GROOVE

³⁄₈″ WD ×
¹⁄₄″ DP
RABBET

2³⁄₄″

13³⁄₄″

13¹⁄₄″

¹⁄₄″

¹⁄₂″

1¹⁄₂″

¹⁄₄″

34¹⁄₈″

BISCUIT
JOINT

³⁄₄″

¹⁄₂″

5¹⁄₂″

6″

6¹⁄₂″

SECTION A

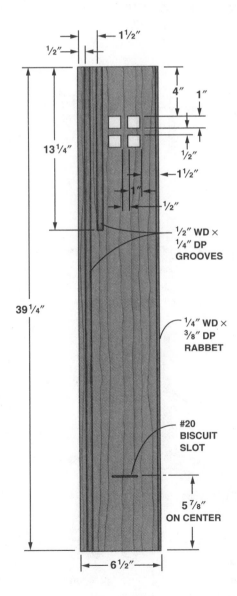

1¹⁄₂″

¹⁄₂″

4″   1″

13¹⁄₄″

¹⁄₂″

1¹⁄₂″

1″

¹⁄₂″

¹⁄₂″ WD ×
¹⁄₄″ DP
GROOVES

39¹⁄₄″

¹⁄₄″ WD ×
³⁄₈″ DP
RABBET

#20
BISCUIT
SLOT

5⁷⁄₈″
ON CENTER

6¹⁄₂″

SIDE LAYOUT

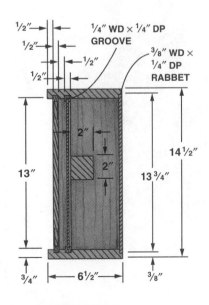

¹⁄₂″

¹⁄₂″

¹⁄₂″

¹⁄₄″ WD × ¹⁄₄″ DP
GROOVE

³⁄₈″ WD ×
¹⁄₄″ DP
RABBET

2″

2″

13″

14¹⁄₂″

13³⁄₄″

³⁄₄″

6¹⁄₂″

³⁄₈″

SECTION B

Saturday Afternoon

4 **Cut the top rail and middle rail.** Lay out the notches in the ends of the middle rail and the top rail, as shown in the *Middle Rail Layout* and *Top Rail Layout*. Cut the notches, then temporarily clamp the parts of the face frame together, carefully positioning the middle rail and top rail on the stiles. Mark the ends of the rails, and remove the clamps. Cut the middle and top rails to length, beveling the ends at 1¼ degrees.

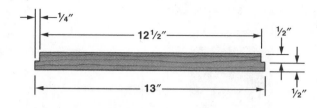

TOP RAIL LAYOUT

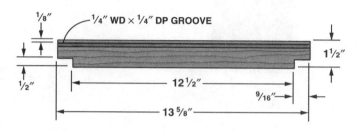

MIDDLE RAIL LAYOUT

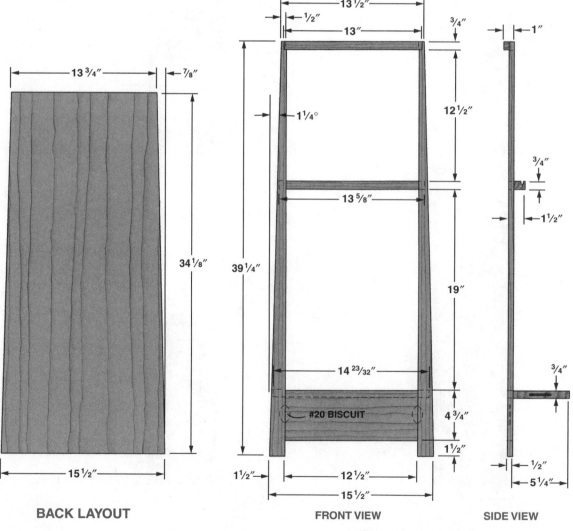

BACK LAYOUT

FRONT VIEW **SIDE VIEW**

FACE FRAME LAYOUT

5 Assemble the face frame. Cut biscuit joints to secure the bottom rail to the stiles. Finish sand the face frame parts, then assemble them with glue. Note that the top rail protrudes from the front surface of the face frame, while the middle rail protrudes toward the back, as shown in the *Face Frame Layout/Side View.* After the glue dries, sand the joints clean and true up any adjoining surfaces that should be flush but aren't.

Saturday Evening

6 Cut the soundholes. The sides have decorative soundholes to help you hear the chimes. Lay out these square soundholes, as shown in the *Side Layout.* Drill a 1-inch-diameter hole through each square to remove most of the waste. Then square the corners of the soundholes with a coping saw or scroll saw. Smooth the cut surfaces with a file.

7 Assemble the clock case. Temporarily clamp the face frame and the sides together. Make sure the sides are square to the face frame, then carefully measure the distance between the sides at the top edge of the bottom rail — this is the shelf length. Cut the shelf to size, beveling the ends at 1¼ degrees. Cut slots for biscuit joints in the shelf and sides, as shown in *Section A.* Finish sand the sides, shelf, face frame, and clock board holders, then glue these parts together.

Sunday Afternoon

8 Cut and attach the back. Place the assembled clock case on the ¼-inch ply-

TRY THIS

PREVENTING TEAR-OUT

When filing across the grain, the file may tear or chip the wood where the teeth "exit" the stock. To prevent this, clamp a scrap board to the exit side of the stock. The top edge of this board should be even with the layout line that you're following as you file. This board backs up the wood, preventing it from tearing. It also helps mark the line and guide the file.

wood, and trace the shape for the back. The shape should match the *Back Layout* fairly closely, but don't panic if the dimensions are slightly different. Cut the back with a band saw or hand saw, then attach it to the clock case with #4 screws.

9 Assemble the top. Measure the top of the clock case, and trim the top so it's about ¹⁄₃₂ inch longer than the case is wide. Bevel the top molding stock at 25 degrees, as shown in the *Front View.* Then cut matching spline grooves in the molding and the top.

Cut the top molding to length, mitering the adjoining ends at 45 degrees. Also make splines from scraps of ¼-inch plywood. Glue the top molding to the top, inserting the splines in the grooves.

Note: The assembled top should fit the clock case snugly, but don't attach it permanently. You want to be able to remove the top easily and slide the clock board out of the case. This will make it a simple matter to install, maintain, and repair the clock movement.

WEEK 2

Friday Evening

10 Make the door frames. Measure the opening for the upper and lower doors, then cut the door rails and stiles to length. Make the doors exactly the same size as the openings — you can shave them down so they fit the opening with a little clearance after you assemble the doors.

Join the door frame members with bridle joints, cutting slots in the ends of the stiles and matching tenons in the rails. Use the *Tenoning Jig* shown on page 120 to hold the parts vertically while you cut the slots and tenons. After cutting the joints, finish sand the rails and stiles, then assemble them with glue.

TRY THIS

KEEPING ASSEMBLIES FLAT

To make sure that the door frames are perfectly flat, clamp the assemblies to a flat surface (such as the table saw) as you glue them up. Protect the surfaces with a sheet of plastic.

Saturday Morning

11 **Cut the rabbets in the doors.** The glass panes rest in ¼-inch-wide, ¼-inch-deep rabbets in the inside edges of the door frames, as shown in the *Top Door Layout* and *Bottom Door Layout*. Cut these rabbets with a router and a rabbeting bit, then square the corners with a chisel.

12 **Hang the doors in the clock case.** Fit the assembled doors to the openings. Lay out the hinge mortises on the face frame and door frames. Cut the mortises and install the butt hinges. **Note:** Use the *Router Plane* shown on page 84 to help cut the hinge mortises to a uniform depth.

Once the doors are hung, install door pulls and magnetic catches.

EXTRA INFO

MAKING BRIDLE JOINTS

1 Cut the bridle joints with a rip blade or combination blade. First, create the ¼-inch-wide slots in the ends of the stiles. Secure each stile in the tenoning jig. Make a single pass, then turn the stile face for face, and make another.

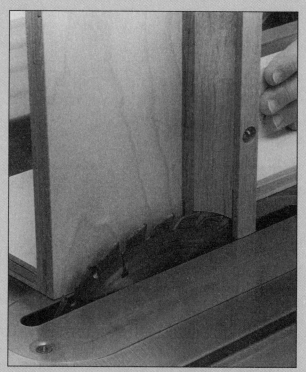

2 The procedure for making the tenons in the ends of the rails is similar. Secure the rails in the tenoning jig, and make a single pass over the saw blade, cutting one cheek. Then turn the rail face for face, and cut the other.

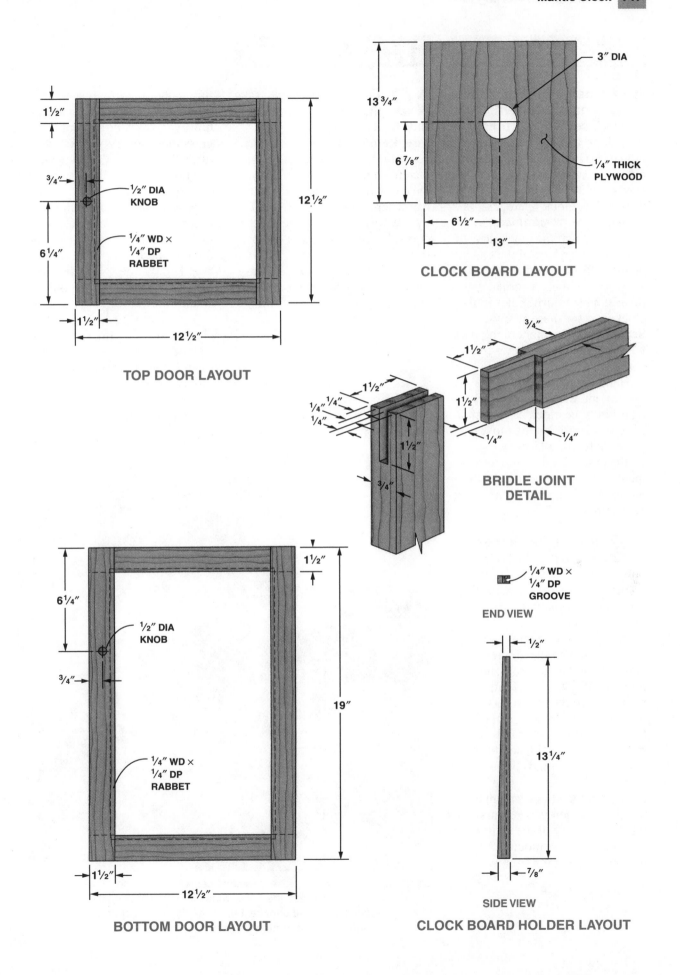

1½"

¾"
½" DIA
KNOB

¼" WD ×
¼" DP
RABBET

6¼"

1½"

12½"

12½"

TOP DOOR LAYOUT

13¾"

3" DIA

¼" THICK
PLYWOOD

6⅞"

6½"

13"

CLOCK BOARD LAYOUT

¾"

1½"

1½"

1½"

¼" ¼"
¼"

1½"

¾"

¼"

¼"

**BRIDLE JOINT
DETAIL**

¼" WD ×
¼" DP
GROOVE

END VIEW

½"

1½"

6¼"

½" DIA
KNOB

¾"

19"

¼" WD ×
¼" DP
RABBET

1½"

12½"

BOTTOM DOOR LAYOUT

13¼"

⅞"

SIDE VIEW

CLOCK BOARD HOLDER LAYOUT

Saturday Afternoon

At Your Leisure

13 Install the clock face and movement. Cut the clock board to size from ¼-inch plywood. Fit it to the holders so it slides easily in and out of the case. Using a hole saw, cut a 3-inch-diameter hole through the clock board, as shown in the *Clock Board Layout.* Attach the clock face to the front surface of the clock board with #2 roundhead wood screws, one in each corner. (You'll have to drill holes in the clock face for these screws.) Secure the movement to the back with the mounting screws that come with it.

Hang the pendulum on the movement, then slide the clock board into the clock case. Install the clock hands on the movement shaft, and place the top on the case. Wind up the movement, and set the pendulum in motion to see how well the clock keeps time.

14 Install the chimes. While the clock is running, secure the chimes to the chime mount with the mounting screws that come with the movement. Remove the back from the clock case, and position the chime mount so the chimes are about ½ inch away from the movement's strikers. Temporarily secure the mount to the top with double-faced carpet tape. Turn the clock hands to rip the chimes and listen to the quality of the sound. If the chimes sound dead or tinny, reposition the chime mount and try again. When you're satisfied with the quality of the sound, secure the chime mount to the top with glue and #8 screws.

15 Finish the clock. Take the top off the clock and slide the clock board out of the case. Remove the clock hands, pendulum, movement, and clock face from the clock board. Store the clock movement in a plastic bag where it won't be affected by sawdust. Also remove the doors, hinges, pulls, and catches from the clock case.

Finish sand any wooden surfaces that may still need it, then apply a finish. After the finish has dried, rub it to the desired luster.

16 Install the glass. Install the glass in the door frames with silicone caulk. Traditionally, glass is held in a glazed door with glass beading, tiny wood molding that's nailed to the door frame. Silicone caulk, however, is faster and holds the glass more securely. The trade-off is that it doesn't look as nice as glass beading when the doors are open.

Replace the back, doors, hinges, pulls, and catches. Attach the clock face, movement, pendulum, and hands to the clock board, and slide it into the case. Finally, place the top on the clock.

Set the clock running and check it daily against a watch or a clock you know keeps good time. If the clock gains or loses time, adjust the position of the bob on the pendulum according to the instructions that come with the movement.

Squeeze out a tiny bead of clear silicone caulk all along the rabbets in the finished door frames. Press the glass panes into the caulk until the glass rests flat against the wood surface. Let the caulk harden, then trim away the excess that squeezes out around the glass.

Pro SKILL: Cutting Tapers

Furniture designers often use tapers as a decorative element. Tapered legs on tables and chairs make these vertical parts seem less heavy without reducing their strength. In the mantle clock, the tapered face frame grows wider toward the bottom. This, in turn, makes the case seem less top-heavy and more stable. In both cases, the taper adds grace and visual interest to the overall design.

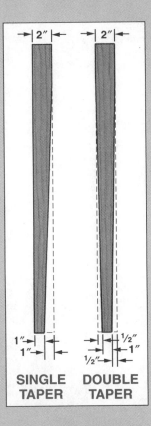

1 To make a taper cut, you must first know the measurements of the tapered part. You should also know whether you will be cutting a *single taper* (on a single side or two adjacent sides) or a *double taper* (with tapers on two or more opposing sides). When making the tapering jig to hold the part as you cut it, always lay out the angled notch as if you were only making a single taper on one side, even though you may cut additional tapers later on.

SINGLE TAPER **DOUBLE TAPER**

2 To cut a taper, lay it out on the stock. This will help you check your setup and monitor the cut. Adjust the fence position so the distance between the fence and the blade is equal to the width of the tapering jig. Place the stock in the notched carriage, and feed it past the saw blade, guiding the jig along the fence.

3 To make a second single taper in an adjacent side, rotate the stock 90 degrees so a straight, *untapered* edge rests against the side of the notch. Repeat the cut, feeding the stock and jig past the blade.

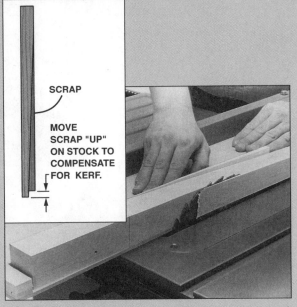

SCRAP

MOVE SCRAP "UP" ON STOCK TO COMPENSATE FOR KERF.

4 To make a double taper, save the wedge-shaped scrap from the first cut. Using double-faced carpet tape, temporarily stick it back on the cut surface to make the stock rectangular again. Rotate the stock 180 degrees so the scrap rests against the side of the notch, and make a second taper cut.

Rocking Footstool

The side frames on this unique footstool have many complex curves. To sand the curved profiles quickly and keep the edges square to the faces, use a drum sander and sanding table.

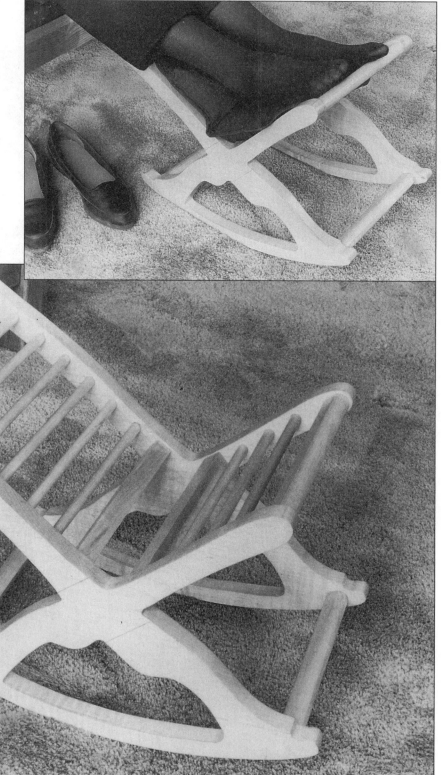

150

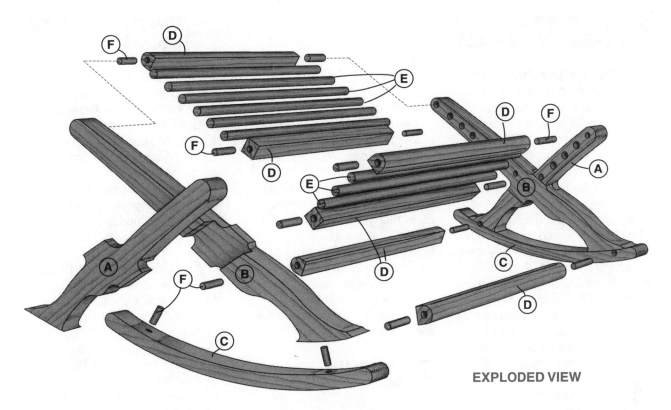

EXPLODED VIEW

MATERIALS LIST

Finished Dimensions in Inches		
Parts		
A. Short leg (2)	$\frac{7}{8}'' \times 3'' \times 20\frac{7}{8}''$	
B. Long leg (2)	$\frac{7}{8}'' \times 3'' \times 26''$	
C. Runners (2)	$\frac{7}{8}'' \times 3'' \times 19''$	
D. Stretchers (6)	$\frac{7}{8}'' \times \frac{7}{8}'' \times 10\frac{1}{4}''$	
E. Rungs (9)	$\frac{1}{2}''$ dia. $\times 11\frac{1}{4}''$	
F. Dowels (16)	$\frac{3}{8}''$ dia. $\times 1''$	

Although he refers to it as a "rocking footstool," craftsman Dr. Gopala Murthy's ingenious stool doesn't really rock like a rocking chair. When you place your feet in the L-shaped cradle, the stool tilts on its curved runners, automatically finding just the right angle to support your feet and lower calves. There's almost no pressure on your ankles; consequently his rocking stool is a good deal more comfortable than the ordinary variety.

Friday Evening

1 Prepare the materials, and cut the parts to size. To make this footstool, you need approximately 4 board feet of 4/4 (1-inch-thick) stock and three 36-inch lengths of ½-inch-diameter dowel rod. The stool shown is made from maple stock and birch dowels, but you can use any cabinet-grade wood. Several mail-order woodworking supply companies sell hardwood dowel stock made from different woods.

Plane the 4/4 stock to ⅞ inch thick, and cut the legs and run-
ners. Cut one or two wide boards 10¼ inches long, and set them aside. Later, you'll use them to make the stretchers.

See Also:
"Cutting Round Stock" on page 240.

2 Cut the lap joints that join the legs. Arrange the short legs and long legs to form an X-shaped frame, as shown in the *Leg-and-Runner Layout.* Make sure they are properly positioned with an angle of 71 degrees between them, then
mark the lap joints on each board. Cut the lap joints on a table saw. Adjust the miter gauge to 71 degrees, then make several passes across a dado cutter to create a 3-inch-wide, ⁷⁄₁₆-inch-deep dado in each leg.

Glue the short legs to the long legs, fitting the dadoes together to make an X-shaped frame. The faces of the legs should be flush with each other.

Saturday Morning

3 Cut the profiles of the legs and runners.

Enlarge the *Frame Pattern.* (This is the profile of the assembled legs and runner.) Trace the pattern on the assembled leg stock and the runner stock.

Attach the runner boards to the leg assemblies with double-sided carpet tape. Each runner must be positioned as shown by the dotted lines in the *Leg-and-Runner Layout.* With the runners secured to the legs, cut the profiles of the runners and the bottom ends of the legs, using a band saw or a saber saw. (This way, the curved ends of the legs will fit the curves of the runners precisely.)

Remove the runners and any scraps of the runner boards from the leg assemblies. Then cut the profiles of the legs.

4 Assemble the legs and runners.

Butt the runners against the bottom ends of the legs where you plan to attach them. Using a straightedge, mark straight lines across the seams between the parts where you

want to install the dowels. (These lines should be roughly parallel to each other.)

Using a square, transfer the marks from the faces of the parts to the adjoining ends and edges. Drill $\frac{3}{8}$-inch-diameter, $\frac{9}{16}$-inch-deep dowel holes in these ends and edges, $\frac{7}{16}$ inch from the faces that you marked. You'll find it's easiest to use a hand-held portable drill for this task. Align the drill bit with the marks you made on the face of the parts as you bore each hole.

Assemble the runners and legs with glue and dowels.

TRY THIS

ELASTIC CLAMPS

To clamp the oddly shaped legs and runners together, wrap lengths of surgical tubing or strips of an old inner tube around the parts, stretching the rubber as you do so. This generates a surprising amount of clamping pressure.

Saturday Afternoon

5 Make the stretchers.

As shown in the *Side View* and *Stretcher Detail,* four of the six stretchers have two rounded edges. Using a table-mounted router, round over the edges of the stretcher stock, then rip $\frac{7}{8}$-inch-wide strips free from the stock. Repeat until you have made four rounded stretchers. Then rip two square stretchers.

6 Drill the holes in the leg frames and stretchers.

Using a portable drill, bore $\frac{3}{8}$-inch-diameter, $\frac{9}{16}$-inch-deep holes in the ends of the stretchers, as shown in the *Stretcher Detail/End View.*

Lay out the locations of the holes on the inside faces of the assembled leg frames, as shown in the *Side View.* Drill $\frac{3}{8}$-inch-diameter, $\frac{9}{16}$-inch-deep holes where you will attach the stretchers and $\frac{1}{2}$-inch-diameter, $\frac{9}{16}$-inch-deep holes where you will insert the rungs.

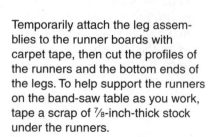

Temporarily attach the leg assemblies to the runner boards with carpet tape, then cut the profiles of the runners and the bottom ends of the legs. To help support the runners on the band-saw table as you work, tape a scrap of $\frac{7}{8}$-inch-thick stock under the runners.

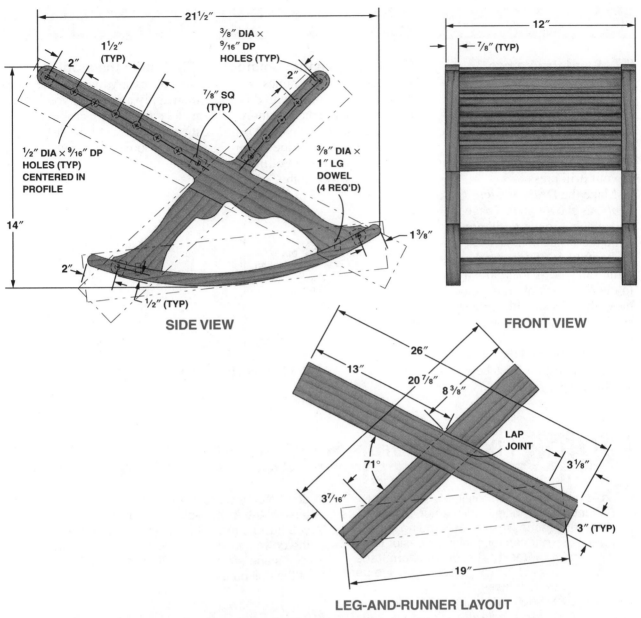

21½"

1½" (TYP)

2"

⅜" DIA ×
⁹⁄₁₆" DP
HOLES (TYP)

2"

⅞" SQ
(TYP)

½" DIA × ⁹⁄₁₆" DP
HOLES (TYP)
CENTERED IN
PROFILE

⅜" DIA ×
1" LG
DOWEL
(4 REQ'D)

14"

1⅜"

2"

½" (TYP)

SIDE VIEW

12"

⅞" (TYP)

FRONT VIEW

26"

13"

20⅞"

8⅜"

LAP
JOINT

71°

3⅛"

3⁷⁄₁₆"

3" (TYP)

19"

LEG-AND-RUNNER LAYOUT

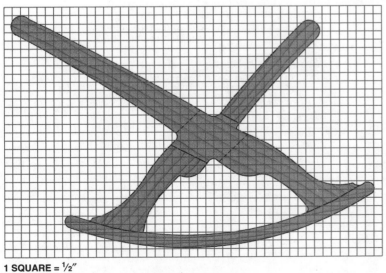

1 SQUARE = ½"

FRAME PATTERN

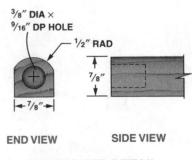

⅜" DIA ×
⁹⁄₁₆" DP HOLE

½" RAD

⅞"

⅞"

END VIEW

SIDE VIEW

STRETCHER DETAIL

Saturday Evening

7 Sand the frames, stretchers, and rungs.
The leg frames are intricately curved, and this makes them difficult to sand. This chore will go a lot faster with a set of small drum sanders that you can mount in your drill press.

Make the *Drum Sanding Table,* as shown on this page, and attach it to your drill press. Sand the inside and outside contours of the leg frames with drum sanders. Work your way up to the finest grit of drum you have, then finish with ordinary sandpaper wrapped around a dowel.

Also finish sand the faces of the leg frames, the stretchers, and the rungs.

Sunday Afternoon

8 Assemble the footstool.
Assemble the frames, stretchers, and rungs with dowels and glue. Clamp the assembly together, making sure there is no warp or twist to it. Wipe off any glue that squeezes out of the joints with a wet cloth.

At Your Leisure

9 Finish the stool. Do any necessary touch-up sanding, then apply a finish. If you wish, make a pad or buy cushions to fit the top surfaces of the stool where you will rest your legs.

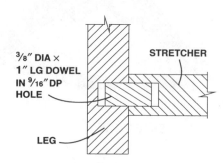

³/₈″ DIA × 1″ LG DOWEL IN ⁹/₁₆″ DP HOLE

STRETCHER

LEG

LEG-TO-STRETCHER JOINERY DETAIL

Quick FIXTURE: Drum Sanding Table

A drum sanding table is just a sheet of plywood with a hole in the center, but it makes all the difference when drum sanding. It increases your control, making it easier to sand a "fair" curve without flat spots or sharp transitions. It also enables you to sand an edge perfectly square to a face.

The table shown is designed to quickly mount on the *Drill Press Table* shown on page 236. The dowels on the underside of the drum sanding table fit the fence slots in the drill press table. If you haven't made this drill press table, arrange the dowels to fit the table you have. Or use cleats and arrange them to fit around the outside of the drill press table.

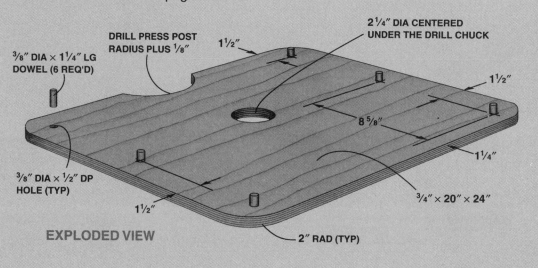

DRILL PRESS POST RADIUS PLUS ¹/₈″

³/₈″ DIA × 1¹/₄″ LG DOWEL (6 REQ'D)

2¹/₄″ DIA CENTERED UNDER THE DRILL CHUCK

1¹/₂″

1¹/₂″

8⁵/₈″

³/₈″ DIA × ¹/₂″ DP HOLE (TYP)

1¹/₄″

³/₄″ × 20″ × 24″

1¹/₂″

2″ RAD (TYP)

EXPLODED VIEW

Pro SKILL: Sanding Curved Surfaces

Sanding curved and contoured surfaces requires more finesse than sanding a flat surface. You must maintain a "fair" curve — a pleasing arc without any flat spots, dips, or sharp transitions. To do this, keep the sander or the wood moving at all times; don't dwell in one place or sand one area overmuch. Work against the rotation of the sander; try not to feed the wood or the sander in the same direction that it revolves. This will give you more control.

1 The most versatile tool for sanding simple curves is a *drum sander*. These range in sizes from ¼ to 8 inches in diameter, but you can perform most curve-sanding chores with a small set from ¾ to 2 inches in diameter. These are sold as accessories for your drill press.

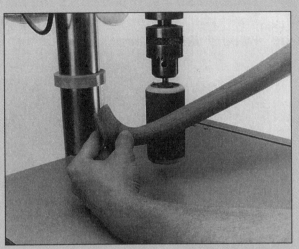

2 Most sanding drums are made from hard rubber to follow a simple curve. However, you can also purchase soft-sided drum sanders, such as this *pneumatic drum*. This allows you to sand *contours*. Adjust the firmness of the abrasive by changing the air pressure inside the drum. The softer the surface, the easier it is for the drum to conform to three-dimensional curves. It also sands more aggressively (removes stock faster).

3 However, if you have a lot of sanding to do, you may want to invest in a *spindle sander*. On this machine, the drums travel up and down or *oscillate* as they spin. This helps keep the abrasive from loading up with impacted sawdust and creates a smoother surface on the wood.

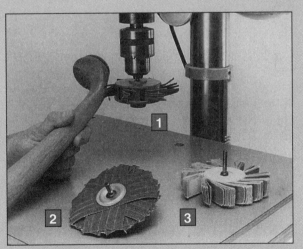

4 For complex surfaces, use an *abrasive mop* (1), *flutter sheets* (2), or a *flap sander* (3) mounted on your drill press. All these accessories reach into crevices and conform to the shape of the work.

Settle Bench

■ **QUICK FIXTURE**
Saw Stand

■ *PRO SKILL*
Handling Long Stock

To handle long boards safely and efficiently, use a saw stand. It's the extra hand you so often need when making large projects like this settle bench.

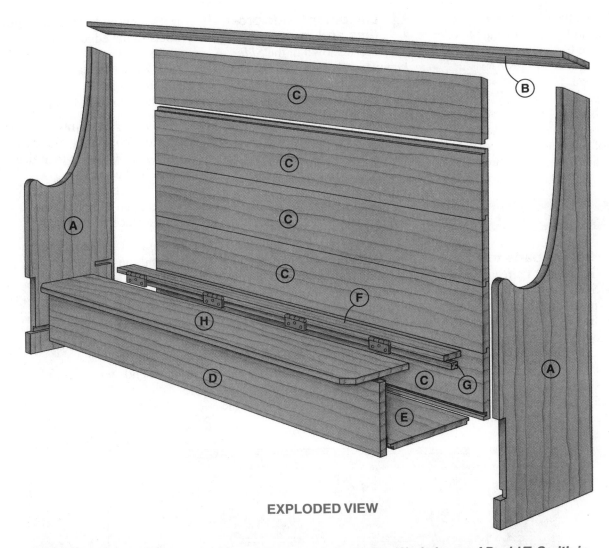

EXPLODED VIEW

MATERIALS LIST

Finished Dimensions in Inches

Parts

A.	Sides (2)	³⁄₄″ × 14″ × 59¹⁄₈″
B.	Top	³⁄₄″ × 5¹⁄₈″ × 60″
C.	Back boards (5)	³⁄₄″ × 11¹⁄₈″ × 59¹⁄₄″
D.	Front	³⁄₄″ × 10¹⁄₂″ × 60″
E.	Bottom	³⁄₄″ × 13¹⁄₈″ × 59¹⁄₄″
F.	Shelf	³⁄₄″ × 3″ × 59¹⁄₄″
G.	Cleat	³⁄₄″ × ³⁄₄″ × 58¹⁄₂″
H.	Seat	³⁄₄″ × 11³⁄₈″ × 58³⁄₈″

Hardware*

6d Cut nails (40–58)

#8 × 1¹⁄₄″ Flathead wood screws (6–8)

1¹⁄₂″ × 2¹⁄₂″ Butt hinges and mounting screws (4 sets)

If you use this project outside, all hardware should be weather-resistant. Substitute galvanized finishing nails for cut nails.

The craftsmen who man the Workshops of David T. Smith in Morrow, Ohio, copied this "settle bench" from a late eighteenth-century design. The original probably sat just inside the doorway or outside on a porch, providing a handy place to sit down and remove muddy footwear. The seat doubles as a chest to store boots and gloves. Some settle benches also had a row of pegs across the back to serve as a coat rack.

Friday Evening

1 Prepare the materials, and glue up the wide stock. To make this bench, you need approximately 62 board feet of 4/4 (1-inch-thick) stock. The bench shown is made from poplar, but you can use any cabinet-grade wood. If you plan to use the bench outside on a covered porch, poplar, cedar, and cypress all weather well. So do mahogany, lauan, and teak, but these imported woods are a good deal more expensive. Avoid redwood. Although it's a traditional "outdoor" wood, it doesn't hold nails as well as other species.

Plane the 4/4 stock to ¾ inch thick, and glue it up edge to edge to make the wide boards you need. If this project will be used outdoors, be sure to use a waterproof glue such as epoxy, polyurethane, or Resorcinol.

See Also:
"Gluing Stock Edge to Edge" on page 74.

Saturday Morning

2 **Cut the parts to size.**
If you don't already have a *Saw Stand,* as shown on page 160, make one to help handle the long boards in this project. Remove the clamps from the stock that you've glued up, and cut all the parts to size. Bevel the edges of the top and the top back board with the blade tilted at 30 degrees as you rip them.

3 **Lay out the side profiles and joinery.** Enlarge the pattern shown in the *Side Layout,* and trace it on the stock. Also mark the rabbets, dadoes, and notches on the inside surfaces of the sides.

Saturday Afternoon

4 **Cut the rabbets, dadoes, and grooves.**
Most of the joints in the settle bench can be made with either a dado cutter or a table-mounted router, using a saw stand to help feed the long boards. Cut:

■ ¾-inch-wide, ⅜-inch-deep rabbets on the back edges of the sides

■ ⅝-inch-wide, ⅜-inch-deep rabbets in the adjoining edges of the back boards, as shown in the *Side View*

■ ⅜-inch-wide, ⅜-inch-deep rabbets in the edges of the bottom

■ A ⅜-inch-wide, ⅜-inch-deep groove in the inside surface of the bottom back board

Several of the joints are easier to make with a handheld router:

■ ¾-inch-wide, ⅜-inch-deep dadoes in the sides

■ A ⅜-inch-wide, ⅜-inch-deep stopped groove in the inside surface of the front

Note that the dadoes for the shelf and the groove in the front are *stopped.* Rout up to the marks for the ends of these joints, then square the stopped ends with a chisel.

See Also:
"Routing Dadoes and Rabbets" on page 59.

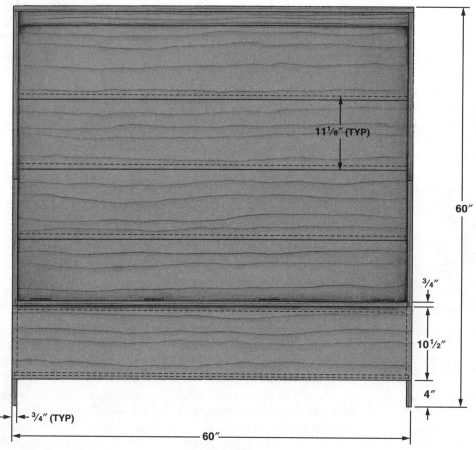

11⅛" (TYP)

60"

¾"

10½"

4"

¾" (TYP)

60"

FRONT VIEW

Saturday Evening

5 **Cut the side and seat profiles.** Using a hand saw and a saber saw, cut the profile of the sides, including the mitered tops and the notch in the front edges. To save time, stack the sides face to face, tape them together, and cut both parts at once. Remember, the sides must be mirror images of each other.

Also chamfer the front corners of the seat, as shown in the *Seat Corner Detail.* Sand the sawed edges.

Sunday Afternoon

6 **Assemble the settle bench.** Finish sand all the parts. Mortise the seat and the shelf for butt hinges. (It's easier to do this before the parts are assembled.)

Fasten the front to the sides with nails, and rest the assembly on its front edges. Insert the bottom and the shelf in their dadoes. Starting with the bottom back board, rest the back boards in the side rabbets. Overlap the edge rabbets, as shown on the *Side View,* and make sure the beveled edge of the top back board is flush with the mitered

ends of the sides. When the back boards are properly fitted and arranged, nail them to the sides. Also nail the top to the sides and the top back board.

Stand the assembly up. Fasten the cleat to the back boards with screws, then nail the shelf to it. Finally, attach the seat to the shelf with hinges.

Note that there's no glue used in the assembly. Many of the wide parts are joined *cross grain* — that is, the wood grain in one part is perpendicular to the grain in the adjoining part. If you glue these parts together, the adhesive will restrict the movement of the wood as it expands and contracts with changes in the weather.

Parts will split, joints will pop, and the assembled bench will be weakened.

TRY THIS

SEASONAL EXPANSION AND CONTRACTION

If you build this bench in the winter, cut the four top back boards 1/8 inch narrower than shown, and assemble them with 1/8-inch gaps between each board. This will allow room for expansion in the summer. The rabbets will disguise the gaps.

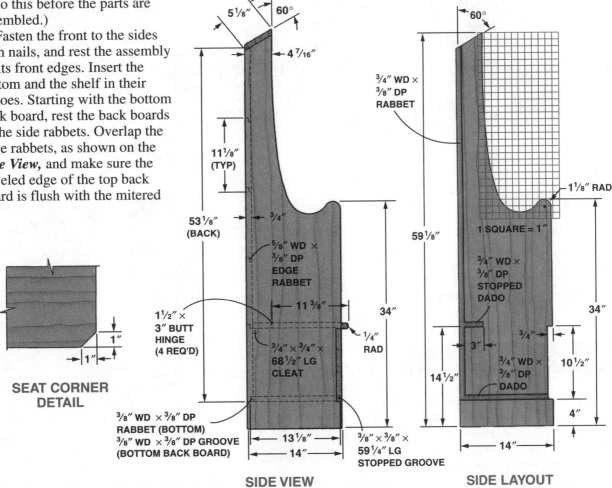

SEAT CORNER DETAIL

SIDE VIEW

SIDE LAYOUT

Nails, when used by themselves, bend or give slightly as the wood moves and the assembly remains sound. I've recommended cut nails for this project because they hold better than common nails (they have more surface area), and the rectangular shanks are reminiscent of hand-forged nails used by eighteenth- and early nineteenth-century craftsmen. When installing these nails in hardwoods, drill pilot holes slightly smaller than the thickness of the nail shanks. Orient each nail so the thickness (short dimension) is perpendicular to the wood grain. This will prevent the wood from splitting.

TRY THIS

MAKING STRONGER NAIL JOINTS

When nailing the parts together, drive each nail at a slight angle. Vary the angle right and left, alternating with each nail. This will lock the parts together.

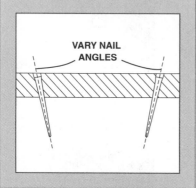

VARY NAIL ANGLES

At Your Leisure

7 Finish the settle bench. Do any necessary touch-up sanding, then apply paint or a finish to the bench. If the project will be used outside, be sure to use an exterior finish.

Quick FIXTURE: Saw Stand

A saw stand is the extra pair of hands that you so often need when working with long boards or large pieces of plywood. It supports the portion of the board that overhangs the workbench or the saw table, yet still allows you to move or feed the work.

The saw stand shown is designed to adjust to any height, between 26 and 45 inches (roughly), allowing you to use it with a wide variety of stationary power tools, including a table saw, radial arm saw, band saw, jointer, planer, drill press, router table, shaper, and scroll saw. The work is supported on *transfer balls* — large ball bearings that roll in any direction. This allows you to move the work in any direction with a minimum of resistance.

To make the saw stand, rout a ⅜-inch-wide. 19¼-inch-long slot in the sliding support post. Drill ⅜-inch-diameter holes in the legs. Attach the top to the post with finishing nails, glue, and gussets to make a T-shaped assembly. Sandwich the post between the legs with a single thickness of paper as a spacer. Attach the legs to one another with the braces. This will make a box-shaped assembly that the support post can slide in and out of.

Attach the legs to the base with glue and screws. Drive #10 x 2-inch flathead wood screws up through the base and into the ends of the legs. Insert the post assembly between the legs, and install a carriage bolt through the legs and post. Secure the bolt with a star knob. When the knob is tightened, it will hold the post at any height you set. Screw a dozen transfer balls to the top.

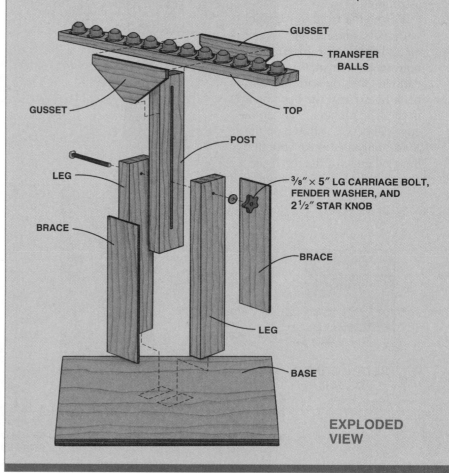

GUSSET

TRANSFER BALLS

GUSSET

TOP

POST

LEG

⅜" × 5" LG CARRIAGE BOLT, FENDER WASHER, AND 2½" STAR KNOB

BRACE

BRACE

LEG

BASE

EXPLODED VIEW

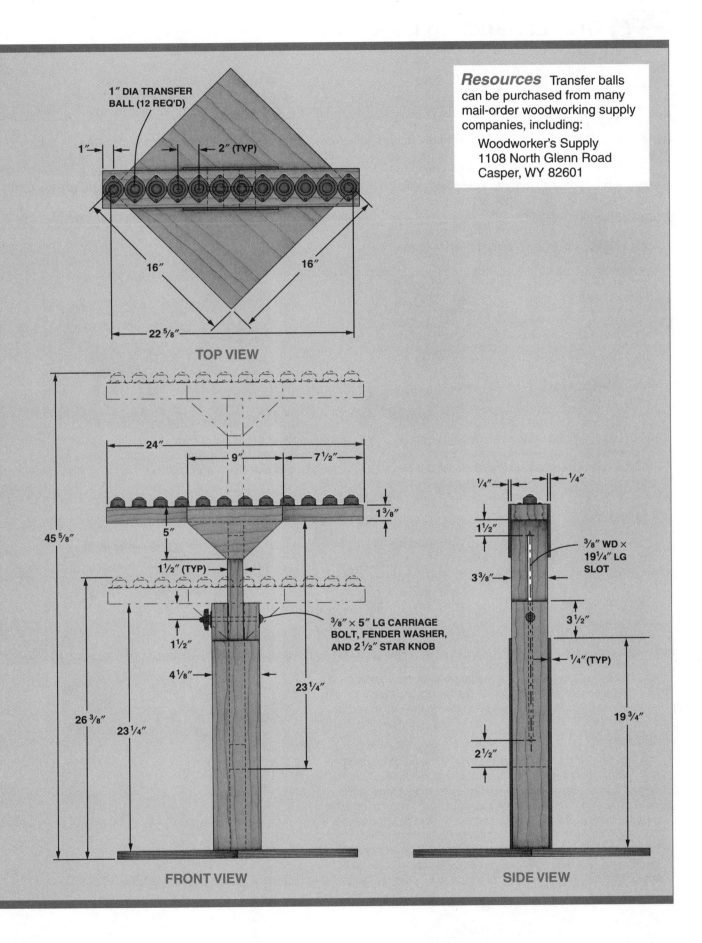

1″ DIA TRANSFER BALL (12 REQ'D)

1″

2″ (TYP)

16″

16″

22 5/8″

TOP VIEW

Resources Transfer balls can be purchased from many mail-order woodworking supply companies, including:

Woodworker's Supply
1108 North Glenn Road
Casper, WY 82601

24″

9″

7 1/2″

1 3/8″

5″

45 5/8″

1 1/2″ (TYP)

3/8″ × 5″ LG CARRIAGE BOLT, FENDER WASHER, AND 2 1/2″ STAR KNOB

1 1/2″

4 1/8″

23 1/4″

26 3/8″

23 1/4″

FRONT VIEW

1/4″

1/4″

1 1/2″

3/8″ WD × 19 1/4″ LG SLOT

3 3/8″

3 1/2″

1/4″ (TYP)

19 3/4″

2 1/2″

SIDE VIEW

Pro SKILL: Handling Long Stock

When working with long boards, you must support the end that overhangs the workbench or saw table. Otherwise, it will be almost impossible to keep the board flat on the table during the entire operation. This not only makes it difficult to make an accurate cut, it also creates potential safety problems. When you have to exert a great deal of force to keep the board on the table, it's much more likely that your hands could slip into the cutter.

Too little support creates other problems as well. A blade could be pinched or damaged when a board tips. A planer will cut a snipe in the end of a board that's not properly supported as you feed it through the machine. And it's much more difficult to joint a straight edge with a jointer if the board isn't adequately supported.

If you don't have shop help at your beck and call, the easiest way to provide this support is with a saw stand. Place the stand wherever you need the most support, usually on the outfeed side of the tool. In some cases, it makes sense to use two or more saw stands.

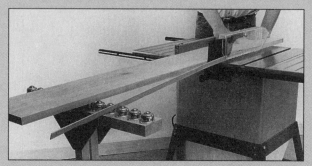

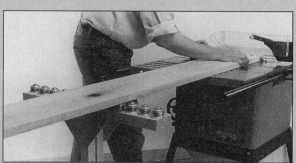

1 To use a support stand when making a rip cut, position the stand several feet behind the saw blade on the outfeed side of the table. If you are sawing thin stock and the boards droop as they pass the edge, lower the stand to compensate. To use the stand when crosscutting a long board, place the stand directly to one side of the saw blade.

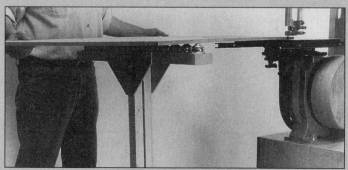

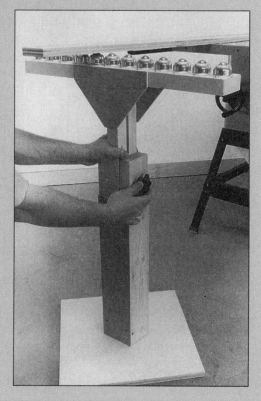

2 When cutting boards that are larger than the worktable of a band saw or scroll saw, place a stand to one side where it will support the bulk of the workpiece during the cut. In some cases, it may be necessary to stop the saw and move the stand during a cut.

3 Whenever you use the saw stand with a tool, you must adjust the height of the stand to the same (or just a little below) height as the tool's worktable. To adjust it to the same height, place a straightedge or a straight board across the table and the transfer balls. Raise or lower the stand until the straightedge lies flat on the table. To compensate for droop in your stock, lower the stand slightly from this point. The amount you need to lower it will depend on the material you're cutting and the distance between the stand and the tool.

Pouting Chair

■ **QUICK FIXTURE**
Finishing Umbrella

■ **PRO SKILL**
Stenciling

No matter what sort of finish you apply to your woodworking projects, dust is a potent enemy. A finishing umbrella offers a simple, inexpensive, and effective shield.

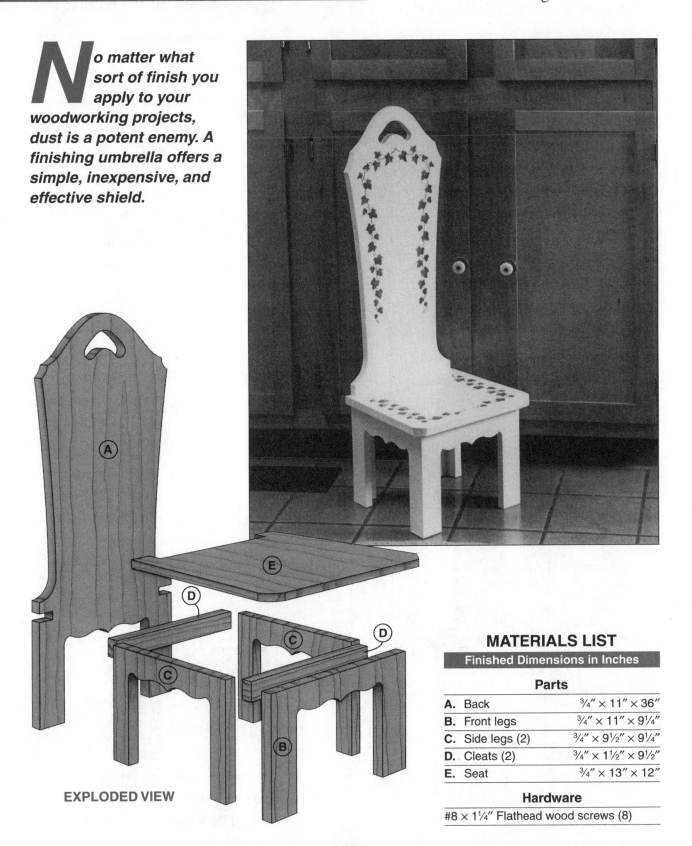

EXPLODED VIEW

MATERIALS LIST

Finished Dimensions in Inches

Parts

A.	Back	$^3/_4'' \times 11'' \times 36''$
B.	Front legs	$^3/_4'' \times 11'' \times 9^1/_4''$
C.	Side legs (2)	$^3/_4'' \times 9^1/_2'' \times 9^1/_4''$
D.	Cleats (2)	$^3/_4'' \times 1^1/_2'' \times 9^1/_2''$
E.	Seat	$^3/_4'' \times 13'' \times 12''$

Hardware

#8 × 1¼″ Flathead wood screws (8)

It's called a pouting chair because it looks like a child's chair and tradition has it that this is where children are sent to think about their bad deeds. But it's not a chair at all; it's a foot stool with a long handle so you can move it wherever you want without having to stoop over to pick it up.

1 Prepare the materials, and cut the parts to size.

To make this pouting chair, you need approximately 8 board feet of 4/4 (1-inch-thick) stock. The chair shown is made from poplar but you can use any cabinet-grade wood. However, if you plan to paint the piece, there's no sense in investing in expensive hardwoods. Poplar, birch, and ash are relatively inexpensive alternatives that you might consider.

When you have selected the lumber, plane it to ¾ inch thick, and cut the parts to the sizes specified in the Materials List.

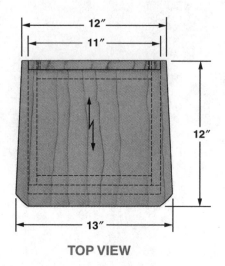

TOP VIEW

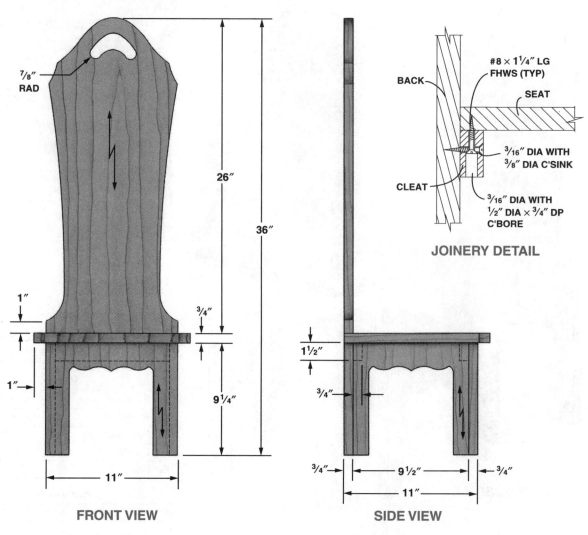

FRONT VIEW

SIDE VIEW

JOINERY DETAIL

2 Cut the leg profiles.
With the exception of the cleats, all the parts have a decorative profile. Enlarge the *Back and Leg Pattern* and the *Seat Pattern.* Trace the leg pattern onto the front leg piece and one of the side leg pieces. Stack the back and front leg pieces face to face with the front leg piece on

top. Hold the
double-face
sure the bot
are flush. A
pieces with
on top.

Cut the
using a ba
saber saw
then take
discard th

You c
the back
the prof
four par
a stack
you co
saw or

Attach the seat to the cleats with flathead wood screws, driving the screws through the cleats and into the underside the seat.

3 Cut the back and seat profiles. Trace the back and seat profiles onto the stock. Cut the shapes with a band saw, saber saw, or scroll saw. To make the handle cutout in the back, you'll have to use either a saber saw or coping saw. Sand the sawed edges.

4 Drill screw holes in the cleats. Bore four screw holes in each cleat — two countersunk holes through the width

and drive the screws through cleats and into the inside surfaces of the back and front legs. The oversize holes will allow the back and front legs to move independently of the cleats. Don't glue these parts in place. The wood grain in the cleats is opposed to the grain in the legs and back. If you glue the parts together, the bond will restrict the wood movement, and the legs may warp or cup.

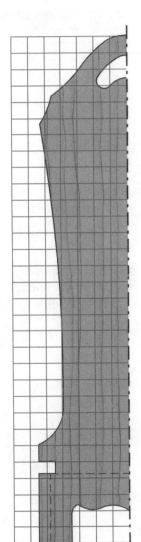

1 SQUARE = 1″

BACK AND LEG PATTERN

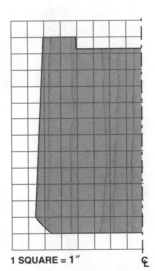

1 SQUARE = 1″

SEAT PATTERN

To make the handle cutout in the back, first drill a ⁷⁄₈-inch hole at both ends of the cutout. Insert the blade of a saber saw or scroll saw through the hole and cut the shape of the handle.

6 **Finish the chair.** Do any necessary touch-up sanding to the assembled chair. Apply paint or a finish to the chair. If you'd like to decorate a painted chair with stencils, apply the decorations directly over the paint. If the chair will get a clear finish, apply the finish over the decorations.

FIXTURE: Finishing Umbrella

When applying a finish, your greatest enemy is the dust in the air. Dust settles on a wet finish, creating dimples and dulling the surface. This is especially unfortunate for woodworkers because woodworking shops are some of the dustiest places on earth.

What can you do, short of building a separate finishing room with its own air filtration system? Quite a bit! A simple dust umbrella dramatically reduces the amount of dust that settles on a wet finish. After you leave the shop and stop stirring up the air currents, most of the dust that ends up on a project settles down. A sheet of plastic just above the wet surface catches this dust. Do your finishing chores last, just before you quit for the evening, and set up the umbrella over the project. You'll have considerably less work to do the next day when sanding between coats or rubbing out the finish.

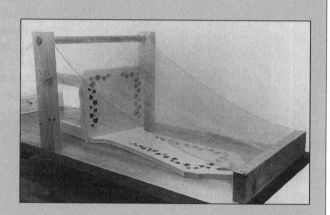

The finishing umbrella shown is designed to roll up on the ends. You can unroll as much of the plastic sheet as you need each time you use it.

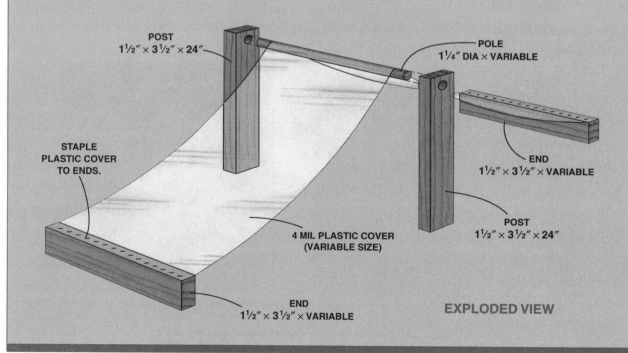

POST
1½″ × 3½″ × 24″

POLE
1¼″ DIA × VARIABLE

STAPLE PLASTIC COVER TO ENDS.

END
1½″ × 3½″ × VARIABLE

POST
1½″ × 3½″ × 24″

4 MIL PLASTIC COVER
(VARIABLE SIZE)

END
1½″ × 3½″ × VARIABLE

EXPLODED VIEW

Pro SKILL: Stenciling

Stenciling is an easy way to dress up painted furniture. Although it's sometimes thought of as a folk or "country" art, it doesn't have to be. Stencils create a wide range of effects, from simple to sophisticated. It all depends on the stencil design and how you apply it.

When repeating a decoration, use a stencil to create the shape. Often, you'll apply a shape over and over again so the repetitive shapes form a decorative pattern. To make a stencil, decide on a design, and enlarge it or reduce it to the size you want. Lay a sheet of Mylar or waxed stenciling paper over the design. (Both materials are available at craft supply stores.) With a sharp bench knife, cut out the design. Where necessary to connect interior parts of the design to the exterior shape, leave "bridges" in the stencil.

For multicolored designs, cut different stencils for each color. You can align two or more stencils on the wood surface by cutting two little triangles near one edge of each stencil. These triangles must be cut in exactly the same spot on each stencil. To make sure they are, stack the stencils, align them, then cut the triangles in all the stencils at the same time.

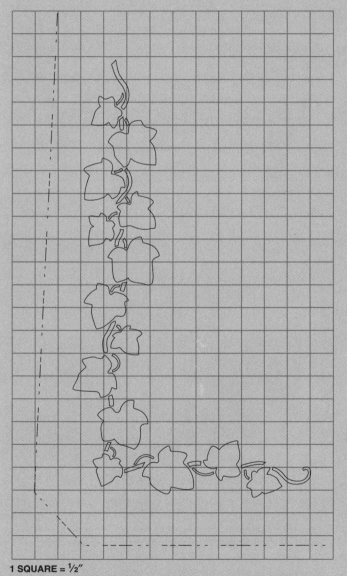

1 SQUARE = ½″

SEAT STENCILING PATTERN

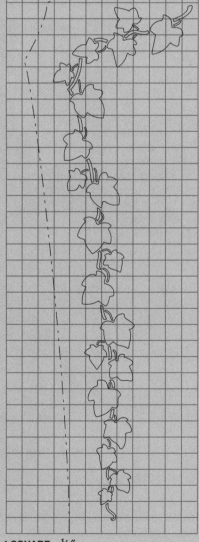

1 SQUARE = ½″

BACK STENCILING PATTERN

(continued)

Pro SKILL: Stenciling — CONTINUED

Tape the first stencil to the wood, and trace the triangles lightly in pencil. Thereafter, line up each successive stencil with those marks. After you've applied the decoration, erase the marks.

Almost any type of paint will work for stenciling, but quick-drying, thick pigments work best. Acrylic artist's paints are especially well suited for wood. After they're dry, they're durable and waterproof.

Dip a stiff brush into the paint, and wipe it on a palette to remove most of the pigment. (The brush should be fairly "dry.") Apply the paint to the wood, brushing in from the edge of the

stencil to the open middle. Keep adding coats of paint until the color is thick enough to cover the surface beneath it. Carefully remove the stencil, lifting it up so as not to smear the paint.

After stenciling, you may want to apply a clear finish to the entire surface. This will help protect the decoration and keep it from wearing. It's wise to test the stencil paint with the finish you're going to use before you try the combination on a real project. If you find the two materials are incompatible, seal the dried decoration with a "wash coat" of white shellac (about a 1-pound cut) before applying the finish.

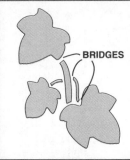

BRIDGES

1 Cut the stencil with a sharp knife, tracing the outline of the pattern. Where necessary, leave "bridges" to hold the stencil together and strengthen the interior parts of the design.

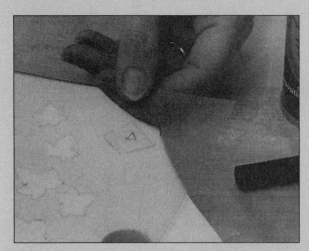

2 To help align successive stencils when making a multicolored decoration, cut triangular openings near one edge. These triangles must be positioned exactly the same on each stencil. Use these as "register marks" to align each stencil on the wood.

3 Apply the stencil paint with a "dry brush," stroking in from the outside of the design toward the middle. If the brush is too wet or you stroke to the outside, the paint may "bleed" under the edges of the template. This will make your design appear fuzzy.

PART SIX

For Dressing
and Sleeping

Pencil Post Bed

■ *QUICK FIXTURE*
Post Sawing Jig

■ *PRO SKILL*
Making Pencil Posts

I cut the tapered posts on this bed with a special tapering jig. This jig not only holds the stock at a slight angle to the blade; it lets you rotate the stock and index it every 45 degrees. This, in turn makes it possible to cut eight tapered surfaces in each post, all precisely the same.

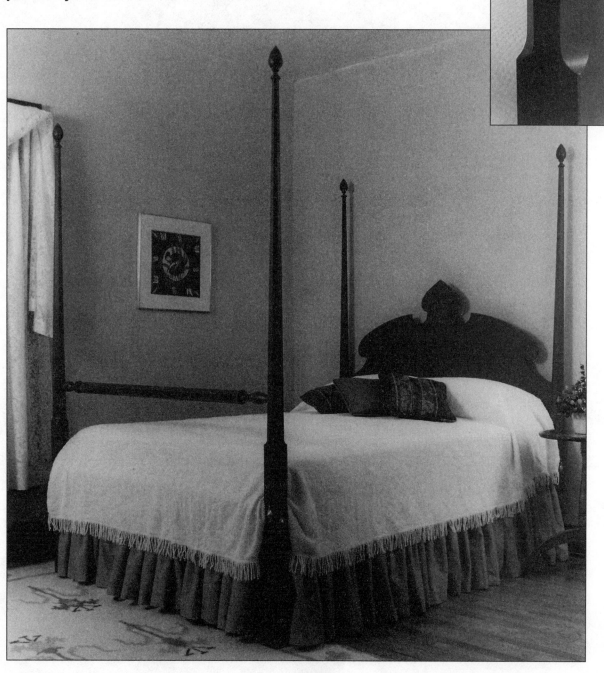

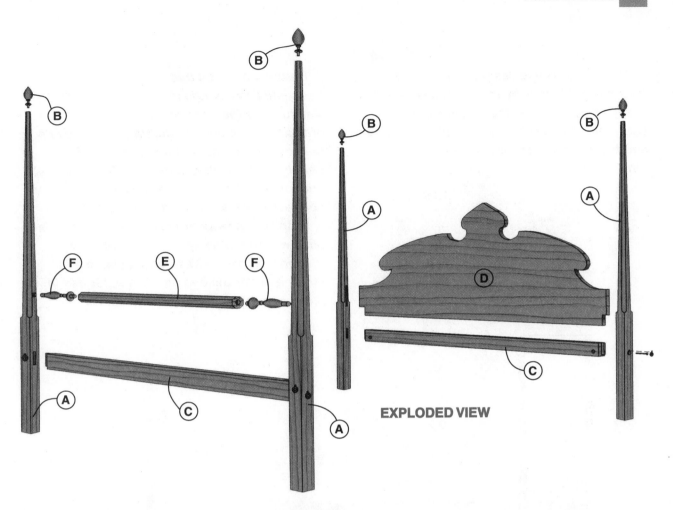

EXPLODED VIEW

MATERIALS LIST
Finished Dimensions in Inches

Parts		Hardware
A. Posts (4)	2½″ × 2½″ × 82″	½″ × 4″ Hex bolts (4)
B. Finials (4)	2¹/₁₆″ dia. × 6″	½″ Square nuts (4)
C. Head/foot rail (2)	2½″ × 3½″ × 59″	½″ Flat washers (4)
D. Headboard	¾″ × 34″ × 59″	Bed bolt covers (8)
E. Blanket rail	2″ × 2″ × 45⅛″	Universal mattress frame with connector brackets and
F. Blanket rail ends (2)	2⁵/₁₆″ dia × 9″	lag screws for both head and foot boards

Resources Purchase the bed bolt covers (#99235) from:

The Woodworkers' Store
4365 Willow Drive
Medina, MN 55340

You can also purchase ready-made finials (#A0803-220) and blanket rails (#A0806) from:

Adams Wood Products
974 Forest Drive
Morristown, TN 37814

Adams' finials and blanket rails aren't the same profile as is shown in the plans, but they will work well with the design.

A bed is an awkward piece of furniture. You have to take it apart just to get it through the bedroom door. For this reason, the headboard and footboard assemblies shown here aren't glued together. Instead, the mortise-and-tenon joints are held together with "bed bolts" — two each in the headboard and footboard assemblies. When you remove the bolts, the posts, rails, headboard, and blanket rail all come apart.

The bed shown is designed for a queen-size mattress (60-inches by 80-inches), but it can easily be adapted to other sizes simply by shortening or lengthening the rails, headboard, and blanket rail. Here are some common bedding sizes:

	WIDTH	LENGTH
Single	36″	75″
Twin	40″	75″ or 80″
Full	54″	75″ or 80″
Queen	60″	80″ or 84″
King	76″	80″ or 84″

Before you begin this project, set up the mattress and box springs in the mattress frame. Measure the distance between the connector brackets at the ends of the frame rails. Ideally, the headboard and footboard assemblies should be 2½ inches wider than the mattress, but you may have to adjust this slightly so the connector brackets contact the posts.

Note: *The headboard and footboard assemblies will also work with the Bed Storage Platform on page 198, allowing you to add storage under the bed or use a water bed in place of a regular spring mattress.*

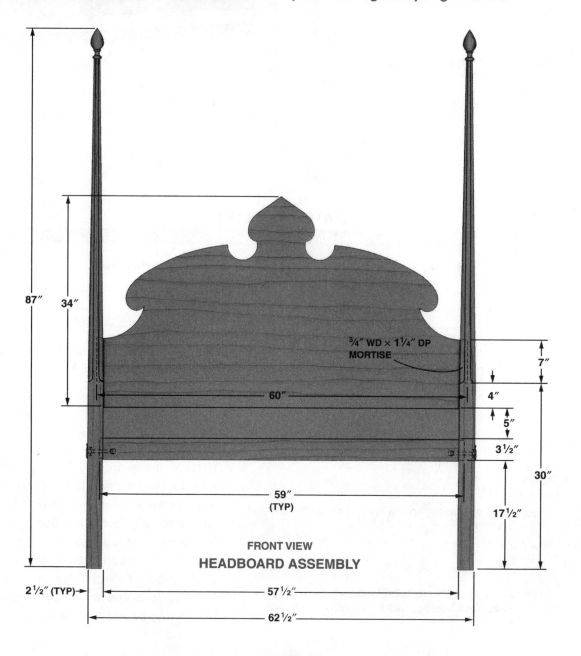

87″ 34″

¾″ WD × 1¼″ DP MORTISE

7″

60″ 4″

5″

3½″

59″ (TYP)

30″

17½″

FRONT VIEW
HEADBOARD ASSEMBLY

2½″ (TYP)→

57½″

62½″

Friday Evening

1 Prepare the materials, and cut the parts to size.

To make the pencil post bed as designed, you need approximately 40 board feet of 12/4 (3-inch-thick) stock and 17 board feet of 4/4 (1-inch-thick) stock. On the bed shown, the parts are all made from poplar, then painted. However, you can use any cabinet-grade wood.

Plane some of the 12/4 to 2½ inches thick, and cut the rails. Rip the remaining 12/4 stock into 3-inch-square posts. Joint

two adjacent sides of each post flat and true and square to one another. Plane the other two surfaces so the posts are 2½ inches square. From this stock, cut the bed posts and turning stock for the finials and blanket rail ends. Plane a 4-foot-long length of this

TRY THIS

QUARTERSAWN LUMBER FOR WIDE PARTS
Make the headboard from quartersawn lumber (in which the annual rings run face to face). Quartersawn stock is more stable than other types of lumber and less likely to cup or warp. As a result, the headboard stays relatively flat.

stock to 2 inches square, then cut the blanket rail to length.

Plane the 4/4 stock to ¾ inch thick, and glue up a piece wide enough to make the headboard.

See Also:
"Gluing Stock Edge to Edge" on page 74.

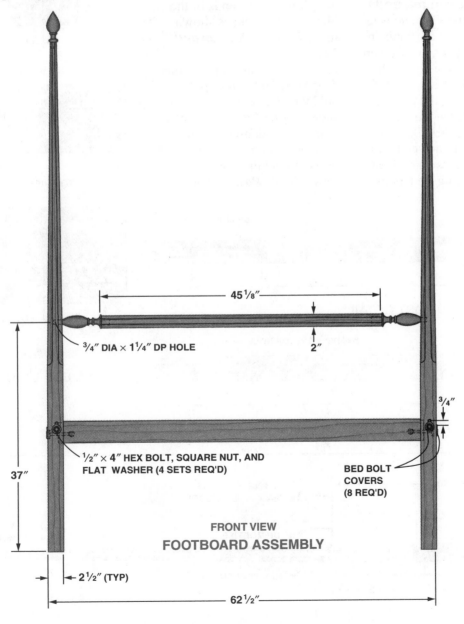

45⅛"

2"

¾" DIA × 1¼" DP HOLE

¾"

37"

½" × 4" HEX BOLT, SQUARE NUT, AND FLAT WASHER (4 SETS REQ'D)

BED BOLT COVERS (8 REQ'D)

FRONT VIEW
FOOTBOARD ASSEMBLY

2½" (TYP)

62½"

Saturday Morning

2 Cut the mortises in the posts. The headboard and rails rest in mortises in the posts. In each post, cut a ¾-inch-wide, 3½-inch-long, ¹³⁄₁₆-inch-deep mortise for the adjoining rail, as shown in the *Post Layout.* In the head posts, make ¾-inch-wide, 7-inch-long, 1¼-inch-deep mortises to hold the headboard, as shown in the *Head Post Detail.*

See Also:
"Routing Mortises" on page 28.

3 Cut tenons in the ends of the rails. Cut tenons in the ends of the rails, as shown in the *Rail End Layout,* and fit them to the mortises in the posts. The rails are too large to safely cut the tenons vertically on the table saw, even if you use a tenoning jig to help support the stock. Instead, use your router or dado cutter to rabbet three surfaces on each end of each rail, creating the tenons.

Saturday Afternoon

4 Drill the holes in the posts and rails. You must make several stopped holes in various parts of this project:

■ 1-inch-diameter, 1⅝-inch-deep holes near the end of each rail, as shown in the *Rail End Layout.* These hold the nuts that fit the bed bolts, allowing you to draw the tenons tight in the mortises.

See Also:
"Boring End Grain" on page 193.

■ 1-inch-diameter. 1½-inch-deep holes in the ends of the blanket rail stock, as shown in the *Blanket Rail Layout/ End View*

■ ¾-inch-diameter, 1¼-inch-deep holes in the foot posts to hold the blanket rail ends, as shown in the *Foot Post Detail*

■ ½-inch-diameter, 1-inch-deep holes in the ends of the posts to hold the finials, as shown in the *Post Layout*

■ ½-inch-diameter bolt holes with 1⅜-inch-diameter, ⅜-inch-deep counterbores in the posts, as shown in the *Post Layout.* These must go through the mortises.

Do *not* drill the ½-inch-diameter holes in the ends of the rails yet.

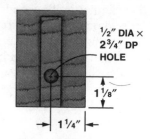

½" DIA × 2¾" DP HOLE

1⅛"

1¼"

END VIEW

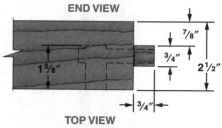

1⅝"

⅞"
¾"
2½"
¾"

TOP VIEW

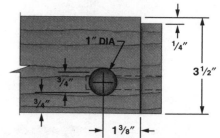

1" DIA

¼"

3½"

¾"
¾"

1⅜"

SIDE VIEW

RAIL END LAYOUT

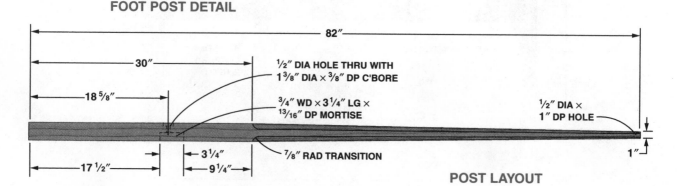

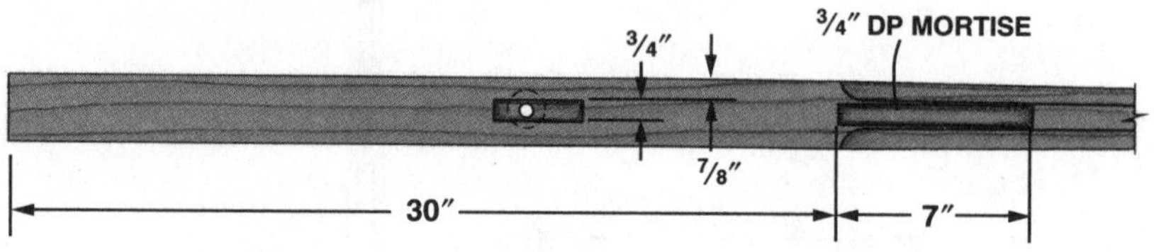

¾"

¾" DP MORTISE

⅞"

30"

7"

HEAD POST DETAIL

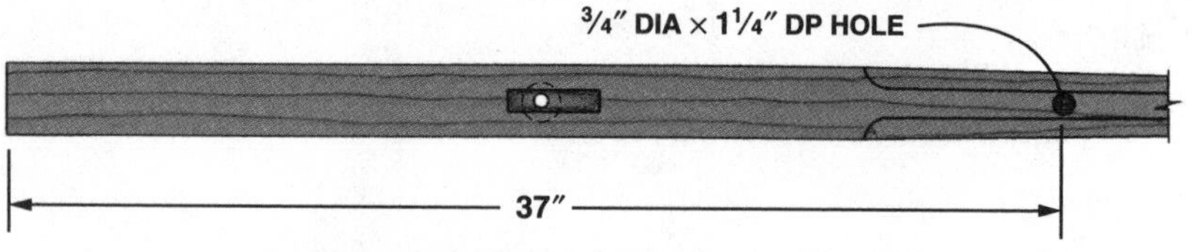

¾" DIA × 1¼" DP HOLE

37"

FOOT POST DETAIL

82"

30"

½" DIA HOLE THRU WITH
1⅜" DIA × ⅜" DP C'BORE

¾" WD × 3¼" LG ×
¹³⁄₁₆" DP MORTISE

18⅝"

½" DIA ×
1" DP HOLE

3¼"

⅞" RAD TRANSITION

17½"

9¼"

1"

POST LAYOUT

5 Rough-cut the tapers in the posts.

Make the *Post Sawing Jig,* and use it to cut the rough tapers in the posts. First make the face tapers on a band saw, then cut the curved transitions at the corners with a coping saw. Go back to a band saw to cut the corner tapers. When you've finished, all four posts should taper from 2½ inches square 30 inches above the floor to 1¹⁄₁₆ inches octagonal at the top.

See Also:
"Making Pencil Posts" on page 179.

TRY THIS

MAKING SMOOTH BAND SAW CUTS

When cutting the tapers, feed the wood slowly. The slower the feed rate, the more cuts per inch and the smoother the cut surface. This reduces the amount of work necessary to plane and sand these surfaces.

Saturday Evening

6 Plane and sand the pencil posts.

The tapered surfaces of the pencil post will be fairly rough after you saw them. Clean them up with a block plane, scrapers, and sandpaper. (Back up the sandpaper with a hard, flat block to maintain a flat surface.) Also sand the curved transitions. When you're finished, the post should taper to approximately 1 inch at the top.

Sunday Afternoon

7 Cut the octagonal shape of the blanket rail.

On a table saw, bevel all four corners on the blanket rail, turning the 2-inch square into an octagon. Each face on the octagonal should be ²⁷⁄₃₂″ wide, as shown on the *Blanket Rail Layout.*

8 Cut the shape of the headboard.

Lay out the profile of the headboard, as shown in the *Headboard Pattern.* Also lay out the 1¼-inch-long, 7-inch-wide tenons, as shown in the pattern and the *Headboard Assembly/Front View.* Cut the profile and the tenons with a saber saw or coping saw. Sand the sawed edges.

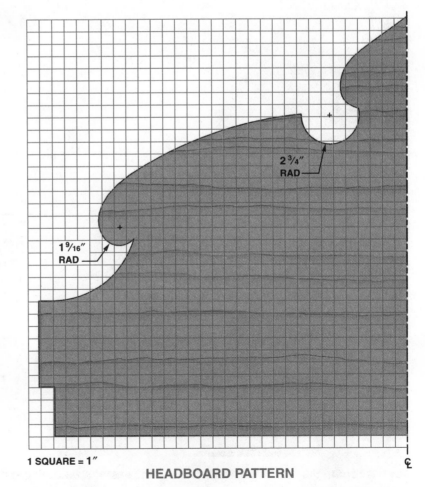

2 ¾″ RAD

1 ⁹⁄₁₆″ RAD

1 SQUARE = 1″

HEADBOARD PATTERN

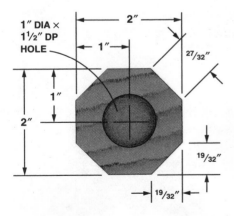

1″ DIA × 1½″ DP HOLE

2″

1″

²⁷⁄₃₂″

1″

2″

¹⁹⁄₃₂″

¹⁹⁄₃₂″

END VIEW
BLANKET RAIL LAYOUT

Quick FIXTURE: Post Sawing Jig

To make the pencil posts, you must cut very gentle tapers — 0.83 degrees, to be ridiculously precise. This carriage holds the long post cocked at the proper angle as you guide it along a resawing fence on your band saw.

Except for the dowel, make the parts of the jig from ¾-inch plywood. Rip the base and the side of the jig from the long edges of the sheet — the factory edges will be relatively straight. Stack the holder parts face to face and cut two identical holders. Drill the hole in the top end, then assemble the parts *except* for the dowel and the holder that supports the post 30 inches from the bottom end.

Leave the dowel loose. To position the remaining holder, mount a square post in the jig. Measure 30 inches from the bottom edge. Place the remaining holder under the post and slide it along the post until it's even with the 30-inch mark. Trace the position of the holder on the

base, then attach it with glue and screws. Don't worry that one end of the holder hangs over the base. You'll cut this off when you make the first pass on the band saw.

Note: As designed, this jig can only be used to cut 52-inch-long tapers in stock that's 2½ inches square and 82 inches long. To change the length of the taper or the size of the stock, you must redesign the jig. When doing this, think of the long "open" edge of the jig as the cut line. With the post in position, the edge of the jig will be in line with the path you want to cut when viewed from above.

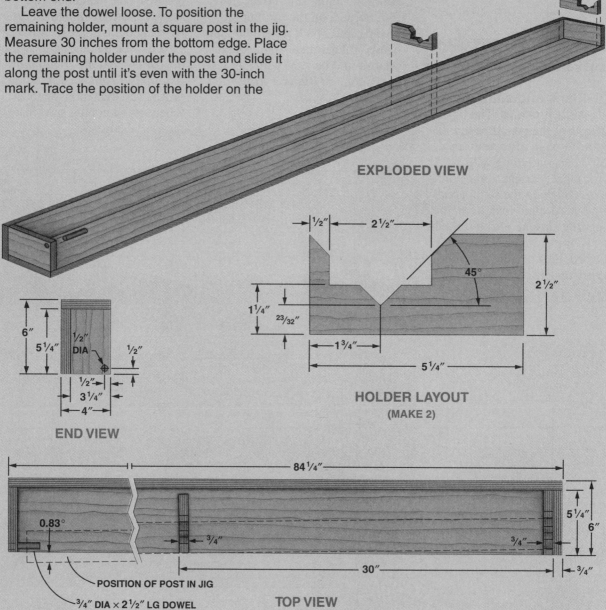

EXPLODED VIEW

HOLDER LAYOUT
(MAKE 2)

END VIEW

TOP VIEW

9 **Turn the blanket rail ends.** Turn the two blanket rail ends, as shown in the *Blanket Rail End Layout.* To help turn the tenons to the proper diameter, make the *Round Tenon Gauge* shown on page 178. Sand the rail ends smooth on the lathe as you make them, but be careful not to sand the tenons. You don't want to remove any more stock once you've turned them to the proper size.

10 **Turn the finials.** Turn the shapes of the finials, as shown in the *Finial Layout.* Once again, use a round tenon gauge to help turn the round tenons on the ends of the finials to the proper diameter. As you make them, sand the finials smooth on the lathe, but don't sand the tenons.

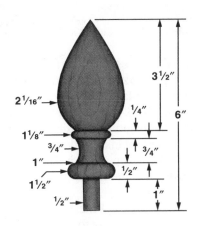

FINIAL LAYOUT

3½″
2 1/16″
¼″
1⅛″
¾″
¾″
1″
½″
1½″
½″
6″
1″

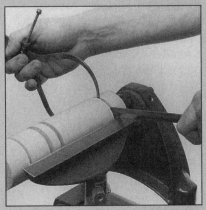

BLANKET RAIL END LAYOUT

9″
4″
½″
1½″
¼″
¼″
1″
1½″
¼″
1¼″
2″
1″
¾″
1″
1¼″
¾″
⅞″
2 5/16″

EXTRA INFO

DUPLICATING FINIALS

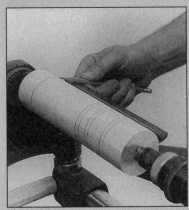

1 After rounding each turning square, mark the locations of the beads, coves, and flats on the surface.

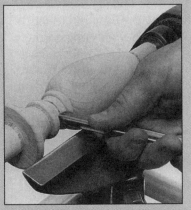

2 Using a parting tool, turn down to the "major" diameters (the crests of the beads), the "minor" diameters (the bottoms of the coves), and the beginnings of the flat or straight areas that form the tenons. Use a caliper to gauge these diameters.

3 Then cut the shapes, stopping when you get to the diameters that you turned with the parting tool. Some craftsmen shade the bottom of the grooves they make with the parting tool. The shading serves as an indicator — they know to stop turning when they start to remove the pencil marks.

Monday Afternoon

11 Assemble the headboard and footboard. Glue the blanket rail ends to the blanket rail. Insert the ends of the tenons on the headboard, rails, and blanket rail assembly into their respective holes in the posts, and clamp the parts together.

Using the counterbored bolt holes in the posts to guide your drill, bore ½-inch-diameter, 2¾-inch-deep holes in the ends of the rails, as shown in the *Rail End Layout*. These holes should pass through the 1-inch-diameter holes near the ends of the rails.

Insert bed bolts in the holes in the posts and rails with the flat washers under the heads. Reaching in through the 1-inch-diameter holes in the rails, thread a nut onto the end of each bolt. Tighten the bolts to hold the headboard and footboard assemblies together.

Stand the headboard and footboard assemblies on the floor beside the mattress frame. Have a helper hold them upright while you mark the locations of the holes in the connecting brackets of the frame. Drill pilot holes at these locations, then secure the headboard and footboard assemblies to the frame with lag screws.

TRY THIS

STABILIZING THE BED

To make the headboard and footboard assemblies as stable as possible, drill the pilot holes for the lag screws slightly higher on each post than your marks indicate. If the bed will rest on a hard floor, drill them about ¹⁄₁₆ inch high. If it will rest on a carpet, drill them ⅛ to ¼ inch high. By doing this, the bottoms of the posts will be slightly lower than the legs of the mattress frame. When you lie on the bed, the frame will transfer a good deal more weight to the posts than it would otherwise. This will plant the posts firmly on the floor and keep them from rocking.

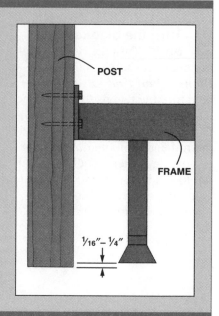

Finally, install bed bolt covers. Use four of these covers to cover the ends of the bed bolts, as shown in the *Headboard Assembly* and *Footboard Assembly*. The other four are just for show. (They would have covered the bed bolts that joined the headboard and footboard to side rails if you had used traditional side rails instead of a mattress frame.) Attach these dummy covers to the end faces of the posts, ¾ inch above the side covers.

At Your Leisure

12 Finish the bed. Detach the headboard and footboard assemblies from the frame, then disassemble the parts. Do any necessary touch-up sanding, then apply finish. Do not finish the surfaces of the mortises and tenons — you may want to mask them off. After the finish has dried and you have rubbed it to the desired luster, reassemble the bed.

Bonus FIXTURE: Round Tenon Gauge

When turning round tenons, make this simple "fixed calipers" from a scrap of ¼-inch plywood. Use it to gauge the diameter of the tenon as you turn. When the gauge slips over the tenon up to the first step, you know you're close — within ¹⁄₁₆ inch of the required diameter, so cut away stock very slowly. When the gauge slips over the tenon up to the round end, stop cutting.

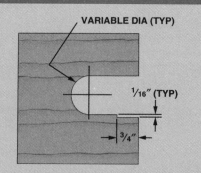

ROUND TENON GAUGE LAYOUT

Pro SKILL: Making Pencil Posts

Not long ago, Scott Phillips, host of *American Workshop,* asked if I would devise a simple method of making pencil posts for an upcoming show. We were both familiar with the traditional method that involves tedious layout and a great deal of hand planing. Scott was after something quicker and easier for his viewers. Here's the method I devised.

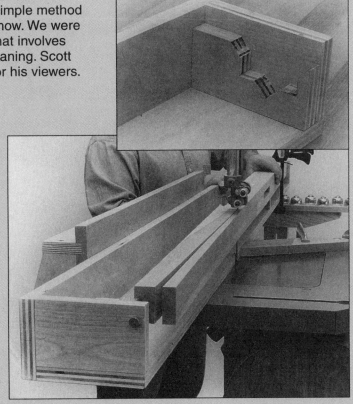

1 Mount the post in the post sawing jig. Place the bottom end in the holder, then insert the dowel in the top end and press it into the hole in the top of the post. The holder not only supports the bottom end of the post, it also indexes it, allowing you to secure it every 45 degrees. Turn the stock so the face you will be cutting is parallel to the band saw blade. Make sure the bottom end of the post butts against the bottom end of the jig, then clamp the post in the jig. Mount a resawing fence on your band saw, 6$\frac{1}{32}$ inches from the blade (equal to the width of the jig plus $\frac{1}{32}$ inch for cleanup). Cut a taper in one face of the stock, guiding the jig along the fence. Rotate the stock 90 degrees and repeat. Continue until you have cut all four *face* tapers.

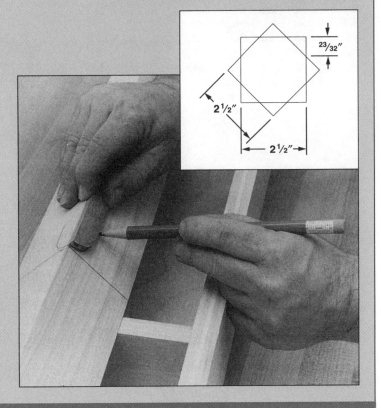

2 If you were to cut the corner tapers using this same method, they would continue almost all the way to the bottom end of the post. This is because the post is wider when measured diagonally from corner to corner than it is when measured across a face. To stop the corner tapers at the same point as the face tapers, you must cut *transition curves* in the corners. First, figure the radius of the curve. Draw two squares the same dimensions as the posts. Center one square over the other and turn it 45 degrees, to make an 8-pointed star. Measure along one of the arms of this star — that's your radius. On this post, the radius is precisely $\frac{23}{32}$ inch, but $\frac{3}{4}$ inch will be close enough. Mark this radius on both faces of each corner, 30 inches from the bottom end of the post. Also draw straight lines up from the curves, 1 or 2 inches long and parallel to the edges of the post.

(continued)

Pro SKILL: Making Pencil Posts — CONTINUED

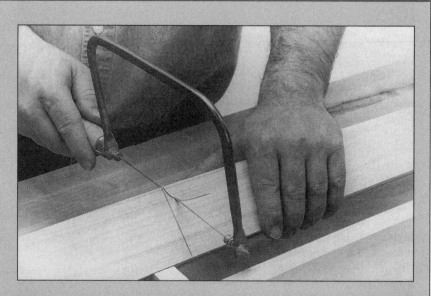

3 Using a coping saw, cut the transition curves in the corners, and follow the straight lines about an inch toward the top of the post. Take it slow, and monitor the layout lines on both faces as you cut each corner. Cut to the waste side of these lines. Later, you can sand or file the shape down to the line.

4 Rotate the stock in the jig so the faces are 45 degrees from the blade. Cut a corner taper, stopping immediately when the band saw blade meets up with the transition curve you cut with the coping saw. *Be careful not to cut into the curve!* Back the jig and post out of the saw, rotate the stock 90 degrees, and cut another corner. Continue until you have made all the corner tapers.

5 Smooth the cut surfaces with a block plane, scraper, and sandpaper. Don't plane or scrape too deeply; all the surfaces of the octagonal taper should appear the same size. **Tip:** The post sawing jig also makes a great holding jig when smoothing the tapers. Just clamp it to your workbench.

Oval Mirror

To make this mirror, you must draw several elliptical curves or "ovals." A double trammel, a special compass that pivots around two points, marks perfect ovals with no need to painstakingly lay out points on the curves.

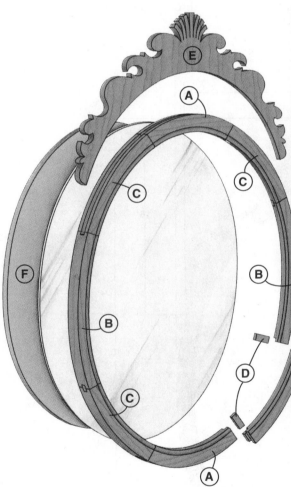

EXPLODED VIEW

MATERIALS LIST
Finished Dimensions in Inches

Parts

A.	Top/bottom frame members (2)	$\frac{3}{4}'' \times 3\frac{1}{2}'' \times 9\frac{5}{8}''$
B.	Left/right frame members (2)	$\frac{3}{4}'' \times 3\frac{1}{2}'' \times 14\frac{1}{2}''$
C.	Diagonal frame members (4)	$\frac{3}{4}'' \times 3\frac{1}{2}'' \times 12\frac{1}{2}''$
D.	Splines (8)	$\frac{1}{8}'' \times 3\frac{1}{2}'' \times \frac{3}{4}''$
E.	Fretwork	$\frac{1}{4}'' \times 21\frac{1}{2}'' \times 16''$
F.	Back*	$\frac{1}{8}'' \times 20\frac{3}{4}'' \times 31\frac{3}{4}''$

*Make this part from plywood or hardboard.

Hardware

$\frac{3}{4}''$ Wire brads (8–10)
$\frac{1}{4}''$ Eye screws (2)
Braided 50-lb. wire for hanging frame (24")
Oval mirror ($\frac{1}{8}'' \times 20\frac{5}{8}'' \times 31\frac{5}{8}''$)

If you cut an oval frame from a solid piece of wood, it will be weak where the wood grain runs across the width of the frame. Furthermore, it will expand more in one direction than another. To strengthen and stabilize the frame for his mirror, craftsman Charles Bales joined eight pieces of clear hardwood end to end to make an octagonal frame, then cut the octagon to an oval shape.

Friday Evening

1 Prepare the materials, and cut the parts to size.

To make this oval mirror, you need about 6 board feet of 4/4 (1-inch-thick) lumber and a quarter sheet (2 feet × 4 feet) of ⅛-inch hardboard. Charles' mirror frame is made from walnut, but you can use any cabinet-grade wood.

Plane the 4/4 stock to ¾ inch thick, and cut the frame members. Miter the ends of top and bottom members at 62 degrees and the side members at 73 degrees, as shown on the *Frame Layout.* Miter one end of each diagonal member at 62 degrees and the other end at 73 degrees.

Resaw the remaining stock in half, and plane it to ¼ inch thick. Glue this stock edge to edge to make a large, wide board for the fretwork. **Note:** The wood grain in the fretwork stock should run top to bottom, which is the *short* dimension of the board (what we normally think of as the width). The grain in the splines also runs through the short dimension.

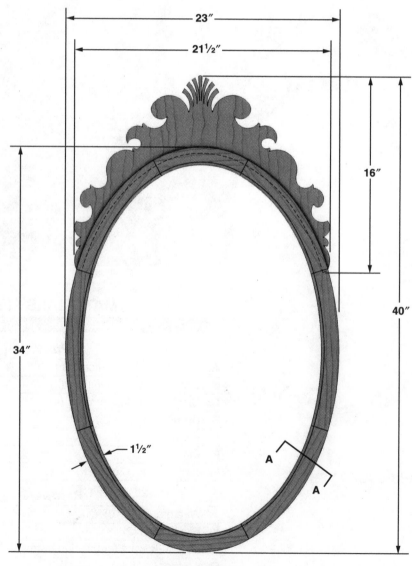

FRONT VIEW

Saturday Morning

2 **Cut spline joints in the frame members.** The frame members are joined at the ends with the splines, as shown in the *Frame Layout.* Cut ⅛-inch-wide, ⅜-inch-deep grooves in the mitered ends of the frame members to accept these splines. These grooves should be ¼ inch from the back surface.

Cut ⅛-inch-thick splines from the scraps that you cut from the frame members. Remember, the wood grain in the splines should run *across* the joints.

3 **Assemble the frame.** Glue the frame members end to end, inserting splines in the grooves you just cut. Clamp the frame together with a band clamp while the glue dries.

To cut the spline grooves, clamp the frame members to a tenoning jig so the mitered end rests flat on the worktable. Use the jig to guide the parts over a dado cutter or a table-mounted router.

Saturday Afternoon

4 **Lay out the oval shapes.** There are four elliptical curves or ovals in this project — the outside curve of the frame, the inside curve, the curved edge of the fretwork that joins the frame, and the shape of the back. Each curve has a different major axis (long dimension) and minor axis (short dimension):

	MAJOR AXIS	MINOR AXIS
Outside Frame	34″	23″
Inside Frame	31″	20″
Fretwork	33″	22″
Back	31¾″	20¾″

Draw these shapes with a *Double Trammel,* as shown on page 185. Drill two pivot holes (A and B) in the beam for each oval. The center-to-center distance from the pencil hole to each pivot hole must be half the major or minor axis.

See Also:
"Drawing Ovals" on page 187.

	HOLE A	HOLE B
Outside Frame	17″	11½″
Inside Frame	15½″	10″
Fretwork	16½″	11″
Back	15⅞″	10⅜″

Note: When marking the ovals on the frame, rest the base

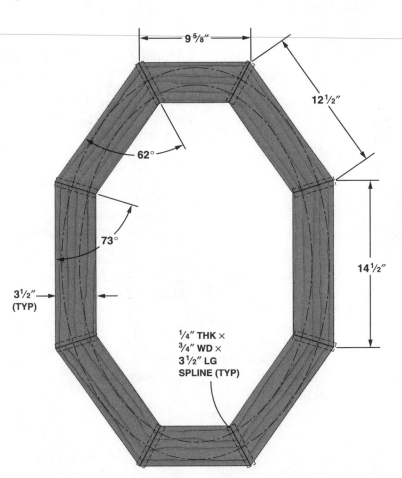

FRAME LAYOUT

9⅝″

12½″

62°

73°

14½″

3½″ (TYP)

¼″ THK × ¾″ WD × 3½″ LG SPLINE (TYP)

of the trammel on a ¾-inch-thick scrap so it's at the same height as the frame members. When marking the curve on the fretwork stock, place the base on a ¼-inch-thick scrap.

5 **Lay out the fretwork.** Enlarge the *Fretwork Pattern,* and trace it on the fretwork stock.

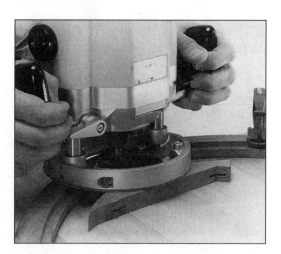

To help balance the router when cutting the rabbet, attach a scrap the same thickness as the frame to the base of the router with double-faced carpet tape.

Saturday Evening

6 **Cut the ovals and the fretwork.** Cut the profiles of the ovals and the fretwork with a scroll saw or a coping saw. Sand the sawed edges smooth.

7 **Round over the outside edge of the frame.** With a router and a piloted ¼-inch-radius roundover bit, round over the outside edge of the frame, as shown in *Section A.*

Sunday Afternoon

8 **Rout the grooves and rabbets in the frame.** Using a router and a piloted rabbeting bit, cut a ⅜-inch-wide, ⅜-inch-deep rabbet in the inside edge of the frame, as shown in *Section A.* With a piloted slot-cutting bit, cut a ¼-inch-wide, ½-inch-deep groove in the outside edge for the fretwork, as

shown in the *Joinery Detail.* Square the ends of the groove with a chisel.

9 **Scratch a bead on the inside edge of the frame.** The inside edge of the oval frame is decorated with a small bead, as shown in *Section A.* This bead isn't cut; rather it's scraped or "scratched." To create the bead, make a *Scratch Stock,* as shown on page 186, and gently scrape around the inside edge, removing a little stock at a time. Keep the scratch stock firmly against the edge as you work. After a few passes, the bead will begin to take shape. Continue scraping until the bead is a uniform depth and shape all around the frame.

Note: A scratch stock creates a much smoother shape if you apply only modest pressure, especially when you start to scrape. If you press too hard, the blade will tear the wood.

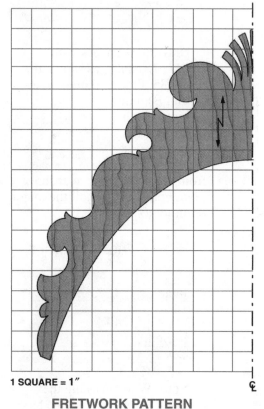

1 SQUARE = 1″

FRETWORK PATTERN

¼″ RAD

¼″

BEAD

¾″

1½″

⅜″ WD × ⅜″ DP RABBET

SECTION A

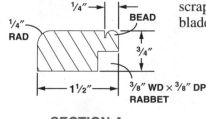

FRETWORK

¼″ WD × ½″ DP GROOVE

WIRE BRAD

BACK

JOINERY DETAIL

Quick FIXTURE: Double Trammel

An ellipse or *oval* is an arc that curves around two points or *foci*. To draw a perfect oval, draftsmen use a *double trammel,* a unique compass that swings around two points. It works much like the "smoke grinders" you often see at craft fairs. The beam fits over two pivots, and the pivots travel back and forth in slots. The slots cross at right angles.

To make a double trammel, rout two T-slots in a plywood base. Insert 5/16-inch-diameter *closet bolts* (also called flange bolts and T-slot bolts) in the slots.

Drill a 9/32-inch-diameter hole near the end of the beam to hold a pencil. A standard pencil is slightly larger than this, but you will be able to

press the pencil into the hole. If not, cut a slot parallel to the length of the beam that splits the hole. This will allow the wood to give slightly as you press the pencil into the hole.

Along the length of the beam drill two 5/16-inch-diameter pivot holes — the positions of these holes depend on the size of the oval you want to draw. Fasten the beam to the base with wing nuts and washers, inserting the bolts in the 5/16-inch-diameter holes.

Note: The size of the base determines the dimensions of the ovals that you can draw. To calculate length of a side on the square base, subtract the minor axis from the major axis and add 1 inch.

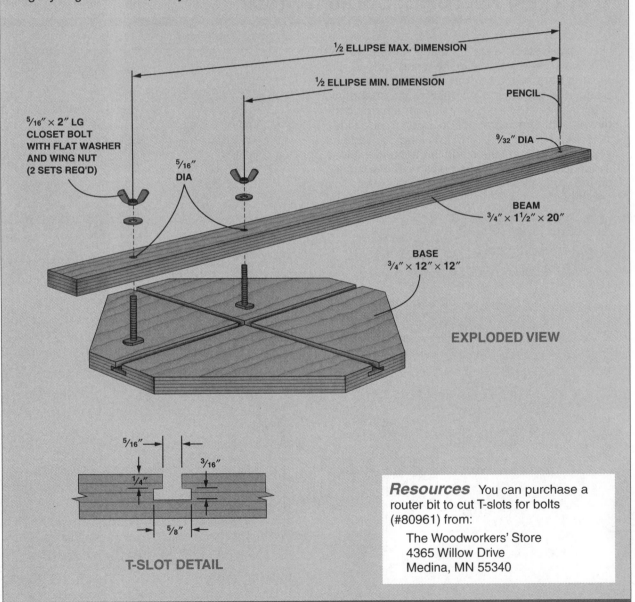

½ ELLIPSE MAX. DIMENSION

½ ELLIPSE MIN. DIMENSION

PENCIL

5/16" × 2" LG CLOSET BOLT WITH FLAT WASHER AND WING NUT (2 SETS REQ'D)

5/16" DIA

9/32" DIA

BEAM 3/4" × 1½" × 20"

BASE 3/4" × 12" × 12"

EXPLODED VIEW

5/16"

3/16"

1/4"

5/8"

T-SLOT DETAIL

Sunday Evening

10 **Assemble the oval frame.** Finish sand the completed frame and fretwork, then glue the fretwork in the grooved edge of the frame.

At Your Leisure

11 **Finish the mirror frame.** Do any necessary touch-up sanding, then apply a finish to the assembled mirror frame. After rubbing out the finish, install an oval mirror in the frame rabbet. Insert the back behind the mirror, then secure both the mirror and the back with wire brads. To hang the mirror, install eye screws in the back of the frame, and stretch braided 50-pound picture-hanging wire between them.

Note: Most glass shops will cut an oval mirror for you. However, many prefer you leave the frame with them so they can fit the mirror to it. If this is the case, you may wish to take the frame to them *before* you attach the fretwork or apply the finish.

Bonus FIXTURE: Scratch Stock

A scratch stock holds a shaped scraper so you can scrape a shape in the wood surface. Cut a blade from an old scraper or a used hacksaw blade, and grind it to a negative of the shape you want to create. Make a handle from a hardwood dowel, cutting a flat rabbet or a step in one side. This step serves as a pilot, following the edge as you scrape. Clamp the blade in the handle. Move it side to side to adjust the position of the shape on the work, and up and down to adjust the depth of cut.

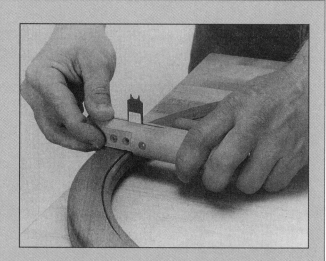

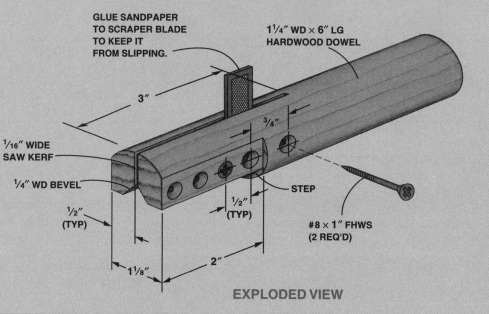

GLUE SANDPAPER TO SCRAPER BLADE TO KEEP IT FROM SLIPPING.

1¼" WD × 6" LG HARDWOOD DOWEL

3"

¾"

1⁄16" WIDE SAW KERF

¼" WD BEVEL

STEP

½" (TYP)

½" (TYP)

#8 × 1" FHWS (2 REQ'D)

1⅛"

2"

EXPLODED VIEW

Pro SKILL: Drawing Ovals

To draw an oval or an elliptical curve with a double trammel, first decide how large to make the shape. Every oval has a long dimension (called the major axis) and a short one (the minor axis).

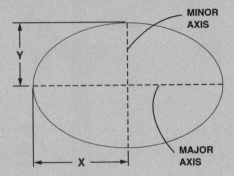

1 Lay out the major and minor axes on your work. The two lines should cross at right angles, and the point of intersection should be halfway along both lines.

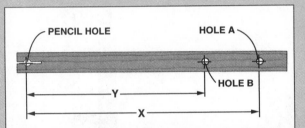

2 The positions of the pivot holes on the beam depend on the size of the oval. The distance from the pencil to pivot hole A must be half the major axis, and the distance to pivot hole B must be half the minor axis. Lay out the positions of the pivot holes on the beam and drill them.

3 Center the base of the double trammel over the axes, aligning the center of the long slot with the major axis and the center of the short slot with the minor axis. Secure the base to the work with double-faced carpet tape. Note that I've attached a spacer to the base the same thickness as the frame.

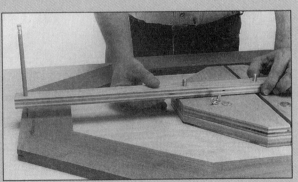

4 Attach the beam to the base. Fit hole A over the bolt that rides in the long slot and hole B over the bolt in the short slot. Tighten the wing nuts that hold the beam so they are snug, then back them off ⅛ turn. Check that the bolts can slide freely in the slots. (The wing nuts may loosen slightly as you draw the oval. This is okay; it will not affect the shape of the oval.)

5 Swing the beam around the base counterclockwise, drawing an oval with the pencil. As you do this, keep a small amount of tension on the beam, pulling out from the base. This will take any play out of the double trammel and keep the curves "fair," with no flat spots or steps.

Clothes Tree

Once in a while, you run across a project that requires you to drill an accurate hole in the end of a post or spindle. If you don't have a horizontal boring machine handy, don't worry. You can do a great job with an inexpensive drill guide and a horizontal boring jig.

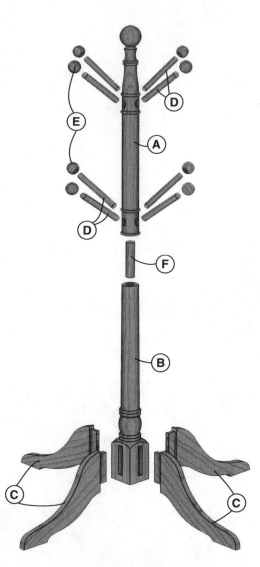

EXPLODED VIEW

MATERIALS LIST

Finished Dimensions in Inches

Parts		
A.	Top post	2¾″ dia. × 30″
B.	Bottom post	2¾″ × 2¾″ × 30″
C.	Legs (4)	¾″ × 5³⁄₁₆″ × 16³⁄₁₆″
D.	Pegs (8)	¾″ dia. × 6″
E.	Beads (8)	1½″ dia.
F.	Dowel	1″ dia. × 6″

Like many craftsmen, Ralph Sprang doesn't have a long-bed lathe to make long turnings. So he turned the 5-foot-long spindle for this clothes tree in two sections. They are joined at a crisp "transition" in the turning, where the shape of the spindle changes from a long, gentle taper to a small bead. In a one-piece turning, there would have been a line at this juncture. By joining the parts here, Ralph made the seam almost impossible to detect.

3/4" DIA ×
3/4" DP HOLE
IN 1½" DIA BEAD

3/4" × 6" DOWEL
(8 REQ'D)

30"

1" × 6"
DOWEL IN
1" × 3¹/₁₆" DP
HOLES IN TOP
AND BOTTOM
POSTS

64"

ROUND
OVER
TOP
EDGE.

30"

3/8" WD × 1¹/₁₆" DP
MORTISE (TYP)

4 3/4"

10"

27 1/8"

FRONT VIEW

Resources Hardwood dowels and beads are available from several different mail-order woodworking supply companies, including:

Woodworker's Supply
1108 North Glenn Road
Casper, WY 82601

Friday Evening

1 Prepare the materials, and cut the parts to size.
To make the posts for this clothes tree, you need two 12/4 (3-inch-square) turning blanks, each about 3 feet long. For the remaining parts, you need two 3-foot lengths of ¾-inch-diameter dowel stock, a short piece (6 inches) of 1-inch-diameter dowel stock, eight 1½-inch diameter hardwood beads, and about 5 board feet of 4/4 (1-inch-thick) lumber. Ralph's clothes tree is made from cherry with maple pegs and beads, but you can use any cabinet-grade wood.

TRY THIS

SQUARING STOCK

To square a turning blank, joint two adjacent faces 90 degrees to one another. Feed the stock through a planer, planing one of the remaining faces. Turn it 90 degrees to plane the last face, and feed it through again *without changing the thickness setting.*

Note: Although hardwood dowels are available in several wood species, beads are commonly offered only in maple or birch. As an alternative, you might turn each bead and peg as a single piece from an 8/4 (2-inch-thick) turning blank.

True up the 12/4 turning blanks, making them 2¾ inches square. Cut the top post to 32 inches long, and the bottom post to 30 inches long.

Plane the 4/4 stock to ¾ inch thick, and cut the stock for the legs. Also cut the pegs and the 1-inch dowel to size.

See Also:
"Cutting Round Stock"
on page 240.

If you use the drill guide to bore the peg mortises, clamp the base of the guide to the stock to prevent it from shifting as you make each hole. If you use a drill press for this task, clamp the stock to the drill press table or it will walk "downhill" as you feed the quill.

Saturday Morning

2 Bore the mortises that join the posts. It's much easier to cut all the joinery while the posts are square. Begin by making the round mortises that join the posts. Make the *Horizontal Boring Jig* on this page. Then using the jig and a drill guide, bore 1-inch-diameter, 3¹⁄₁₆-inch-deep holes in the adjoining ends of the posts, as shown in the *Front View.*

3 Drill the peg mortises in the top post. Lay out the locations of the ¾-inch-

diameter, 1¹¹⁄₁₆-inch-deep round peg mortises, as shown in the *Peg Mortise Layout (in Square Stock).* Note that on the square stock, these mortises are ⅜ inch above the locations shown in the turned post. This is because the mortises are angled. As you cut away stock from the spindle, the mortise locations shift toward the bottom end of the post, as shown in the *Peg Mortise Layout (in Turned Post).*

You can drill these mortises on a drill press, but you'll find

it's just as accurate to make them with a portable drill and drill guide. Before you drill the lower set of mortises, insert the dowel in the round mortise in the end of the post. The drill bit will bite into this dowel slightly as you make the mortises. Mark the dowel and the post end so you put the dowel back in the same position when you assemble the clothes tree.

Quick FIXTURE: Horizontal Boring Jig

This fixture is used with a drilling guide and a portable drill to bore precise holes in the ends of legs, posts, and turning stock. The sides or legs of the jig hold it to the work, while the top provides a flat, steady platform for the drilling guide.

To make the jig, create a wide slot in the top, cutting diagonally from one corner. Assemble the legs in a V-shape, then attach the top to them.

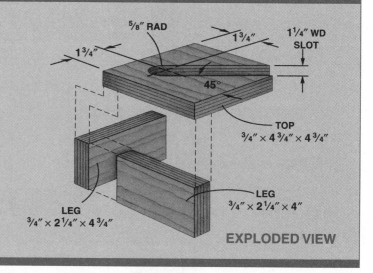

5⁄8" RAD

1¾"

1¾"

1¼" WD SLOT

45°

TOP
¾" × 4¾" × 4¾"

LEG
¾" × 2¼" × 4"

LEG
¾" × 2¼" × 4¾"

EXPLODED VIEW

Saturday Afternoon

4 **Drill the round mortises in the beads.** On a drill press, drill ¾-inch-diameter, ¾-inch-deep mortises in the wooden beads. Align each bead to drill parallel to the grain.

5 **Rout the leg mortises in the bottom post.** The legs are joined to the bottom post by mortise-and-tenon joints. Rout ⅜-inch-wide, 1¹⁄₁₆-inch-deep, 4¾-inch-long mortises in each face of the bottom post turning blank, as shown in the ***Bottom Post Layout.***

See Also:
"Routing Mortises" on page 28.

The challenge in drilling a bead or a wooden ball is to position it directly under the bit and prevent it from rolling. To do this, clamp a ¾-inch-thick scrap board to the table of the drill press. Drill a ¾-inch-diameter, ½-inch-deep hole in the board, then rest the bead in the hole. Hold the bead in a clamp as you drill.

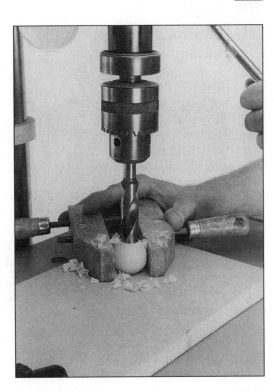

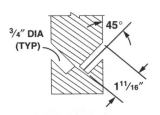

PEG MORTISE DETAIL
(IN SQUARE STOCK)

¾″ DIA (TYP) 45° 1¹¹⁄₁₆″

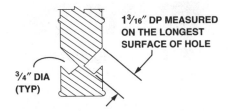

1³⁄₁₆″ DP MEASURED ON THE LONGEST SURFACE OF HOLE

¾″ DIA (TYP)

PEG MORTISE DETAIL
(IN TURNED POST)

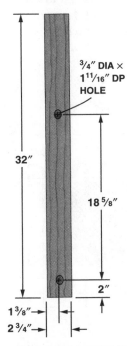

¾″ DIA × 1¹¹⁄₁₆″ DP HOLE

32″

18⅝″

2″

1⅜″

2¾″

PEG MORTISE LAYOUT
(IN SQUARE STOCK)

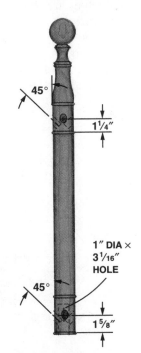

45°

1¼″

1″ DIA × 3¹⁄₁₆″ HOLE

45°

1⅝″

PEG MORTISE LAYOUT
(IN TURNED POST)

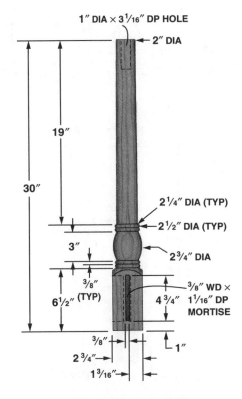

1″ DIA × 3¹⁄₁₆″ DP HOLE

2″ DIA

19″

30″

2¼″ DIA (TYP)

2½″ DIA (TYP)

3″

2¾″ DIA

⅜″

6½″ (TYP)

⅜″ WD × 1¹⁄₁₆″ DP MORTISE

4¾″

⅜″

1″

2¾″

1³⁄₁₆″

BOTTOM POST LAYOUT

Saturday Evening

6 **Turn the posts.**
Temporarily, plug the round mortises in the ends of the post blanks with scraps of 1-inch-diameter dowel. Mount the blanks on a lathe, and turn the shapes shown in the *Top Post Layout* and *Bottom Post Layout*. When turning the top post, remove stock very slowly in the vicinity of the peg mortises. You don't want the chisel to catch on the edge of a hole and tear out the wood.

When you have turned the shapes, finish sand each post on the lathe. Part the scrap from the top end of the top post, and sand the ball shape perfectly round.

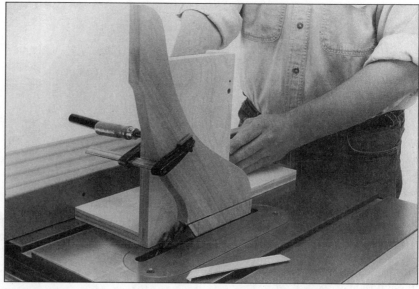

When making the tenons on the ends of the legs, clamp each leg in a tenoning jig to cut the cheeks and shoulders. Then remove the leg from the jig, and cut the tops and bottoms of the tenons freehand, using a band saw or a dovetail saw.

Sunday Afternoon

7 **Cut the leg profiles.**
Enlarge the *Leg Pattern* and trace it on one of the leg boards. Stack the leg boards face to face with the marked board on top. Tape the stack together so the ends and edges are flush, then cut the entire stack on a band saw. (If you don't have a band saw, you can cut the legs two at a time with a saber saw.) Sand the sawed edges.

8 **Cut the tenons in the legs.** To create the tenons on the ends of the legs, cut 1-inch-long cheeks and ³⁄₁₆-inch-wide shoulders in all four surfaces of each leg. Fit the tenons to the mortises in the bottom post.

See Also:
"Cutting Tenons" on page 121.

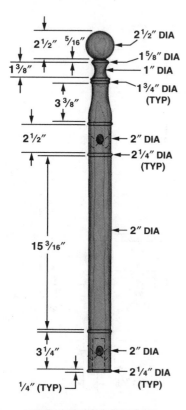

TOP POST LAYOUT

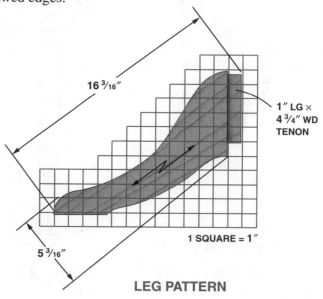

LEG PATTERN

Sunday Evening

9 **Round over the legs.** Using a table-mounted router and a ¼-inch-radius roundover bit, round over the top edges of the legs, as shown in the *Front View.*

10 **Assemble the clothes tree.** Finish sand all the wooden parts, then assemble the parts with glue. First, attach the pegs and beads. Insert the dowel in the round mortise in the end of the top post and — before the glue has a chance to set up — insert the

pegs in their mortises. (That way, if the dowel isn't perfectly aligned, you can reposition it when you insert the pegs.) Attach the legs to the bottom post, then join the top and bottom assemblies.

Note: Because the legs aren't square, they are difficult to secure with ordinary clamps. Instead, wrap lengths of surgical tubing or strips of an old inner tube around the legs after you glue them to the post. This will secure them until the glue dries.

At Your Leisure

11 **Finish the clothes tree.** Do any necessary touch-up sanding, then apply a finish to the assembled tree. Because the surfaces of the posts are fairly intricate, use something that's easy to sand between coats. A wiping varnish or oil is easy to sand and rub because it's applied in such thin coats. And if you apply several coats, it's reasonably durable.

Pro SKILL: Boring End Grain

Drilling into the ends of boards — cutting parallel to the wood grain — requires more power and creates more friction. It takes more work to cut the wood fibers in two than it does to shave them. Consequently, your choice of bits and drilling technique is more important.

Brad point bits and spade bits are your best choices for drilling end grain. Avoid Forstner bits and multispur bits — these tend to overheat and catch on the wood. Turn the bit at a slower speed than you would normally use, and feed it at a moderate rate to help keep it cool.

1 Mark the location of the holes on the end of the stock. If you want to position a hole in the precise center, use a center finder or a straightedge and a center head to draw two lines across the end. On square stock, the lines should stretch diagonally from corner to corner; on round stock, they should cross at approximately 90 degrees. Where the lines cross is the center of the stock.

2 Clamp a horizontal boring jig to the end of the work. The marks for the holes should show through the slot. Attach a drill guide to your portable drill. Place the guide against the top of the jig, align the bit with the mark, and bore the hole.

Ring Holder

How do you shape the very end of a turning when it's too small to mount to a faceplate? Fasten it to a screw chuck.

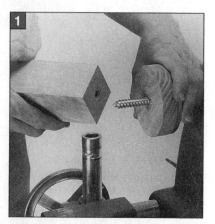

Craftsman Marion Curry was tired of losing track of her wedding ring every time she took it off to do the dishes or apply a finish. So she made these attractive "ring holders" — tiny turned stands with a neck slightly smaller than the average ring finger. "If you keep one of these handy," says Marion, "you'll know where to put your wedding ring when you take it off and where to look for it when you want to put it back on."

Saturday Afternoon

1 **Mount the turning blank in the lathe.** To make a ring holder, you need a turning blank 2 to 3 inches square and 5 to 6 inches long. Any wood species will do, provided it's free of defects that might cause it to come apart on the lathe.

Make the *Screw Chuck,* as shown on page 196, and attach it to your lathe faceplate. Mount the stock to the screw chuck, then mount the faceplate on the lathe.

Find the center of the stock on one end, and drill a 7/16-inch-diameter, 1¾-inch-deep hole in it. Turn the blank onto the lag screw in the screw chuck. Then mount the assembly to your lathe.

194

2 Round the blank. Engage the tailstock center at the other end of the blank so you're turning between two centers. Turn the blank round.

3 Turn the shape of the ring holder. Once the stock is round, make the cove, beads, and flats that form the shape of the ring holder. You can follow either *Ring Holder #1 Layout* or *Ring Holder #2 Layout,* if you wish, or turn a shape of your own design.

It's best to turn as much of the shape as you can with the live center engaged — this provides more support. Advance the tailstock until the live center bites into the stock. Then round the turning blank.

Don't turn the bottom 2 inches of the blank (the portion resting against the screw center). This is waste; you'll cut it off when you complete the holder. By doing this, the holder won't have a large hole in the bottom.

TRY THIS

FINDING THE DYNAMIC CENTER

The tailstock should engage the *dynamic center* of the blank, the end of the turning axis. Usually this is pretty close to the geometric center, but if the end of the blank that rests against the screw center isn't perfectly square or the mounting hole is a hair off-center, the dynamic center and the geometric center may be different. To find the dynamic center, simply advance the tailstock until it touches the end of the blank. As long as the tailstock is aligned precisely with the turning axis, it will contact the blank at the dynamic center.

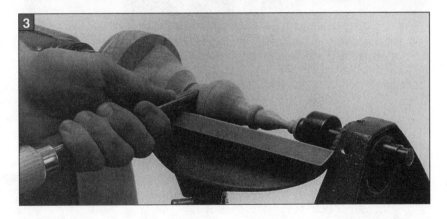

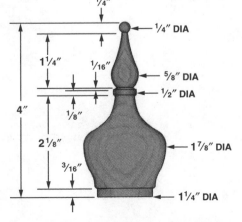

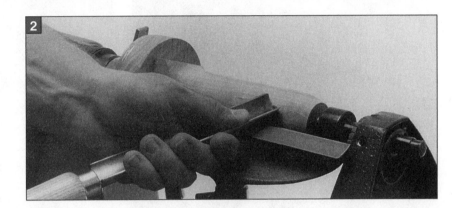

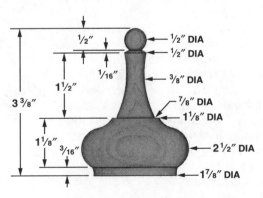

RING HOLDER #1 LAYOUT

RING HOLDER #2 LAYOUT

4 **Turn the end of the holder.** Part the waste at the top of the turning, cutting almost through the blank. Leave a ¼- to ⅜-inch-diameter neck. Back the tailstock and the live center away from the stock and sever the waste with a hand saw. Then shape the very end of the turning.

5 **Sand and finish the ring holder.** Sand the ring holder smooth on the lathe, beginning with 100-grit sandpaper and working your way up to 220-grit. Then apply a finish on the lathe.

6 **Remove the waste from the bottom of the ring holder.** Part the ring holder from the waste at the bottom, leaving a small neck as you did before. Cut through the neck with a hand saw. Sand the very bottom of the ring holder and apply a finish to it.

Part the waste from the top of the turning and back off the live center so the stock is held by the screw chuck only. Turn the very top of the ring holder. Use a very light touch, otherwise the turning may whip as it spins.

Finish sand the ring holder on the lathe. The friction of the lathe against the abrasive builds up a lot of heat, especially when using the finer grits. Protect your fingers by wrapping the paper around a pad of steel wool. When you have sanded the holder, apply a finish.

Quick FIXTURE: Screw Chuck

A screw chuck lets you turn with either one center or two, as needed. It's an expensive gizmo, especially when you consider that you'll only use it for a handful of projects — like the ring holder. However, you can easily make your own. Cut a round disc out of stock that is truly flat and uniform in thickness. Drill a ½-inch-diameter hole with a ¾-inch-diameter, ⁵⁄₁₆-inch-deep counterbore through the center. With a chisel, cut the counterbore to a hexagonal shape. Insert a ½-inch × 2½-inch lag screw in the hole, pressing the head into the counterbore. Attach the disc to a faceplate.

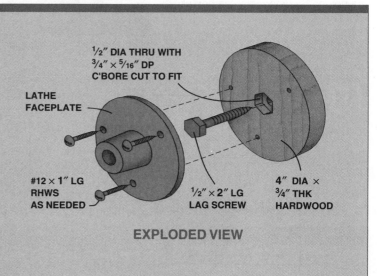

½" DIA THRU WITH
¾" × ⁵⁄₁₆" DP
C'BORE CUT TO FIT

LATHE
FACEPLATE

#12 × 1" LG
RHWS
AS NEEDED

½" × 2" LG
LAG SCREW

4" DIA ×
¾" THK
HARDWOOD

EXPLODED VIEW

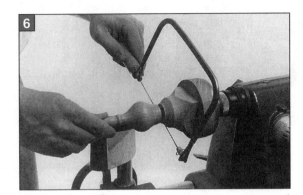

6

Part the waste from the bottom of the ring holder, but don't completely remove it. Leave a small neck. Then turn off the lathe, let it come to a complete stop, and saw through the neck with a hand saw.

Pro SKILL: Finishing on the Lathe

One of the most appealing aspects of lathe turning is that you can actually finish your work right on the lathe. This makes the lathe the only power tool where you can begin and end a project without ever having to use another tool.

You can apply almost any finish on the lathe, but penetrating finishes such as tung oil seem to work best. Master turner Rude Osolnik gave me a recipe that I've used for years — add 1 tablespoon of spar varnish to 1 cup of tung oil. This builds a gloss faster and is decidedly harder than tung oil alone, but it retains the deep luster of tung oil.

1 When applying finish on a lathe, take care not to apply too much, otherwise the spinning shape will throw it everywhere. Dip a small rag in the finish, squeeze out most of the liquid, then hold the rag against the project as it spins at low speed. Keep the loose corners of the rag away from the turning, but don't wrap it around your fingers, just in case the rag catches on the wood. Some turners recommend applying a finish with abrasive pads, claiming the fine abrasive on a green pad (equal to about 320 grit) or a dark gray pad (600 grit) create an ultra-smooth surface.

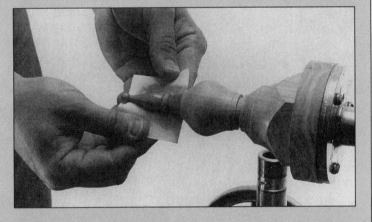

2 If you want an *instant* finish (one that requires no drying time), apply hard wax to the turning. Most turners prefer pure carnauba (available through most mail-order finishing suppliers), but you can also use ordinary paraffin. Hold the block of wax against the spinning shape, and coat as much of the surface as you can. Then spread the wax out, and work it into the crevices with an abrasive pad. The friction of the pad on the wood melts the wax and lets it penetrate the wood. After a few applications of wax, the turning will develop a deep shine. **Note:** Because the wax never forms a hard film, you shouldn't use this finish on objects that will see a lot of wear and tear.

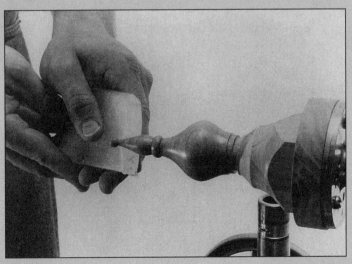

Bed Storage Platform

■ **QUICK FIXTURE**
Circular Saw Guide

■ **PRO SKILL**
Cutting Plywood

Cutting large sheets of plywood in a small shop can be a daunting task. However, a simple circular saw guide cuts it down to a manageable size.

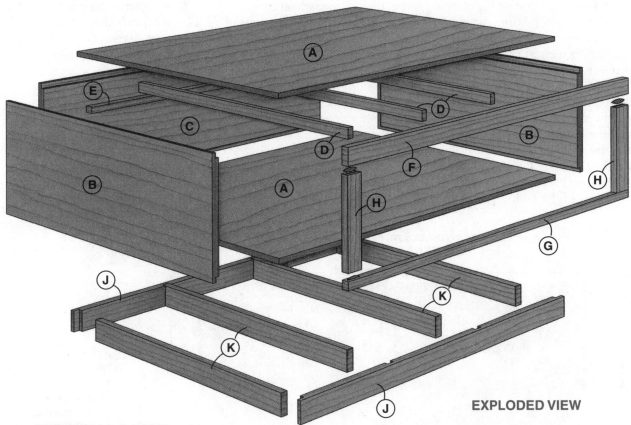

EXPLODED VIEW

MATERIALS LIST

Finished Dimensions in Inches

Parts (for 4 units)

A.	Top/ bottom* (8)	¾″ × 28⅞″ × 39¼″
B.	Sides* (8)	¾″ × 16″ × 29¼″
C.	Back* (4)	¾″ × 16″ × 39¼″
D.	Braces (12)	¾″ × 1½″ × 28½″
E.	Cleat (4)	¾″ × ¾″ × 38½″
F.	Face frame top rail (4)	¾″ × 2¼″ × 40″
G.	Face frame bottom rail (4)	¾″ × 1″ × 40″
H.	Face frame stiles (8)	¾″ × 2″ × 12¾″
J.	Plinth front/back (8)	¾″ × 3″ × 37″
K.	Plinth sides/ stretchers (16)	¾″ × 3″ × 26″

Make these parts from plywood.

Hardware

#8 × 1½″ Flathead wood screws (150–200)

#10 × 1½″ Roundhead wood screws (32)

#00 Biscuits (16)

⁵⁄₁₆″ × 2″ Carriage bolts, hex nuts, and flat washers (8 sets)

This simple storage platform makes good use of the otherwise wasted space beneath a bed. It comes apart in four easy-to-build, easy-to move units. Each unit is a reinforced box, open on one side. Arrange the boxes so the open sides faces out, allowing you to reach the space inside. If you wish, fit the boxes with pull-out shelves or drawers.

The boxes can be built to any size to support different sizes of mattresses. They are strong enough to support both standard bedding and water beds. And you can bolt or screw almost any type of headboard or footboard to them.

Friday Evening

1 Decide the size of the platform and figure the dimensions of the parts.

The size of the storage units you build will depend on the size of your bedding and the height at which you want the platform to hold your bed. As shown in the drawings, the platform is designed to hold a queen-size water bed. The mattress that rests upon it is 80 inches long, 60 inches wide, and 8 inches thick. The bed height that my wife and I decided on was 27 inches. So the overall size of the assembled platform is 80 inches × 60 inches × 19 inches.

To figure the size of the platform you want to build, measure the bedding you want to rest on it. (There's a chart of standard bedding sizes on page 172 in the Pencil Post Bed chapter.) Also decide the height of the bed. The length of each platform unit is half the length of the bedding, and the width is half the bedding width. The height of the platform units is the bed height less the thickness of the bedding. From these overall sizes, you can figure the specific dimensions of each part.

Remember to allow for the base or *plinth* when calculating the height of the platform. The plinth is 3 inches tall and 3 inches shorter and narrower than the units themselves. This creates a 3-inch-tall, 3-inch-deep toe space all around the assembled platform so you won't stub your toes on the units.

2 Prepare the materials, and cut the solid wood parts to size. The amount of materials needed to make the platform depends on its size, of course. I made the queen-size platform you see here from five sheets of 3/4-inch plywood and about 30 board feet of 4/4 (1-inch-thick) lumber. The platform shown is made from birch plywood and poplar lumber, but you can use any cabinet-grade materials.

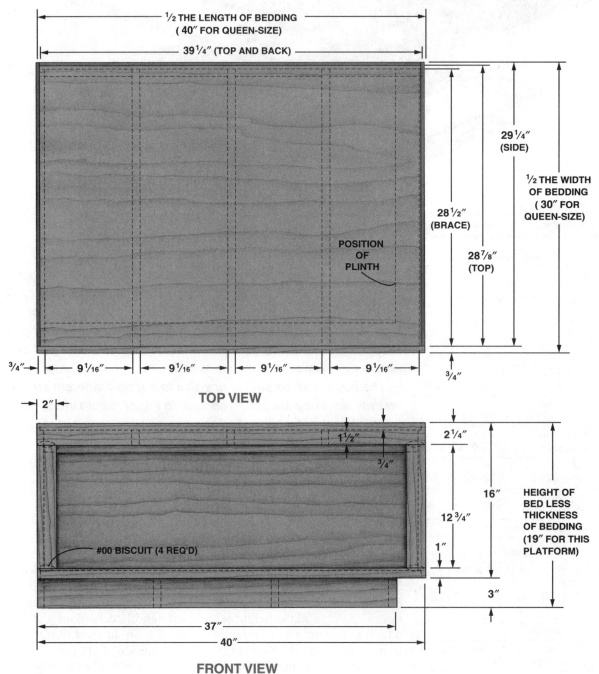

TOP VIEW

FRONT VIEW

Plane the 4/4 stock to ¾ inch thick, then cut all the solid wood parts to size — face frame members, plinth members, braces, and cleat.

Saturday Morning

3 **Cut the plywood parts to size.** Cutting up 4 × 8-foot sheets of plywood in a small shop can be a chore, but you can save time and effort by making a *Circular Saw Guide,* as shown on page 202. Use the guide, along with a circular saw and a high-quality plywood blade, to cut the plywood parts to size.

Bonus FIXTURE: Cutting Grid

When cutting plywood with a circular saw, the sheet should be supported on both sides of the cut line. It mustn't bend or droop as you make the cut. To properly support it, make a simple grid from 2×4s, and lay it across the saw horses.

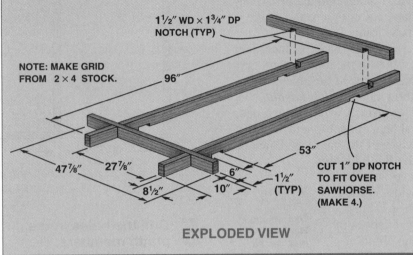

1½" WD × 1¾" DP NOTCH (TYP)

NOTE: MAKE GRID FROM 2 × 4 STOCK.

96"

47⅞" 27⅞"

8½" 10" 6"

1½" (TYP)

53"

CUT 1" DP NOTCH TO FIT OVER SAWHORSE. (MAKE 4.)

EXPLODED VIEW

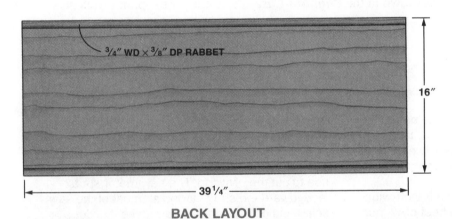

¾" WD × ⅜" DP RABBET

16"

39¼"

BACK LAYOUT

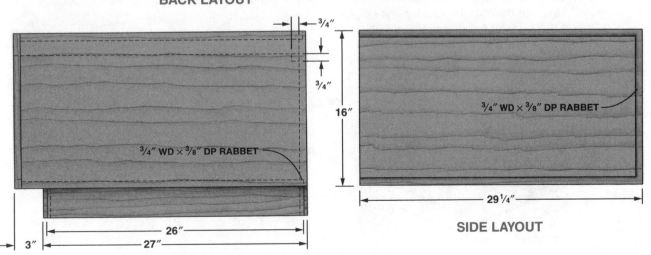

¾"

¾"

16"

¾" WD × ⅜" DP RABBET

26"

27"

3"

SIDE VIEW

¾" WD × ⅜" DP RABBET

16"

29¼"

SIDE LAYOUT

Saturday Afternoon

4 Cut the joinery in the case and plinth parts.

The plywood cases and the plinths they rest upon are joined with rabbets and dadoes. Using a dado cutter or a router, make these joints:

■ ³⁄₄-inch-wide, ³⁄₈-inch-deep rabbets in the top, bottom, and back edges of the sides, as shown in the *Side Layout*

■ ³⁄₄-inch-wide, ³⁄₈-inch-deep rabbets in the top and bottom edges of the back, as shown in the *Back Layout*

■ ³⁄₄-inch-wide, ¹⁄₄-inch deep rabbets and dadoes in the plinth fronts and backs, as shown in the *Plinth/ Top View*

See Also:

"Routing Dadoes and Rabbets" on page 59.

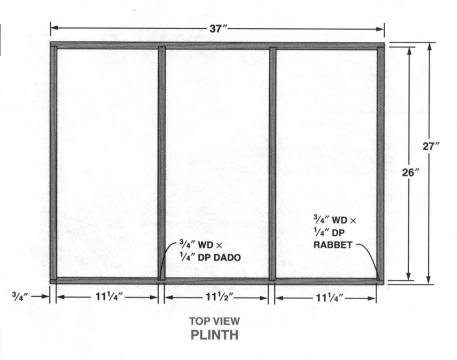

TOP VIEW
PLINTH

5 Drill the holes in the plinth members.
The assembled plinth is screwed to the bottom of the plywood case, as shown in the *Plinth-to-Case*

Joinery Detail. Drill ³⁄₁₆-inch-diameter pilot holes with ³⁄₈-inch-diameter, 2-inch deep counterbores through the *width* of the plinth stretchers.

Quick FIXTURE: Circular Saw Guide

A circular saw guide lets you make perfectly straight cuts with a handheld circular saw. The straightedge guides the saw, while the base makes it easy to position the straightedge before each cut.

To make the straightedge, cut a 3-inch-wide strip from the *factory* edge of a sheet of ³⁄₄-inch plywood. As it comes from the factory, the edges of plywood are straight enough that you can use them to guide a saw. Cut the base from ¹⁄₄-inch plywood, making it a little wider than necessary. Glue the parts together so the *sawed* edge (not

the factory edge) of the straightedge is flush with one edge of the base.

After the glue dries, cut the base to width using the same circular saw and blade you will use to cut the plywood. The saw motor should face toward the straightedge so most of the saw's sole rests on the base as you make this cut.

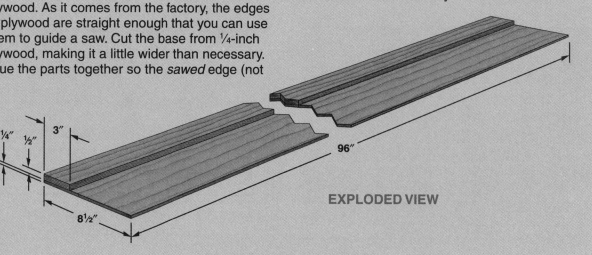

EXPLODED VIEW

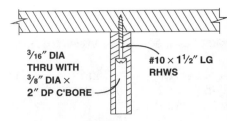

3/16" DIA THRU WITH 3/8" DIA × 2" DP C'BORE

#10 × 1 1/2" LG RHWS

PLINTH-TO-CASE JOINERY DETAIL

The precise placement of these holes is not important, but you should drill two holes in each stretcher near the ends.

6 Cut the biscuit joints in the face frame members. The parts of the face frames are joined with biscuits, as shown in the *Front View.* Cut slots for #00 biscuits in the ends of the stiles and the edges of the rails.

Note: On traditional face frames, the ends of the rails attach to the edges of the stiles. On these face frames, it's just the other way round. In this particular case, the nontraditional arrangement is stronger — the stiles support the top rail like posts support a beam.

Saturday Evening

7 Assemble the cases. Finish sand the parts you have made. Assemble one case at a time, securing the parts with glue and flathead screws. Start by attaching the bottom, sides, and back. Then fasten the cleat to the inside surface of the back and the braces to the inside surface of the top. (The front edges of the braces must be flush with the front edge of the top.) Finally, attach the top to the case.

As you work, countersink and counterbore the screw holes so the heads rest slightly below the plywood surface. Cover the screw heads with wooden plugs.

Sunday Afternoon

8 Assemble the plinths and face frames. Assemble the face frames with biscuits and glue, then set them aside.

Attach the plinth fronts and backs to the plinth stretchers with glue and screws. Once again, countersink and conterbore the screw holes. However, you need only cover the screw heads on the plinth front; those on the back won't show.

Important Note: As you assemble the parts, make sure that the counterbores in the stretchers all face the same direction.

Sunday Evening

9 Attach the face frames to the cases. Finish sand the face frames, then attach them to the plywood cases with glue and screws. Counterbore and countersink the screw holes, then cover the screw heads.

At Your Leisure

10 Attach the plinths. Sand the joints flush and clean, being careful not to sand through the veneered surface of the plywood parts. Also sand the wooden plugs flush with the surfaces of the cases. Do the same for the plinths.

Turn the cases bottoms up and arrange them as you will assemble them to make the platform. Mark the inside corners. Attach the plinths to the case bottoms with roundhead wood screws. The back and one side of each plinth should be flush with the inside corner of its case.

11 Finish the units. Do any necessary touch-up sanding, then apply paint or a finish to those wooden surfaces that will show when the platform is assembled. Do not finish the top surfaces or the inside surfaces of the units. The exposed wood will absorb and release moisture quickly, helping to protect stored bedding and linens from mildew.

12 Assemble the platform. Arrange the units in your bedroom so the backs and sides butt against one another, making a platform. Make sure the top surfaces are flush. Then, working from inside the units, drill two 5/16-inch-diameter holes through the adjoining backs and sides. The precise locations of these holes is not important, but they should be near the ends of the parts and centered between the tops and bottoms. Insert carriage bolts in these holes and secure them with hex nuts to tie the units together.

TRY THIS

CEDAR LINERS

If you plan to store linens in the platform, cut sheets of 1/4-inch *cedar closet liner,* and lay them in the bottoms of the units. This flakeboard material is made from chips of aromatic red cedar. Although the tradition that cedar repels insects is largely a myth, the aromatic oils in the wood do keep cloth goods smelling sweet and fresh.

Pro SKILL: Cutting Plywood

Cutting up unwieldy 4×8-foot sheet materials is a big job; there's no getting around it. Large shops often have panel saws to perform this task, but these require more space and money than most of us can spare. Craftsmen in small shops have to resort to more clever strategies. Here are two effective methods for cutting sheet materials.

1 Many woodworkers prefer to *double-cut* plywood and particleboard, "busting them down" with a circular saw and trimming them to final dimensions on a table saw. Lay out the first set of cuts, making the parts slightly wider than needed. Also be sure that each part has at least one *factory edge.* Slice the sheets into easily manageable sizes with a circular saw.

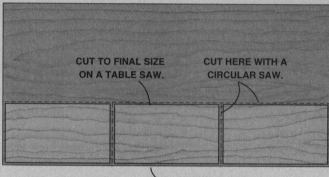

CUT TO FINAL SIZE ON A TABLE SAW. CUT HERE WITH A CIRCULAR SAW.

FACTORY EDGE

2 Then trim the smaller sheets to size on a table saw. Use the factory edge as the guiding edge for the first cut; thereafter, use either a factory edge or a table-sawed edge for the remaining cuts. You may want to make the first table saw cuts wide, then turn the stock and trim the factory edge. Although factory edges make good guides, they are often dented and chipped.

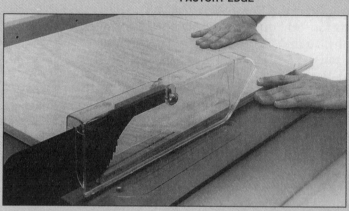

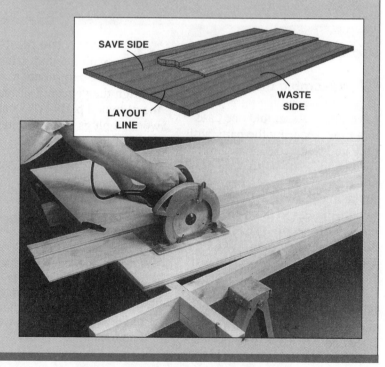

SAVE SIDE

WASTE SIDE

LAYOUT LINE

3 If you don't want to cut each part twice, use a circular saw guide to guide your cuts. Lay out the parts on the sheet, and position the guide on the "save" side of the layout line (opposite the waste), positioning the edge of the base even with the line. Clamp the guide to the plywood, and rest the circular saw on the base so the saw motor faces the straightedge. Make the cut, keeping the saw's sole firmly against the straightedge. **Note:** For this to work well, you must equip your circular saw with a high-quality combination or plywood blade. You cannot make finished cuts with blades designed for construction work.

PART SEVEN

For Yard
and Garden

Butterfly House

When making repetitive router cuts to form a decorative pattern of slots in the front of this butterfly house, it helps to make a template to guide the router. This lets you repeat the cuts precisely without having to lay out or set up each cut.

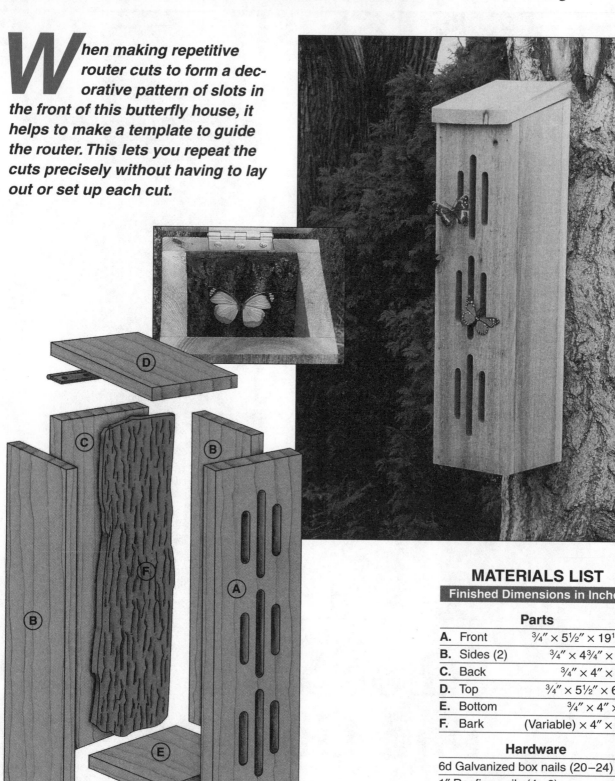

EXPLODED VIEW

MATERIALS LIST
Finished Dimensions in Inches

Parts

A.	Front	$3/4'' \times 5\frac{1}{2}'' \times 19\frac{15}{16}''$
B.	Sides (2)	$3/4'' \times 4\frac{3}{4}'' \times 21''$
C.	Back	$3/4'' \times 4'' \times 21''$
D.	Top	$3/4'' \times 5\frac{1}{2}'' \times 6\frac{3}{4}''$
E.	Bottom	$3/4'' \times 4'' \times 4''$
F.	Bark	(Variable) $\times 4'' \times 21''$

Hardware

6d Galvanized box nails (20–24)

1″ Roofing nails (4–6)

$1\frac{1}{2}'' \times 3''$ Hinge and mounting screws

A "butterfly house" protects butterflies from predators. It also serves as a hibernation box for certain species and encourages them to stick around your garden through the cold months. The insects crawl through the slots in the front of the box and cling to the bark on the inside. The hinged top on the box lets you spy on the guests while they're sleeping or hibernating.

Saturday Morning

1 Prepare the materials, and cut the parts to size. To make the butterfly box, you need about 4 board feet of 4/4 (1-inch-thick) lumber. Select a wood that holds up well outdoors, such as cypress, redwood, or cedar. Don't use pressure-treated lumber; the chemicals used to treat the wood may affect the butterflies. The butterfly house shown is made from a single 1×6×8-foot board of rough-sawn western red cedar.

Plane the 4/4 stock to ¾ inch thick, and cut the parts to size. Miter the top ends of the sides at 75 degrees, as shown in *Section A*. Also bevel the top ends of the front and back and both ends of the top at 75 degrees.

2 Drill a hole in the bottom. Drill a ¼-inch-diameter hole through the bottom, centered in the board. This will allow any rainwater that blows into the box to drain out.

Saturday Afternoon

3 Cover the back with bark. Take a walk through a nearby forest and look for a fallen tree or limb. Or look through a pile of firewood that's been weathering for a year or two. In most wood species, the bark comes loose after the cambium that holds it in place dies and decays. It should peel off easily. (Don't peel the bark from live trees, of course. And respect sensitive natural environments where the caretakers would rather you not disturb the natural cycle.)

Using a band saw or a coping saw, cut a piece of bark large enough to cover the back. Fasten it to the back with roofing nails.

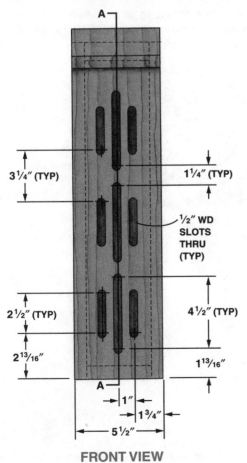

FRONT VIEW

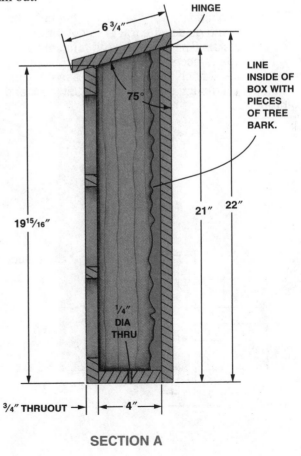

SECTION A

Saturday Evening

4 **Rout the slots in the front.** Make a *Routing Template* to help rout three ½-inch-wide slots — two short and one long slot. Using a straight bit, rout slots through the front, repeating the pattern three times, as shown on the *Front View.*

5 **Assemble the box.** Join the front, back, sides, and bottom with box nails. Attach the top to the back with a hinge. **Note:** If you're building the house from redwood, you should know that redwood does not hold nails well. You may want to attach the parts with brass or stainless steel screws instead.

At Your Leisure

6 **Hang the butterfly house.** Fasten the assembled house to a post or fence by driving a screw through the back. The house should hang about 5 feet above the ground near your garden or whatever vegetation the butterflies prefer.

TRY THIS

WINTER CARE AND FEEDING

If your butterflies emerge from hibernation during an exceptionally warm winter day, place a bowl of sugar water near the house to keep them busy. They will retreat back into shelter as the evening cools.

Quick FIXTURE: Routing Template

This template fits over the front of the butterfly house and guides the router to cut three ½-inch-wide slots. The cutouts in the template are ⅝ inch wide to accommodate a ⅝-inch-diameter *guide collar.* Attach the collar to the base of your router, then mount a ½-inch straight bit to extend through it.

Clamp the template to the work and rout the slots, guiding the bushing against the sides of the cutouts in the template.

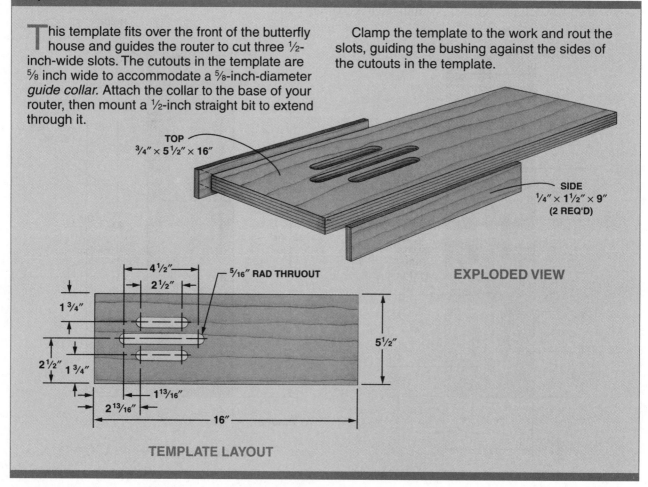

TOP
¾" × 5½" × 16"

SIDE
¼" × 1½" × 9"
(2 REQ'D)

EXPLODED VIEW

4½"
2½"
1¾"
⁵⁄₁₆" RAD THRUOUT
2½"
1¾"
5½"
1¹³⁄₁₆"
2¹³⁄₁₆"
16"

TEMPLATE LAYOUT

Pro SKILL: Pattern Routing

To rout a pattern, follow a template with a handheld router. The template may be any size or shape; the router will duplicate the template pattern precisely.

There are two common routing accessories to follow a template:

- A *guide bushing*
- A *pattern-routing bit*

1 *Guide collars* are round, hollow bushings that mount to the base of a router. The bit extends through the collars. As the collar traces the shape of a template, the bit cuts a similar shape. However, because the bit and the collar are not the same diameter, the routed pattern will be a slightly different size than the template. Compensate for this when making the template. Subtract the diameter of the bit from the diameter of the bushing and divide by 2. The edge of the template must be offset from the shape you want to rout by this amount.

2 A *pattern-routing bit* has a pilot bearing mounted above the flutes, between the cutter and the shank. (This is called an *overbearing*.) The bearing is the same diameter as the bit. The bit traces the template exactly — the routed pattern is the same size as the template pattern. However, there are fewer sizes and types of bits available — only large straight bits and core-box bits are commonly available with overbearings. Also, the template must be as thick as the cutting flutes are long for the bearing to make contact during both shallow and deep cuts. This limits the depth of cut.

3 Cut the routing template with a band saw, scroll saw, or coping saw. (In some cases, you may wish to rout the template. The cutouts in the template shown are routed.) Sand the sawed edges smooth, otherwise the guide collar or the pattern-routing bit will trace every imperfection and duplicate it in the work. Mount the template to the work with double-faced carpet tape or clamps. If you clamp the template, check that the clamps don't interfere with the router. Adjust the bit to cut no more than ⅛ inch deep and make the first pass, keeping the collar or bearing firmly against the template. Lower the bit another ⅛ inch and make another pass. Continue until you have routed the pattern to the desired depth or have cut through the board.

4 You can also use flat objects as templates. This technique is especially handy when repairing furniture or "carpenter gothic" house trim. Affix the old, broken part to a board and trace the outline with a pattern-routing bit. The bit will cut a perfect copy.

Child's Folding Table and Chair

The Achilles heel of every table saw is its miter gauge. It's not a particularly accurate tool for crosscutting, especially when sawing long boards. A cutoff sled is a vast improvement. Jobs like cutting the slats for this table and chair go faster and you get better results.

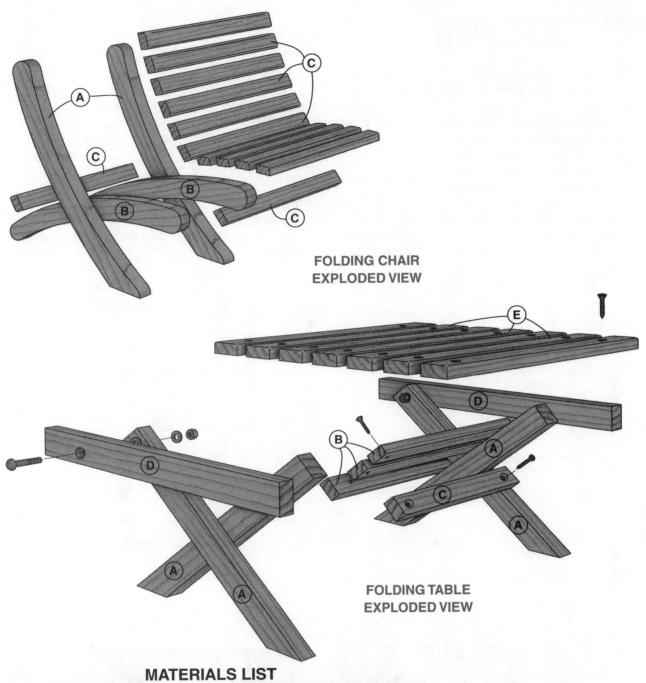

FOLDING CHAIR EXPLODED VIEW

FOLDING TABLE EXPLODED VIEW

MATERIALS LIST

Finished Dimensions in Inches

Table Parts

A.	Legs (4)	¾″ × 1⅜″ × 13⅜″
B.	Rails (3)	¾″ × 1⅜″ × 9½″
C.	Short rail	¾″ × 1⅜″ × 8″
D.	Aprons (2)	¾″ × 1⅜″ × 13¾″
E.	Top slats (7)	¾″ × 1⅜″ × 12″

Table Hardware

#8 × 1¼″ Flathead wood screws (22)

¼″ × 1¾″ Carriage bolts (2)

¼″ Flat washers (4)

¼″ Stop nuts (2)

Chair Parts

A.	Back legs (2)	¾″ × 4″ × 22¼″
B.	Seat legs (2)	¾″ × 3⅛″ × 18¾″
C.	Slats/rails (12)	¾″ × 1⅜″ × 12″

Chair Hardware

#8 × 1¼″ Flathead wood screws (24)

"I was surprised to find when I went looking for outdoor children's furniture," Joe Zwiesler told me, "that there is very little available." So Joe, an accomplished craftsman, decided to make his own. This folding table and chair set is simple enough to build in a day, but it's sturdy enough to stand up to the abuse that kids dish out.

Saturday Morning

1 Prepare the materials, and cut the parts to size.

To make the table, you need about 4 board feet of 4/4 (1-inch-thick) lumber, and to make the chair, you need 6 board feet of the same. The table and chair shown are made from white cedar, but you can use any clear wood. Cedar, cypress, redwood, mahogany, and teak all hold up well in the weather.

Plane the stock to ¾ inch thick, then cut the parts to the sizes shown in the Materials List. Miter the bottom ends of the table legs at 45 degrees.

MAKING THE TABLE

2 Drill pivoting holes in two of the legs and the aprons.

The table top is attached to one of the leg assemblies to

pivot. This allows you to fold the leg and top flat. Drill ¼-inch-diameter holes through the legs, as shown on the *Top/Pivoting Leg Assembly/Side View.* In the aprons, drill ¼-inch-diameter holes with ⅝-inch-diameter, ¼-inch-deep counterbores.

3 Round over the top corners of the slats.

To prevent the kids from getting

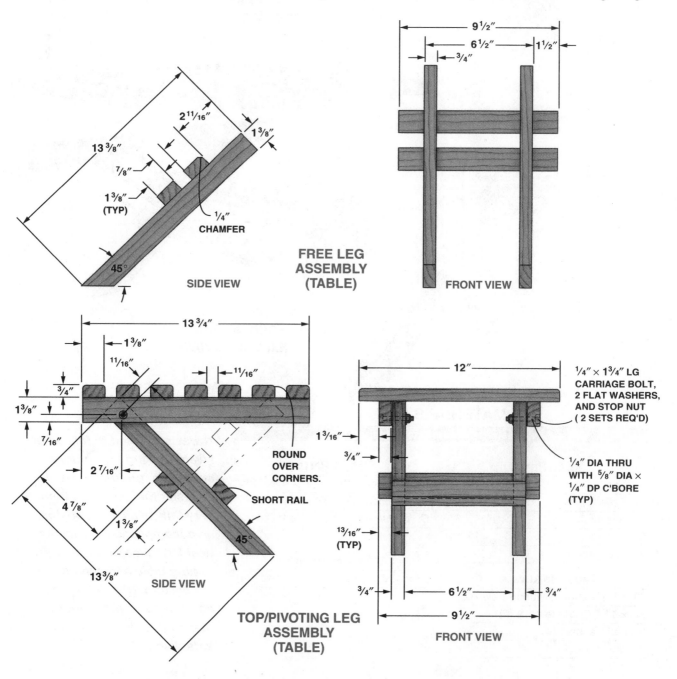

splinters, round over the top corners of the slats. You don't need to rout or shape them; just hit the corner with a block plane or a rasp, then sand them smooth.

4 Chamfer the top rail.
Using a table saw or a router, cut a ¼-inch-wide chamfer in one edge of one rail. This will become the top rail in the free leg assembly.

5 Assemble the table.
Lightly sand the parts, making sure the surfaces are smooth and free of splinters. Using screws, attach the rails to the legs, as shown in the *Free Leg Assembly* and *Top/Pivoting Leg Assembly* drawings. Make sure the chamfered rail becomes the top rail in the free leg assembly, with the chamfered edge facing up. Also screw the top slats to the aprons. Countersink each screw so

the head rests flush with or just below the wood surface.

Attach the pivoting leg assembly to the top assembly with carriage bolts. Secure the bolt with stop nuts — these nuts will prevent the bolts from working loose.

To set up the table, slide the free leg between the rails on the pivoting leg. Let the top rest on the chamfered corner of the top rail on the free leg.

Quick FIXTURE: Cutoff Sled

Many years ago, I made a cutoff sled for crosscutting chores and was amazed to find how much better it worked than a miter gauge. I still use one today — I haven't found anything I like as well. The long fence on the sled backs up both long and short boards. And because the boards don't drag across the table, there's no tendency for them to pivot or "walk" as they're fed into the blade.

Make a guide from hard maple to fit the slots in your table saw as closely as possible. (You can also use UHMW [ultra-high molecular weight] plastic for this part — it slides effortlessly and wears like iron.) Attach it to the base, parallel to a long edge. The distance from the guide to the edge should be a fraction of an inch more than the distance from the miter gauge slot to the blade. Trim this edge the first time you use the sled.

Fasten the fence to the base with carriage bolts. Note that the bolt holes in the fence are slightly larger than the bolts. This lets you adjust the fence a few degrees right or left so you can get it perfectly square to the blade. The nuts are recessed in counterbores so they won't catch on the saw guard.

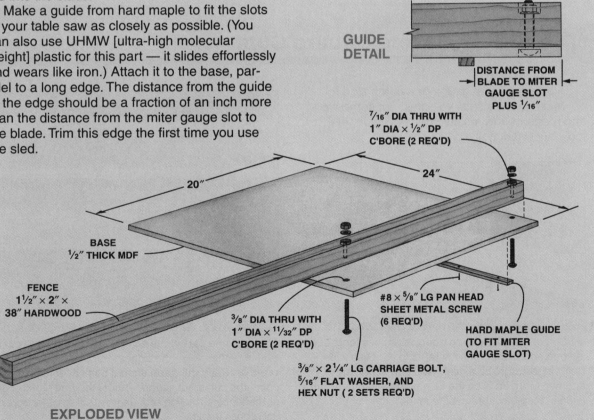

GUIDE DETAIL

DISTANCE FROM BLADE TO MITER GAUGE SLOT PLUS ¹⁄₁₆″

⁷⁄₁₆″ DIA THRU WITH 1″ DIA × ½″ DP C'BORE (2 REQ'D)

24″

20″

BASE
½″ THICK MDF

FENCE
1½″ × 2″ × 38″ HARDWOOD

³⁄₈″ DIA THRU WITH 1″ DIA × ¹¹⁄₃₂″ DP C'BORE (2 REQ'D)

#8 × ⁵⁄₈″ LG PAN HEAD SHEET METAL SCREW (6 REQ'D)

HARD MAPLE GUIDE (TO FIT MITER GAUGE SLOT)

³⁄₈″ × 2¼″ LG CARRIAGE BOLT, ⁵⁄₁₆″ FLAT WASHER, AND HEX NUT (2 SETS REQ'D)

EXPLODED VIEW

Saturday Afternoon

MAKING THE CHAIR

6 **Cut the leg profiles.** Lay out the shapes of the legs, as shown in the *Back Assembly/ Side View* and *Seat Assembly/ Side View*. Stack each set of legs face to face, making two stacks. Tape the boards together with the ends and edges flush, then cut the profiles with a band saw or saber saw. Sand the sawed edges.

7 **Round over the corners of the slats.** As you did when building the table, round over the top corners of the slats. "Soften" the corners with a block plane or a rasp, then sand them.

8 **Assemble the chair.** Lightly sand the chair parts. Attach the slats and rails to the legs with screws, as shown in the

Back Assembly and *Seat Assembly* drawings. Once again, countersink the screws.

To set up the chair, insert the seat assembly between the rails on the back assembly.

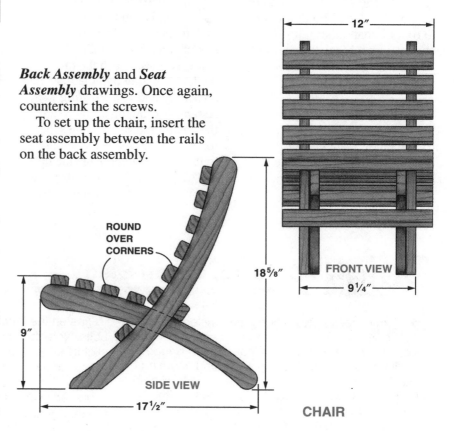

SIDE VIEW

FRONT VIEW

CHAIR

Pro SKILL: Making Square Cuts

To adjust a miter gauge or a cutoff sled to make square cuts, you must cut some wood and measure the results, then fine-tune your tools accordingly.

1 Select a straight scrap about 18 inches long. Joint one edge, and rip the scrap 3 to 4 inches wide. Both edges must be straight and parallel to one another. Mark an X on the face of the scrap near the middle, then saw through the mark.

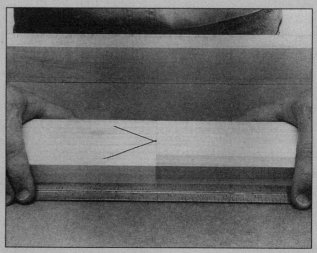

2 Flip one part of the scrap over and butt the cut ends together. Align the edges with a straightedge. The seam between the parts should be tight. If it gaps at any point, the cut is not square. Adjust the angle of the gauge or the fence a fraction of a degree, cut another scrap, and check again.

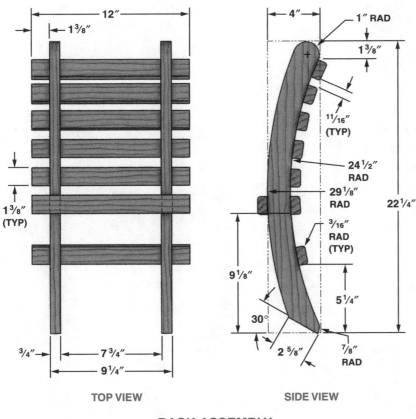

TOP VIEW SIDE VIEW

BACK ASSEMBLY

12″

1 3/8″

1 3/8″
(TYP)

3/4″   7 3/4″

9 1/4″

4″

1″ RAD

1 3/8″

11/16″
(TYP)

24 1/2″
RAD

29 1/8″
RAD

3/16″
RAD
(TYP)

22 1/4″

9 1/8″

5 1/4″

30°

2 5/8″

7/8″
RAD

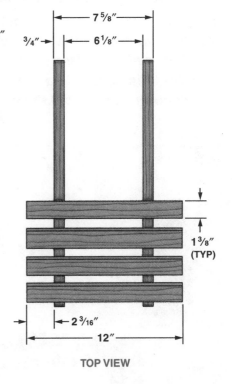

TOP VIEW

7 5/8″

3/4″   6 1/8″

1 3/8″
(TYP)

2 3/16″

12″

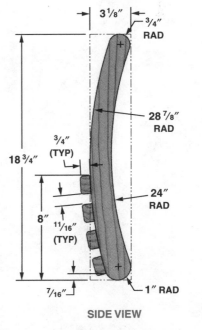

SIDE VIEW

SEAT ASSEMBLY

3 1/8″

3/4″
RAD

28 7/8″
RAD

3/4″
(TYP)

18 3/4″

24″
RAD

8″

11/16″
(TYP)

7/16″

1″ RAD

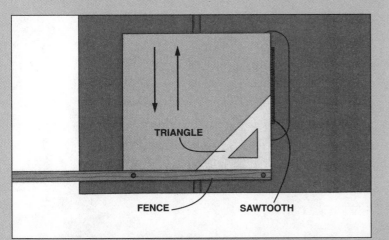

TRIANGLE

FENCE   SAWTOOTH

3 For a quick check, here's a trick that Bob Moran, author of *Woodworking: The Right Technique,* showed me. Rest the base of a large drafting triangle against the miter gauge face or sled fence and the side against one tooth on the blade. Slowly push the sled forward, then pull it back again. The side of the triangle should remain in contact with the tooth. If a gap opens between them or the triangle slides sideways, you've got problems.

Bird Feast

The four sides of the hip roof on this bird feeder present a thorny assembly problem. They are joined at odd angles, making them difficult to clamp together with standard clamps. To glue up these parts, I had to make an assembly jig to hold them.

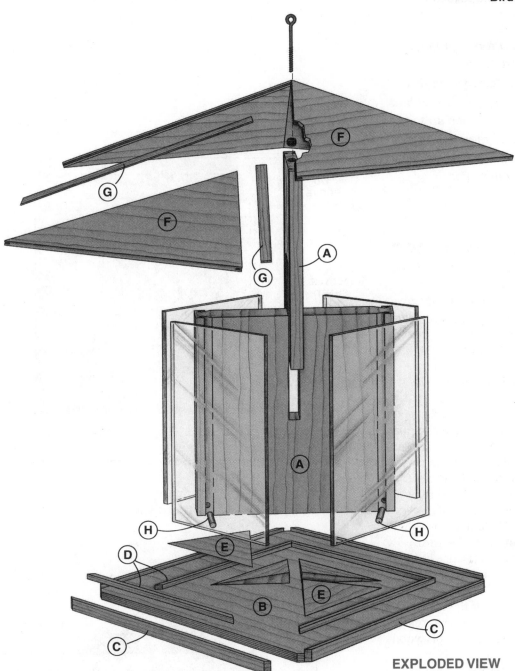

EXPLODED VIEW

MATERIALS LIST

Finished Dimensions in Inches

Parts

A.	Walls (2)	$\frac{3}{4}'' \times 10'' \times 12''$
B.	Bottom*	$\frac{1}{2}'' \times 13\frac{3}{4}'' \times 13\frac{3}{4}''$
C.	Edge trim (4)	$\frac{1}{4}'' \times \frac{3}{4}'' \times 13\frac{1}{2}''$
D.	Seed dams (4)	$\frac{1}{4}'' \times \frac{3}{8}'' \times 9\frac{3}{4}''$
E.	Wedges (4)	$\frac{3}{4}'' \times 2\frac{7}{8}'' \times 5\frac{3}{4}''$
F.	Roof sides (4)	$\frac{1}{2}'' \times 16\frac{1}{8}'' \times 9\frac{1}{4}''$
G.	Splines (4)	$\frac{1}{8}'' \times \frac{3}{4}'' \times 10''$
H.	Dowels (4)	$\frac{1}{8}''$ dia. $\times \frac{3}{4}''$

Make this part from exterior plywood.

Hardware

#10 × 2″ Flathead wood screws (4)

$\frac{1}{8}'' \times 6\frac{3}{8}'' \times 11\frac{5}{8}''$ Acrylic plastic sheets (4)

$\frac{1}{4}''$ Threaded insert

$\frac{1}{4}'' \times 4''$ Eye bolt

This feeder offers four large compartments, each dispensing a different seed mixture, attracting a variety of bird species. It's designed so that you can either mount it on a post or hang it from a tether — whichever you prefer.

Friday Evening

1 **Prepare the materials, and cut the parts to size.**
To make the "bird feast," you need about 8 board feet of 4/4 (1-inch-thick) lumber and a small piece of exterior plywood. Choose a wood that holds up well in the weather — cedar, cypress, redwood, and mahogany are all good choices. (The feeder shown is made from mahogany.) Avoid pressure-treated lumber; the chemicals used to treat the wood may affect the birds.

Plane the 4/4 lumber to ¾ inch thick, and cut the walls, trim, dams, splines, and wedge stock to the sizes listed in the Materials List. (You need cut only two pieces for the wedges. Later you'll resaw these to make four parts.) Also cut the plywood bottom.

Note: Ordinarily, the wood grain in the splines should run edge to edge, across their width. But these splines are only for alignment; they aren't necessary to reinforce the roof joints since the roof doesn't support much weight. And because of the manner in which you must assemble the roof, ordinary splines might snap off. I suggest you cut them so the grain is parallel to the edges. (Or, use ⅛-inch plywood, if you have it.)

Plane the remaining stock to ½ inch thick, and set it aside to make the roof.

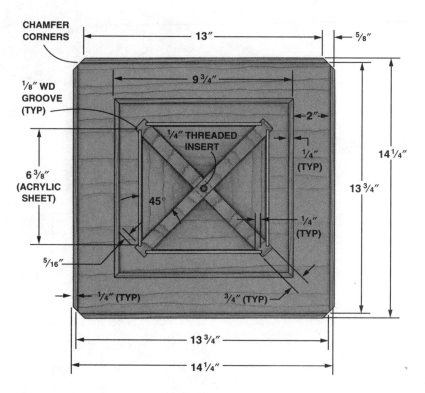

TOP VIEW
(WITHOUT TOP)

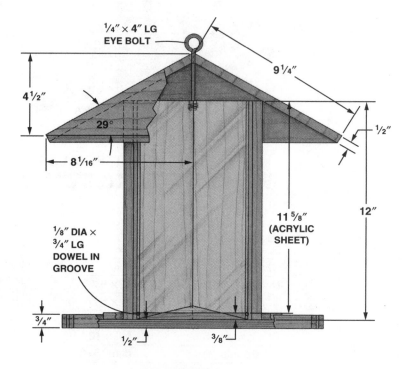

SIDE VIEW

Saturday Morning

2 Cut the compound miters that join the roof sides. The four roof sides are joined with compound miters — joints that are both mitered and beveled. To make these miters on a table saw, set your miter gauge to 48¾ degrees and tilt the blade to 20 degrees, as shown in the *Roof Side Layout.* Attach an extension to the face of the miter gauge; this will give you more control. Cut all the right-hand miters, then the left.

3 Cut the spline grooves in the roof sides. Don't change the tilt of the saw blade — let it remain at 20 degrees — but adjust the depth of cut to make the spline grooves in the edges of the roof sides. Guide the sides along the fence as you cut the grooves.

4 Cut the grooves in the walls. Tilt the saw blade to 45 degrees, and cut the ⅛-inch-wide grooves near the edge of the walls. These grooves hold the plastic sheets.

5 Cut the slots in the walls. The walls are joined with a large cross-lap — two slots that fit over one another. Lay out the slots as shown in the *Wall Layout,* then cut them with a band saw or saber saw.

6 Drill holes in the walls. Small dowels in the walls hold the plastic sheet a fraction of an inch above the bottom of the feeder. This allows the seed to slip underneath the plastic as the birds eat it. Mark the bottom end of each wall, then lay out the locations of the dowel holes. These ⅛-inch-diameter holes must pass through the grooves, as shown in the *Wall Layout.* Drill the holes through the walls.

Cut the spline grooves in the mitered edges of the roof sides with the saw blade tilted at 20 degrees — the same setting used to make the compound miters. An ordinary combination blade will cut a groove approximately ⅛ inch wide.

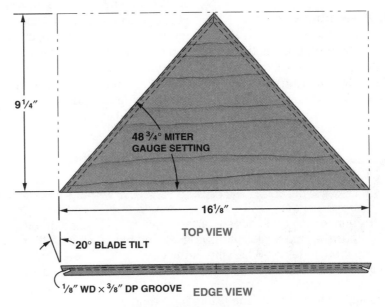

ROOF SIDE LAYOUT

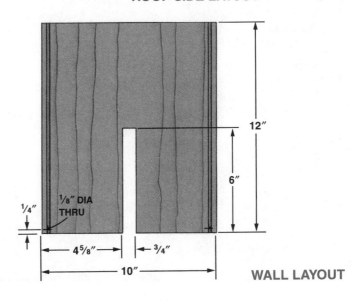

WALL LAYOUT

7 **Cut the wedges.** There is a wedge at the bottom of each compartment in the feeder. This provides an inclined surface that helps feed the seed under the plastic. To make these wedges, tilt the band saw table to 15 degrees, and resaw the wedge stock to make tapered pieces. Miter the ends of each piece, as shown in the *Wedge Detail.*

Note: If you don't have a band saw, you may omit the wedges; the feeder will work fine without them. However, there will be a little bit of seed in the back of each compartment that the birds won't be able to reach.

8 **Assemble the roof.** Temporarily, assemble the parts of the roof, holding them together with masking tape. Make an *Assembly Jig* to keep the roof sides from spreading apart. Check that the stops rest

snug against the bottom edges of the assembled roof.

Take the roof apart, and lay out the pieces with the outside surfaces facing up. Butt the mitered edges together (all except for one joint), and stick masking tape across the seams. Turn the roof sides over, and apply waterproof glue to the mitered edges and grooves. Fold the parts together, and tape the last seam. Then insert the splines in the grooves. Place the assembled roof in the assembly jig to hold the parts together as the glue dries.

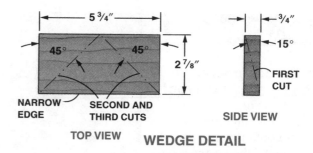

WEDGE DETAIL

TRY THIS

WORKING TIME

When there are lots of parts to assemble at once, or the nature of the assembly requires more time, use a glue with a long *working time* (also called *open assembly time*). The glue shouldn't start to cure until you've completed the assembly. For this roof, I used resorcinol glue. Resorcinol offers 15 to 30 minutes working time.

Quick FIXTURE: Assembly Jig

When joining odd-shaped parts or joining parts at odd angles, it may be difficult to clamp them together. When this is the case, build an assembly jig. This fixture doesn't clamp the parts; instead, it braces the assembly. The two adjoining parts and the fixture form a rigid triangle. Once braced, apply weight or pressure to the part to clamp them.

The assembly jig for the feeder roof consists of a plywood base and four stops. To position the stops precisely, temporarily assemble the roof sides with masking tape and place it on the base. Butt the stops against the edges and mark their positions.

To clamp the roof in the jig, place a weight at the peak. I used a bag of lead shot that I keep around for just such a task. You might also wrap band clamps or lengths of surgical tubing around the jig and the glued-up parts.

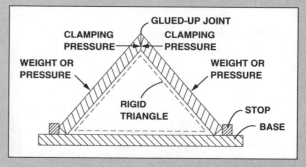

EXPLODED VIEW

An assembly jig creates a rigid triangle and prevents the parts from slipping as you apply pressure to the glued-up joint.

9 Assemble the feeder.

Using waterproof glue, assemble the walls to make an X-shape, and fasten them to the bottom with flathead wood screws. Also glue the wedges, dams, and trim in place.

When the glue dries, chamfer the corners of the bottom. There should be a small gap between the ends of the trim at each corner. This will allow the rain water to drain out.

Install a threaded insert in the top of the feeder where the walls cross. Slide the plastic sheets into their grooves. Sand the seams in the roof clean, and drill a ¼-inch-diameter hole through the peak, as shown in the *Top/ Top View*. Fasten the roof to the feeder by inserting an eye bolt through the hole and into the insert. *Don't overtighten the eye bolt.* It should hold the roof snug, but not too tight.

At Your Leisure

10 Hang or mount the feeder.

To hang the feeder, simply attach a rope, wire, or chain to the eye bolt. To mount it on a post, drill a ⅜-inch-diameter, 2-inch-deep hole dead center in the bottom, up into the wall assembly. Install a ⅜-inch hanger bolt in the top of a post, as shown in the *Post Mounting Detail.* Place the feeder on the post, inserting the hanger bolt in the hole in the bottom.

¼" DIA HOLE THRU

⅛" × ¾" × 10" SPLINE (4 REQ"D)

← 16⅛" →

TOP VIEW
TOP

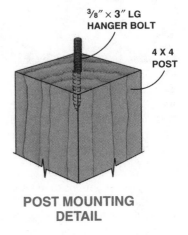

⅜" × 3" LG HANGER BOLT

4 X 4 POST

POST MOUNTING DETAIL

Pro SKILL: Compound Miters

In a compound miter joint, the adjoining surfaces are mitered and beveled. The assembled parts "slope" rather than rest flat on an edge or face. The angle of the slope and the number of sides in the assembly determine the miter angle and bevel settings.

1 To cut a compound miter on a table saw, angle the miter gauge and tilt the blade. To make matching right and left compound miters in the ends of a board, make the first cut in one end, then flip the board, and move the miter gauge to the slot on the opposite side of the saw. If you're cutting a part with two parallel edges (such as a frame member), the miter gauge should face forward for both cuts, but a different edge should rest against the miter gauge and a different face should rest against the table for each cut.

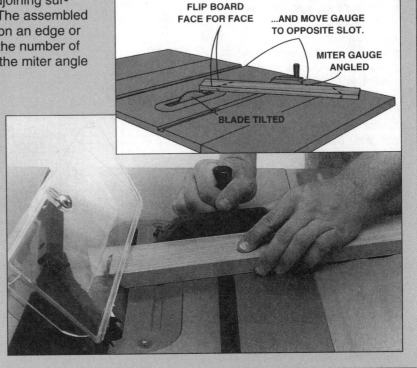

FLIP BOARD FACE FOR FACE

...AND MOVE GAUGE TO OPPOSITE SLOT.

MITER GAUGE ANGLED

BLADE TILTED

(continued)

Pro SKILL: Compound Miters — CONTINUED

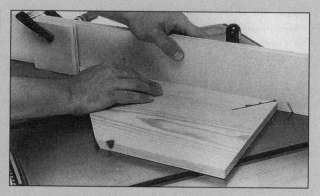

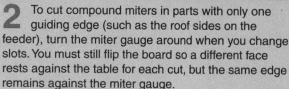

2 To cut compound miters in parts with only one guiding edge (such as the roof sides on the feeder), turn the miter gauge around when you change slots. You must still flip the board so a different face rests against the table for each cut, but the same edge remains against the miter gauge.

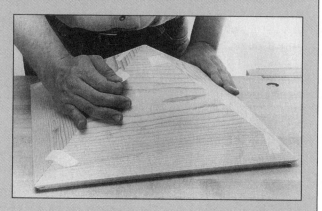

3 However you make the miters, you should test the setup *before* you cut good stock. To do this, make a small frame and tape the parts together. If the joints gap on the inside, decrease the blade tilt. If they gap on the outside, increase it. If the slope is greater than expected, decrease the miter gauge angle. If it's less than expected, increase the angle.

COMPOUND MITER SETTINGS

To find the settings for a compound miter in a four-sided assembly, follow the arc to the desired slope. (The slope is measured from horizontal, as the assembly sits on a bench.) Read the miter setting on the horizontal scale and the bevel setting on the vertical scale. For example, the roof of the bird feeder has a slope of 29 degrees. The corresponding miter setting is 48¾ degrees and the bevel setting is 20 degrees.

If you know how to pound on a scientific calculator and produce an intelligible result, you can use these formulas:

$$tanMG = 1 \div cosS$$
$$tanBT = cosMG \times tanS$$

Where:

S is the slope angle
MG is the miter gauge setting
BT is the blade tilt setting

PART EIGHT

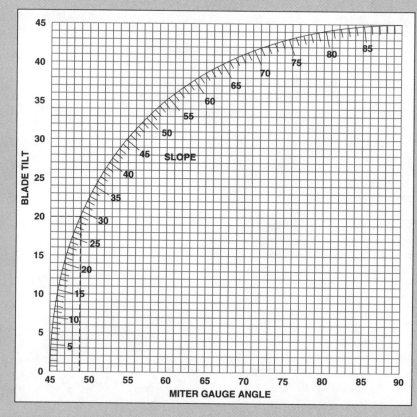

For Celebration
and Decoration

Potpourri Box

*H*ave you got a scroll saw or another wood-working tool that vibrates more than you'd like? Vibrations can be extremely annoying, especially when you have a piece that requires lots of delicate cuts, like the top on this box. Fortunately, an old lathe turner's trick will suck the vibrations right out of the machine.

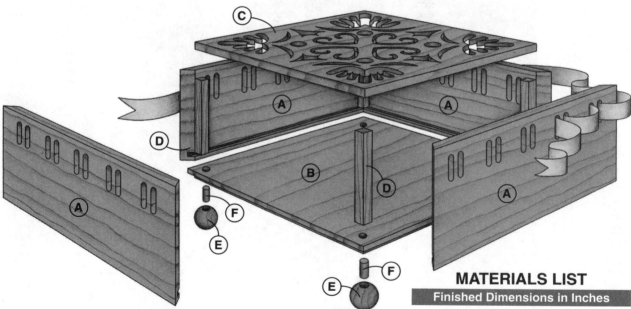

EXPLODED VIEW

MATERIALS LIST

Finished Dimensions in Inches

Parts

A.	Sides (4)	¼″ × 3″ × 6″
B.	Bottom	¼″ × 5¹¹⁄₁₆″ × 5¹¹⁄₁₆″
C.	Top	¼″ × 5⁷⁄₁₆″ × 5⁷⁄₁₆″
D.	Glue blocks (4)	¼″ × ¼″ × 2½″
E.	Beads (4–optional)	⅝″ dia.
F.	Dowels (4–optional)	⅛″ dia. × ½″

Hardware

½″ Ribbon (30″)	

Peter Holt, chief craftsman and proprietor of "English Accents," took time off from his handmade furniture business to make this decorative box for his wife. It's designed to be filled with aromatic herbs. The pattern on the top is pierced to allow the fragrance of the potpourri to escape into the room.

Saturday Morning

1 Prepare the materials, and cut the parts to size.

To make this box, you need less than a board foot of 4/4 (1-inch-thick) stock, provided you resaw the wood before you plane it.

> See Also:
> **"Resawing"**
> on page 107.

The parts are small enough to make from scrap wood. The box shown is made from cherry, but you can use any clear wood.

Resaw the 4/4 stock in half, then plane it to ¼ inch thick. Cut the parts to the sizes shown in the Materials List. As you do, miter the ends of the sides at 45 degrees.

2 Cut tongue-and-groove joints in the sides and bottom.

The ends and edges of the bottom are rabbeted to form a tongue around its perimeter. This tongue fits into grooves in the sides. Using a rip blade, cut ⅛-inch-wide, ⅛-inch deep grooves in the sides near the bottom edge, and ⅛-inch-wide, ⅛-inch-deep rabbets in the ends and edges of the bottom, as shown in the **Bottom Joinery Detail**. **Note:** A standard-size blade cuts a kerf reasonably close to ⅛ inch wide.

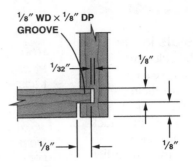

⅛" WD × ⅛" DP GROOVE

1/32"   ⅛"

⅛"   ⅛"

BOTTOM JOINERY DETAIL

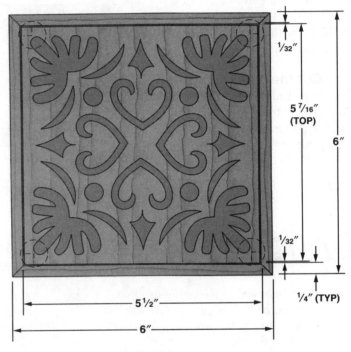

1/32"

5 7/16" (TOP)

6"

1/32"

¼" (TYP)

5½"

6"

TOP VIEW

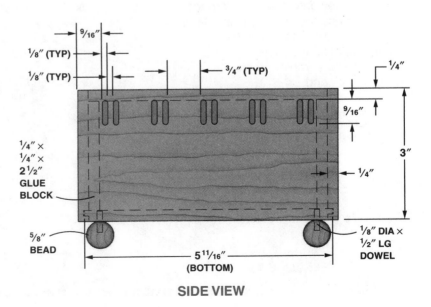

9/16"

⅛" (TYP)

⅛" (TYP)

¾" (TYP)

¼"

9/16"

3"

¼" × ¼" × 2½" GLUE BLOCK

¼"

⅝" BEAD

⅛" DIA × ½" LG DOWEL

5 11/16" (BOTTOM)

SIDE VIEW

Saturday Afternoon

3 Cut the slots in the sides. The sides are slotted so you can weave a ribbon in and out of them — a clever decorative detail, I thought. To cut these slots, stack the sides so the ends and edges are flush and tape them together. Lay out the slots on the top part in the stack. Drill ⅛-inch-diameter holes to mark the beginning and end of each slot, then remove the waste between the holes with a scroll saw or a coping saw.

4 Cut the pattern in the top. Enlarge the *Top Pattern* and trace it on the top. Cut the pattern with a scroll saw or coping saw.

TRY THIS

TRANSFERRING PATTERNS

Perhaps the easiest way to transfer a pattern to wood is to enlarge it on a copier, then stick the copy to the wood with spray adhesive. Most quick-print shops have copiers that enlarge and reduce.

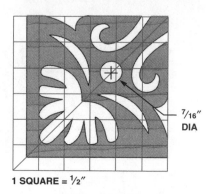

7/16″ DIA

1 SQUARE = ½″

TOP PATTERN

Saturday Evening

5 Drill dowel holes in the beads and bottom. The optional wooden beads that form the box feet are attached to the bottom with dowels. Drill ⅛-inch-diameter holes through the bottom near the corners, and ⅛-inch-diameter, ¼-inch-deep holes in the beads.

6 Assemble the box. Finish sand the wood parts. Glue the sides together. As you assemble the sides, insert the bottom in its grooves. However, don't glue the bottom in place. It should "float" in the grooves, free to expand and contract.

To reinforce the corner joints and support the top, attach glue blocks to the sides. Secure the beads to the bottom with dowels and glue.

Quick FIXTURE: Vibration Eliminator

More than any other stationary power tool, the scroll saw is plagued by vibration. The standard cure for this annoying problem is a rubber mat. But contrary to the claims of advertisers, these "anti-vibration pads" don't reduce vibration; they only isolate it. Perhaps the best way to reduce the shaking is to attach a massive stand to the saw — mass dampens vibrations.

Or, you can employ an old turner's trick and *sandbag* the machine. (Turners sandbag lathes to reduce vibration when making delicate turnings.) Sand not only adds mass, it has the unique physical property of *hysteresis* — it actually absorbs vibrations. Make this special mounting box slightly larger than the scroll saw base. Locate the bolt holes to match the saw base. Then fill the box with sand and bolt your saw to it to make it run smooth as silk.

⅜″ DIA (TYP)

VAR.

VARIABLE

⅜″ HEX NUT AND FLAT WASHER (4 SETS REQ'D)

4″

⅜″ DIA WITH 1″ DIA × ¼″ DP C'BORE ON BOTTOM (TYP)

EXPLODED VIEW

⅜″ × 5 ½″ LG CARRIAGE BOLT (4 REQ'D)

At Your Leisure

7 Finish the box. Do any necessary touch-up sanding, then apply a finish to the *outside* surfaces of the box. Leave the inside unfinished. This will help prevent the herbs inside the box from mildewing.

8 Weave a ribbon into the box and fill it with herbs. Select a ½-inch wide ribbon, and weave it in and out of the slots near the top edge of the box. The ribbon should be on the outside of the box where it goes around the corners. Tie off the ribbon and fill the box with fragrant potpourri.

Pro SKILL: Making Interior Cuts

An interior cut is one that doesn't begin or end at the perimeter of the workpiece — all the cutouts in the top of the Potpourri Box are interior cuts. To make them, you must begin somewhere in the middle of the stock, and cut away the waste from the interior without sawing through to an edge or end.

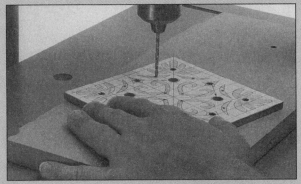

1 To make an interior cut, first drill a small hole, or *saw gate,* in the waste portion of the pattern. If you can, size this hole and position it to create one of the curves in the pattern. If you can't, drill the hole well inside the cut lines.

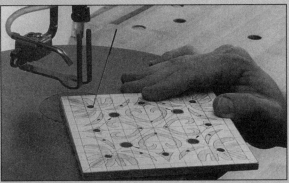

2 Disengage the scroll saw blade from one of the clamps. Thread the blade through the saw gate, and secure the free end in the clamp once again.

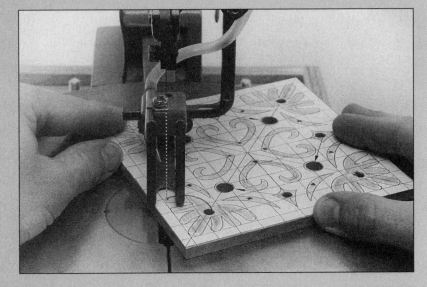

3 Cut out from the saw gate to the pattern line. Cut the interior pattern, removing the waste. When you've completed the cut, release one end of the blade from its clamp and pull the blade from the cutout.

Autumn Wreath

To sand the faces of the small wooden leaves in this wreath, I used a small parts holder. This kept me from scraping away the ends of my fingers on the abrasives.

MATERIALS LIST

Finished Dimensions in Inches

Parts

A. Cottonwood leaves (5)	$\frac{1}{4}'' \times 6\frac{1}{2}'' \times 7\frac{1}{2}''$
B. Maple leaves (5)	$\frac{1}{4}'' \times 5\frac{1}{2}'' \times 5\frac{1}{2}''$
C. Elm leaves (5)	$\frac{1}{4}'' \times 3'' \times 4''$
D. Oak leaves (5)	$\frac{1}{4}'' \times 4'' \times 6''$

I know a member of the International Wood Collectors Society who, every time he gets a new hardwood sample, carves it in the shape of a leaf of the tree from which it came. One Thanksgiving, his wife arranged this wonderful collection around the centerpiece of the table. This was my inspiration for the Autumn Wreath.

Saturday Morning

1 Prepare the materials, and cut the parts to size.

To make the wreath, you need about 3 board feet of 4/4 (1-inch-thick) lumber provided you resaw the wood before you plane it. If you just plane the wood, you'll need 6 board feet. The wreath looks best if you use different species and colors of wood. I selected cherry, walnut, maple, red oak, and mahogany, but you can use any clear wood. In fact, because the parts are small, this might be a good project to use up all the scraps of expensive woods that you've been saving forever.

Resaw the 4/4 stock in half, then plane the pieces to ¼ inch thick. Cut them into blanks of the sizes listed in the Materials List. Note that you need five blanks for each leaf.

2 Cut the leaf profiles.

Stack each blank by size, making four piles with 5 blanks

in each pile. Tape the piles together with the ends and edges flush. Enlarge the *Elm Leaf Pattern, Maple Leaf Pattern, Oak Leaf Pattern,* and *Cottonwood Leaf Pattern.* Trace the patterns on the top blank in each stack. Saw the profiles on a scroll saw or band saw, cutting all five blanks in each stack at once. Sand the sawed edges, then take the stacks apart.

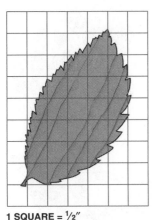

1 SQUARE = ½"

ELM LEAF PATTERN

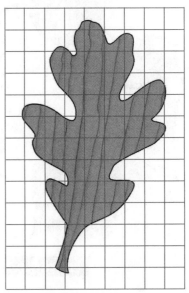

1 SQUARE = ½"

OAK LEAF PATTERN

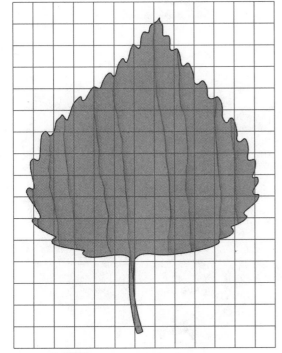

1 SQUARE = ½"

COTTONWOOD LEAF PATTERN

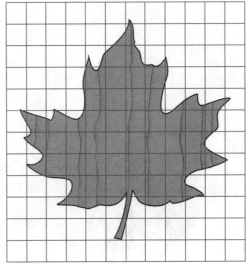

1 SQUARE = ½"

MAPLE LEAF PATTERN

TRY THIS

SAWING SMOOTH EDGES

There are a lot of intricate surfaces in these leaf profiles and it will take you forever and a day to sand them if you use a rough-cutting saw or saw blade. If you can, use a scroll saw with a *precision ground* *blade* or a *double-skip tooth fret blade*. Both of these leave very smooth surfaces and will reduce your sanding time considerably.

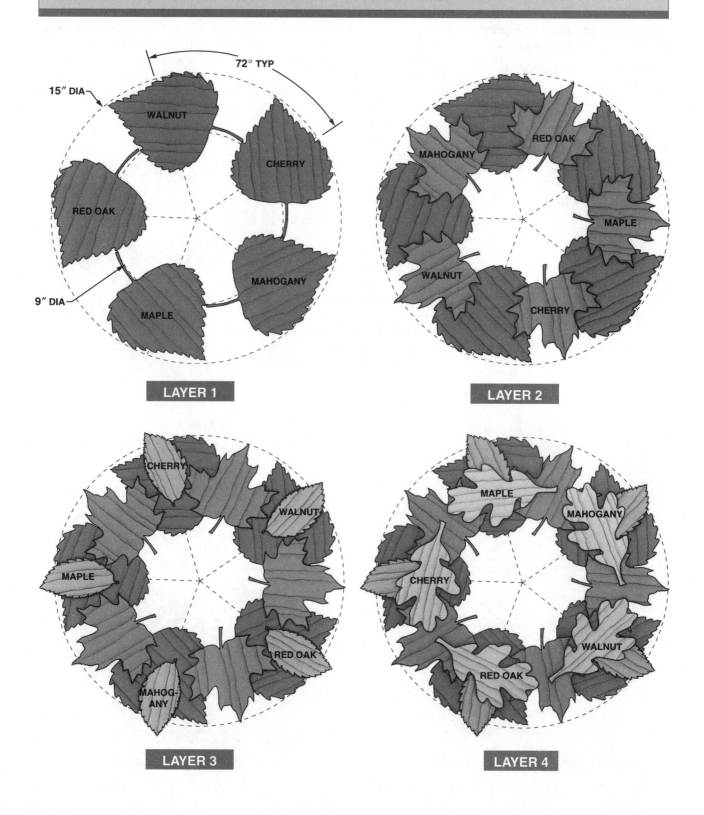

Saturday Afternoon

3 Finish the leaves. I found it easier to finish the leaves *before* I glued them together. There are just too many intricate surfaces to bother with once the wreath is assembled.

Finish sand the leaves. If you want a flat look, apply a wipe-on finish such as tung oil. If you'd rather have something glossy, use lacquer or shellac.

The type of finish you apply and the number of coats may extend this project past the weekend. For example, if you want to apply three coats of tung oil, it will take you two or three days. But you can squeeze in several coats of shellac or lacquer in a day's time because these materials dry quickly.

Sunday Afternoon

4 Assemble the wreath. Rub out the finish on the leaves but *don't* wax them. Arrange them in a circular shape and glue them together. You can arrange them in any pattern that appeals to you, or you can copy the pattern shown.

To copy this pattern, scribe two concentric circles, 9 inches and 15 inches in diameter, on a large sheet of paper. Divide the circles into five equal sections, each pie-shaped section is 72 degrees of the circle. Lay out the cottonwood leaves as shown in *Layer 1.* Lay the maple leaves on top of the cottonwood, arranging them to span the gaps between the cottonwood leaves, as shown in *Layer 2.* Then place the elm leaves between the maple leaves, as shown in *Layer 3.* Finally, lay the oak leaves on top of the maple and elm leaves, stretching from maple leaf to maple leaf, as shown in *Layer 4.*

As you place the second and third layers of leaves, glue them to the layer beneath them. Because the leaves are finished, you shouldn't use an ordinary wood glue; it won't bond to the surfaces properly. Instead, use epoxy, mastic, or silicone caulk.

Quick FIXTURE: Small Parts Holder

When machining small parts, your fingers may come dangerously close to moving blades, cutters, and abrasives. To prevent this, attach the small part to a holder, then use the holder to manipulate the part.

Although you can make a holder from almost any material, I prefer to use small pieces of clear plastic, as shown. This lets you see the work as it progresses. Attach the parts to the holder with double-faced carpet tape.

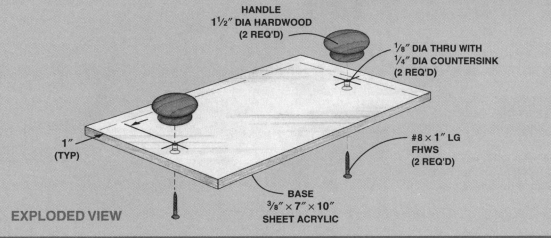

HANDLE
1½″ DIA HARDWOOD
(2 REQ'D)

⅛″ DIA THRU WITH
¼″ DIA COUNTERSINK
(2 REQ'D)

1″
(TYP)

#8 × 1″ LG
FHWS
(2 REQ'D)

BASE
⅜″ × 7″ × 10″
SHEET ACRYLIC

EXPLODED VIEW

Pro SKILL: Pad Work

One of the most time saving techniques I've ever run across is "pad" work. To make several parts all the same, stack them up in a "pad," tape them together so they won't shift, and machine the entire pad. This saves time when sawing, sanding, drilling, and routing, depending on the part you're making.

Perhaps the most important step in pad work is stacking. The individual parts cannot shift while you're working or they will be ruined. Many craftsmen simply wrap masking tape around the stacks, but I've had too many disappointing experiences with this method — the parts move when you cut most of the tape away. Instead, I prefer double-faced carpet tape between the layers. You have to be careful how much tape you use, however. This stuff has an iron grip and you can snap small pieces when you try to pry them apart. For delicate work, like the leaves in the wreath, I use just two or three ½-inch squares of tape between layers.

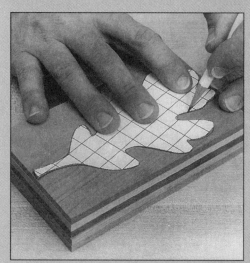

1 One of the ways in which pad work saves time is layout. You need only mark the top part in each stack.

2 Cut, drill, rout, or sand the entire pad. Frequently, you can perform several successive operations on a pad. For example, when making the leaves, you can saw the profile in the pad, then smooth the edges.

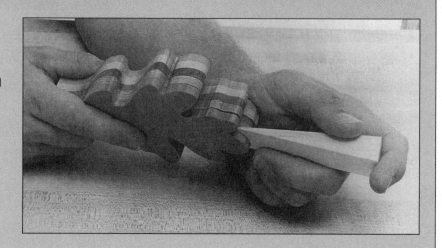

3 When you've completed the operations, take the pad apart and discard the tape. This is sometimes easier said than done. Remember, the carpet tape has an iron grip. To pry the pieces apart without damaging them, make a long, gently tapered wooden wedge. Insert the wedge between the pad layers and gently drive the wedge into the pad.

Treat Tree

As it comes from the factory, a traditional drill press is a limited tool. Sophisticated drilling techniques, such as the automatic spacing method I used to make this Treat Tree are impossible. A simple table and fence converts your press to a much more capable machine.

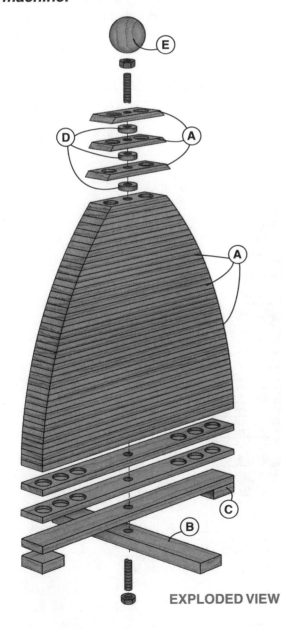

EXPLODED VIEW

MATERIALS LIST

Finished Dimensions in Inches	
Parts	
A. Branches (46)	$5/16'' \times 1 1/4'' \times 12''$
B. Base	$11/16'' \times 1 1/4'' \times 9''$
C. Feet (2)	$11/16'' \times 1 1/4'' \times 1 1/4''$
D. Spacers (3)	$1 1/4''$ dia. $\times 5/16''$
E. Bead	$1 1/2''$ dia.
Hardware	
$1/4''$ dia. $\times 16 5/8''$ Threaded rod	
$1/4''$ Hex nuts (2)	

*The branches of this "tree" fan out to make a cone shape.
Each branch is drilled with shallow holes to hold small candies.
When the tree is no longer needed, the branches fold flat for
easy storage.*

Friday Evening

1 **Prepare the materials,
and cut the parts to size.**
To make this decorative tree, you
need about 4 board feet of 4/4
(1-inch-thick) lumber, provided
you resaw the branch stock
before planing it. The tree shown
is made from maple, but you can
use any cabinet-grade wood.

Cut enough rough stock to
make the base and feet, and

plane it to $^{11}/_{16}$ inch thick. Resaw
the remainder, cutting the boards
in half, and
plane them to
$^{5}/_{16}$ inch thick.
Cut the
branches, base,
and feet. Set some $^{5}/_{16}$-inch-thick
scraps aside to make the spacers.

> See Also:
> **"Resawing"**
> on page 107.

Saturday Morning

2 **Drill the pivot holes in
the branches and base.**
All the branches pivot on a $^{1}/_{4}$-
inch-diameter rod that runs up
through the center of the tree.
Drill $^{1}/_{4}$-inch-diameter holes
through the center of each
branch. To save time, stack the
branches in groups of six or
seven, tape the stacks together
so the ends and edges are flush,
and drill the entire stack at once.
Also drill a $^{1}/_{4}$-inch-diameter
pivot hole with a $^{7}/_{16}$-inch-
diameter, $^{1}/_{4}$-inch-deep counterbore through the center of the
base, as shown in the *Front View.*

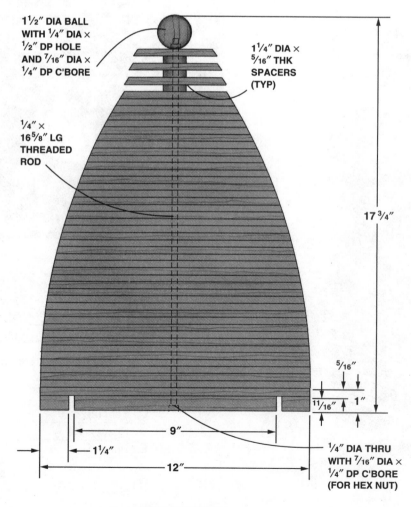

FRONT VIEW

3 **Cut the shape of the tree.** Stack the base and branches on the threaded rod as shown in the *Cutting Diagram,* and secure them with hex nuts. Rest the assembly flat on a workbench. Enlarge the *Tree Pattern,* and trace it on the assembly. Cut the profile of the tree with a band saw or saber saw, then sand the sawed edges.

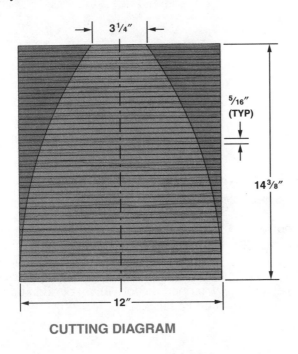

3¼″

5/16″
(TYP)

14³/8″

12″

CUTTING DIAGRAM

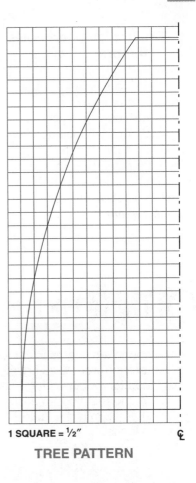

1 SQUARE = ½″

TREE PATTERN

EXTRA INFO

DRILLING EVENLY SPACED HOLES

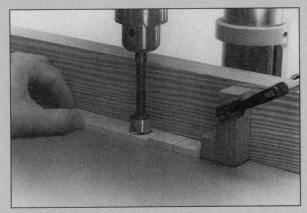

1 To drill the stopped holes in the branches, guide them along the fence on the drill press table. Clamp a stop to the fence, and place two 1¼-inch spacers between the stop and the bit. When the spacers are butted against the stop, the distance from the center of the bit to the edge of the first spacer should be ¹³/16 inch. Butt a branch up against the first spacer and drill a stopped hole near one end.

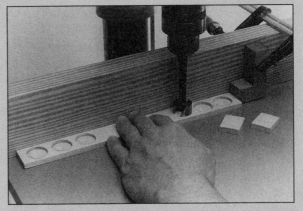

2 Turn the branch end for end, and drill a hole near the other end. Remove the first spacer, and drill two more holes. Repeat until you have drilled all the holes. Drill six holes in the bottom 20 branches, four holes in the next 15 branches, and two holes in the remainder.

4 Drill the stopped holes in the branches.

The branches have stopped holes in the top surfaces to hold candies. Number the branches on the bottom surface with a pencil, and remove them from the threaded rod. Using a Forstner bit, drill 1-inch-diameter, ⅛-inch-deep flat-bottomed holes in all the branches, as shown in the *Branch Layout.*

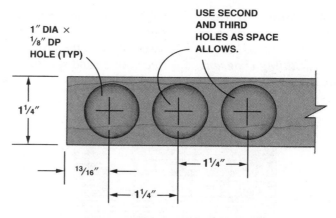

1″ DIA × ⅛″ DP HOLE (TYP)

USE SECOND AND THIRD HOLES AS SPACE ALLOWS.

1¼″

¹³/₁₆″

1¼″

1¼″

BRANCH LAYOUT

Quick FIXTURE: Drill Press Table and Fence

Although a drill press is an essential tool for precision woodworking, most presses are designed for metalworking and have some serious shortcomings in a wood shop. The most glaring problem is the table — it's too small and has no fence.

You can remedy this by building an auxiliary table that mounts to the existing one. The table shown offers a generous work surface. It also has a movable fence that mounts face up (when you need a short fence) or edge up (when you need a tall fence).

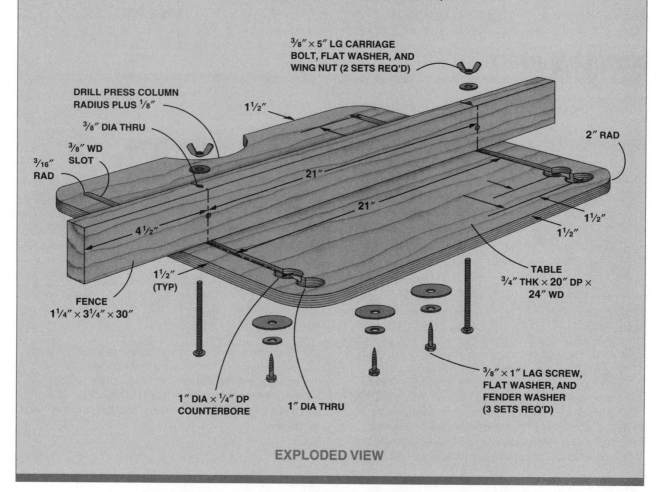

⅜″ × 5″ LG CARRIAGE BOLT, FLAT WASHER, AND WING NUT (2 SETS REQ'D)

DRILL PRESS COLUMN RADIUS PLUS ⅛″

⅜″ DIA THRU

⅜″ WD SLOT

³/₁₆″ RAD

1½″

2″ RAD

21″

21″

1½″

1½″

4½″

TABLE ¾″ THK × 20″ DP × 24″ WD

1½″ (TYP)

FENCE 1¼″ × 3¼″ × 30″

1″ DIA × ¼″ DP COUNTERBORE

1″ DIA THRU

⅜″ × 1″ LAG SCREW, FLAT WASHER, AND FENDER WASHER (3 SETS REQ'D)

EXPLODED VIEW

Sunday Afternoon

5 **Make the spacers.** Cut square scraps of ⁵⁄₁₆-inch-thick stock to make three spacers. Stack the squares and tape them together with the ends and edges flush. Using a compass or a hole template, lay out a spacer on the top part in the stack. Drill a ¼-inch-diameter hole through the center of the circle, cut the circular shape of the spacers, and sand the sawed edges.

6 **Drill the bead.** The bead needs a hole and a counterbore to hold a hex nut. Drill a ¼-inch-diameter, ½-inch-deep hole with a ⁷⁄₁₆-inch-diameter, ¼-inch deep counterbore. For a tip on how to drill a bead dead center, see page 191 in the Clothes Tree project.

7 **Assemble the tree.** Glue the feet to the bottom branch. Press hex nuts into the counterbores in the base and the bead, securing them with epoxy or cyanoacrylate ("Super") glue. Turn the threaded rod into the base and stack the branches on it in order. Put spacers between the last four branches. Tighten the bead/hex nut assembly onto the top end of the rod.

Tighten or loosen the knob as the wood shrinks and swells with the seasons.

At Your Leisure

8 **Finish the tree.** Take the bead, base, spacers, and branches apart. Set the rod aside and do any necessary touch-up sanding to the wooden parts. Apply a nontoxic finish, let it dry, then assemble the tree again.

Pro SKILL: Nontoxic Finishes

Most finishes harden to relatively benign substances with low toxicity. A very few of the chemicals that remain, such as the heavy metal salts that are used as dryers, can be poisonous, but these are imbedded in the hardened finish.

Usually, this residual toxicity poses no threat. But if these chemicals are ingested, they can be dangerous. When chewed or abraded by knives and forks, the finishes can flake off and be swallowed. Or, the mild acids in saliva and food juices may leach the finish out of the wood. For these reasons, projects that come in contact with food and children, or those that are in prolonged contact with the skin require *nontoxic* finishes. These include not only projects like the Treat Tree, but also serving bowls, cutting boards, eating utensils, toys, infant's furniture, and wooden jewelry.

The traditional nontoxic finish is *mineral oil*. Unfortunately, this is no finish at all. It doesn't harden and does little to protect or beautify the wood. Instead, consider:

■ *Walnut oil,* which does dry but does not form a hard film. Walnut oil is available at most health food stores, and several commercial finishes are made with nut oils.

■ *Salad bowl finishes,* which are manufactured from FDA-approved chemicals. They're durable, but not especially hard films. These are available from most mail-order woodworking suppliers.

■ Some brands of *water-based varnishes and lacquers,* which are marketed as nontoxic. However, because they chip and flake, they're not recommended for eating utensils.

■ *Shellac,* which is so safe that the FDA approves its use in medicines. And you can purchase it at almost any hardware store.

■ *Food dyes,* which, when diluted with water, make good stains. They are surprisingly colorfast. A wash coat of shellac (shellac diluted 1 to 1 with denatured alcohol) seals the dye in the wood so it won't leach out.

Time Bomb Clock

To cut the dowels that pretend to be the sticks of dynamite in this phony bomb, I cradled them in a V-jig. The jig prevents the stock from rolling, keeping the work aligned with the blade or bit.

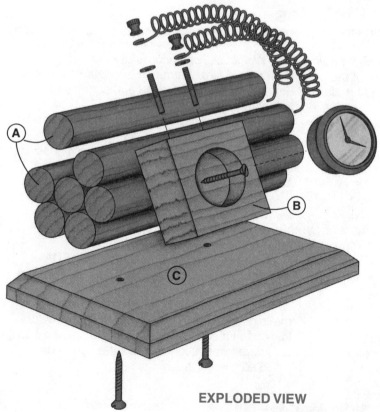

EXPLODED VIEW

MATERIALS LIST

Finished Dimensions in Inches

Parts

A.	Dynamite sticks (7)	¾" dia. × 4"
B.	Battery box	¾" × 2" × 2"
C.	Base	½" × 3" × 4½"

Hardware

#8 × 1½" Flathead wood screws (3)
14-gauge Solid wire (24")
#10 × 1" Roundhead machine screws (2)
#10 Flat washers (2)
#10 Knurled nuts (2)
1⅜" Clock insert

Resources Small clock inserts may be purchased from most mail-order woodworking supply companies, including:

The Woodworkers' Store
4365 Willow Drive
Medina, MN 55340

I've probably received more comments on this project than any other in the book. After a lifetime of wrestling with deadlines, this is the mental picture I get every time I look at a clock or a calendar. Judging from the reaction of folks who have seen this timepiece, it's an image many of us share.

Friday Evening

1 Prepare the materials, and cut the parts to size.
To make the time bomb clock, you need one 3-foot length of ¾-inch-diameter dowel stock, a few scraps of wood, and an odd sense of humor. You can use any hardwood species, of course, but this project looks best when made from light-colored woods. The clock shown is made from birch dowels and maple scraps. Once you've gathered the materials, cut the parts to size.

2 Paint the dowels. Finish sand the dowels, then paint them bright red to look like tiny sticks of dynamite.

Saturday Morning

3 Drill the battery box.
The clock fits in a 1⅜-inch-diameter, ⅜-inch-deep round mortise in the battery box. Drill this hole with a Forstner bit. You can also use a 35-mm-diameter boring bit commonly sold for installing European-style cabinet hinges. If you don't have a large Forstner bit, these are much less expensive.
Also drill two ³⁄₁₆-inch-diameter, ⅝-inch-deep holes in the top edge of the battery box, about 1 inch apart. These will hold the wire terminals.

4 Chamfer the base. Cut a ⅜-inch chamfer all around the perimeter of the base, as shown in the *Side View.*

5 Apply a finish to the battery box and base.
It's easier to finish the battery box and base *before* you assemble the clock. If you use shellac, lacquer, or a water-based varnish, you can apply two or three coats before tomorrow. You can also get a second coat of paint on the sticks of dynamite.

Sunday Afternoon

6 Coil the wire. Cut the wire into 12-inch lengths, then wrap each length around a pencil. Slide the coiled wire off the pencil.

7 Assemble the clock.
Finish sand the battery box and base. Glue the dynamite sticks together to form a hexagonal bundle, as shown in the *Side View.* Because these parts

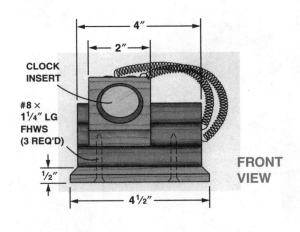

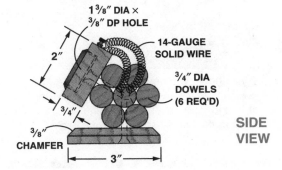

Quick FIXTURE: V-Jig

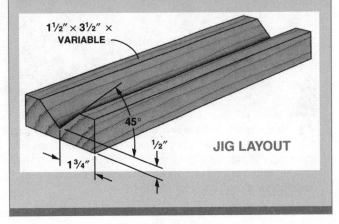

A V-jig cradles round stock in a V-groove that's cut in one surface. To cut the groove, tilt the table-saw blade to 45 degrees. Rip one side of the groove, turn the stock end for end, and rip the other. I make these jigs from short lengths of 2×4 stock in batches so I always have a few around.

are painted, ordinary wood glue may not hold them. Use a fast-setting epoxy or cyanoacrylate ("Super") glue instead.

Wait for the glue to dry, then fasten the battery box to the bundle with a flathead wood screw, driving the screw through the round mortise in the box. Also screw the base to the bundle. Countersink the heads of the screws.

Cut the heads off the round-head bolts, and glue them into the holes in the top of the battery box to make the battery terminals. Drill two $\frac{1}{16}$-inch-diameter holes in the end of the middle stick in the dynamite bundle. Glue one end of each coiled wire in these holes, and fasten the other ends to the battery box terminals with knurled nuts.

Finally, set the clock to the correct time, and insert it in the round mortise.

Carrying A Good Joke Too Far This goes without saying, but if I don't say it, I may hear about it — don't send this project through the mail or board an aircraft with it.

Pro SKILL: Cutting Round Stock

Round stock wants to roll, creating both safety and accuracy problems. More than once, I've cut off a small length of dowel and the saw has pitched it at me when it's rolled into the blade. Or I've needed to cut two or more flats only to have the stock roll after the first cut, making it difficult to align the next cut. A V-jig solves both these problems neatly by cradling the stock so it can't roll.

1 Here's the setup I used to cut up long dowels when making time bomb clocks. I used two V-jigs fastened to a miter gauge extension. The long V-jig feeds the dowel, while the shorter one holds the cutoff portion after it's sawed. A stop (clamped to the fence) positions the dowel for each cut.

2 With the dowel held in a V-jig, you can perform most of the cutting tasks that you ordinarily do with flat stock — mitering, ripping, cutting dadoes and grooves. You can even create tenons or narrow "necks" by feeding the dowel into a dado cutter, then slowly turning it in the V-jig.

3 Should you need to secure a dowel in a V-jig for an operation, lay short strips of hanger strap over the dowel, and screw them to the sides of the jig, as shown.

PART NINE

For Child's Play

Play Table

Parts of this play table were assembled with biscuits — flat, football-shaped wafers of compressed wood. These save time over traditional joinery and — in most applications — are just as strong.

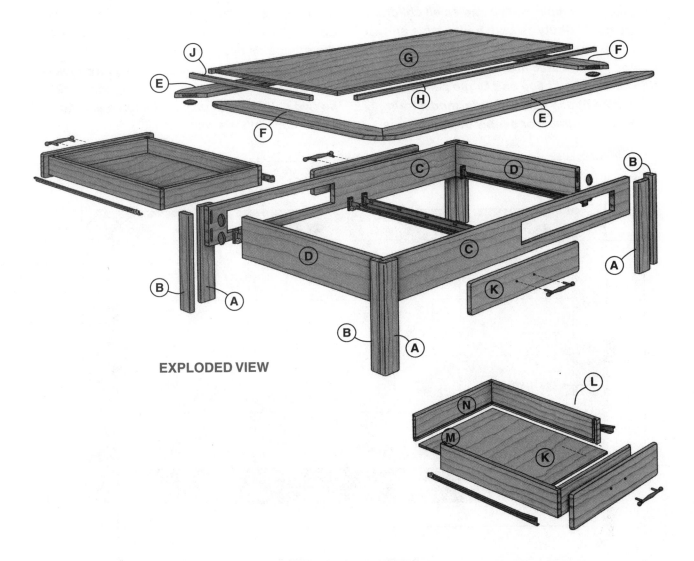

EXPLODED VIEW

MATERIALS LIST

Finished Dimensions in Inches

Parts	
A. Front/back legs (4)	³⁄₄″ × 2¹⁄₂″ × 17¹⁄₄″
B. Side legs (4)	³⁄₄″ × 1³⁄₄″ × 17¹⁄₄″
C. Front/back aprons (2)	³⁄₄″ × 7″ × 46¹⁄₂″
D. Side Aprons (2)	³⁄₄″ × 7″ × 22¹⁄₂″
E. Front/back trim (2)	³⁄₄″ × 3″ × 51³⁄₄″
F. Side trim (2)	³⁄₄″ × 3″ × 29¹⁄₄″
G. Top*	³⁄₄″ × 22¹⁄₂″ × 45″
H. Front/back top banding (2)	³⁄₈″ × ³⁄₄″ × 45³⁄₄″
J. Side top banding (2)	³⁄₈″ × ³⁄₄″ × 23¹⁄₄″
K. Drawer faces (4)	¹⁄₂″ × 5″ × 20″
L. Drawer fronts/backs (4)	¹⁄₂″ × 3⁷⁄₈″ × 17¹⁄₂″
M. Drawer sides (4)	¹⁄₂″ × 3⁷⁄₈″ × 23″
N. Drawer bottoms* (2)	¹⁄₄″ × 17¹⁄₂″ × 22¹⁄₂″

Make these parts from plywood.

Hardware

#20 Biscuits (12)

#8 × 1¹⁄₄″ Flathead wood screws (16)

21″ or 22″ Extension slides, rear brackets, and mounting screws (4)

Drawer pulls (4)

5¹⁄₈″ × 11¹⁄₄″ Lego and/or Duplo panels (12–optional)

Resources Extension slides are available from most woodworking supply companies, including:

Woodworker's Supply
1108 North Glenn Road
Casper, WY 82601

Order #878-316 (slides) and #859-210 (rear brackets).

Craftsman Paul Garbon invented this play table for folks with small houses and small children. It does double-duty as both a play table and an attractive coffee table. One side of the reversible top Paul stained and finished. To the other side he attached Lego and Duplo panels. (You might also attach game boards, model train tracks, a race track, or simply designate one side of the table as the "play" side and the other as the "good" side.) With the finished side up, the project is a piece of fine furniture. With the other side up, it's a play station. The drawers in the table provide storage for toys or game pieces. They pull out from opposite sides so two children can play at the table and not get in each other's way.

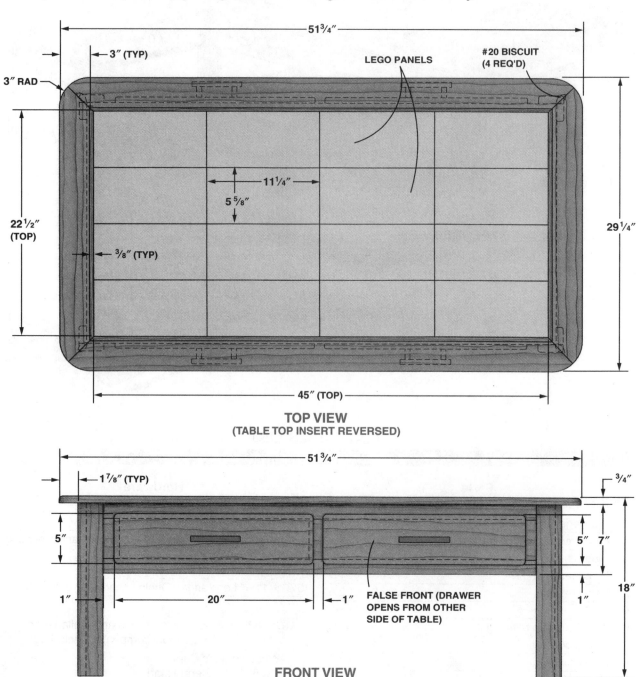

TOP VIEW
(TABLE TOP INSERT REVERSED)

FRONT VIEW

Friday Evening

1 Prepare the materials, and cut the parts to size.
To make the play table, you need about 23 board feet of 4/4 (1-inch-thick) material, a quarter sheet (2 feet by 4 feet) of ¾-inch plywood, and a quarter sheet of ¼-inch plywood. Paul's table is made from red oak and oak-veneer plywood, but you can use any cabinet-grade wood and matching plywood.

Plane the 4/4 stock to ¾ inch thick, and cut the stock for the legs, trim, and side aprons to the sizes shown in the Materials List. Miter the ends of the trim at 45 degrees. Cut the bandings an inch or so longer than specified,

and make the front and back aprons about ½ inch wider than specified.

Plane the remaining stock to ½ inch thick, and cut the drawer parts. Also cut the plywood top and drawer bottoms.

Saturday Morning

2 Make the cutouts in the front and back aprons.
The front and back aprons have rectangular cutouts for the drawers. To make these cutouts, rip a 1½-inch-wide strip from the top of each board, then a

4-inch-wide strip, then another 1½-inch wide strip. Cut a 3¼-inch long part from one end of the 4-inch-wide board, then a 24¼-inch-long part from the other end. Glue the parts back together, as shown in the *Apron Layout,* leaving out the 19-inch-long piece. If you carefully match the grain so the pieces go back together in the same way they were cut apart, you won't be able to see the glue joints.

See Also:
"Gluing Stock Edge to Edge" on page 74.

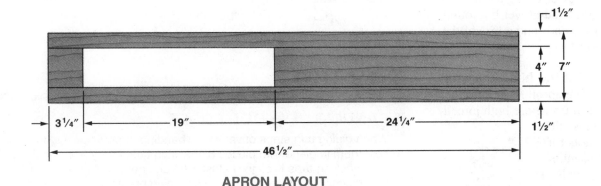

APRON LAYOUT

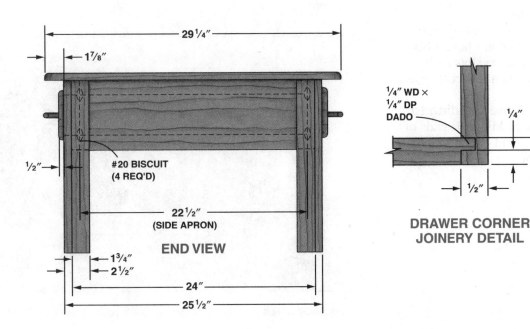

END VIEW

DRAWER CORNER JOINERY DETAIL

3 Cut the drawer joinery.

While the glue is drying on the aprons, make the joinery for the drawer parts. Using a dado cutter or table-mounted router, cut:

■ ¼-inch-wide, ¼-inch-deep grooves in the drawer front, backs, and sides to hold the bottom

■ ¼-inch-wide, ¼-inch-deep dadoes near the ends of the drawer sides to hold the front and back

■ ¼-inch-wide, ¼-inch-deep rabbets in the ends of the drawer backs and front to join the sides

Saturday Afternoon

4 Round over the drawer faces.

Using a router and a ⅜-inch roundover bit, round over the ends and edges of the drawer faces.

5 Cut the biscuit joints.

The apron frame and the top trim frame are both joined with biscuits. Cut slots for #20 biscuits in the ends of the trim and the side aprons and faces of the front and back aprons. If you don't have a biscuit joiner, cut the slots with your router and a slot-cutting bit.

See Also:
"Biscuit Joinery"
on page 248.

6 Attach the banding to the top.

Miter the ends of the banding, and glue it to the plywood top.

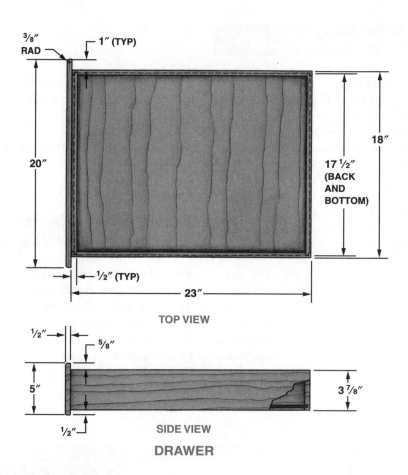

TOP VIEW

SIDE VIEW

DRAWER

TRY THIS

BANDING PLYWOOD EDGES

When gluing thin strips of veneer or banding to plywood edges, hold them in place with pieces of masking tape every 2 to 3 inches. The masking tape is slightly elastic. If you stretch it tight, the multiple pieces will generate enough clamping pressure to get a good glue bond.

Saturday Evening

7 **Assemble the legs, trim frame, apron frame, and drawers.** Finish sand the legs, aprons, trim, and drawer parts. Glue together:

■ The legs to make four L-shaped assemblies

■ The front, back, and side aprons, with biscuits. Remember, the cutouts for the drawers must be on opposite sides.

■ The trim frame members, with biscuits

■ The drawer fronts, backs, sides, and faces. Insert the bottoms in their grooves as you assemble the drawer, but don't glue them in place. They should "float" in the grooves.

Sunday Afternoon

8 **Round the corners of the trim frame.** Using a coping saw or a saber saw, cut a 3-inch radius on the outside corners of the trim frame, as shown in the *Top View*. This will help prevent injury when the kids are playing at the table.

9 **Assemble the sub-assemblies.** Do any necessary touch-up sanding to the assemblies you've made so far. Attach the legs to the outside of the apron frame with glue and screws. Then glue the trim frame to the top edges of the aprons. The trim frame only covers half the thickness of the aprons.

When the trim and aprons are assembled, the aprons should form a ³⁄₈-inch-wide ledge all around the inside edge of the trim. The top will rest on this ledge.

Also glue the false drawer faces to the front and back aprons.

Sunday Evening

10 **Install the top and drawers.** Attach the drawer pulls to the drawers and the false drawer faces. Mount the rails for the extension slides

---

Quick FIXTURE: Biscuit Slot Template

If you don't have a biscuit joiner, you can make biscuit joints with your router. Most mail-order woodworking supply companies sell ⁵⁄₃₂-inch slot-cutting bits to rout biscuit slots. This template is designed to guide the router with the aid of a pilot bearing as you cut these slots. The space between the stops in the template depends on the cutter diameter (CD), the pilot bearing diameter (BD), and the biscuit length (BL). Use the formula shown to figure the spacing. For example, if you want to install #20 biscuits (2½ inches long) using a 1⅞-inch-diameter cutter and a ½-inch-diameter pilot bearing, make the space 1⅝ inches wide.

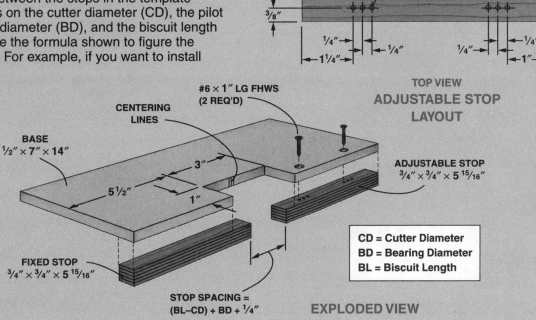

inside the table, and the slides themselves to the drawers. Insert the slides in the rails, and test the action of the drawers. They should slide in and out easily. If necessary, adjust the position of the rails for the best possible action.

When the drawers work to your satisfaction, lay the top in place. If the fit is tight, sand or plane the edges until the top lifts out and plops back in easily.

At Your Leisure

11 **Finish the table.** Remove the drawers, drawer pulls, and extension slides from the table. Set the hardware aside and do any

Pro SKILL: Biscuit Joinery

A "biscuit" or plate is a flat, oval-shaped spline made from compressed hardwood. When installed in short slots, they span the seam between two adjoining parts, tying them together. Stress tests show that, in certain applications, this arrangement is as strong as a mortise-and-tenon joint.

Biscuits come in three sizes, #0, #10, and #20.

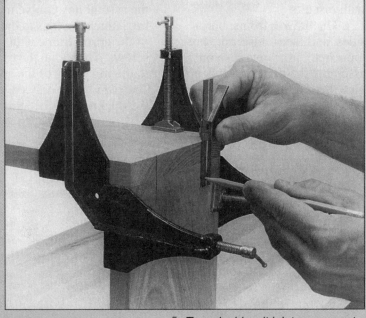

1 To make biscuit joints, you must cut pairs of matching slots for the biscuits in the adjoining parts. Temporarily, clamp the parts together and draw short lines across the seam where you wish to install the biscuits.

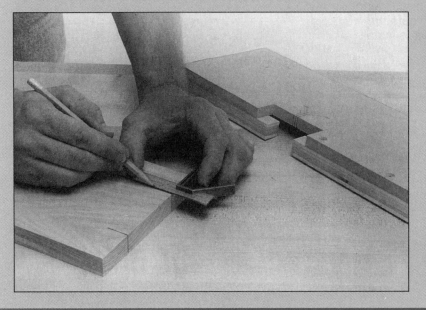

2 If you're using a routing template to make the slots, mark the center of the notch in the template. Extend the short lines you drew on the stock an inch or so perpendicular to the surface where you will cut the slots.

necessary touch-up sanding. Then apply a finish. Since children will be abusing this project, I suggest something extremely durable, like polyurethane or spar varnish.

12 Install the Duplo and Lego panels. If you're making this project to provide a play surface for young Duplo or Lego enthusiasts, attach the panels to the "play" side of the top. These panels have short legs that are designed to be screwed to a surface. However, Paul found he could create a more solid playing surface by cutting the legs off and gluing the panels to the top with contact cement.

Resources You can purchase Duplo and Lego panels from:

Lego Shop-At-Home Service
P.O. Box 1310
Enfield, CT 06083-1310

3 Clamp the template to the work, aligning the marks on the board with the center of the notch. Make sure the clamps won't interfere with the router.

4 Insert a ⁵⁄₃₂-inch slot cutter in the chuck. Adjust the depth of cut, then cut the slots, keeping the pilot bearing against the stock between the stops.

5 Apply glue to the mating surfaces and the insides of the slots. Insert the biscuits in the slots, then clamp the parts together. Because the biscuits are a little loose in the slots, you can adjust the position of the parts slightly to align them perfectly. You have only a minute or two to do this, however. The water in the glue causes the compressed biscuits to swell, and in a few moments they expand to fill the slots. **Note:** If you need more working time to align the parts, use epoxy or a slow-set polyurethane glue.

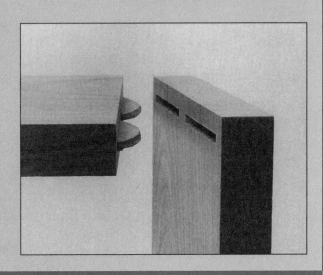

Marble Race

*T*he ramps that channel the marbles are suspended by ladders. To make these ladders, I had to drill almost 200 holes, all precisely spaced and aligned. Sounds like a formidable task, doesn't it? But with a simple indexing jig, you can create all these holes in less than an hour.

250

MATERIALS LIST

Finished Dimensions in Inches		
Parts		
A. Ramps (8)		¾″ × 2″ × 20″
B. Stops (8)		⅛″ × ½″ × 2″
C. Long ladder supports (12)		¾″ dia. × 18″
D. Short ladder supports (12)		¾″ dia. × 9″
E. Rungs (96)		¼″ dia. × 2¾″
F. Dowel (12)		¼″ dia. × 1″
G. Bases (6)		¾″ × 6″ × 6″

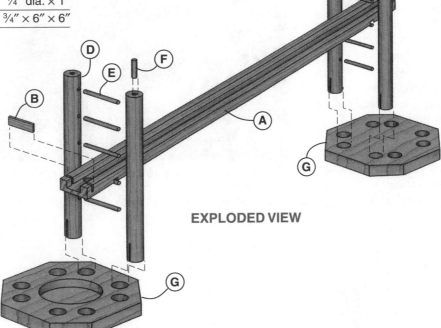

EXPLODED VIEW

This marble race consists of four components — long ladders, short ladders, bases, and ramps — that can be assembled in many different configurations. In fact, I quickly found when I kid-tested this project that it's a lot more fun to plan new configurations and put the parts together than it is to race the marbles. Building the first race takes two kids about half an hour of intense concentration. After that, there's about three hours of arguments, labor strikes, riots, and nonbinding arbitration as the configuration is altered again and again in a quest for the ultimate marble race. The whole notion of actually racing marbles seems fairly unimportant, although quite a few test marbles roll down the ramps while the construction engineers duke it out.

With that in mind, how many ramps, ladders, and bases should you build? Obviously, the more parts there are, the more configurations you can make. The materials list shows the parts needed for what I found was a "basic" set — 8 ramps, 6 long ladders, 6 short ladders, and 6 bases. With this, you can make configurations in which the supports have as many as 16 rungs (by attaching a short ladder to a long one) and the marbles drop 27 inches. A more "advanced" set might consist of 11 ramps, 8 long ladders, 8 short ladders, and 8 bases. This would allow you to combine long ladders to make supports with 22 rungs, and the marble would drop 36 inches.

Hint: If the Rube Goldbergs among you decide to modify this design so you can make even taller supports, bear in mind that the tallest support should always have an even number of rungs. The number of ramps needed will be half the number of rungs in the tallest support.

Saturday Morning

1 Prepare the materials, and cut the parts to size.

To make the basic set shown in the Materials List, you need about 4 board feet of 4/4 (1-inch-thick) stock, about 30 linear feet of ¾-inch-diameter dowel stock, and 24 linear feet of ¼-inch-diameter dowel stock. Choose a clear, durable hardwood. The marble race shown is made from ash and maple dowel stock.

Plane the 4/4 stock to ¾ inch thick, and cut the ramps and bases to size. Then plane a scrap to ½ inch thick, and cut the stops. Cut the ¾-inch-diameter dowel stock to make the long and short ladder supports, and the ¼-inch-diameter dowel stock to make the rungs and the dowels.

To quickly cut the rungs to size, attach a *resawing fence* to your band saw. Position the fence 2¾ inches from the blade — this becomes a stop that automatically gauges the length of the rung before you cut it. Use a square scrap of wood to feed the dowel stock into the blade, as shown.

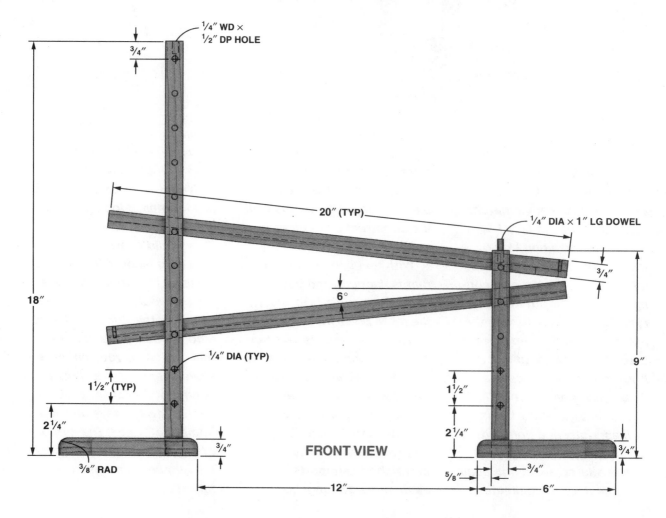

FRONT VIEW

2 **Make the jigs.** The marble race is a mass production project. There are many cuts to make and holes to drill, but they are all repetitive. Consequently, if you make a few jigs to help you do the repetitive operations, you can blaze through this project in an afternoon. Really! After I cut the parts to size and made the jigs, it took less than four hours to complete the

marble race. You need four simple fixtures:

■ A *Hole Indexing Jig* on this page to drill the holes in the ladder supports for the rungs

■ A *Ladder Gauge and Drilling Guide* on page 255 to help assemble the ladders and drill the holes in the ends of the supports

■ A *Notch Jig* on page 257 to hold the bases as you cut the

octagonal shape and drill the mounting holes. This jig also holds the ladders so you can cut slots in the ends of the supports.

■ A *Pattern Routing Template* on page 258 to scoop out a recess in one of the bases.

Most of these jigs are just a single piece of wood that you can cut or machine in just a few minutes.

Quick FIXTURE: Hole Indexing Jig

When drilling the rung holes in the ladder supports, you must space the holes precisely 1½ inches on center. Although you could measure and mark all the ladder supports, this would be ridiculously time-consuming. It's quicker and more accurate to make a *hole indexing jig.*

To make the jig, first make a simple *V-jig* to hold round stock. (There are plans and instructions for making a V-jig on page 239.) On a table saw, cut ⅛-inch-wide saw kerfs across the V-groove every 1½ inches. There should be as many slots as there are holes to drill. Since you must drill 11 rung holes in each ladder support, cut 11 slots in the V-jig.

Finally make a ⅛-inch-thick stop to fit the slots. Before drilling a hole, insert the stop in a slot, and butt the round stock up against it to position the stock in the jig.

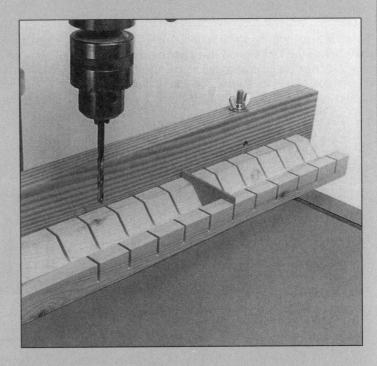

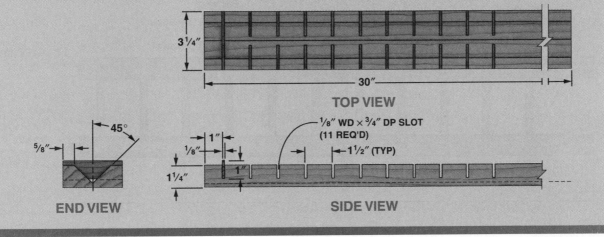

3¼"

30"

TOP VIEW

45°

⅝"

⅛" WD × ¾" DP SLOT
(11 REQ'D)

1"

⅛"

1¼"

1"

1½" (TYP)

END VIEW

SIDE VIEW

Saturday Afternoon

3 **Drill the holes in the ladder supports.** Mark a line down the length of each ladder support, then mark the locations of the rung holes on a single long support. (There's no need to mark all the supports —

you just need one to check your setup.)

Position the hole indexing jig on your drill press and drill ¼-inch-diameter, ⅜-inch deep rung holes in the long support you've measured and marked, moving

the stop in the jig to position each hole. If your setup is correct, the bit should hit the mark each time. When you're satisfied with the setup, drill the remaining supports, both long and short.

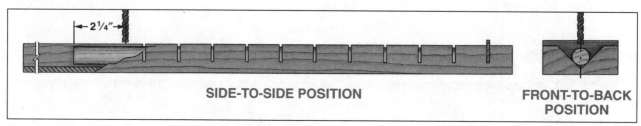

SIDE-TO-SIDE POSITION

FRONT-TO-BACK POSITION

Place the hole indexing jig on your drill press table. If you've made the *Drill Press Table and Fence* shown on page 236, rest the jig against the fence. Insert the stop in the first slot, and place the support you've measured and marked in the jig. Mount a drill bit in the chuck, and posi-

tion the jig side to side so the bit is directly above the mark for first rung hole (the hole 2¼ inches from the bottom end). Position it front to back so the bit is directly above the point of the V-groove in the jig. Clamp the jig to the fence or the table.

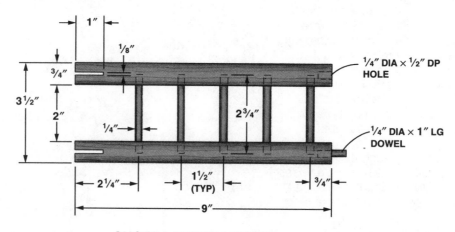

SHORT LADDER LAYOUT

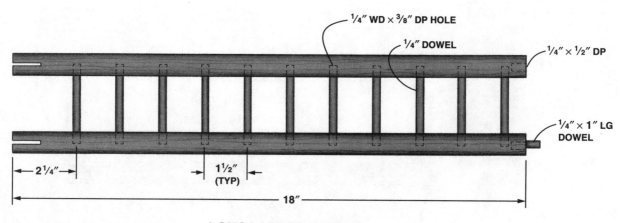

LONG LADDER LAYOUT

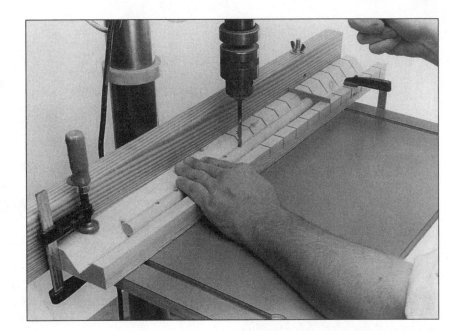

Once the jig is positioned, turn the support so the line you've drawn down its length is directly under the bit. Set the depth stop on the drill press to bore the holes just ³⁄₈ inch deep. Drill the first hole, move the stop on the jig to the next slot, and repeat. Continue until you've drilled all the holes in all the supports.

Bonus FIXTURE: Ladder Gauge and Drilling Guide

When you assemble the ladders, the supports must be exactly 2 ³⁄₄ inches on center. Otherwise, the ladders may not fit the holes in the bases. This jig serves as a gauge to measure this distance. It also serves as a drill guide when boring holes in the top ends of the ladder supports.

Make the fixture from a block of hard wood. Carefully measure and mark the positions of the holes. Drill the ³⁄₄-inch-diameter counterbores first, then the ¹⁄₄-inch-diameter through holes.

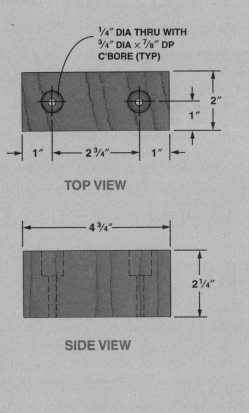

¹⁄₄" DIA THRU WITH
³⁄₄" DIA × ⁷⁄₈" DP
C'BORE (TYP)

2"

1"

1" — 2 ³⁄₄" — 1"

TOP VIEW

4 ³⁄₄"

2 ¹⁄₄"

SIDE VIEW

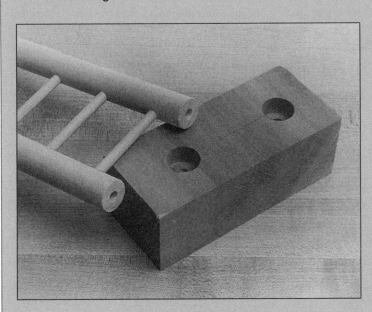

4 Assemble the ladders.
Sand the supports with 100-grit sandpaper. Then assemble the supports and rungs with glue. If any glue squeezes out of the joints, wash it off with water, and set the ladders aside to dry.

TRY THIS

BRUSHING AWAY EXCESS GLUE

An inexpensive foam brush makes a good tool to scrub away glue squeeze-out. Just dip the brush in water from time to time to clean it and keep it wet. The pointed tip lets you reach into corners and crevices.

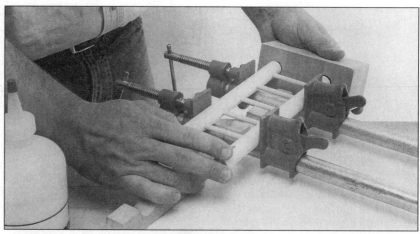

As you glue the ladder supports and rungs together, check that both the top and bottom ends of the supports slip into the ¾-inch-diameter holes in the ladder gauge and drilling guide. If the supports are too far apart to fit the holes, press the supports and rungs together with a clamp or a vise before the glue dries. If they are too close together, pry them apart.

5 Cut the octagonal shape of the bases. Cut the corner off the bases to create octagonal shapes. Use the notch jig to hold the bases as you saw them, guiding the jig along the table saw fence.

6 Drill the mounting holes in the base. Lay out the positions of the ¾-inch-diameter mounting holes in one base. Using the notch jig to position the bases on the drill press, drill the mounting holes in the base that you've marked. Check that the ladders fit the holes reasonably well. If so, drill the mounting holes in the remaining bases.

To cut the shapes of the bases, position the table saw fence 9 inches away from the blade. Place a base in the notch in the notch jig, and feed the base past the saw blade, guiding the jig along the fence. Take the base out of the jig, turn it 90 degrees, and repeat. Continue until you have cut all the corners off all the bases.

TRY THIS

DRILLING CLEAN HOLES

To prevent the wood grain from tearing when the bit exits the base, rest the base and the notch jig on a scrap of plywood. This will back up the base as you drill it.

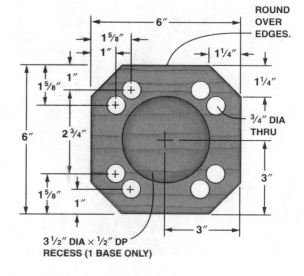

BASE LAYOUT

ROUND OVER EDGES.

6"

1⅝"
1"

1"

1⅝"

6"

2¾"

1⅝"

1"

1¼"

1¼"

¾" DIA THRU

3"

3"

3½" DIA × ½" DP RECESS (1 BASE ONLY)

Mark the positions of the mounting holes on a single base. Place that base in the notch jig and position the jig so the mark for one of the holes — any hole, it doesn't matter which — is directly under the bit. Secure the jig to the drill press table. Drill the first hole, lift the base out of the notch, turn it 90 degrees, put it back in the notch, and drill the next hole. Repeat until you have drilled four holes. Then flip the base face for face and repeat, drilling another four holes.

Bonus FIXTURE: Notch Jig

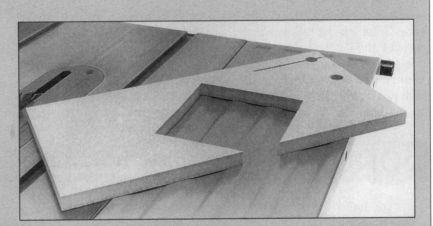

When machining odd-shaped parts or sawing, sanding, or drilling at odd angles, it helps to hold the parts in a notch jig. This particular jig holds both the bases and the ladders for various cutting and drilling operations.

Measure and mark the shape of the base and the locations of the holes on the notch jig. Cut a notch to hold the base with a band saw, then drill the mounting holes.

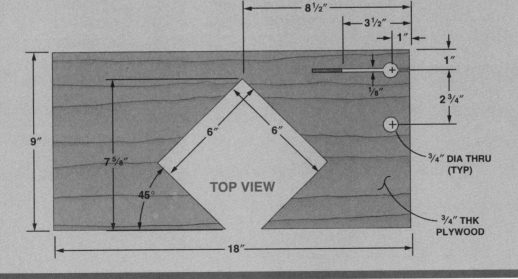

TOP VIEW

8½"
3½"
1"
1"
⅛"
2 ¾"
9"
7 ⁵/₈"
6"
6"
45°
18"
¾" DIA THRU (TYP)
¾" THK PLYWOOD

7 **Rout the recess in the "last" base.** One base has a recess in the surface to catch the marbles. You could rout this recess in all the bases, but it's a time-consuming chore and you really only need it in one base — the last base, at the end of the race. Select a base, and attach the pattern routing template to it. Then rout the recess with a core box bit, as shown in the **Base Layout.**

8 **Round over the edges of the bases.** Using a table-mounted router and a piloted roundover bit, round over the top edges of the bases, all around the circumference.

9 **Make the ramps.** Drill a 1-inch-diameter hole in each ramp, near one end, as shown in the **Ramp Detail/Top View.** Then cut the following grooves and dadoes:

■ A 1-inch-wide, $^7/_{16}$-inch-deep groove down the center of each ramp to create a channel for the marbles

To rout a recess in a base, attach the pattern routing template to it with double-faced carpet tape. Mount a ½-inch core box bit in your router and install a $^5/_8$-inch guide bushing. Rout the recess, using the template and the guide bushing to guide the router. Make the recess in several passes, cutting no deeper than ⅛ inch with each pass.

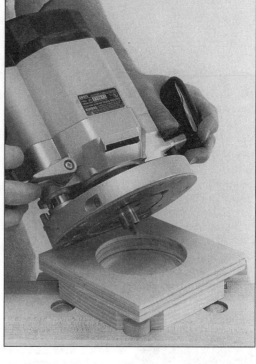

■ ¼-inch-wide, ¼-inch-deep dadoes in the bottom faces of the ramps to fit over the rungs in the ladders, as shown in the **Ramp Detail/Side View**
■ A ⅛-inch-wide, ½-inch-deep dado that just touches the

outside edge of the hole in each channel, nearest the end.

Finish sand the channels, then glue the stops in the ⅛-inch-wide dadoes.

Bonus FIXTURE: Pattern Routing Template

One base has a recess to collect the marbles at the end of the race. To cut this recess, make a simple routing template to guide a ½-inch router bit and $^5/_8$-inch guide collar. Simply cut a 3¾-inch-diameter hole in the plywood template with a hole saw.

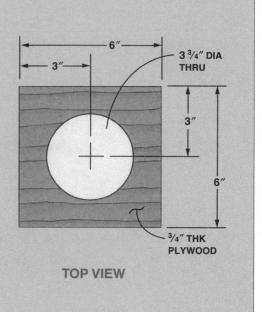

6"
3"
3 ¾" DIA THRU
3"
6"
¾" THK PLYWOOD

TOP VIEW

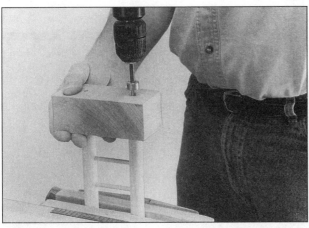

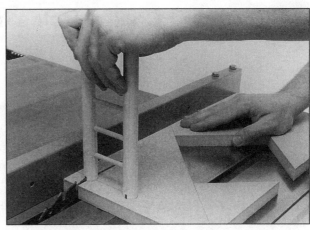

Place the ladder gauge and drilling guide over the top end of each ladder. Using a hand-held drill, bore a ¼-inch-diameter, ½-inch-deep hole in the top end of each support. Use a stop collar to stop the drill bit at the proper depth.

To cut the slots in the bottom ends of the ladder supports, insert a ladder into the holes in the notch jig. Feed the ladder over the blade, guiding the jig along the fence and cutting a single slot. Then turn the ladder 180 degrees and cut the second slot.

10 Cut the slots and install the dowels in the ends of the ladder supports. Using the ladder gauge and drilling guide to position and guide a hand-held drill, bore holes in the top ends of the ladders, as shown in the *Long Ladder Layout* and *Short Ladder Layout.* Glue dowels into just one hole in the top of each ladder.

The bottom ends of the ladder supports are slotted, as shown in the *Long Ladder Layout* and *Short Ladder Layout.* This allows them to flex and makes it easier to fit the ladders to the holes in the bases, even if the holes or supports aren't precisely 2¾ inches on center. Cut these slots using the notch jig to hold and guide the ladders over the table saw blade.

At Your Leisure

11 Finish the marble race. Finish sand the bases, ladders, and ramps. Then apply a nontoxic finish to all wooden surfaces. You have several choices — shellac, "salad bowl" finishes, and some brands of water-based varnishes are nontoxic. If you wish to add color to the marble race, food dyes diluted with water make excellent nontoxic stains. And they are surprisingly colorfast.

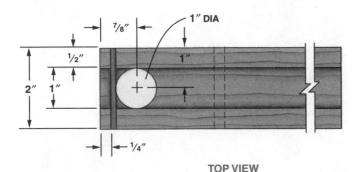

TOP VIEW

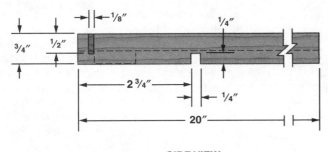

SIDE VIEW

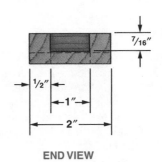

END VIEW

RAMP DETAIL

Pro SKILL: Drilling Holes in Round Stock

When drilling round stock, you must take extra care to hold and position the stock. Not only do you have to prevent the stock from rolling, you must also make sure that the holes are properly aligned along the length of the stock and that you drill through the diameter, or center, of the stock.

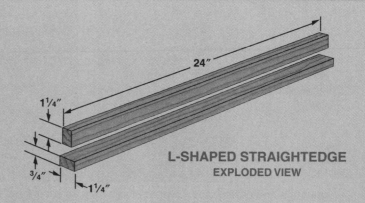

24"

1¼"

¾"

1¼"

L-SHAPED STRAIGHTEDGE
EXPLODED VIEW

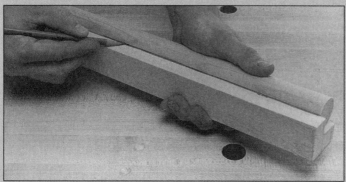

1 When boring a series of holes, such as the rung holes in the ladder supports or the round mortises in a chair leg, the holes must be arranged in a straight line down the length of the cylinder. To make sure that they are, make an L-shaped straightedge from two scraps of wood, as shown. Rest the round stock in the inside corner of the straightedge, and scribe a line down the length.

2 To prevent the stock from rolling, cradle it in a V-jig. To make sure you drill through the diameter, position the V-jig so the point of the V-groove is directly underneath the point of the drill bit. Clamp the jig to the drill press table to prevent it from shifting as you work.

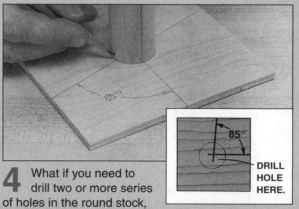

85°

DRILL
HOLE
HERE.

3 Measure along the line you have marked down the length of the round stock and mark the positions of the holes you want to drill. Then place the round stock in the V-jig and rotate it so the line is directly under the bit. Drill the hole with the bit centered on the line.

4 What if you need to drill two or more series of holes in the round stock, each series a precise number of degrees away from the others? To do this, first lay out the angles on a piece of cardboard or scrap of thin plywood. Where the angles cross, drill a hole the same diameter as the round stock. Insert the round stock in the hole, and mark the surface where the angled lines meet it. Using an L-shaped straightedge, draw lines down the length of the cylinder at each of these marks.

Arch Blocks

To cut the 10-sided form quickly and accurately, I laid out the odd-shaped profile on the stock and followed the lines with a table saw duplicator. If I had been making several sets of arch blocks, I could have made duplicate forms in minutes, using the first form as a template.

MATERIALS LIST

Finished Dimensions in Inches		
Parts		
A. Arch blocks (7)		$1\frac{3}{4}'' \times 3\frac{1}{4}'' \times 4''$
B. Support blocks (2)		$1\frac{3}{4}'' \times 3\frac{5}{16}'' \times 3\frac{1}{4}''$
C. Support block bases (2)		$\frac{3}{4}'' \times 3\frac{5}{16}'' \times 4''$
D. Form*		$\frac{3}{4}'' \times 9\frac{1}{2}'' \times 11\frac{5}{16}''$
E. Form handle		$\frac{3}{4}'' \times 3'' \times 6''$

* Make this part from plywood.

Hardware
#8 × 1½″ Flathead wood screws (6)

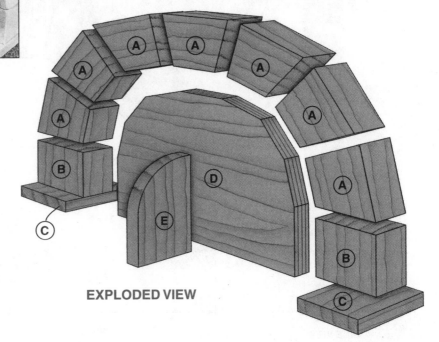

EXPLODED VIEW

When Fred Weissborn of Cincinnati, Ohio, showed me his design for this set of blocks, I thought it was a great educational toy. On the surface, it looks like Fred designed it to teach coordination and spatial relationships. Arrange the blocks over and around the form, then carefully slip the form from under the blocks leaving a stable arch, not unlike what architects and engineers have been doing for 2,000 years. What could be more educational?

But after making a set for a nephew with a radio-controlled car, I found the arch quickly became an action toy. Once the arch is in place, drive the car toward the opening at full speed. If the car makes it through the arch without hitting the blocks, turn it around and try again. If the car doesn't make it — and it usually doesn't — well, the crash is spectacular.

Friday Evening

1 Prepare the materials, and cut the parts to size.
To make this set of arch blocks, you need approximately 3 board feet of 8/4 (2-inch-thick) stock and 2 board feet of 4/4 (1-inch-thick) stock. The blocks shown are made from hard maple to ensure their durability. However, you can use any clear wood that does not chip or splinter easily.

Plane the scrap of 8/4 stock to 1¾ inches thick and the 4/4 stock to ¾ inch thick. Cut the support blocks, support block bases, form, and form handle to size. Rip a piece of 1¾-inch-thick stock 3¼ inches wide and 30 inches long to make the mitered arch blocks. Also prepare a 30-inch-long scrap of 2×4 lumber, jointing it straight and true. You'll need this scrap to check your setup before you cut the blocks.

Saturday Morning

2 Cut the arch blocks.
The ends of the arch blocks must be mitered at 12.9 degrees. It's very difficult to set this miter angle accurately using the small scales on most table saw miter gauges. But you can fine-tune the setup by clamping a straight-edge to a carpenter's square to create the desired angle, then using this to adjust the gauge.

To check your setup, cut seven mitered blocks all the same length from the 2×4 scrap, and

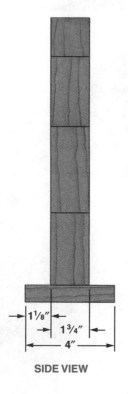

SIDE VIEW

1⅛″
1¾″
4″

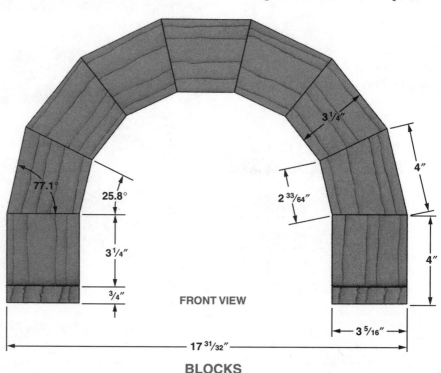

FRONT VIEW

3¼″
77.1°
25.8°
3¼″
¾″
2 ³³⁄₆₄″
4″
4″
3 ⁵⁄₁₆″
17 ³¹⁄₃₂″

BLOCKS

arrange them on a flat surface to form an arch. Tape the mitered ends together so they won't shift and pull apart. Lay a straight-edge across the bottom of the arch. The blocks on either end of the arch should rest flat against the straightedge.

When you're satisfied with the setup, cut the 3¼-inch-wide maple stock to make seven arch blocks, all 4 inches long on the long side. Use a miter gauge extension and stop to make sure the parts are precisely the same length.

See Also:
"Miter Gauge Extension and Stop" on page 79.

Saturday Afternoon

3 **Cut the form.** Arrange the arch blocks and support blocks on a flat surface to form an arch. Tape the adjoining ends together on both sides of the assembly so you can pick up the arch and move it. Remember, the ends must remain snug against one another.

Arrange the arch on the form stock. Space the ends of the support blocks ¾ inch from the bottom edge of the form stock. (To be precise, use the support block bases as spacers.) Using the assembled arch as a template, trace the *inside* profile on the form stock.

Using double-faced carpet tape, attach a scrap of wood to the form stock, aligning the edge of the scrap with one of the layout lines on the form. Cut along the line, using the scrap and a *Table Saw Duplicator* to guide the cut. Move the scrap, and cut another line. Continue until you have cut the entire profile.

See Also:
"Cutting and Duplicating Odd Shapes" on page 266.

TRY THIS

SIZING THE FORM

I've found the form is easier to use if it's slightly smaller than the inside circumference of the arch. (This makes it easier to slip the form from under the blocks.) To make it so, attach the guiding scrap to the form on the *inside* edge of each layout line. Presuming you have set up the table saw duplicator correctly, the circumference of the completed form will be smaller than the arch by the width of a pencil line.

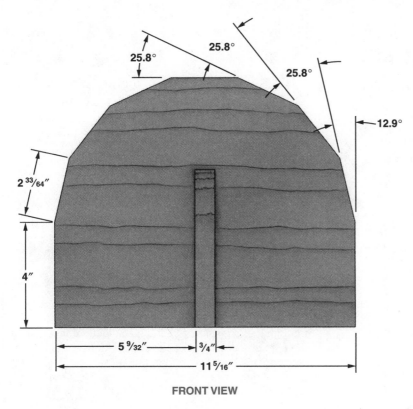

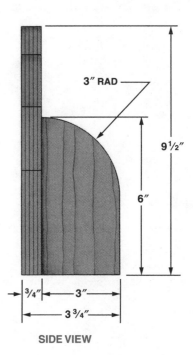

FRONT VIEW

SIDE VIEW

FORM

EXTRA INFO

SETTING UP THE MITER ANGLE AND CUTTING THE BLOCKS

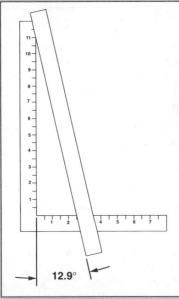

12.9°

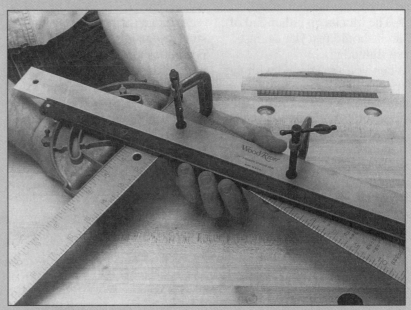

1 Clamp or tape a straightedge to a carpenter's square so the edge touches the 10⅞-inch mark on the long blade and the 2½-inch mark on the short blade. The angle between the straightedge and the long blade will be as close as you'll ever get to 12.9 degrees.

2 Set the miter gauge by aligning the bar with the straightedge and the face with the square, as shown.

3 To begin cutting the arch blocks, miter the end of the stock. Note which edge is resting against the miter gauge extension as you make the first cut.

4 Attach a stop to the miter gauge extension 4 inches from the kerf where the blade passes through the extension. Flip the stock face for face so the opposite edge rests against the extension. Butt the stock against the stop, and make another cut. Flip the stock, and cut again. Continue until you have made seven 4-inch-long blocks.

4 **Cut the profile of the form handle.** Mark the curved edge of the form handle, as shown in the *Form/Side View.* Cut the curved profile on a band saw, and sand the sawed surface smooth.

5 **Assemble the form and support blocks.** Attach the bases to the support blocks with glue and wood screws. Also attach the handle to the form. Countersink and counterbore the screws, then cover their heads with wooden plugs. When the glue dries, sand the plugs flush with the surrounding wood surface.

6 **Finish the blocks and form.** Finish sand the blocks and form, rounding the edges and corners. Then apply a *nontoxic* finish to all wooden surfaces — shellac, "salad bowl" finish, or special brands of water-based varnishes. If you wish to add color to the blocks, make colored stains by diluting food dyes with water.

Quick FIXTURE: Table Saw Duplicator

When cutting odd shapes and angles on the table saw, it's often quicker to use a "duplicator" than it is to fuss around with your miter gauge, setting and re-setting the angle and stop for each cut. This fixture lets you make the cut by following your layout lines.

The duplicator is a horizontal fence extension that overhangs the blade. To make the extension, attach a ¼-inch-thick strip of clear acrylic plastic to a wooden cleat with wood screws.

Note: In a pinch, you can use ¼-inch plywood instead of ¼-inch plastic, but the clear plastic lets you see the cut as you make it. The plywood blocks your view.

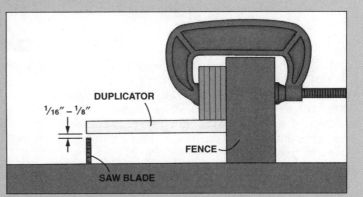

DUPLICATOR

1/16" – 1/8"

FENCE

SAW BLADE

To mount the duplicator on your table saw, first adjust the blade height. Clamp the cleat to the fence so the plastic extension is about 1/16 to 1/8 inch above the blade. Position the fence so the edge of the extension is even with the tips of the saw teeth that point *away* from the fence.

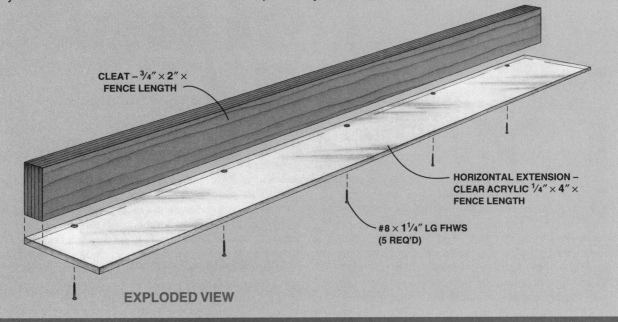

CLEAT – ¾" × 2" × FENCE LENGTH

HORIZONTAL EXTENSION – CLEAR ACRYLIC ¼" × 4" × FENCE LENGTH

#8 × 1¼" LG FHWS (5 REQ'D)

EXPLODED VIEW

Pro SKILL: Cutting and Duplicating Odd Shapes

Every now and then you run across an odd shape or profile with straight sides that you must cut or duplicate accurately to complete a project. The ten-sided form in this project is a good example. It can be a time-consuming task to cut all these angles with a miter gauge. Instead, use a table saw duplicator.

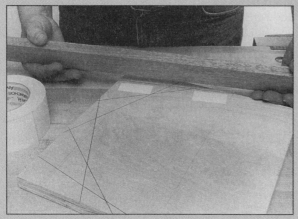

1 Lay out the shape or profile you want to cut on the stock. Take your time; measure and mark the wood as precisely as possible. Layout is the key to accuracy in this operation. Because you're following your lines exactly, the more precise the layout, the more precise the sawed shape. When you have laid out the shape, joint a long scrap of wood perfectly straight. Align the straight edge with one of the layout lines, and secure the scrap to the stock with double-faced carpet tape.

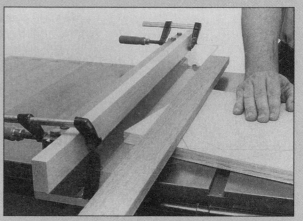

2 Place the stock on the table saw with the scrap against the duplicator. Feed the stock past the blade, guiding it along the edge of the horizontal extension. **Note:** Even when cutting a short side, use a long scrap to guide the work. This will keep the stock from turning or twisting as you cut it.

3 Remove the scrap from the stock, and align it with another layout line. Secure the scrap to the stock, and make another cut. Repeat until you have completed the profile. **Note:** The distance from the layout line to the edge of the stock must be less than the width of the horizontal extension. If there's too much stock on the waste side of the line, trim it with a band saw or saber saw before using the duplicator.

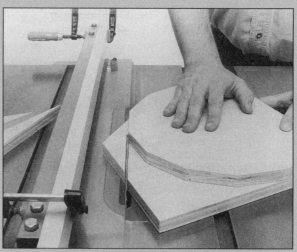

4 Once you've completed a single shape, you can use it as a template to create precise duplicates, as long as the sides are long enough to safely guide the work. Attach the shape to the stock with double-faced carpet tape. Then feed the stock past the blade, guiding the straight edges of the shape along the horizontal extension.

Stegosaurus

■ **QUICK FIXTURE**
Sanding Sticks

■ **PRO SKILL**
Making Moving Parts

The spines on the back of this animated toy dinosaur look like they'd be a nightmare to shape and sand. But a cabinetmaker's rasp and a set of sanding sticks make short work of this chore.

EXPLODED VIEW

MATERIALS LIST

Finished Dimensions in Inches	

Parts

A.	Sides (2)	$3/4'' \times 6^1/8'' \times 11^1/8''$
B.	Head and tail	$3/4'' \times 6^3/4'' \times 19^7/8''$
C.	Spacer	$7/8'' \times 2'' \times 4^3/4''$
D.	Upper forelegs (2)	$3/4'' \times 1^1/2'' \times 3^3/8''$
E.	Lower forelegs (2)	$3/4'' \times 1^1/4'' \times 3^5/8''$
F.	Upper hind legs (2)	$3/4'' \times 2'' \times 4^1/4''$
G.	Lower hind legs (2)	$3/4'' \times 1^1/2'' \times 3^5/8''$
H.	Cam	$1^3/4''$ dia. $\times 3/4''$
J.	Wheels (4)	$2^1/2''$ dia. $\times 3/4''$
K.	Axles (2)	$1/2''$ dia. $\times 3^7/8''$
L.	Pivots (2)	$1/2'' \times 2^3/8''$
M.	Axle pegs (12)	$7/32''$ dia. $\times 1^1/4''$
N.	Cross dowels (2)	$1/8''$ dia. $\times 1^1/4''$
P.	Bead	$1''$ dia.

Hardware

1" Wire brad

$3/16''$ Nylon rope (48" length)

As this wooden dinosaur is pulled along, the legs pump back and forth while the head, spines, and tail bob up and down. This is another creation of David Wakefield, the author of Animated Toys *and* Making Dinosaur Toys in Wood. *I was thrilled when David agreed to contribute a project to this book; he's an imaginative and prolific toy designer. His business,* Howling Wolf Woodworks *in Athens, Ohio, looks a great deal like Santa's workshop.*

Friday Evening

1 Prepare the materials.
To make David's Stegosaurus, you need about 3 board feet of 4/4 (1-inch-thick) lumber. You can use any cabinet-grade wood, but avoid open-grain woods because these collect dirt, harbor bacteria, and splinter more easily than closed-grain woods. Maple is the traditional choice for children's toys, but David prefers cherry because it works easily and has a rich color.

You'll also need some dowel stock, hardwood wheels, axle pegs, and a bead. These are commonly available in birch and maple only.

Plane the 4/4 stock to ⅞ inch thick, and cut a small piece to make the spacer. Plane the remainder of the stock to ¾ inch thick.

2 Lay out the patterns.
Make photocopies of the *Side Pattern, Spacer Pattern, Head and Tail Pattern, Upper Foreleg Pattern, Lower Foreleg Pattern, Upper Hind Leg Pattern,* and *Lower Hind Leg Pattern,* enlarging each pattern the specified amount, if necessary. Most small printers have enlarging/reducing copiers. Apply a spray adhesive to the backs of the patterns. (The adhesive used to mount sanding discs works well.) Stick the patterns to the stock, paying careful attention to the grain direction. The grain must be parallel to the long dimension of each piece. Using a band saw, bust the stock down into small, easy-to-manage

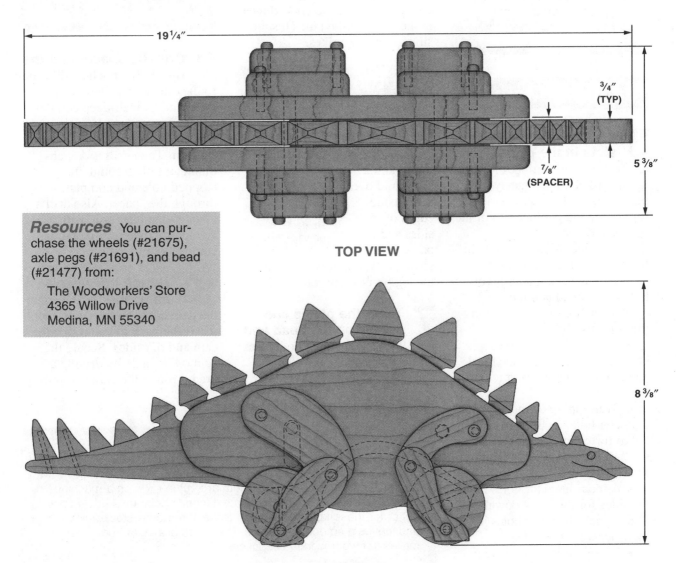

TOP VIEW

SIDE VIEW

Resources You can purchase the wheels (#21675), axle pegs (#21691), and bead (#21477) from:

The Woodworkers' Store
4365 Willow Drive
Medina, MN 55340

pieces, each with a single pattern stuck to it.

Also lay out the cam. If you're using ready-made wheels, lay out the holes in the wheels. If you're making your own wheels, lay out the wheels *and* the holes.

TRY THIS

PAD OPERATIONS

The sides and leg pieces must be made in pairs. You can save time by sticking two ³⁄₄-inch-thick boards face to face with double-faced carpet tape, then applying one pattern to the top board. Saw, drill, and sand these parts as a "pad" (see "Pad Work" on page 232), then take them apart just before assembly.

Saturday Morning

3 **Drill the holes and slots in the parts.** There are an enormous number of holes in this project. Fortunately, they're all laid out and marked for you on the photocopies of the patterns. Drill:

- A ⁷⁄₁₆-inch-diameter hole in the spacer for the front axle
- A ⁷⁄₁₆-inch-diameter pivot hole in the head and tail
- ⁷⁄₁₆-inch-diameter holes in the sides for the axles
- ¹⁄₂-inch-diameter holes between the spines on the head and tail to make it easier to cut the profile
- Overlapping ¹⁄₂-inch-diameter holes in the head and tail to form the slot. Shave the sides of the slot straight with a chisel.
- ³⁄₈-inch-diameter holes in the sides for the pivot dowels
- ³⁄₈-inch-diameter holes in the wheels for the axles
- A ³⁄₈-inch-diameter hole in the cam to fit it over the axle

- A ¹⁄₄-inch-diameter hole in the head and tail to make the eyes
- ¹⁄₄-inch-diameter holes in the legs where they pivot on the axle pegs
- ⁷⁄₃₂-inch-diameter holes in the sides, legs, and wheels where they hold the axle pegs

4 **Cut and sand the patterns.** Using a band saw or a scroll saw, cut the profiles of the parts, then sand the sawed edges.

5 **Reinforce the tail spikes.** Drill ¹⁄₈-inch-diameter, 1¹⁄₄-inch-deep holes in the bottom edge of the tail, running up into (but not through) the two tall spikes. Glue the cross dowels in the holes in the tail. This will strengthen the spikes.

Saturday Afternoon

6 **Round the outside edges of the sides and legs.** Using a table-mounted router and a ¹⁄₄-inch roundover bit, round over the outside edges of the sides and leg parts. Use a small parts holder to safely hold the leg parts when routing them.

See Also:
"Small Parts Holder" on page 231.

7 **Taper the plates and spikes on the head and tail.** With a rasp, taper both faces of the plates and spikes. They should be about ¹⁄₈ inch thick on

TRY THIS

QUICK-ACTING RASP

Tapering the plates and spikes can be a long, tedious process with an ordinary rasp in which the teeth are cut in rows on a machine (called *machine stitching*). A hand-stitched cabinetmaker's rasp is better for these kinds of shaping tasks. It removes stock quickly and leaves a smoother surface. These are available from most mail-order woodworking suppliers.

the top edge. You don't want them to come to a point; they would weaken them overmuch. It might also be dangerous to children.

8 **Assemble the body of the dinosaur.** Finish sand all the wooden parts, then glue together the sides, spacer, and pivot dowels. As you assemble the parts, install the head and tail over the pivot dowels. (Make sure the head faces in the proper direction!) However, don't glue the head and tail in place. It should move up and down on the pivot dowels freely.

Sunday Afternoon

9 **Drill the spacer and the bead.** To attach a pull rope to the dinosaur, drill a ¹⁄₂-inch-diameter, ³⁄₈-inch-deep counterbore in the underside of the spacer, as shown in the *Spacer Pattern*. Then drill a ¹⁄₄-inch-diameter hole through the stopped hole and completely through the spacer. Also drill a ¹⁄₄-inch-diameter hole with a ¹⁄₂-inch-diameter, ¹⁄₂-inch-deep counterbore in the bead.

10 **Attach the wheels, cam, and legs.** Center the cam between the sides, then insert the back axle through the cam and the sides. Secure the cam on the axle by driving a brad through the cam and into the axle. Insert the front axle through the sides and the spacer, then glue the wheels to the axles.

Peg the upper forelegs and hind legs to the sides. Glue the pegs in the sides, but be careful not to get any glue on the legs. They should pivot freely on the pegs. Then peg the lower leg parts to the upper legs and the wheels.

At Your Leisure

11 **Finish the dinosaur.**
Do any necessary touch-up sanding, then apply a nontoxic finish to the wooden surfaces of the assembled stegosaurus. When the finish dries, insert one end of a rope into the hole in the spacer and the other in the hole in the bead. Knot the ends to secure the rope.

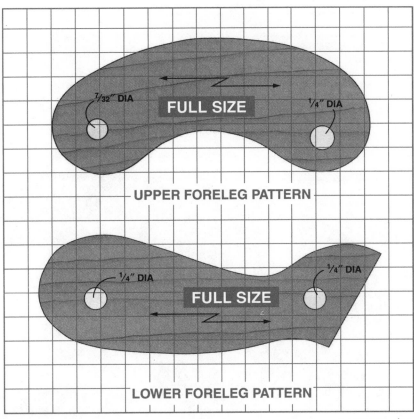

UPPER FORELEG PATTERN

LOWER FORELEG PATTERN

1 SQUARE = 1/4"

Quick FIXTURE: Sanding Sticks

Sanding intricate shapes can be a time-consuming job without a set of sanding sticks to help you reach the nooks and crannies. Shown are three common shapes — round, rectangular, and wedge. You can make other shapes to suit your needs.

Cut the shape from wood, then cover it with soft leather or felt when possible. The soft surface conforms to the irregularities in the wood surface and helps the sandpaper cut more quickly and more evenly.

Use sanding sticks to reach into areas that you can't get to with a sanding block. Select the stick that best conforms to the surface.

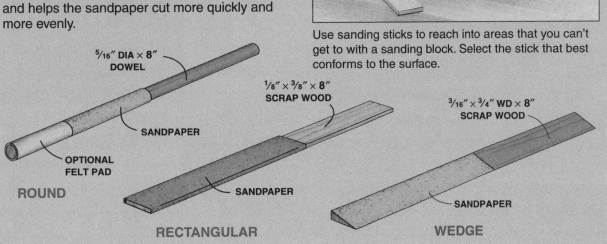

ROUND

RECTANGULAR

WEDGE

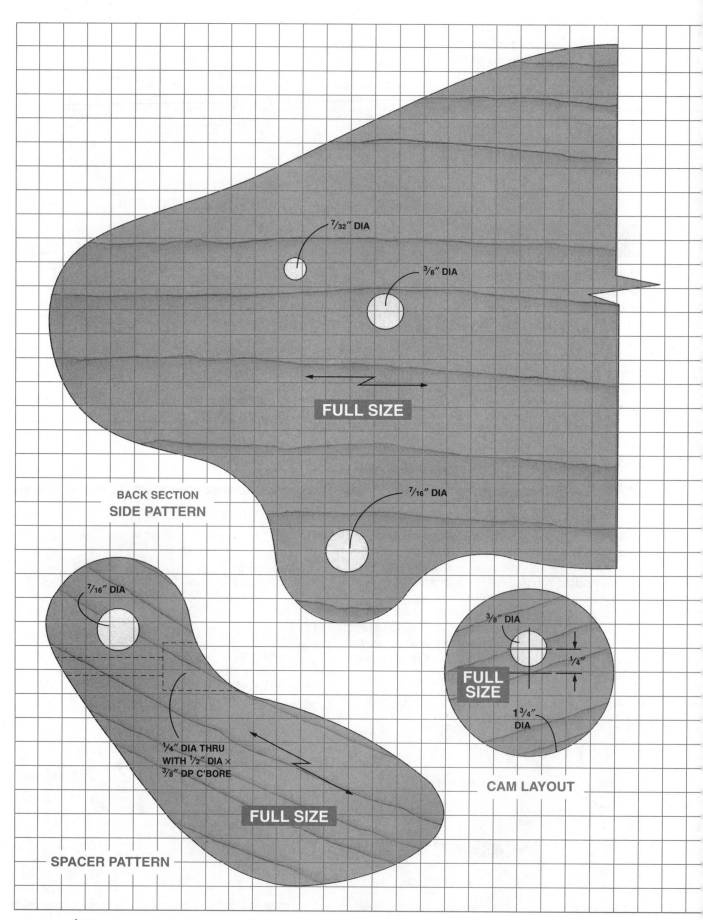

⁷/₃₂″ DIA

³/₈″ DIA

FULL SIZE

BACK SECTION
SIDE PATTERN

⁷/₁₆″ DIA

⁷/₁₆″ DIA

³/₈″ DIA

¹/₄″

FULL
SIZE

1³/₄″
DIA

CAM LAYOUT

¹/₄″ DIA THRU
WITH ¹/₂″ DIA ×
³/₈″ DP C'BORE

FULL SIZE

SPACER PATTERN

1 SQUARE = ¹/₄″

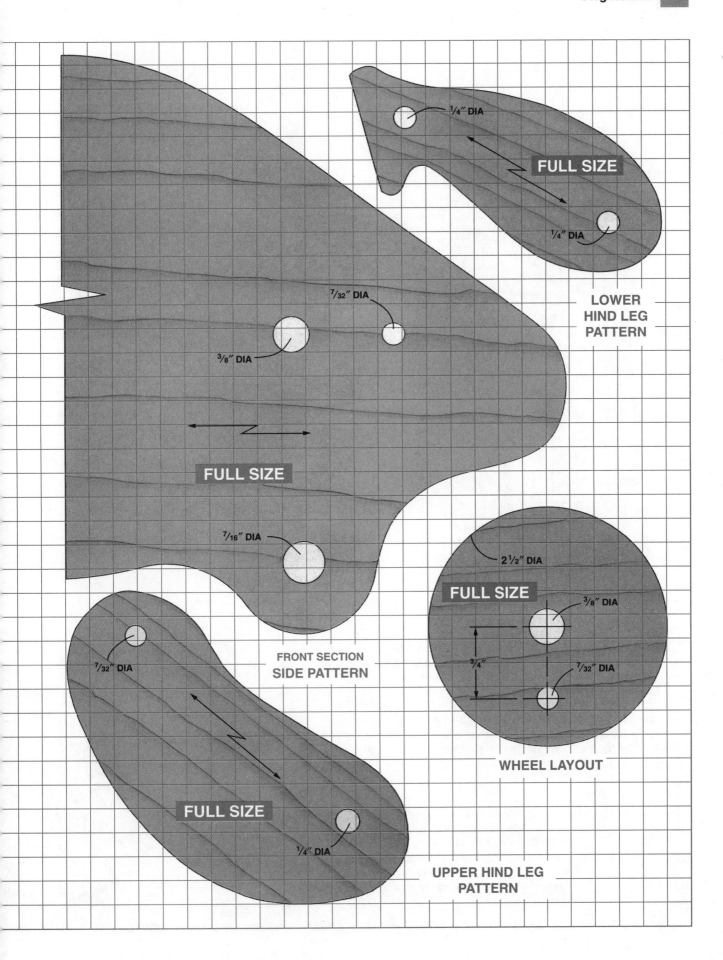

1/4″ DIA

FULL SIZE

1/4″ DIA

LOWER HIND LEG PATTERN

7/32″ DIA

3/8″ DIA

FULL SIZE

7/16″ DIA

2 1/2″ DIA

FULL SIZE

3/8″ DIA

3/4″

7/32″ DIA

FRONT SECTION SIDE PATTERN

WHEEL LAYOUT

7/32″ DIA

FULL SIZE

1/4″ DIA

UPPER HIND LEG PATTERN

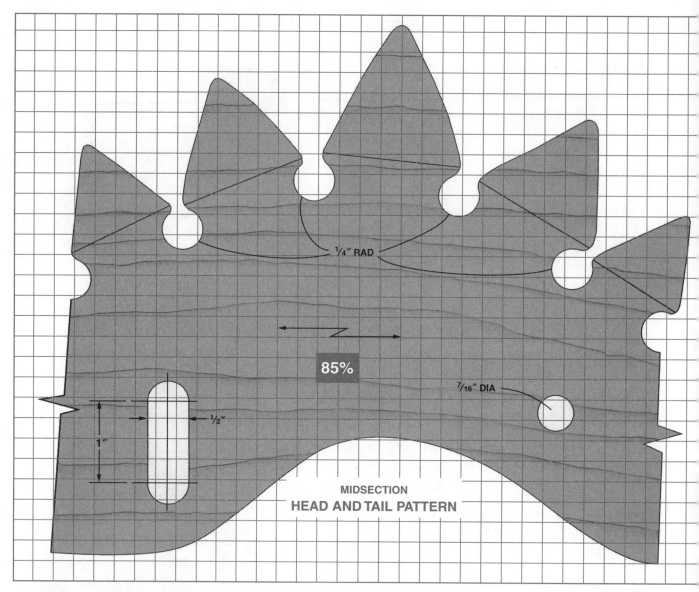

¹⁄₄" RAD

85%

⁷⁄₁₆" DIA

¹⁄₂"

1"

MIDSECTION
HEAD AND TAIL PATTERN

1 SQUARE = ¹⁄₄"

Pro SKILL: Making Moving Parts

When making an animated toy or an assembly that moves, typically one or more parts turn on a *pivot*. In the Stegosaurus, for instance, the head and tail swing up and down on a pivot dowel. To prevent premature wear, these pivots should be made from an extremely hard wood such as maple or birch.

1 You can further prevent wear by sanding the wooden surfaces that will rub together as smooth as you can get them. Then mask the part of the pivot that will be glued with tape and apply a paste wax to the remainder. This reduces friction between the pivot and the moving part.

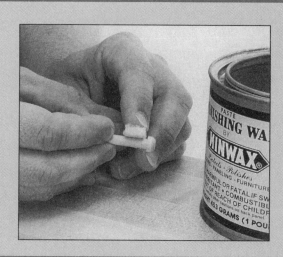

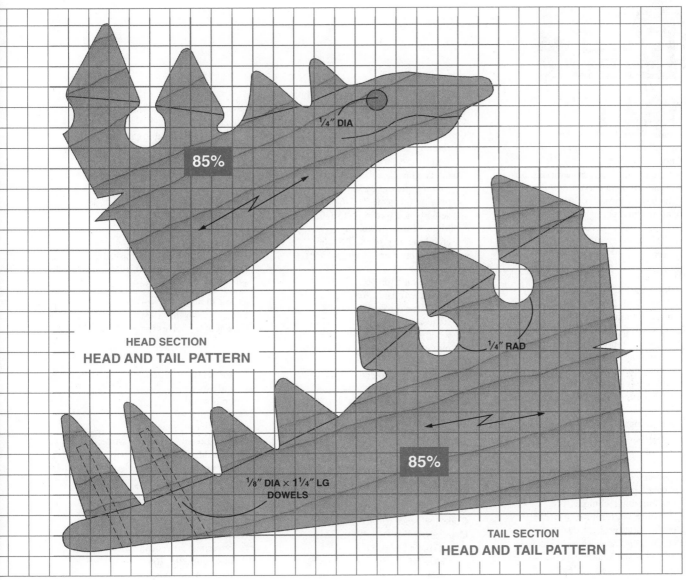

¼" DIA

85%

HEAD SECTION
HEAD AND TAIL PATTERN

¼" RAD

85%

⅛" DIA × 1¼" LG
DOWELS

TAIL SECTION
HEAD AND TAIL PATTERN

1 SQUARE = ¼"

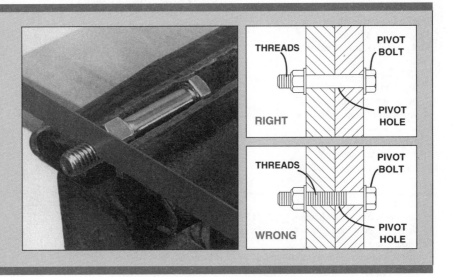

2 If you expect that the pivot will see an unusual amount of use, make it from a metal bolt instead of a wooden dowel. When selecting pivot bolts, make sure the portion of the bolt inside the pivot hole is *unthreaded.* Otherwise the threads will eat away at the wood every time the part moves, enlarging the hole. In many cases, you may have to purchase much longer bolts than needed, and cut away some of the threaded portion. **Tip:** Use a *stop nut* to secure the pivot. This type of nut won't work itself loose.

THREADS

PIVOT BOLT

PIVOT HOLE

RIGHT

THREADS

PIVOT BOLT

PIVOT HOLE

WRONG

Index